How to Do *Everything* with Your

iMac
Fourth Edition

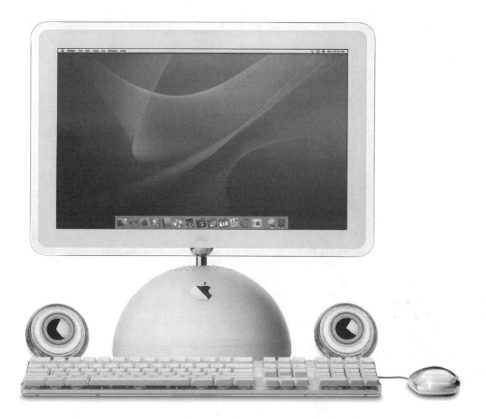

How to Do *Everything* with Your

iMac
Fourth Edition

Todd Stauffer

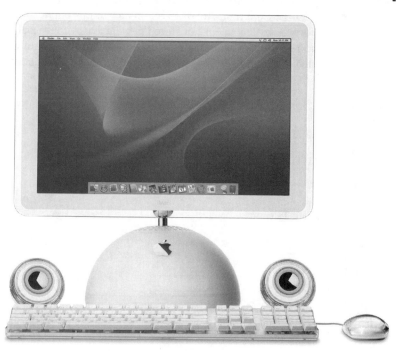

McGraw-Hill/Osborne

New York   Chicago   San Francisco   Lisbon
London   Madrid   Mexico City   Milan   New Delhi
San Juan   Seoul   Singapore   Sydney   Toronto

The McGraw·Hill Companies

McGraw-Hill/Osborne
2100 Powell Street, 10th Floor
Emeryville, California 94608
U.S.A.

To arrange bulk purchase discounts for sales promotions, premiums, or fund-raisers, please
contact **McGraw-Hill**/Osborne at the above address. For information on translations or book
distributors outside the U.S.A., please see the International Contact Information page immediately
following the index of this book.

How to Do Everything with Your iMac, Fourth Edition

1234567890 FGR FGR 01987654

ISBN 0-07-223188-2

Publisher	Brandon A. Nordin
Vice President &	
Associate Publisher	Scott Rogers
Executive Editor	Jane Brownlow
Project Editors	Judith Brown, Paul Tyler
Acquisitions Coordinator	Agatha Kim
Technical Editor	Clint Rogers
Copy Editor	Judith Brown
Proofreader	Paul Tyler
Indexer	Claire Splan
Composition	Apollo Publishing Services
Illustrator	Melinda Lytle
Series Design	Mickey Galicia
Cover Series Design	Dodie Shoemaker

This book was composed with Corel VENTURA™ Publisher.

About the Author

Todd Stauffer is the author or co-author of over three dozen books on computing, including the previous editions of *How to Do Everything with Your iMac, How to Do Everything with Your iBook*, and *Blog On: The Essential Guide to Building Dynamic Weblogs.* He's a regular contributor to *MacAddict* and has written for publications as diverse as *Working Woman* and *Hamptons* magazine. Todd is the publisher of the *Jackson Free Press*, a news and culture magazine in Jackson, Mississippi, where he lives with writer Donna Ladd and entirely too many cats.

Contents at a Glance

Contents

Acknowledgments

The original *How to Do Everything with Your iMac* was the result of a fairly unique idea: a big book about a little computer. With the help and support of some great people, I took a stab at putting together a book that I hoped would help many readers get the most—for business, pleasure, or education—out of their iMac.

But the iMac product line is changing swiftly; new Mac OS versions are coming out, and even more exciting capabilities are being built into and bundled with the iMac. Those changes, coupled with the success of the first, second, and third editions, have us at it again to bring you this fourth edition covering all the latest applications and capabilities of the iMac, and folding in info about the popular—and similar—eMac and iBook product lines.

My thanks go first to Heidi Poulin, project editor on the first edition, who helped shape the original content and much of the structure that continues into this edition. Likewise, thanks to Bob LeVitus for his technical review and preface for the original edition.

Jane Brownlow, acquisitions editor for all four editions, was largely responsible for the success of the first edition and made it possible for me to write the others. My thanks to her for flexible deadlines as we tried to get this book done in a way that could touch on nearly every aspect of computing with a consumer Mac.

For the fourth edition, thanks go to Clint Roberts for an efficient technical edit, Judith Brown for her capable copy editing (and soft management touch), and Paul Tyler for managing us through the page proofs stage.

I'd also like to thank everyone who contributed to the book for Voices from the Community and other sidebar material, including my sometimes writing partner Kirk McElhearn, as well as Richard T. White, Joe Zoller, Mary Bischoff, and Jim Eaton. Thanks also to Warren Williams, president of the AppleWorks Users Group, for his help in reaching some of these users so they could contribute. (I encourage anyone who is interested in using AppleWorks to its fullest to investigate **http://www.awug.org/** to learn more about the AppleWorks Users Group and their resources. It's a great group and service.)

My thanks to the staff members of the *Jackson Free Press*, who kept both their visible annoyance and relief to a minimum when I disappeared into "book mode" for this project. Finally, special thanks to Donna Ladd, for her support, love, and partnership through the thick and thin of all sundry adventures.

Introduction

The original idea of *How to Do Everything with Your iMac* was a simple one. The iMac is a complete computer with a wonderful bundle of applications that enable you to do just about anything you need a computer to do. So, I wanted my book on the iMac to be as comprehensive as possible, teaching the reader how to be productive while enjoying this exciting little tool.

It was a risk, though, because the prevailing winds suggested that iMac owners might want thin books with only the basics to get up and running with their easy-to-use iMac. A 500-page book on the iMac? To some, it didn't make sense. Would readers buy this book?

The results speak for themselves, with the first three editions of the book selling over 100,000 copies—a runaway best-seller in the computer-book business. The folks at McGraw-Hill/Osborne were tickled enough to create an entire series of *How to Do Everything* books.

Now, we've put together this fourth edition, largely to tackle all of the new software and capabilities that Apple continues to pile onto the iMac. Not the least of these is Mac OS X—arguably the first all-new Mac OS since the advent of the Macintosh. In its current "Panther" iteration, Mac OS X is a modern, elegant, but complex operating system that can be fun to learn and, at times, a bit frustrating to manage or troubleshoot. (That makes for at least one good reason to get a book about it!)

In the third edition of this book we covered both Mac OS 9 and Mac OS X. For the fourth edition, we're focusing exclusively on Mac OS X because, well, that's what Apple has done. All of Apple's consumer Macs have shipped with Mac OS X for well over a year, and the transition to Mac OS X as the mainstay operating system for most Mac users is essentially complete. You'll find that Mac OS X is full featured, offers great advantages, and, frankly, requires every page that I have available to give to it. (For those of you still working with Mac OS 9 or with "Classic" applications, the appendix discusses some of the differences and how to get them to work together.)

In *How to Do Everything with Your iMac, Fourth Edition,* perhaps the most dramatic change we've made is to extend the book's focus to cover the iBook and eMac as well as the iMac. All of Apple's consumer Macs include almost identical bundles of software applications, so you'll find that much of the coverage is identical. But there are certain quirks and features that make each of these Mac models unique, too, so I'll touch on them throughout the book.

Coverage of the Internet is arranged to get you up and running more quickly, starting with Chapter 5's quick guide to the Internet. That's in addition to Chapters 18, 19, and 20, where you'll find extensive coverage of e-mail, the World Wide Web, and Apple's .Mac features, which make it easy to transfer files online, create web pages, and display images and movies on the Web.

Chapter 21 covers the complexities of networking and enabling multiple users to access your Mac; Chapter 22 includes coverage for increasing the speed of your Internet connection and even putting together a wireless Internet and/or networking connection for your Mac.

In this book you'll learn, in detail, how to accomplish important computing tasks with your iMac, from the first time you press the Power button. Since the iMac comes bundled with AppleWorks, I show you how to create documents, reports, memos, spreadsheets, databases, and charts. And I mean how to *use* them in real-world situations to oversee projects, turn in to teachers, present to your clients, or manage your hobbies.

You'll see how to create slide-show presentations; how to use templates and assistants for all sorts of things; how to manage your calendar, task list, and contacts with aplomb; how to create databases to track just about anything—sports teams, weddings, recipes, projects, or classroom assignments.

The Mac is about creativity and fun, too. You can draw, paint, and even create a newsletter or high-end report. You'll learn about QuickTime, digital audio, digital video, and even a little about creating your own movies, managing a library of digital photos or digital songs, and burning your own audio CDs or creating your own photo albums and having them printed professionally. Plus, there's an entire chapter on Apple's latest "iApp." Called GarageBand, it can only be described as a music studio on your Mac—tons of fun regardless of your knowledge of music theory (or lack thereof).

Beyond that you'll learn about printing documents, adding fonts, scanning photos, backing up data, adding a removable drive, synchronizing with your iPod or handheld computer, customizing your settings, and troubleshooting your Mac when things go wrong.

The book communicates all this information very simply. It has four major parts: Get Started, Get Your Work Done, Get Online, and Improve and Maintain Your Mac. The book is both a reference and a tutorial. It's arranged so you can move quickly to an interesting topic you look up in the index, or you can just read straight through to get a complete understanding of a given topic. Plus, special elements help you along the way, including notes, tips, shortcuts, and cautions. And every chapter includes special "How to…", "Did you know…," and "Voices from the Community" sidebars that explore one special feature to show you how to make the most of your Mac.

An important note: throughout the book I'll refer to "Mac OS 9" and "Mac OS X" generically—in most cases, when I say that, I'm discussing a feature or issue that has been present in those operating systems since they were introduced. But don't let that generic approach confuse you; it's always a good idea to have the latest versions of Mac OS 9 (at the time of writing, Mac OS 9.2) and Mac OS X (version 10.3, currently). See Chapter 23 for details on updating your Mac OS versions. You should also look into Apple's Mac OS X Up-to-Date program (**http://www.apple .com/macosx/uptodate/**) to determine whether you're eligible for free or inexpensive upgrades to the Mac OS.

Want to reach me? You can, through my web site for this book. It's **http://www.macblog .com/imac_book/**. You'll also find bonus material on that page and elsewhere on the MacBlog.com site that includes news, opinion, and discussions on all sorts of Mac topics, including answers to frequent questions. Other corrections, explanations, discussion, and frequently asked questions will also be posted on that site, so please visit regularly or whenever you have a question.

Part I

Get Started

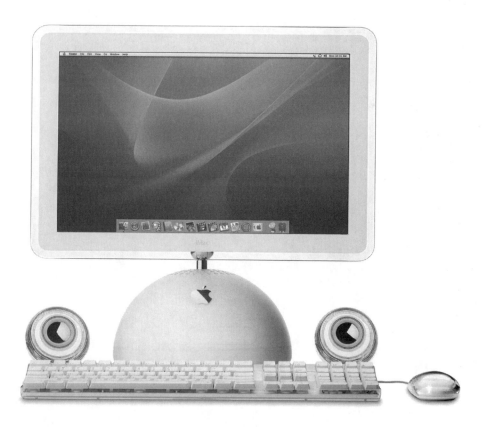

Chapter 1

Welcome to iMac (and eMac and iBook)

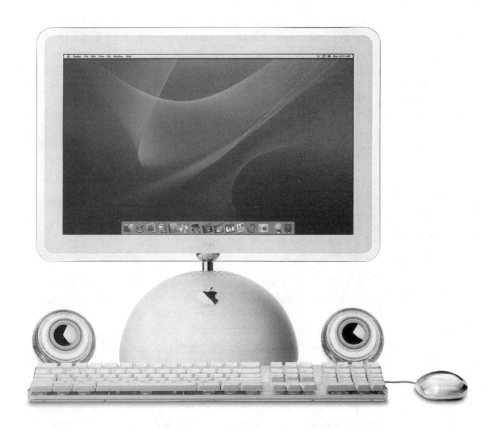

How to...

■ Prepare yourself for using your Mac

■ Figure out all the parts of the Mac

■ Set up your Mac

■ Start, restart, and put your Mac to sleep

In 1998, Apple Computer set out to create a slightly different sort of computer from those that had been seen in the past—one designed specifically for consumer users who wanted to get on the Internet. They called it the iMac, to suggest that it was the first "Internet" Macintosh marketed. It used a lot of the parts and software that a regular Macintosh computer uses, but it offered enough differences to make it a whole new idea. And it was a very exciting idea—a friendly, easy-to-use computer that can still do just about anything at all.

Since that time, Apple has upgraded the iMac to a PowerPC G4 processor, moved to a thin flat-panel design, and has continued to improve the technology featured in the iMac, so that it now includes, for instance, media drives that can create CDs and (in many cases) DVDs of data or movies. At the same time, Apple has broadened its consumer options by offering the iBook laptop computer as a sort of portable iMac and the eMac as an inexpensive all-in-one design that's great for home or school.

With today's consumer Macs, what makes them unique is not only the attractiveness and functionality of the designs. What can really set them apart is the complete bundle of software that comes with these Macs, including Mac OS X—the *operating system*, which is the heart and

How to ... **Care for the Case**

Wondering how to clean your consumer Mac's case? The plastics on the iMac, eMac, and iBook are durable, but they can still be scratched by abrasives or hard-edged objects. Of course, any computer case can be scratched, but the Mac will look a little worse for the wear since it's designed to be more attractive than most computers.

To clean the case, Apple recommends you shut down the Mac, pull its plug (from the wall socket or surge protector), and wipe the case with a dry, lint-free cloth. Avoid using water or liquid cleaners, since the Mac's case has seams where liquid could conceivably penetrate the case and damage the electronics.

To clean the screen, use a slightly damp, clean, lint-free cloth or a cloth from packets designed specifically to clean computer monitors (you can get them at computer and office-supply stores). Don't spray liquids directly on the Mac (spray water lightly on the cloth itself), and don't use any harsh cleaners.

soul of the Mac—and the iLife bundle of applications that includes iMovie, iPhoto, iTunes, and, on many models, iDVD and GarageBand. On top of that, Apple includes AppleWorks for creating all sorts of documents, iCal for managing your calendar, and all of the Internet applications you'll need so that you can gather information and communicate with others online.

As the title of this book suggests, if you have an iMac, eMac, or iBook, you can do just about anything you can do with any other sort of computer. You're ready to go.

Understand Apple's Consumer Macs

The iMac, eMac, and iBook offer a number of distinguishing features beyond looks. The latest models are all powerful computers, based on Apple's PowerPC G4 processors. Ease of use was important when Apple originally created the iMac, and that focus continues with the current model as well as the spin-offs. A big part of the theory behind the design of all of Apple's consumer Macs is that they are "all-in-one," with a display built in and a relatively compact footprint. (In the case of the iBook, they're also ultraportable.) These Macs are designed to help you get on the Internet, connect peripherals, and even attach to a network easily. They have all the important stuff built in—a modem, Ethernet port, graphics—plus two easy, modern ways to add extras: Universal Serial Bus ports and FireWire ports. Moreover, Macs come with applications already installed that you can use for a variety of home or home-office tasks.

These Macs are also designed to work collaboratively with other computers over the Internet or a local area network of Macs or PCs. And they offer some special ways to transmit, share, and translate files that other computers use so you can share and edit them with others.

What Is the Internet?

It's obvious just from the "i" in iMac's and iBook's name that the Internet will be a huge focus of this book and your experience with the computer, so you'll need to know what it is. The Internet is the name given to a global system for connecting computers to one another; once connected, these computers can share documents and transfer files. The result has been electronic mail, message areas, and the World Wide Web.

NOTE   *The eMac is no less capable of getting on and making use of the Internet—it was named with an "e" because it was originally marketed as an education-only model. It proved popular with all Mac users, because it offers most of the powerful features of the iMac but includes a CRT display, which makes it cheaper than the iMac with its LCD flat-panel display.*

The Internet began as a government project to move data over long distances, with redundancies to survive some sort of wartime or natural disaster. Eventually, it became an important way to connect university computing centers and, later on, individuals. In the early 1990s the corporate world caught on, and soon, electronic mail and messaging became popular ways to use a personal computer.

So what makes it the Internet? Any computer using a particular language called the Transmission Control Protocol/Internet Protocol (TCP/IP) can connect to the Internet. All you need is a modem or a network connection and an Internet connection through an Internet service provider (ISP). The ISP gives you an address on the Internet, called an *IP address*, which gives your Mac a unique identity on this global network. Once you have an address, you're ready to send and receive Internet documents.

NOTE *To learn more about using the Mac with the Internet, see "Get Online with the Setup Assistant" later in this chapter, as well as Chapter 5 and Chapters 18 through 20, where I discuss the Internet in detail.*

Consumer Macs Are Still Macs

Although Apple's professional-level Mac desktop and laptop models are called the Power Macintosh and PowerBook, respectively, they're largely similar to the consumer Macs. The only differences tend to be in terms of capacities and speeds. The professional-level Macs have the very latest processors and offer the most expansion in terms of system memory and storage for documents and applications. Functionally, they're mostly identical to the iMac, eMac, and iBook.

The iMac, eMac, and iBook do not run software specifically written for DOS, Windows, Windows 95/98, or Windows NT/2000, although many programs are written in both PC and Macintosh versions. Sometimes you'll even find both versions on the same CD-ROM.

And that's not to say the Mac can't run PC software at all—it just can't run PC software right out of the box. Special software programs, such as Microsoft's Virtual PC, allow you to run those programs on your Mac (see Chapter 23). That software, called *emulation* software, can trick Windows programs into believing that they're being run on a Windows-based machine, even as they're being run on your Mac. It's a neat tool and it can be done pretty inexpensively.

And note that computers that use Intel-compatible processors and DOS, Windows, or Windows NT are often called "PCs" for the sake of convenience and to differentiate them from iMacs and other Mac models. I'll follow that convention despite the fact that your Mac is a "personal computer."

Consumer Macs Use the Latest Hardware

Get your iMac, eMac, or iBook home and there's a decent chance that you'll soon want external peripherals for it. You may want a printer, a document scanner, and a digital camera, or you may want to connect your Mac to other computers and copy files between them. Part of the excitement of the Mac stems from its Universal Serial Bus (USB) and, on recent models, FireWire ports that can be used to connect high-speed peripherals.

USB is incredibly easy to use—you pretty much just plug things in and they work. Plus, it's a standard that the latest Mac and PC computers can both use. That means many USB devices are compatible with Macs right out of the box. That said, some USB devices require special *driver software*, so read the box carefully, ask a salesperson, or just focus on USB devices that show up in the Mac section of the store. If it has a Mac or iMac logo on the box, then it likely includes the software drivers you need.

NOTE *In some cases, you'll need a Mac OS X–specific driver if you wish to work with the device in Mac OS X. See Chapter 23 (or Chapter 12, if the device is a printer) for details.*

If you have any consumer Mac model made in summer 2000 or later, your Mac includes additional ports, called FireWire ports. These high-speed ports are included for copying data between your Mac and a digital camcorder so you can edit video. But that's not all FireWire is good for. It is also popular for connecting other devices, including high-speed external hard disks and removable disks. You'll find that many external devices are available with FireWire connections. As an added bonus, FireWire is easy to set up, with the same "hot-pluggability" that USB offers.

You need to watch out for peripherals made for older Mac computers. These days, all of Apple's new products use USB ports, but older Mac-compatible printers and scanners may use either *serial* ports or *SCSI* ports for their connections. That's not the end of the world—actually, some of those other peripherals made for older Macintosh computers can still be used, but you'll need an adapter and some know-how. We'll discuss various peripherals in Chapter 23.

Meet Your Mac: A Quick Tour

Before you get into the heart of setting up your Mac, let's take a quick look at it to get an idea what everything is and how things connect. You'll find that the Mac has some interesting and surprising nooks and crannies.

Explore Your iMac

The iMac started it all when it was introduced as a little Bondi Blue beach ball with a built-in screen and a new approach to consumer computing. Since then, a number of different models have come along, up through today's flat-panel iMac models and their increasingly impressive displays. Let's take a quick tour of the models.

Tray-Loading iMac G3

The original iMac is called the "tray-loading" iMac because it has a CD-ROM drive with a pop-out tray where you place the CD. These are all-in-one models with a 15-inch CRT (cathode-ray tube) display. They range in processor speeds from 233 MHz to 333 MHz, and the second round of them came in a number of different "fruity" colors. These original iMacs are still viable under certain circumstances, although they're notable for their lack of FireWire, which means they can't be used to communicate with fast external hard disks or with digital camcorders for editing movies.

Slot-Loading Macs

In fall 1999, Apple introduced a new line of iMacs that all feature slot-loading CD-ROM or DVD-ROM drives. At that time, the distinction between the low-end and high-end models was made by calling the higher-end models iMac DV, which suggested that they had DVD-ROM drives and FireWire ports. All slot-loading iMacs also feature improved, higher-fidelity sound thanks to improved integrated speakers. These Macs were also designed to avoid using an internal fan, so they run quieter than most other computers.

In early 2001, Apple again changed things around, offering iMacs that could feature a CD-ROM, DVD-ROM, or a CD-RW (rewritable) drive, and in summer 2001, all Macs began shipping with CD-RW drives as the standard. Still in the same slot-loading enclosure, these models also included larger hard drives, more RAM, and faster processors.

iMac G4

In early 2002, Apple introduced the flat-panel iMac G4 with a 15-inch LCD (liquid crystal display). The iMac G4 offers the user the choice of a CD-RW/DVD "Combo" or DVD-RW "SuperDrive" in most configurations. The SuperDrive can be used in combination with iDVD software to write DVD movies that can be played back on consumer equipment. The flat-panel iMac models are all adept at running Mac OS X and can be upgraded with quite a bit of internal memory. In July 2002, Apple introduced the 17-inch iMac, which features a larger flat-panel display; in fall 2003, Apple introduced the even more impressive 20-inch iMac G4 model.

In fall 2003, the iMac G4 models became the first consumer Macs to offer Double Data Rate (DDR) RAM and support for USB 2.0 peripherals, which use the same connection as USB, but at speeds that slightly exceed standard FireWire.

Explore Your eMac

Introduced in spring 2002 as an education-only model, the eMac was made available to the public later that summer. It proved popular because it offered similar power and capabilities to the iMac, but at a lower price because it uses a less-expensive CRT display. The eMac has shipped with CD-ROM, CD-RW, Combo, and SuperDrive configurations, and PowerPC G4 processors. All eMac models have supported both Ethernet and AirPort networking, making them handy for home- or small-business networks. The eMac ships with a similar bundle of software to that of the iMac and, overall, represents a great value, even if it doesn't quite have the same exotic looks of the flat-panel iMac.

Explore Your iBook

Apple has made two different generations of iBook in terms of design—the original iBook and the second-generation "iceBook" models. While the original mission of a relatively rugged and lightweight portable has remained the same, the execution has differed between the models.

Original iBook

Aimed initially at home and education users, the original iBook has been called everything from a "power purse" to a high-tech toilet seat. The unique design was meant to make the iBook rugged and rubberized while making it portable—hence, it has a small plastic fold-out handle. In terms of technology, the original iBook models had only a CD-ROM drive and support for USB peripherals only, although they supported AirPort and Ethernet networking connections. The iBook 366 model, introduced in September 2000, included a FireWire port and a special AV port for video-out connections, making it useful for presentations.

The "iceBook" iBook

The second-generation iBook actually has a number of different models. It began powered by a PowerPC G3 processor, for instance, and now has a PowerPC G4 processor; it's also available in models that have 12-inch and 14-inch displays. The original purpose of the design, however, was to be both sleeker and lighter than the original iBook—the 12-inch models are around five pounds and the 14-inch models about six pounds, which are both less than the original 12-inch iBooks.

These iBooks also offer a higher screen resolution and the option of a CD-RW/DVD Combo drive. All "iceBook" models include FireWire and video out.

Before You Set Up Your Mac

If you've just gotten your Mac and you're waiting for me to tell you how to get started, this is your section. I'll also talk about some relevant issues for users who have their Mac running— stuff not necessarily covered by the manual you got from Apple. Let's take a quick look.

Get a Surge Protector

Not enough people get surge protectors for their computers, and I suggest you run out and buy one right now (or at least later today) if you plan to start or continue using your Mac. The surge protector is designed to let you plug in a number of peripherals while stopping power surges from reaching your valuable equipment. It keeps your Mac from getting fried, basically, when a power surge occurs thanks to a lightning strike, power outage, or problem with your (or your power company's) wiring.

You need to get the kind of surge protector that includes protection for the phone line, too. In my experience, extreme surges occur more frequently over phone lines than over power lines. Since your phone line will probably almost always be plugged into your Mac's modem port if you plan to use the modem for Internet or faxing, it's possible for such a surge to go straight into the modem, causing it to cease functioning. In fact, this could affect your entire Mac.

A good surge protector costs at least $25, probably more depending on the features. Don't get an $8 protector and think you're done—often, those are just power strips (giving you more plug receptacles), not protectors. Check the box to see if the manufacturer offers a guarantee or equipment replacement insurance. If so, there's a decent chance the protector actually works well.

NOTE *Some iBook users don't use a surge protector, thinking that the iBook's external power supply will protect them from surges. While it's true that the iBook's external power supply is more likely to be lost to a surge, it's not a guarantee that a power surge won't damage internal components on your iBook. Furthermore, the power supply can be pricey, so a surge protector is still an important precaution.*

Keep Glare to a Minimum

Another important consideration before you set up your Mac is where the windows are in the room where you're working (or playing) on your Mac.

In general, avoid having a window directly in front of the Mac (that is, when you sit at the Mac, the window is at your back) or directly behind the Mac (when you look at the Mac's screen, you can see the window behind it). The reason for this is simple—glare and eyestrain. If the window is directly behind you, then sunlight will glare off the screen and make it harder to see text and images on your Mac. If the window is directly behind the Mac, your eyes will have trouble adjusting to the varying levels of light, causing strain and fatigue.

Along those same lines, it's always a good idea to look away from your monitor for a minute or more every 15 minutes. That means looking out the window (which should be directly to your right or left if possible), reading a bit, or just letting yourself relax and perform eye exercises, raise a dumbbell, get up for some water, or do whatever you do to relax.

Don't Forget the Ergonomics

It's also important—especially if you plan to use your Mac for an extended period of time—to consider the ergonomic implications of your setup. While I'm not a doctor or chiropractor, I can pass on some general advice. You might want to consult an expert regarding your setup, especially if you're experiencing any pain or strain from repetitive movements.

First, your hands and legs should generally approach the table and chair that support your Mac at a 90-degree angle. That means elbows at 90 degrees and knees at 90 degrees with your feet flat on the floor, if possible. Adjust your table and/or chair if neither of these angles is correct.

Next, you shouldn't look far down or far up at your monitor—don't crane your neck, in other words. If you're looking down on your monitor, make a trip to the computer store to purchase a stand to raise the Mac. (You can also lower your adjustable chair, if you have one, as long as that doesn't adversely affect your sitting and typing position.) The top of the Mac's screen should be level with your eyes when you're looking straight ahead.

In fact, looking straight ahead is exactly what you want to do. Do you have a desk that positions the monitor off to the side at an angle? They should be illegal. You should look *directly* at a monitor that is in front of you, not to one side. Otherwise you'll have your neck and/or back cocked sideways for minutes or hours at a time—not a good thing. It's like driving cross-country while looking out the driver-side window. That would start to hurt after a while, wouldn't it?

> **NOTE** *With the flat-panel iMac, Apple has a design that allows you to move the display up or down in different configurations. This is probably helpful from an ergonomic standpoint, as it encourages you to choose a good height for the display and shift it frequently. With an eMac or older iMac, you'll want a stand to bring the display's height up a bit. The eMac has an accessory stand available from Apple, while the older iMac has a number of stands available from third parties.*

Do you have lots of padded mouse and wrist accessories? Don't let them allow you to get lazy. The ideal wrist position is actually over the keys slightly, not resting on the wrist pad—at least, according to most things I've heard and read. If you took piano class as a kid, you know how you're supposed to hold your hands. Keep them aloft for a while. When you're tired, don't rest your wrists on little gel things—quit typing.

Finally, the second you start to feel pain or strain, get ahold of your doctor. (Repetitive strain injuries are serious and often covered by health insurance policies.) You may be able to get add-on keyboards, mice, or some other solution for working with your Mac. Or your doctor may prescribe a vacation to the Bahamas for two weeks.

> **NOTE** *The iBook can be a bit more of a problem ergonomically, particularly if you spend a great deal of time using it. The best advice is to get an external keyboard and mouse, as well as a stand that raises your iBook's display. Use those external devices when you're at home (or in the office) where you use the iBook the most; then, when you're traveling, you can use the iBook's keyboard and mouse for shorter durations.*

Know Your Mac's Ports

While Chapter 23 will dig deeper into the fundamentals of upgrading a Mac, I want to touch briefly on the ports on the side of your Mac that you'll want to use for getting your Mac set up and configured for use. It turns out that all of Apple's consumer Macs—the iMac, eMac, and iBook—offer the same labeling and some special ports in common, so you should find that it's relatively easy to find the ports discussed here.

For connecting your keyboard and mouse, you'll use USB. Today's iBook has two USB ports, the iMac G4 has three, and the eMac has three. (Earlier models had fewer.) They're labeled with a small pitchfork-like icon.

Interestingly, USB 1.1 (the low-speed standard) and USB 2.0 (the high-speed standard currently on the iMac G4) use the same style connector. If your Mac supports USB 2.0 peripherals, you should use the ports on the side of your Mac for high-speed connection, as the ports on the side of your keyboard are likely to be USB 1.1.

Currently, all consumer Mac models use FireWire 400, which is the original FireWire standard. FireWire ports are used for high-speed peripherals (like external hard disks) and for digital video cameras. They're all labeled with a radioactive-looking "Y" symbol.

Note that not all consumer Macs have FireWire—the earliest iMac and iBook models did not have FireWire ports. Because it's integral to the use of iMovie and digital camcorders for video editing, Apple now makes FireWire standard on all its Mac models, including portables.

NOTE *Consumer Macs may soon begin to support FireWire 800, which is simply a faster standard. Unlike USB 2.0, FireWire 800 also uses a different connector from its slower sibling, FireWire 400, so you'll find that you need a different cable in order to connect a FireWire 800 device to your Mac.*

If you're connecting your Mac to a phone cable so that you can use the phone line for Internet access or for sending and/or receiving faxes, you'll want to pick the correct port. The phone line is labeled with a small phone icon (as shown to the left).

Meanwhile, the Ethernet port, which is similar in configuration to the phone line port—but a bit larger—is designed to accept a Category 5 Ethernet cable. Its label looks like <···> (as shown to the right).

Set Up Your Mac

Now for the moment of truth. When you've accounted for surges, glare, and ergonomics, the setup instructions that come with your Mac are perfectly acceptable.

1. Pull the Mac out of the box, place it on the table, and adjust its display (iMac or iBook) or its stand (optional on the eMac), if desired.

NOTE   *Technically the iMac and eMac are portable, but they're still heavy, at 30–45 pounds depending on the model. I recommend using two hands with your consumer desktops. On older iMacs, hold it by the handle and place a hand under the iMac near its CD drive; on eMac, support its base with two hands. The flat-panel iMac can be lifted by its metal neck, although you'll likely find that it's ideal to support its base with another hand as well.*

2. Plug the power cord into the power socket on the back of the Mac, then plug it into your surge protector.

3. Will you be using the Mac's modem for Internet or fax connections? Use the phone wire that came with the surge protector (or another that you have around the house), and connect the phone wire from your wall socket to the Phone In socket on your surge protector. Use the phone cord that came with your Mac to stretch from the Phone Out on the surge protector to the modem socket on the Mac. (Note: you can use a small phone splitter from a hardware or electronics store if you want to place a telephone next to your Mac.)

4. For your iMac, eMac, or an iBook that you'll use with an external keyboard, plug the Mac's keyboard cord into one of the USB ports on the side or back of the Mac.

5. Plug your Mac's mouse into the appropriate USB port on the keyboard (depending on whether you work the mouse with your left hand or right hand).

TIP   *Some iBook users opt to use the built-in keyboard but attach an external mouse for use when they have enough desktop space. Just plug the mouse into an available USB port on the side of your iBook.*

6. Press the Power button on the front or side of the Mac. (It's on the keyboard for an iBook.) You should see a small light appear on the Power button (on certain models), or a small light illuminates on the display to show that the Mac is powering up.

That's it. If all goes well, your Mac should fire up and be ready to go. You'll see the Apple logo screen, followed by the Mac OS X progress window. Soon, if this is the first time you've turned on your Mac, you'll be greeted by the Setup Assistant.

NOTE   *If you don't see anything on the screen, if you see something blinking, or if it's been, say, 20 minutes and nothing is happening and the power light is either amber or off, turn to Chapter 24 to troubleshoot your Mac.*

Get Online with the Setup Assistant

Once the Mac has started up, you'll be greeted by the Setup Assistant. The Mac OS X Setup Assistant is designed to walk you through some of the basic settings that your Mac needs to operate without making you dig too deep into all the configuration controls. The Setup Assistant, instead, asks you plain questions and helps you enter the answers. Here are some of those steps:

1. The Mac OS X Setup Assistant begins with the "Welcome" screen, where you begin by choosing your country and clicking the Continue button. Click the Go Back button anytime to return to a previous screen.

2. Next, answer with the type of keyboard layout you want to use and click Continue.

3. On the next screen, enter your Apple ID if you have one. (You can also enter a .Mac membership name and password, if you have that.) If you don't have an Apple ID, you can either create one (choose Create an Apple ID for Me) or you can skip it for now (choose Don't Create an Apple ID for Me) and click Continue.

NOTE *An Apple ID is used for a variety of reasons, most of which involve buying something— purchases from the iTunes Music Store or buying prints through iPhoto. You'll also need one to access portions of Apple's Support site on the Internet. It's handy to have an Apple ID, but you can sign up later if you want to skip it for now.*

4. After the initial screens, you'll be asked to enter registration information and answer some demographic questions. Don't forget to check No next to the "I would like…" options if you don't want to be contacted by Apple or third parties.

5. The next screens are more interesting. On the Create Your Account screen, enter your full name in the Name entry box, followed by a shorter user name in the Short Name box. This will be your name on the Mac OS X system, and it will be the name of your personal *home* folder, where your documents and preferences will be stored. Next, enter a password in the Password and Verify boxes (since you can't see what you type, you'll enter it twice). Remember that passwords are case sensitive, so if you use any capital letters, you'll always have to type those letters as capitals. In the Password Hint entry box, enter a hint that doesn't give away your password, but that you can use to help remember it, if desired. Click Continue.

NOTE *The password and user name are necessary if you decide to create multiple users or to access your Mac from another Mac on a network, as discussed in Chapter 21. (You'll also sometimes use it when installing new software.) Remember to keep your password from being easily guessed by combining numbers and letters, preferably using nonsensical words.*

6. Once you've created a user account, you'll set up your Internet account. If you have your own account, select the I'll Use My Existing Service option and click Continue. If you don't yet want Internet access, you can select I'm Not Ready to Connect to the Internet and skip a few steps. If you want to set up a new Earthlink account, choose the option I'd Like a Free Trial Account with Earthlink, or I Have a Code for a Special Offer with Earthlink, whichever is appropriate.

NOTE

If you choose to set up your existing service, you'll be asked how you connect—telephone modem, cable modem, DSL modem, local network (Ethernet), or local network (wireless). You'll then need to enter some vital numbers and make choices—see Chapters 5 and 22 if you're not sure what to do for those steps. In most cases, you'll need to know how your Internet service provider recommends that you set up Internet access.

7. Next up, after you've stepped through Internet setup, you'll be back at the step that enables you to get an Apple ID or sign up with your .Mac registration. (You won't see this step if you skip signing up for Internet access.) Choose either the Use My .Mac Membership option or Create My Apple ID, as appropriate, and then click Continue. You'll be walked through any additional necessary steps.

8. If you've configured Internet access, the next step is to send your registration to Apple. Click Continue on the Now You're Ready to Connect screen. After a moment, the assistant will report success or failure.

9. Now, if you've set up an Internet account, you'll next configure an e-mail account on the Set Up Mail screen. You can either use a .Mac account (if you've configured one), or you can add a POP or IMAP account. You'll need to know something about your e-mail setup from your ISP (or company or organization). See Chapter 18 for details.

10. With your Internet and e-mail choices made, you can next choose your local time zone on the Select Time Zone screen, followed—if you haven't set up Internet access—by the Set Your Date and Time screen. (Use the arrows next to the "digital" date and time entries to change them to the current date and time.) Click Continue and you'll be reminded to register if you haven't already. Then, the Mac OS X desktop will appear and you're ready to compute.

Did you know?

Software Update

If you created an Internet account using the Mac OS X Assistant, Software Update will automatically launch the first time you access your desktop and check special Apple computers via the Internet for updates to your Mac OS X software. If Software Update finds new versions of your software, the Software Update icon flashes in the Dock at the bottom of the screen. Click it, and a listing will appear in the Software Update window. Place check marks next to the items you want to install, then click Install. A window will appear asking for your password. Enter it in the Password box and click OK. Now, the updates will be downloaded and installed automatically. Note that these updates can take a long time if you have a modem connection, so if you'd like to ignore Software Update for now, click Cancel in the Software Update window and it will disappear. (See Chapter 24 for more on Software Update.)

Mac: About, On, Off, Sleep

Once you get past the assistants, you're greeted with the desktop—the space that shows your hard drive icon, a few words across the top of the screen, and a little Trash can. I'll discuss this area in more depth in Chapters 2 through 4. For now, we need to talk about a few important commands.

Which Mac OS Do You Have?

The first command to cover is About This Computer. Throughout this book, I'll be referring to different versions of the Mac OS. In order to know if a particular feature is available to you, you'll need to know if you have Mac OS X 10.1, 10.2, 10.3, or a later (or earlier, such as Mac OS 9.1) version of the Mac OS. To find out, move your mouse pointer to the top of the screen and point it at the little Apple logo. Click the mouse button once. A menu appears.

Now, move the mouse down the menu until it points at About This Mac. Click the mouse button again. The About This Mac window appears. This window tells you some other things about your Mac, including how much system RAM (random access memory) it has and the type of processor your Mac has installed.

Turn Off Mac

You've already turned on your Mac successfully using the Power button on the Mac or on the Mac's keyboard. But what about turning off the Mac? There are a couple of different ways to do that, and it's important to turn it off correctly.

Let's start with the one way *not* to turn off your Mac. Don't just cut power to the machine. That means don't just pull the cord out of the wall or surge protector, and it means don't just throw the power switch on the surge protector. If your Mac ever crashes, you may have to resort to this sort of thing, but not yet.

Instead, shut down your Mac gracefully by choosing Shut Down from the Apple menu (the one that looks like an Apple logo).

 *Another way to shut down is to tap the* POWER *key on your Mac's keyboard, if it has a* POWER *key. A dialog box appears, allowing you to do a number of power-related things. To shut down, just click the Shut Down button with your mouse.*

You may notice that after choosing Shut Down, your Mac jumps through a few hoops. It will ask all open application programs if they need to save anything, then it tells them to quit. During that process, the application may ask *you* if you want to save something. Once all that business has been taken care of, the Mac quits all those programs, writes some last-minute things to the hard disk, and shuts itself down. To start up again, tap the Power button.

Restart Mac

Sometimes you don't really want Mac to shut all the way down. Instead, you simply want it to restart—maybe you've just installed a new program or you're experiencing odd behavior because of an errant program or similar issue. In that case, you'll choose Restart from the Apple menu (in

How to ... Put Mac to Sleep

Here's the cool option. You know how it takes a minute or so for your Mac to start up when it's completely off? Well, you can choose to put the Mac to *sleep* instead, so that it wakes up more quickly and is ready to work. The best part is that the Mac is still using very little power, even though it's turned on and working. (In some cases, it can even wake up to accept an incoming fax!)

On most of today's iMacs and eMacs, you can put it to sleep by simply pressing the Power button on the front or the side of the Mac. Your Mac should immediately power down, plus, the Power button or the light on your Mac's display may strobe, almost as if the Mac were snoring. You can put an iBook to sleep by simply closing its lid.

You can also put the Mac to sleep by choosing Sleep from the Apple menu. Alternatively, if your Mac has a POWER key on its keyboard, you can press that key, then click the Sleep command that appears in the dialog box on screen.

To wake up your Mac, just tap any key on your keyboard. The screen will light back up (it may also shimmer a bit). You're ready to compute.

Mac OS X). You can also tap the POWER key on your keyboard, if you have such a key, and choose Restart. Your Mac goes through the same procedure as when you issue the Shut Down command, except that the power is never turned off to the Mac, and the Mac OS starts right back up again after the contents of system memory are cleared.

Chapter 2

Get Acquainted with Your Mac

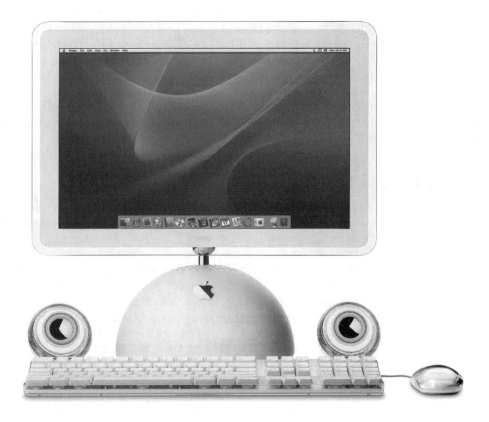

How to...

- Figure out what the desktop is for
- Learn how to use the mouse
- Click and drag on the screen
- Get to know icons and windows
- Work with (and eject) disks
- Set volume and other preferences with menu bar icons
- Get some Help

If you've worked your way through Chapter 1, then, hopefully, you've gotten past the Setup Assistant, you have an Internet account, and all your settings are in order. Now let's take a look at what you see once you've powered up your Mac. Your Mac is a combination of hardware—things on the outside that you touch and push like the CD or DVD drive, the mouse, and the keyboard—and software—the computer code that creates the *interface* on the screen, which is made up of icons, menu items, and windows. That interface is created by the *operating system*, the low-level computer instructions that give the Mac its on-screen personality. That operating system is Mac OS X, which we'll be exploring in this chapter and this part of the book.

In this chapter you'll see how those things come together. You'll learn how to move around on the screen, work with the mouse and keyboard, insert and work with CDs and DVDs, and work with the internal hard disk.

What Is the Desktop?

Let's begin at the beginning. After you've pressed the Power button (or POWER key) and your Mac has started up, you'll see one of two things: the login screen or the desktop. If you see a login screen, you'll need to enter your user name and password, as detailed in Chapter 21.

In most cases, you'll see the desktop. The *desktop*, for all practical purposes, is the background pattern or color you see on the main screen of your Mac when it first starts up. Think of it in terms of 3-D: you'll see the little hard disk picture(s), the menu bar, and the Trash picture. All these items can be thought of as sitting *on top of* the desktop, as shown in Figure 2-1.

If it's called the desktop, then clearly this is supposed to have some relationship to a typical desk, right? Sort of. The desktop represents the top of a desk, but there's stuff on it that you wouldn't normally put on top of your desk, like a trash can and a hard disk. But for the most part, the metaphor holds up.

So what are you looking at? The desktop metaphor is made possible by three major elements: icons, menus, and windows. Each represents a real-world idea you'd find near, or on, a desk.

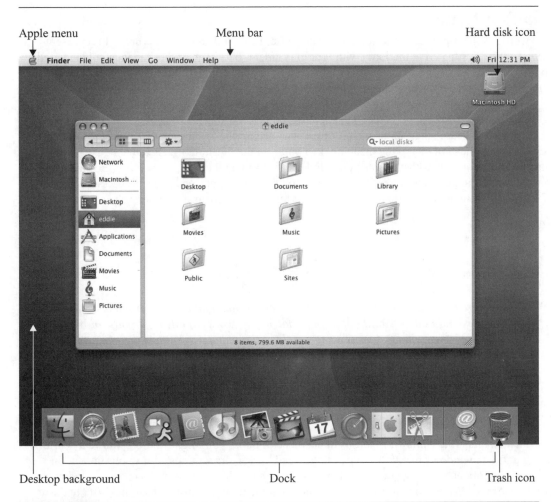

Apple menu   Menu bar   Hard disk icon

Desktop background   Dock   Trash icon

FIGURE 2-1   The Mac OS X desktop, which is the pattern behind other interface elements
that make up your virtual "workspace"

What's an Icon?

Icons are the small pictures that represent parts of your Mac or files on your computer. The
Macintosh HD icon, for instance, represents the hard disk that's inside your Mac's case. A hard
disk is used for storage—it's sort of a virtual filing cabinet. The icon, then, allows you to open
that filing cabinet and root around in the file folders.

What's a Menu?

The words at the top of the Mac screen (Finder, File, Edit, and so on, in Figure 2-1) represent *menus*—they're situated in the long, white (or gray) menu bar. Each of these menus holds related commands that allow you to accomplish things on your Mac, almost as if they were the drawers full of pencils, staplers, and scissors you'd find in a desk.

In Mac OS X, the menu bar offers two special menus, shown in the following illustration. Both of these menus will appear no matter what application you're using on your Mac. One is the Apple menu; the other is the "application" menu, which is named for the application that's currently active. Point at the application menu (the menu marked Safari in the illustration), click the mouse button, and you'll see commands that enable you to hide the current application, show all applications, and in most cases, quit that application. Point and click on the Apple menu and you can access a number of quick preferences and shortcuts to help make your computing tasks simpler.

Apple menu
| Application menu

TIP   *If you're familiar with Microsoft Windows (or, for that matter, most graphical interfaces for Unix and Linux), you'll notice that Mac menus work slightly differently. In Windows, each individual window has its own menu bar within that window. On the Mac, the menu bar is always at the top of the screen, and it changes whenever you change applications. It may seem like the Mac menu bar is always the same, but the menu bar actually changes every time you load or switch to a different application.*

What's a Window?

Our final element, the *window*, is sort of like a piece of paper you might find on your real-world desktop. It's in windows that you'll type things, read things, draw things, and so on. In fact, on the Mac, just about anything you do will take place in a window. If you'd like to see a window, point your mouse at the Macintosh HD icon and click the mouse button twice quickly. (That's called a *double-click*, and it almost always *opens* the item you double-clicked.) We'll talk about windows in greater depth later in this chapter.

Using the Mouse and Keyboard

The most basic skill requirement for using a modern computer is using a mouse and keyboard. The mouse, perhaps, is primary on the Macintosh, since Macs were designed from the outset to use the little guy.

Depending on the age of your iMac or eMac, you have one of two mouse designs. The earlier iMac mouse was a round disk with one large button, called the Apple USB Mouse (you can see the name on the underside of the mouse). This mouse is interesting to users because it can be a little tough to orient—"up" is where the mouse cable connects to the mouse, and you need to orient "up" so that it's pointed in the general direction of your Mac. (Not pointed *toward* the Mac, but

Did you know?

The Dock

There's probably another question you may be asking about now—what's the Dock? That area down at the bottom of the screen is a new feature in Mac OS X, and it has some interesting capabilities. As you'll see later in this chapter, the Dock is where you'll always find the Trash can in Mac OS X; in Chapter 3, you'll see that the Dock is one way to switch to the Finder. In fact, the Dock is many things—you can start applications from it, switch to running applications using it, and even place your own items on the Dock. For now, just remember that it's there and it's an important part of the Mac experience. In Chapter 4, you'll see how to use and customize the Dock to its fullest.

oriented in that direction, so that when you push the mouse toward its own cable, you're seeing the mouse pointer move straight up on the screen.)

The oval mouse (called the Pro Mouse) is interesting in two respects. First, it's an *optical* mouse, meaning it doesn't have a rolling ball that registers movement. This results in good tracking on a normal tabletop, even without a mouse pad. (It can also give very bad results, depending on the surface.) Second, the mouse doesn't appear to have a button—that's because the whole top of the mouse acts as the button. When resting your hand naturally on the mouse, pressing down with your fingers will cause it to "click."

> **NOTE** *For the sake of convenience, I'll refer throughout this chapter, and elsewhere in the book, to "pressing the mouse button." In the case of the Pro Mouse, this simply means the top portion of the mouse is under your fingers. You'll get used to this movement fairly quickly.*

On an iBook, of course, you don't have a mouse (although you can plug one into an available USB port on the side of the iBook). Instead, the iBook has a built-in *trackpad*, which you use for moving the pointer around on the screen. To use it, touch the trackpad and glide your finger over it. Under the trackpad is a button, which you'll use for selecting items, as described next.

> **NOTE** *At this writing Apple has introduced a wireless version of its Pro keyboard and mouse— they use Bluetooth technology, which is a relatively new wireless standard for input and output devices like keyboards, mice, and even printers, PDAs, and mobile phones. In practice, using these devices is similar to using their cabled cousins except that you've got to replace the batteries every so often.*

Click with the Mouse

The mouse is used to point at, grab, carry, and activate items on the desktop. When you move the mouse with your hand or glide your finger over the trackpad, a little arrow on the screen moves around with you to indicate where the mouse is currently pointing. That arrow is called the *mouse pointer,* or simply "the pointer," and it's something you'll get to know very well. No matter what you want to do with your Mac, you'll likely do it by placing the pointer over an icon (or menu item or window) on your screen and clicking the button.

NOTE *Mouse and trackpad movements are relative, not absolute. That means if you pick up the mouse (or, on a trackpad, pick up your finger) and put it down in a different place, the location of the pointer on the screen won't change. Only moving the mouse or moving your finger in a particular direction will move the pointer in that direction.*

There are three basic actions that the mouse or trackpad allows you to perform: select, open, and drag-and-drop. Each of these is a combination of pointing and clicking the button:

- **Select** To select an item, move the pointer until it's touching that item, then press and release the button once. A selected icon becomes highlighted, a selected window comes to the *foreground* (it appears "on top" of other windows), and a selected menu drops down to show you its contents. In the case of a menu, you move your pointer down to the menu item and click again to select that menu item. You'll also find interface buttons and menus within applications that need to be selected.

- **Open** Icons like the Macintosh HD are opened (to reveal their contents) by moving the pointer over the item and double-clicking the button. (Click it twice in rapid succession.) Other icons can be opened, too, like document, folder, and application icons.

NOTE *You can also open icons and folders in the Finder using a sequence of commands: select the item (point at the icon and click once), then point at the File menu and click once, and then point at the Open command and click once.*

- **Drag-and-drop** On the desktop and in the Finder, you can drag icons around to move them from one place to another. Place the pointer on an item, click and hold down the button, and move the pointer. Now you're dragging. To drop the icon in its new location, let go of the button.

NOTE *By default, you have another way of "clicking" when you're using an iBook's trackpad— you can tap the trackpad itself to perform a click. This can take some getting used to— tap once to click once, tap twice for a double-click, and tap and hold to drag an item. (This last operation definitely requires some dexterity.) You may also find that this tapping capability is a bit annoying; you can turn it off by accessing System Preferences, which we'll discuss in detail in Chapter 4.*

You'll also find that the on-screen pointer changes sometimes to reflect different things that are happening. It turns into a little rotating beach ball, for instance, when the Mac is busy doing something that can't be interrupted in the current application. It turns into an *insertion point* (also called an *I-beam*)—a capital "I"—when the mouse is hovering over a window (or sometimes a portion of a window, such as part of an electronic form) where you can type. Click the mouse once in that window, and the insertion point is placed in the document. Type with the keyboard and your words appear:

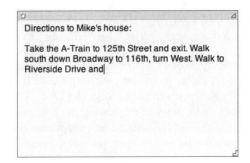

Directions to Mike's house:

Take the A-Train to 125th Street and exit. Walk south down Broadway to 116th, turn West. Walk to Riverside Drive and|

Special Keyboard Keys

Most of the time, you'll find that typing on your keyboard is like typing on any computer terminal, typewriter, or word processor. But there are special keys on the Mac's keyboard and special key combinations you'll use for various things.

The special keys are the CONTROL, OPTION, and ⌘ (Command) keys. These keys, along with the more familiar SHIFT key, can be used in various combinations to perform special commands in your application or in the Finder.

You'll see these special keyboard commands throughout this book. In order to use them, you'll need to hold down all of the keys at once, then release them all together. For instance, ⌘-S can be used to save a document in most applications: press ⌘ first and then the S key, release them together, and the command will execute.

NOTE   *Some of the most common keyboard commands for working with everyday applications are discussed in Chapter 6; others are discussed throughout the text.*

This brings up a fourth instance where you can use the mouse to perform some interesting tasks. Hold down the CONTROL key, click the mouse/trackpad button, and then release them both. Do this in the right place (usually when pointing at an object in the Finder or in an application) and you'll get a *contextual menu*—a special "pop-up" menu of options regarding that object, as shown in the accompanying illustration. In essence, Mac OS X is offering a special set of menu commands that are relevant to the object you've chosen.

NOTE *If you're used to Microsoft Windows, you'll notice that the Mac mouse only has one button. This* CONTROL-*click scheme is sort of like "right-clicking" in Windows.*

If you have a Mac made in the spring of 2001 or later, you'll also notice some other keys on your extended keyboard. On the far right, above the number pad, are three audio keys (VOLUME DOWN, VOLUME UP, and MUTE) along with an EJECT key. The EJECT key is used to eject media in the CD or DVD drive, and it works whether you're viewing the Finder or not. The volume keys also work whether or not you're in the Finder, with some exceptions. (For instance, the keys will occasionally not be recognized when you're playing a full-screen game.)

NOTE *On an iBook, these special keys share a role with the* function keys. *When you press one of the volume keys (*F3 *and* F4*), for instance, the volume level will change on the iBook. But if you want to access the functionality assigned to* F3 *and* F4 *instead of changing volume, you first press the* FN *key (in the bottom-left corner of the keyboard) and then press one of those function keys. Now, it will register as* F3 *or* F4*, or whichever key you press. Also, note that you can use the* FN *key along with other keys on the keyboard to emulate a number pad (see the letter keys* U, I, O, *and so on) or for* PAGE UP *and* PAGE DOWN *commands (see the arrow keys). By pressing the* FN *key, in other words, you'll activate the secondary function of those keys, which is represented by the smaller label on the bottom-right corner of those keys.*

Mouse and Keyboard Connectors

Your iMac's or eMac's mouse and keyboard both connect to the Mac using one of the two (or three) Universal Serial Bus (USB) ports on the side of the Mac. The keyboard is plugged into the Mac, and then the mouse is plugged into one side of the keyboard. (You can also plug your mouse into the USB port on the Mac's side, but the keyboard is a better choice.) Likewise, if you want to add an external keyboard or mouse to your iBook, you can do so by plugging into one of the USB ports on the side of the iBook.

If one or both of these plugs works loose, don't worry about it too much. USB is called a *hot-pluggable* technology, which basically means that it's OK to connect and disconnect devices while your Mac is running. Bottom line: if one of the devices comes unplugged, plug it back in. It should work right away. That's not quite true with USB or FireWire-based hard drives and such sophisticated devices, which need to be *mounted* and *ejected* to work with. But for basic input devices—or output, like a printer—you can plug and unplug them with few worries (except for the obvious...you usually can't use an unplugged device!).

NOTE *You'll see more about this in Chapter 23, but Apple's USB keyboard is actually a USB hub. That means its second USB port can be used for connecting another USB device, such as a joystick, trackball, or even an image scanner or digital camera.*

Work with Icons and Windows

I mentioned that icons are the small pictures on your Mac screen that represent parts of your Mac's internal filing system. And while icons represent different parts, windows are the way you view those parts—when you open a file folder or a document, you'll view its contents using a window. Let's look at icons and windows each in turn.

In Depth with Icons

You can often tell right away what a given item is based on the way its icon looks. You'll encounter about five different types of icons on your Mac, and each gives you an idea of what it does based on its general appearance.

Audio CD

- **Hardware icons**   These icons appear on the desktop to help you interact with some of the hardware in or attached to your Mac. Whenever you start up your Mac, for instance, the internal hard disk is recognized and the Macintosh HD icon is placed on the desktop. Similarly, if you pop a CD-ROM into your Mac's CD-ROM or DVD-ROM drive, that CD's icon appears on the desktop. *Hardware icons generally look like the devices they're representing—the disk icons look like little disks.*

Library

- **Folders**   Open your Macintosh HD and a window appears that shows you more icons— most of them will be folders. Folder icons are used by the Finder to help you manage your documents and applications. You can create a storage system by creating new folders that organize your documents and applications. *Folder icons look like file folders.*

Image Capture

- **Programs**   Application programs like AppleWorks or Internet Explorer have their own icons, too. When you "open" an application (by pointing to its icon and double-clicking the mouse), you start up that application, loading all of its menu commands and, probably, a document window. You can then start creating. *Program icons are often the least standardized—they tend to be unique icons designed by the application programmers.*

Memo_Sales.rtf

- **Documents**   Document icons are created whenever you save a document from an application. If you create a report in AppleWorks, for instance, a new document is created when you invoke the Save command, and a new icon appears in the Finder. Just as with a document in a physical filing system, you can move that document icon to a folder where you want it stored. *Documents often, although not always, look like pieces of paper or some variation on that theme—a piece of paper with a special logo, for instance.*

- **System icons**   This is a catchall category that we won't discuss too much right now. The Mac OS features many special icons that perform certain tasks behind the scenes on your Mac. For instance, there are system icons that represent the fonts you use in your documents and the special files used to manage the preferences settings on your Mac. You'll read more about system icons in Part IV of this book.

Converter.plugin

Accounts.prefPane

AppleGothic.dfont

Memo_Sales.rtf alias

- ■ **Aliases**   An *alias* is a special "empty" icon that doesn't really represent a file or a device—instead, it *points* to that file. For instance, an alias allows you to have a pointer to a document or application on your desktop while the actual document or application is stored deep in your hard disk's file folders. Instead of being an entire *copy* of a file, an alias is simply an icon that represents the file. *An alias looks like the document or application it points to, but it has a special, curved arrow as part of the icon.*

Icons will respond to the mouse or trackpad actions described early in this chapter. They can be selected, opened, and moved around the screen using drag-and-drop. In fact, you'll find that there's often reason to drag an icon over another icon and drop the first icon on the second icon. For instance, you can drop a document icon on top of a folder icon to store that document in that folder. Similarly, you can drop a document icon onto an application icon to start that application and view the document.

Open Up Windows

So what do you do with these icons? In many cases, you *open* them. When you open them, a window appears. For instance, if you double-click the icon for a document that was created in the Mac's text editor, TextEdit, a window appears that reveals that document's contents, as shown in Figure 2-2.

Any window has standard parts that make it easy to deal with. All of these parts allow you to move things around, resize them, stack windows—do different things while you're working with the windows. Here's what the different parts do:

- ■ **Close button**   Click this to close the window. Note that you're dealing with an application's window, so closing the window doesn't necessarily quit the application. You'll often have a different command to quit (usually in the menu that's named for the application, such as the TextEdit menu).

- ■ **Minimize button**   Click this button to minimize the window to the Dock. This is one way to decrease window clutter. The minimized window will appear as a *tile* on the right side of the Dock, where you can click it to work with it again.

- ■ **Maximize button**   Click this button to resize the window to optimum size (in many cases). Click it again to revert to the original size.

- ■ **Title bar**   This part of the window tells you what the window represents. It's also used to drag the window around the screen: click and drag on the title bar, then release the mouse button to drop the window. (Most windows can also be quickly *minimized*—sent from the screen and represented on the Dock as an icon—when you double-click the title bar.)

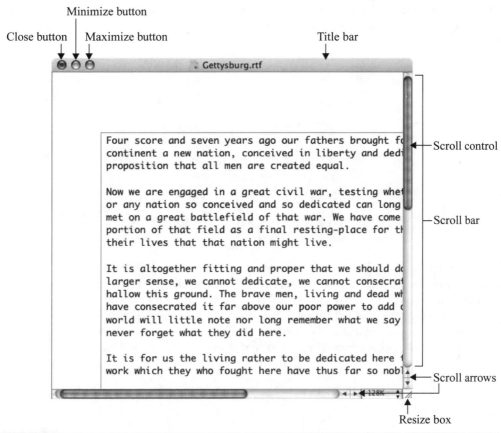

Minimize button

Close button   Maximize button   Title bar

Scroll control

Scroll bar

Scroll arrows

Resize box

FIGURE 2-2   The parts of a window in Mac OS X

- ■ **Scroll bar**   This bar shows you that the window can be scrolled. If more information is in the window than can be shown at once, a scroll control will appear, which you can drag to see the rest of the window's contents.

- ■ **Scroll control**   Click and drag the scroll control to scroll the window's contents up and down (or side to side, if you use the bottom scroll bar).

- ■ **Scroll arrows**   Click the arrows to scroll up and down or side to side within the window.

- ■ **Resize box**   Click and drag the resize box to make the window larger or smaller.

You'll also encounter some different sorts of windows, called *dialog boxes*. These windows are designed so that the Mac OS can ask you questions or get you to provide information. Usually, dialog boxes require you to click Cancel or OK after you've finished entering information (these tend to look like alerts, which I'll cover momentarily). They don't always, though.

As shown in this illustration, some dialog boxes have to be dealt with in order to move on from the document in question. These are called dialog *sheets*, because they pop out from under the title bar of the document window in question, making it clear which window the dialog sheet's options will affect:

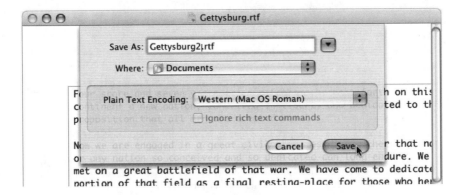

Another type of dialog box is called an *alert*. These messages appear when the Mac OS or an application needs to get your attention because something immediate is happening. This can range from something wrong with a printer or peripheral to a problem with a crashed or misbehaving application. Alerts are like regular dialog boxes, except they don't often give you many options or settings—you simply respond to the question. You can usually dismiss an alert by clicking the Cancel or OK button, although sometimes you'll have to make a more specific choice:

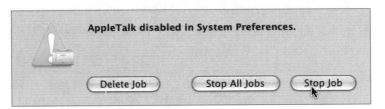

Hard Disks, CDs, DVDs, and Peripherals

Your hard disk is where you'll store most of your documents and any new applications that you install on your Mac. The hard disk is a small box inside your Mac that uses magnetic technology to write down the ones and zeros that make up "digital data." Visually, this digital data is represented by folder, application, document, and system icons that are displayed when you double-click the disk icon in the Finder.

CD and DVD discs are slightly different. CD-ROM and DVD-ROM are *read-only* technologies because you can't actually save any files to the discs, delete files stored on the discs, or move things to different folders on the discs. Instead, you can only copy from the CD-ROM or DVD-ROM to another disk, start up an application, or open a document directly from the CD-ROM or DVD-ROM. (CD-ROM stands for Compact Disc–Read-Only Memory; DVD-ROM stands for Digital Versatile Disc–Read-Only Memory.)

Storage vs. Memory

Storage disks are different from main memory in any computer. Main memory is called *Random Access Memory (RAM)* and actually consists of little computer chips—usually arranged on a special plug-in module—that hold digital information. RAM is sort of the short-term memory of your Mac. Anything currently on the screen, anything being printed, and some behind-the-scenes work goes on in RAM. (In Chapter 1 you saw how to get the About This Mac information, which tells you the current installed amount of RAM.)

But your Mac can easily forget what's in RAM, since RAM is wiped clean whenever you power down your Mac. In fact, if a power surge, a kicked power cord, or some other uncontrollable circumstance cut power to your Mac, you'd also lose whatever was in RAM at that time. RAM needs power in order to remember things.

That's why you have storage disks. Hard disks and removable disks (like writable CDs or Iomega Zip disks) are used for writing things down and saving them long term. Whenever you create a document using your Mac, you'll want to save it to a disk—that lets you keep the document over the long term. The same goes for applications. If you bought and wanted to use Microsoft Office, you'd need to "install" the application by copying it to your hard disk. That way it's easily accessible to your Mac—your Mac will remember, long term, how to run Microsoft Office.

Most modern iMacs, eMacs, and iBooks can also handle CD-R (CD-Recordable) and CD-RW (CD-Rewritable) discs, which do allow you to store data on the discs. CD-R media can be written to once, and then the data is preserved for the life of the disc; CD-RW can be written to, erased, and written to again. This can all be handled from within the Mac OS, as you'll see in Chapter 3. Likewise, Macs with a "SuperDrive" can write to DVD-R and DVD-RW media as well—a recordable DVD offers tons of storage space (up to 4.7GB) while not taking up any more physical space than a CD. Having a SuperDrive means a more expensive Mac, however, so they're not quite as common.

Of course, not every disc you deal with is a data disc. You can also listen to music stored on audio CDs on your Mac, and you can watch DVD movies on Macs equipped with DVD players.

SuperDrive-equipped Macs can do another trick—they can not only play back video DVDs, they can create them. Chapter 16 covers using iMovie and iDVD to edit digital video movies and "burn" them to a DVD that can be played in a conventional DVD player.

The Hard Disk Icon

The hard disk icon is always there on the desktop by default (although you can change that, as detailed in Chapter 4). As the Mac starts up, it looks for the hard disk and other storage disks that are attached to the machine. Any disks found are *mounted* on the desktop. That is, the icon is made to appear on the desktop, available for you to use. If you insert a disk (like a CD) after startup, the

Mac OS places the CD's icon as close to the top-right corner as it can get without covering up another icon.

To peer into the hard disk's contents, you can point the mouse at the icon and double-click. This opens the main-level window that shows all of the folders used to store things on your Mac. The hard disk icon can be renamed—you can even change the look of the icon—but you can't throw the icon away or store it inside a folder or on another storage device.

When a disk is recognized, it's also mounted and displayed in the Sidebar of the Finder window, so that you can get to it even if it's not on the desktop. You'll learn more about the Finder window in Chapter 3.

The Trash

Basically, the Trash is the way you delete things from your hard disks, removable disks, or desktop. To delete items, you simply drag-and-drop their icons onto the Trash. When you've dropped something on the Trash icon, that icon changes to reflect the fact that the Trash has items in it. That doesn't mean that items have been deleted yet, though—the Trash has to be emptied first, which is something we'll discuss in Chapter 3.

The Trash icon is also used for something else—ejecting CDs and other removable disks. It takes some getting used to, but after you've dragged a CD or removable disk icon to the Trash, it will pop out of its drive (or the CD-ROM drive will open up). You'll even notice that when you do drag items to the Trash to be ejected, its icon changes to reflect that:

Disks are not deleted or erased when dragged to the Trash. In order to erase entire disks (or discs, in the case of CD-RW and DVD-RW media), you use the Disk Utility application, as discussed in Chapter 24.

If you've used Microsoft Windows 95/98/Me, you'll find that the Trash is very similar to the Recycle Bin in Windows. The major difference is that entire folders are stored, intact, in the Mac's Trash, while the Windows Recycle Bin will usually do away with folders.

CDs and DVDs

CD and DVD icons appear when you insert a CD or DVD into the CD or DVD drive of your Mac. How you insert the disc depends on what type of Mac you have. Some iMac and iBook models offer a "slot-loading" CD or DVD drive. In this case, you insert a CD or DVD the same way you slide them into the slot on a car-stereo CD player. If there's no CD or DVD currently in the Mac, just slide your disc into the open slot. After you've placed it part of the way in, it will be pulled the rest of the way in by its mechanism.

The original iMac, the iMac G4, eMac, and earlier iBooks offer tray-loading CD/DVD players. On earlier tray loaders, such as the original iMac and early iBooks, you press the button on the front of the drive to pop it open, then you insert a disc and close the drive. On newer models, such as the iMac G4 and the eMac, you press the EJECT key on your keyboard to open the drive and access the tray.

When the Mac has recognized the disc, it puts a new icon on the desktop to represent that disc. If the disc is a CD-ROM or DVD-ROM (that is, if they're *data discs* designed to store data files that your Mac can access in the form of icons), you can double-click the icon to open a Finder window and view the files.

NOTE *While DVD drives are generally more useful for playing DVD movies, the computer industry is slowly moving toward storing software on DVD-ROM discs, which offer much greater capacity than CD-ROM discs. Eventually, you'll start finding more and more software—especially games, education, and reference titles—available in DVD-ROM format.*

If the disc is an audio CD, you'll see a generic audio CD icon, probably named "Audio CD." In that case, double-clicking the CD icon will open a window in the Finder that allows you to see the songs on that disc. (You may have to switch back to the Finder first, because iTunes will launch automatically when you insert the audio disc, by default.)

If the disc is a DVD video, inserting it will cause the movie to be launched and displayed in the DVD Player application. If you quit DVD Player and/or switch to the Finder, you can double-click a DVD icon to reveal its contents—movie data—in a Finder window.

NOTE *In order to play DVDs, you must have a DVD-capable drive in your Mac. Some models have only CD-ROM drives; others have CD-RW drives that cannot read DVDs. Still others have "combo" drives, which are CD-RW and DVD capable, and the SuperDrive, of course, can read CDs and DVDs as well as write to recordable CD and DVD media.*

Since a commercial CD-ROM or DVD-ROM is read-only, you can't drag an icon from the desktop or a Finder window to the disc icon or window. You can drag icons the other way, though, causing the items on the disc to be copied to a Finder window or the desktop.

NOTE *Some Mac models have CD-RW drives that do let you copy items to the disc. If you insert a CD-R or CD-RW disk in a Mac that's so equipped (or a DVD-R or DVD-RW disc in a SuperDrive), you'll be able to drag files to it much as if it were an external disk. The only difference is that you have to "burn" a CD-R, CD-RW, DVD-R, or DVD-RW disc before it can be ejected and used elsewhere or stored.*

To eject the CD or DVD, you can do one of two things. You can select the disc icon with your on-screen pointer and then choose File | Eject in the Finder or press ⌘-E. That ejects the disc. Or, as mentioned before, you can drag the disc icon to the Trash. That ejects the disc; it doesn't erase it.

Removable Disks

If you have an Iomega Zip drive or some other sort of external storage drive, those disks will appear on your desktop as well. Usually you just pop the disk into the drive, and, after a short delay, its icon appears on the desktop. It works just like a CD, with the exception that you'll be able to save files to removable storage disks by dragging and dropping files on that disk.

You eject removable disks the same way you eject a CD: select the disk and choose Special | Eject, or drag the disk's icon to the Trash.

Get Help from the Mac OS

The Help Viewer system is based on web technology using *hyperlinks*, which allow you to move from topic to topic in the Help Viewer system by clicking the blue, underlined text. This makes it easy to learn about a topic, then click to see a related topic.

In order to see help, open the Help menu and choose the *Application Name* Help command. This works both in the Finder (Help | Mac Help) and in other applications, such as iMovie (Help | iMovie Help). While some other applications will use their own help systems, the Help Viewer (see Figure 2-3) is the standard set by Apple.

For other applications, you may see other types of help. In Classic applications (those that were written for Mac OS 9 but that run in the emulated "Classic" mode in Mac OS X), you may see the Apple Guide system, for instance, or in Internet Explorer you'll see Microsoft's own help system. See the Appendix for more on Classic help systems.

You can also often get to the Help Viewer by holding down the CONTROL key and clicking in most application and Finder windows. In the contextual menu that appears, there's usually a Help entry that you can select. And, you'll find small question mark buttons (?) throughout the Mac OS interface that you can click to get help.

Browse for Help

With the Help Viewer open, you have a couple of choices. You can either browse for help or search for it. To browse, begin by clicking on the hyperlinks—the blue or gray underlined words—on the page. Clicking a hyperlink causes the Help Viewer to show you that topic. This method is a little like using the table of contents in a book. Click the topic that seems most appropriate. When the document for that topic appears in the Help Viewer, you can click the subtopic that seems most appropriate for your situation.

The browsing screen shows you topics that seem to be related to the original topic that you clicked. After you've clicked the subtopic, you'll most likely see an instructional document that walks you through that topic. While you're reading the instructions, you'll see different types of hyperlinks:

■ If you see a link that says "Tell Me More," the Help Viewer will return you to a browsing screen filled with similar topics.

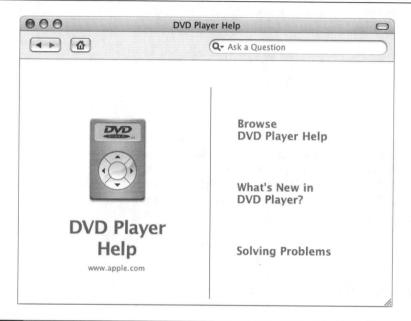

FIGURE 2-3   The Help Viewer is the main online Help system for your Mac.

- If the link says "Open…for me," the link is designed to automatically open the item or command that is being discussed in that help document. For instance, "Open System Preferences for me," when clicked, would open the System Preferences application.

- The third type of link points to a web site on the Internet. These links often begin with "Go…". If your Internet connection is running, you can click one of these links to load your web browser and view the help that's online. (If you have a modem-based connection, you may need to initiate that connection in the Internet Connect application before you can view help that's web-based.)

To leave a particular page, you can either click the Back button in the Help Viewer (which returns you to the list of topics), or you can click a link that takes you to another, related topic. Click and hold the Back button and you'll see a menu of previous articles that you can select from. Or, click the Help Viewer's close box to close help and return to your application.

Search for Help

If the table of contents approach doesn't work for you, you can search directly for a topic using keywords. In the Search entry box at the top of the screen, enter a few words that suggest the issue you want to learn about. You don't need to enter complete sentences—something like "application menu" or "mail merge" should be good enough. (You *can* enter a full question, though, which may help your search succeed.)

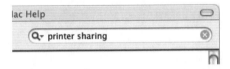

Then press RETURN. After your Mac thinks things over, the Help Viewer will display the search results page. You'll notice that the search results include little bars in a second column. These bars represent the *relevance* of the subtopics—the larger the bar, the more relevant.

When you see a topic that looks good, double-click its name to see a Help document. If you don't see the results you're looking for, you can try different keywords or a different search question—just type it in the Ask entry box and press RETURN.

If you start out in an application-specific Help system, such as iMovie's help, you can click the small magnifying glass in the Ask entry box to select Search All Help. This enables you to conduct the same search using all of the Help Viewer help systems—Mac Help, iTunes Help, AppleScript Help, and so forth.

Menu Bar Icons

One quick concept we should touch on before moving on to the Finder in the next chapter brings together two things we've discussed in this chapter—menus and icons. Mac OS X makes it possible for you to access certain commands and features quickly by using something called a *menu bar icon*—a small menu at the top of the screen that's indicated by an icon. The icon you'll see by default is the volume control. (On most recent Macs, this menu controls the same levels that you can also control using the volume keys.)

The clock, too, is a menu—click it once to see a menu that includes the current date and commands that you can use to change the clock's appearance or set the day and time.

There are other menus you can access in this way. Some of the Mac's networking and Internet features can be accessed via menu bar icons, as can controls for your display, your battery (on iBooks), and even for applications such as iChat. But we'll cover those when we get to them, because you'll need to activate them first. For now, know that those small icons are there for a reason—quick access to important commands.

Chapter 3

Manage Your Files

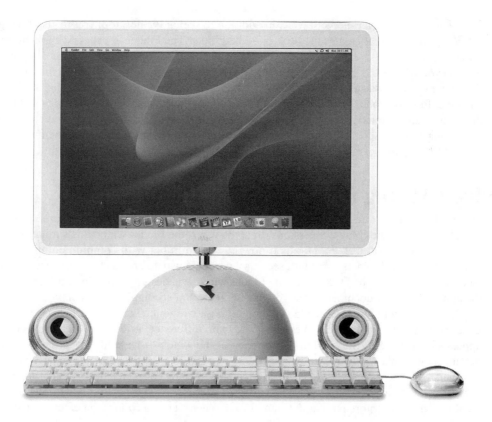

How to...

- Use the Finder window
- Explore your home folder
- Manage folders, files, and icons
- Build aliases
- Burn data to recordable CDs
- Delete icons with the Trash
- Launch documents and applications
- Search for files
- Perform advanced searches

When you first start up your Mac, in addition to seeing the desktop, you're also seeing the application that creates the desktop—the Finder. The Finder is a special application that's always active and can't easily be "quit." It's the Mac OS's built-in application for dealing with the files on your hard drive, your CD/DVD drive, and removable media. You'll find that the Finder is the center of your Mac experience—you use the Finder to manage your applications, documents, and other files. As you'll learn in this chapter, the Finder helps you manage the icons that represent those applications and documents. You'll rename them, move them, copy them, and create folders for storing them in a logical way. We'll also discuss how to delete items, copy them to recordable CDs or DVDs, and search for files to locate them quickly.

Finder 101: Dig into the Finder Window

One of the most unique aspects of Mac OS X is its Finder window, which is something of a departure from earlier Mac OS versions. In some ways, the Finder window is similar to a web browser window—at least insofar as it now has a button bar with common commands and frequently accessed folders. As you'll see, it's a powerful way to browse through your Mac's files (see Figure 3-1), which is the point. The Finder window is designed to help you locate and access the applications and documents that you use to create and accomplish tasks on your Mac.

The Finder window in Mac OS X 10.3 and higher—which we're covering here—is a bit different from earlier Mac OS X versions. The main difference, aside from the "brushed metal" appearance, is the *Sidebar*, the left-side portion of the window that holds icons. Those icons are default choices that Apple makes to help you get started. They're for accessing important items to help you maneuver quickly. At the top of the Sidebar are any connected drives and disks (or discs), as well as the Network icon, which you can use to access any computers that are accessible on a local area network (more on that in Chapter 21.) Whenever you connect an external disk or insert

3

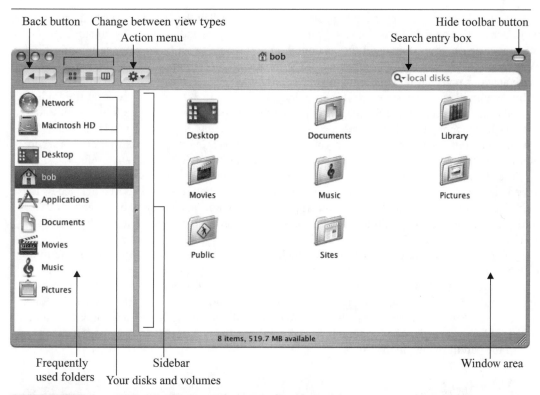

Back button   Change between view types   Hide toolbar button
              Action menu   Search entry box

Frequently   Sidebar   Window area
used folders   Your disks and volumes

FIGURE 3-1   The Finder window offers some handy shortcuts for managing your files.

some sort of removable media (a CD, DVD, or Iomega Zip disk, for instance), it appears at the top of the Sidebar. In this example, I've attached an external FireWire disk and inserted a data CD:

As I touched on in Chapter 2, a big part of the metaphor that the Mac OS uses to help you get work done relies on the idea of folders. You use folders to store and organize the documents and tools you use on your Mac to get things done like you would use a filing cabinet in your office. With that in mind, the bottom portion of the Sidebar contains commonly used folders. Most of these are your personal folders found in your *home* folder; in fact, that's the folder you're looking at by default when you open a new Finder window. (In Figure 3-1, you can see that the folder named bob is selected in the Sidebar. That means the contents of Bob's home folder—subfolders such as the Documents and Movies folders—are currently being displayed.) Your home folder—which is created when you first set up your Mac after unpacking it and turning it on—is where you'll store all of your personal documents, and it's where Mac OS X stores any preferences.

The other folders on the bottom of the Sidebar give you quick access to some of the subfolders stored inside your home folder—Documents, Movies, Music, Pictures—as well as quick access to the folder that holds your desktop and the Applications folder. This is where, by default, you'll find the applications that you'll use to create documents, access the Internet, and accomplish all sorts of tasks using your Mac.

Of course, the common folders on the Sidebar will sometimes have subfolders (sometimes called *child folders*) that you need to dig into. To do that, simply double-click a folder icon in the window area of the Finder window. That should cause the subfolder to open and its contents to appear in the window. To return to a *parent folder*, you can do one of three things: click the Back button in the Finder window, press ⌘–UP ARROW, or hold down the ⌘ key and click the name of the folder at the top of the Finder window. A small menu appears that enables you to choose one of the parent folders in that hierarchy.

 *In the Finder's Columns view, you can simply single-click a parent folder in one of the earlier columns to see its contents.*

Select Items in the Finder

Selecting icons, double-clicking icons, and dragging and dropping icons are covered in Chapter 2, and that process works in Finder windows just as it works on the desktop. But what if you want to gather more than one icon at a time? There are two ways to do it. First, you can select more than one icon at a time by dragging a box around the items. Here's how:

1. Place the mouse pointer just above and to the left of the first icon you want to select.

2. Hold down the mouse button and drag the mouse pointer toward the icon you want to select.

3. Once the first icon is highlighted, keep dragging diagonally to expand the box you're creating. As you expand the box, every item inside the box becomes highlighted.

4. When you've highlighted everything you want to highlight, release the mouse button.

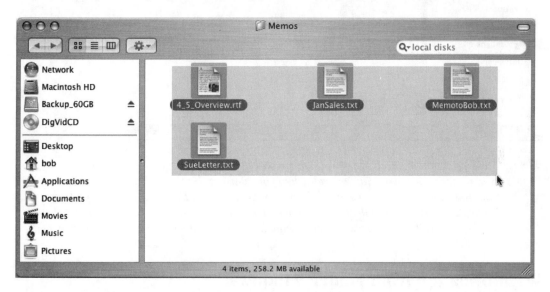

(As you can see, your aim doesn't have to be perfect as long as it covers all the icons you want to select.) Now you have multiple items highlighted. Click and drag one of the items and they all come along. You can treat them all as if they were a single icon, moving them *en masse* to a different folder, to the Printer icon, to the Trash, opening them all using the File | Open command,

and so on. To deselect them, just click anything else on the screen (such as part of the desktop or a different icon).

If you want to add icons that aren't grouped together on the screen, you can add them individually by holding down the ⌘ key as you select each icon. Now, each time you click another icon with the ⌘ key held down, it is added to all the other highlighted items, as shown here:

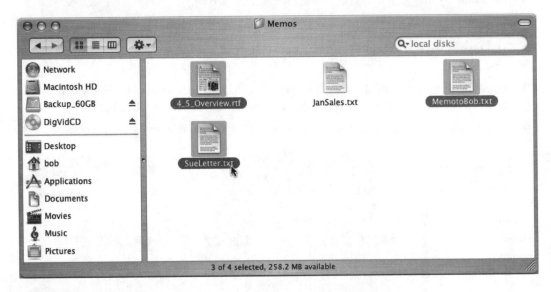

NOTE *These selection methods work well when you're viewing icons, as we've done in these examples, but they work just as well when you're using the Finder windows in List or Columns view—two options we'll discuss in the section "Finder 201: Change How Folders Are Displayed in the Finder." You can drag a rectangle around items in List view windows as well, and you can select additional items in List view or Columns view using the SHIFT key.*

Get Information from Finder Windows

One of the main concerns you may have as a computer owner is maintaining your hard drive and making sure you have enough space to store new files. (It's a constant struggle that may keep you up nights.) Often, the only answer is to delete older files that you don't use anymore—at least once your drive gets a little closer to full. But how can you tell if your drive is getting full?

Look at the bottom of a Finder window, and you'll see some information about the current folder as well as the disk that folder is on. Specifically, you'll see how many items are in that folder and how much storage space is left on that particular disk. (If items are highlighted, you'll see the number selected out of the total, as in 6 of 15 selected.) This works just as well with

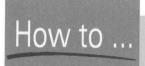

Understand Your Mac's Folders

There are two basic ways to open a new Finder window. One method is to choose File | New or press ⌘-N while the Finder is active. Doing so opens a new Finder window that, by default, displays the contents of your home folder. (You can also quickly open a Finder window by clicking the Finder icon in the Dock.)

Another common approach is particularly comfortable for those of us accustomed to using older versions of the Mac OS: you can double-click the desktop icon for your hard drive. When you do, however, you'll see a different set of folders. Instead of opening to your home folder, double-clicking your hard disk icon opens a window that displays the *root level* of that hard drive. Here's a quick look at those folders:

- The Applications folder is where the Mac OS X installer places Mac OS X native applications, including utilities and Internet applications. As discussed in Chapter 23, you'll typically install your own applications in this folder. This is the same folder you can access by clicking the Applications folder in the Sidebar of a Finder window.

- The Library folder is where important system-level files—preferences, fonts, and other important items—are stored. If you're installing such items (like fonts or application support files) so that any user account on your Mac has them available, you'll generally put them inside a subfolder of the Library folder.

- The System folder is really designed to be off-limits to regular users. This is where Apple's installation applications place important files that keep Mac OS X running.

- The Users folder is where each user's home folder is stored. Even if you're the only user of your Mac, you'll still find a subfolder within the Users folder with your name on it. Your home folder is the primary place for you to store personal documents and files. The Users folder also has a special subfolder called Shared, where you can place files that you'd like other users of the Mac to be able to access (assuming there are other users).

For everyday computing, most of these root-level folders aren't terribly important. You'll spend a lot of your time accessing the subfolders within your home folder, and you'll occasionally open the Applications folder to launch a new application. These folders come more into play when you're adding capabilities to your Mac or troubleshooting problems, so you'll find that we discuss them a lot more in Part IV of the book.

(It's worth noting that these aren't the only folders at the main level on your hard disk. Mac OS X also has a number of hidden files that are used by the operating system for various tasks and reasons. Some of those are discussed in Chapter 24. If you ever get a glimpse of these folders—such as `private`, `sbin`, `tmp`, `usr`, and others—in an application or utility program, it's important to leave them intact.)

a CD-ROM or removable disk, too. (Note in this example that I'm getting extremely low in storage space on my iMac's main hard disk.)

4 items, 258.2 MB available

Finder 201: Change How Folders Are Displayed in the Finder

Managing the way your Finder windows appear can go a long way toward helping you find files. To change the way you view a Finder window, open that window and select it in the Finder, then choose the appropriate view from the View menu. Mac OS X has three different ways that folders can be viewed:

- **Icon**   In this view, the window is filled with icons that can be arranged any way you like. This is the default view in most cases.

- **List**   If you have a lot of items in a particular folder window, this is the way to go. Viewing as a list gives you three advantages. First, you get a whole lot of files on the screen at once in a very orderly manner. Second, you can use the little triangles to look inside subfolders without doing a lot of double-clicking. Third, you get extra info about the files, like the date modified, size, and so on.

- **Columns**   Unique to Mac OS X, the Columns view enables you to see the contents of a folder and its subfolders in separate columns within a single Finder window.

You can switch between the views by selecting a Finder window and then either choosing a command from the View menu (such as View | as Icons or View | as List) or by clicking one of the three View buttons that appears in the toolbar of the Finder window. From left to right they are Icon, List, and Columns views.

Customize List View

Once you have a folder in List view, you can do some other things to make that folder work better for you. At the top of the window, you'll find column listings for the different information that's offered about each file. Place the mouse pointer between two columns, and it changes to a little cursor with an arrow coming out of each side. That's your cue that you can drag the column divider to change the width of the column.

Want to change the order of List view columns? Go up to the column head name and click and hold the mouse button. Now drag the mouse pointer to the left or right. The pointer changes to a

How to ... Drop Files in List View

One peril of using the List view (and this occasionally happens in some other views as well) is that it can be tough to drop items in the open folder window, especially if you have a lot of subfolders in that window (or if you're trying to drag something *from* a subfolder in that same window). Here's the trick: if you want to drop something in the current folder, drag it to the little information bar at the top of the window, just below the title bar. Release the mouse button to drop the item. This drops it in the main folder instead of in one of the subfolders.

hand and you can move the column to wherever you'd like it in the window. Let go of the mouse button to drop the column in place.

To order the window according to a particular column, just click that column's heading name. To view your files organized by the date that the files were modified, for instance, just click the Date Modified column head. You can also change the order of that listing by clicking the column head again to change the sort direction, which is indicated by the small arrow.

	Q local disks		
Date Modified ▼		Size	Kind
Nov 24, 2003, 12:07 AM		--	A
Nov 8, 2003, 10:06 PM		--	F
Nov 5, 2003, 4:46 PM		--	F

To add columns of information to the List view, choose View | Show View Options. In the View Options window, you can place check marks next to any columns you'd like to see, such as Date Created and Comments or Label. Note also that you can set several other options: at the top of the window, you can select This Window Only if you only want the options to apply to the selected folder, or All Windows if you want the change applied to all windows when shown in List view. Once you've made your decision, simply close the window by clicking its close button.

Arrange Items in Other Views

If you're not in List view, there's still some arranging you can do. In Icon view, you can select the Finder window, then choose View | Arrange. That brings up a menu that lets you choose how you'd like your icons arranged—by name, by size, and so on.

If you simply want your Icon views to appear a bit more uniform (but without rearranging the files), you can select the window in the Finder, then choose View | Clean Up. This will move the icons or buttons around so that they're equally spaced and as many as possible fit in the open window.

With any Finder window, you can click the maximize button to automatically reshape the window to display all or as many files as possible.

Auto-Arrange the View

Choosing View | Arrange by Name rearranges your Finder windows just that one time. Would you like the window to be arranged all the time? That's easy enough. Select the window in the Finder, then choose View | Show View Options. In the View Options dialog box, you can choose to have the window automatically arrange icons. The choices are

- **None** The icons will not be auto-arranged.

- **Snap to Grid** The icons won't be put in any particular order, but they will always appear in uniform rows and columns, no matter where you drag-and-drop them within the window.

- **Keep Arranged** This option allows you to force the window to automatically keep icons in order at all times, even when new icons are dropped into the folder. Choose the radio button next to this option to activate it, then choose *how* to arrange the icons from the pull-down menu.

Explore Columns View

If you've worked with previous versions of the Mac OS, you know that the traditional way to maneuver through folders is to double-click the hard disk icon, which opens a window that shows subfolders, which you double-click...and so on. In Mac OS X, the traditional way isn't always the best. Instead, you can opt to use the Finder window and its special Columns view for quickly locating and working with files. To get into Columns view, select View | Columns from the Finder menu, or click the Columns button in the View portion of the Finder window toolbar.

In Columns view, you can quickly move throughout the entire hierarchy of your hard disk. Simply click a disk or item to start with, and then single-click folders to display them in the next column. When you finally reach a document or application, single-clicking it will bring up information about that item in the rightmost column, as shown in Figure 3-2.

You can drag-and-drop an item from one column to another, if that happens to help you. (For instance, in Figure 3-2, you could drag an item from the Spring Project folder that's displayed in the third column back to the Memos folder icon in the second column.) You can also drag items from the window area to one of the folders in the Sidebar and drop it on the folder to move it (or copy it) to that folder. If you need to drag an item to another folder that isn't visible, however, you'll find that a second Finder window, also in Columns view, might be the easiest way to accomplish that. To open a new Finder window, press ⌘-N or select File | New Finder Window.

The wider you drag out the Finder window, the more columns you can display. Also, if you view your Mac at 1024 x 768 resolution, you'll see more columns than at 800 x 600. See Chapter 4 for details on screen resolution.

Back button   Change to Columns view   Hide toolbar button

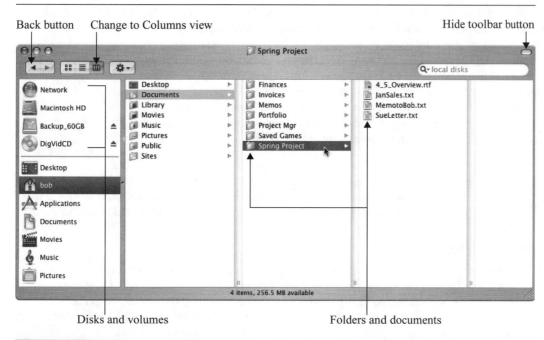

Disks and volumes   Folders and documents

FIGURE 3-2   Mac OS X Finder window, showing Columns view

Finder 301: Create Folders, Copy Files, Rename Icons, and Create Aliases

Before you get too busy moving things around, you'll need to create some folders you can move things into. You'll also find that it's often important to duplicate items or create aliases to those items. The Finder is designed to help you do just that.

> TIP
>
> *Mac OS X now implements an "undo" command that's more effective throughout the Finder than it ever has been. After most any accidental operation—copying, moving, renaming, and others—you can immediately choose Edit | Undo or press ⌘-Z immediately after that operation to reverse it. (In fact, you can undo a number of steps if that helps you.) You can use the command Edit | Redo or ⌘-Y to immediately redo something that you've just undone.*

Create a New Folder

You'll probably learn pretty quickly that it's a good idea to create folders of your own and store them on your hard drive or within other folders. For instance, you may wish to create subfolders within the Documents folder inside your home folder. That way, you can begin to organize your documents for easy retrieval. Doing this also makes it easier to copy your important files to a removable drive for safekeeping.

To create a new folder, open and select the window where you'd like the folder to appear. (If you want it to appear on the desktop, you don't need to select a window.) Then, choose File | New Folder. You can also just press ⌘-SHIFT-N in the Finder.

When the folder appears, its name is already highlighted. Just type to give the folder a new name. When you're done naming it, press RETURN. Now you have a new folder (as shown in the example to the right).

Employee Files

> **TIP** *You can drag folders to the bottom portion of the Sidebar in any Finder window to add that folder as one of the icons there. That makes it easy to access a commonly used folder, and it creates a drag-and-drop target. More on customizing the Finder window in Chapter 4.*

Rename Icons

You can rename a folder or any other sort of icon by clicking once on its name (not its icon) and waiting a second or so. Then, the name becomes highlighted, ready for editing. (You can also click once on an icon to select it, then press RETURN to begin editing the name.) With the name highlighted, you can press DELETE to clear the current name and begin typing a new one. When you're done editing the name, press RETURN again to make the name change final.

Move Icons

A big part of using the Finder is mastering drag-and-drop. You'll move files and folders around a lot in the Finder—from one folder to another, for instance. You do that by dragging the icon in question from one part of the Finder and dropping it on another part. For instance, you can drag an icon from one Finder window to another, or from a Finder window to the desktop, or vice versa. You can also drag-and-drop icons onto folder icons—even if the icon and folder are in the same Finder window—to move the item to the target folder (see Figure 3-3).

In most cases, dragging an icon to another location *moves* that icon to the new location—it will no longer be in the folder where it started. If you drag an icon to another *disk*, however, whether that disk is a remote disk (via a network) or a removable disk, such as a Zip or CD-RW, then you actually create a duplicate of the file, which is placed in the target folder. So, you'll now have two copies—the original and a duplicate.

Create a Duplicate

You can create duplicates on the same disk, if desired. All you have to do is select the item and choose File | Duplicate. You could also select the item and press ⌘-D.

Duplicating creates an exact copy of the file, except that no two items can have the same name and be stored in the same folder, so the duplicate gets the appendage "copy" added to its name. Now, if you like, you can move that duplicate to another folder and rename it.

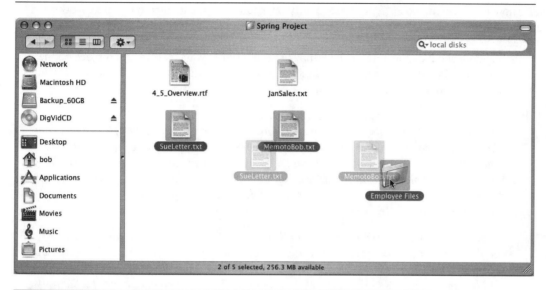

3

FIGURE 3-3 Dragging icons to a subfolder in the same Finder window moves those items to that subfolder.

Remember this is a duplicate of the original and it no longer has a relationship to the original file. For instance, if you had a memo document called Memo to Bob and you created a duplicate,

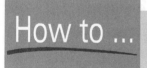 **Use Spring-Loaded Folders**

By default a feature called *spring-loaded folders* can kick in to help you with some of your dragging and dropping. Here's how it works. If you pick up and drag a file or folder to another folder, then hover over that folder for a few seconds, the folder will spring open in a new window. Now, you can drop the file to place it in that folder, or you can hover over another folder, wait, and it will pop open. You'll find this is handy for placing a file somewhere in your hierarchy of folders without first opening and finding that targeted subfolder.

If you happen not to like this feature, it can be turned off. Choose Finder | Preferences and click the General icon. You'll see a check box for the Spring-Loaded Folders and Windows option toward the bottom of the Preferences window. Click to remove the check mark, and the feature is turned off. Click the close button on the Preferences window to close it.

you'd now have two memos. If you subsequently opened the duplicate memo in AppleWorks and edited it to say "Dear Sue," the original Memo to Bob would not be altered. Only the copy is affected.

Another note about duplicating—it takes up space. Every file you create takes up space on the hard disk in your Mac. If you create many duplicates, you'll be filling up your hard disk. Instead, you might want to consider creating aliases.

SHORTCUT *There's a quicker way to duplicate a file. Pick up the original icon you want to duplicate and drag it to the location where you want the duplicate to appear. Now, when you're in the final spot for the duplicate, hold down the OPTION key. Did you see the pointer turn into a plus sign? That means when you let go of the mouse button, a duplicate will be created. Keep holding down the OPTION key and release the mouse button. Your duplicate is made. (If you create the duplicate in the same folder, note that the word "copy" will be appended to the file's name.)*

TIP *Want yet another way? You can use the Copy and Paste commands in the Finder to duplicate files. (And you can use the Cut and Paste commands to move them.) The keyboard command for Copy is ⌘-C; for Cut (which would remove the file from the current folder but let you paste it elsewhere), it's ⌘-X; and for the Paste command to put the file in its new location, press ⌘-V.*

Create an Alias

In Mac parlance, an alias is simply an icon that points to another file. There are a few advantages to creating aliases for your important files:

- **Convenience** Say you have the real AppleWorks icon buried three folders deep on your hard disk. If you like, you can create an alias icon for AppleWorks right on your desktop. (Of course, you can also add it to the Dock, which is probably handier.)

- **Size** Aliases are very small files—unlike a duplicate, an alias isn't a complete copy of the file. It's basically just an icon that stores a reference to the original item. So you can have many aliases in different folders on your Mac and still not be taking up too much storage space.

- **Safety** Why is it safer to create aliases? Because if you (or a coworker, partner, or kid) throw away an alias, the original item doesn't get destroyed. If I take that AppleWorks alias I created and trash it, for instance, then AppleWorks itself is unharmed back in the Applications folder. However, if I had dragged the actual program out to the desktop and trashed it, I'd be in trouble. The actual program would have been deleted.

Convinced? If so, get started creating aliases. In the Finder, select the file for which you'd like an alias. Then, choose File | Make Alias or press ⌘-L in Mac OS X.

3

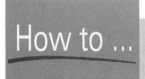 **Burn a Data CD**

Mac models that include an internal CD-RW drive (or a CD/DVD-RW SuperDrive) can be used to create data CDs directly from the desktop. You begin by inserting a blank CD-R or CD-RW disc in your Mac's CD/DVD slot or tray. When the disc is recognized by the Mac, you'll see a dialog box asking what application you should use to open the disc—select Open Finder from the Action menu.

Now, you'll see the disc's icon appear on the desktop. You can name the icon as you would any sort of folder or disk, then you can drag items to the CD icon to add them to the disc. Once you've dragged all the items to the disc that you plan to add, you're ready to burn the CD. In Mac OS X, choose Finder | Burn Disc or simply drag the disc to the Trash icon. (Note that these files are actually stored on your hard disk at first, so in order to burn a data CD or DVD you need enough space on your hard disk to replicate that CD or DVD before it can be created.)

In the dialog box that appears, click Burn if you'd like to continue the process. Now, just sit back and wait while the data is burned to the CD-R or CD-RW disc. When you're done, the disc will eject and you're ready to label it, share it with a friend, or store it away as a backup.

If the disc is a CD-RW (rewritable), remember that it can be erased and used again, if desired. (You can't add individual files to it; you've got to delete the entire disc and start again. For more flexibility in creating CDs, you'll need a third-party application such as those described in Chapter 23.) To erase a CD-RW disc, you'll need to use the Disk Utility application, which is discussed in Chapter 24.

An alias appears, complete with italicized text and the word "alias" appended to the name. Now you can move the alias anywhere you want to and rename it, if desired.

Want to create an alias that immediately appears in its final resting place? Here's how: Drag the original icon to the place where you want the alias to appear—you can use the spring-loaded folders or just drag it to the desktop. Now, instead of letting go, hold down the OPTION *and* ⌘ *keys. See the pointer turn into a little curved arrow? That means when you drop the icon, it'll create an alias instead of moving the original. Keep holding down* OPTION *and* ⌘, *then let go of the mouse button. Voilá! Your alias is ready.*

Find the Alias's Original

Sometimes an alias just isn't good enough—you need to deal with the real file. If that's the case, you can select the alias's icon and choose File | Show Original (or press ⌘-R). This will cause the folder containing the alias's original file to appear in the Finder.

Fix an Alias

Aliases can break sometimes—suddenly, the alias will no longer point to its original file. This happens for a variety of reasons, but mostly it happens because you move, delete, or otherwise mangle the original file. For instance, sometimes when you install a new version of an application that you've been working with, the new application is installed in a fresh new folder inside the main Applications folder, perhaps with a slightly different filename. If you delete the old version, an alias to that old version wouldn't automatically know to launch the new version instead.

If an alias can't find its original, a dialog box appears:

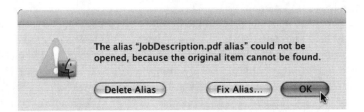

If you don't need the alias anymore, you can click Delete Alias and the alias will trouble you no longer. (Actually, it's simply been moved to the Trash, not permanently deleted.) If you want to continue to use the alias, click Fix Alias and the Fix Alias dialog box appears. Now, find the file you want the alias to point to, select it in the dialog box, and click Choose. Now the alias is pointing to the chosen file. (The Fix Alias dialog box works just like the Open dialog box, which is discussed in Chapter 6.)

Finder 401: Delete Stuff

The Mac OS really only offers one way to delete Finder icons—by moving them to the Trash. (There are a few different ways to move stuff to the Trash, but it all must go through it.) Actually, this is a good thing, because it makes you think carefully about what you're doing before you make a mistake and accidentally delete something. Plus, the Trash offers a way to recover files before they're permanently deleted, even if they've already been thrown away.

Toss Icons

If you're pretty sure you don't need a particular item anymore, you can drag it straight from its current location in the Finder to the Trash. Just drag the icon over the Trash until the Trash icon (or, in Mac OS X, the Trash *tile* in the Dock) becomes highlighted, then release the mouse button. The item is dropped and the Trash takes on a "full" appearance—some wadded paper appears in the icon. You can throw out multiple files just as easily: select them all by dragging a box around them or holding down the SHIFT key, then drag the group to the Trash.

> **NOTE** *Just because the Trash icon has a paper wad in it, that doesn't mean you can't put anymore trash in it. You can continue to place items in the Trash for as long as is practical. The only real limit is when you need to regain hard disk space by emptying the Trash.*

If this is all too much mousing for you, there are three other ways to move files to the Trash:

- With the file(s) selected in the Finder, choose ⌘-DELETE to move items to the Trash.
- Select the file(s) in the Finder and choose File | Move to Trash from the menu.
- CONTROL-click on a file, then choose Move to Trash from the contextual menu.

> **NOTE** *In some cases, you may encounter a warning that tells you that you don't have sufficient privileges to move an item to the Trash. This happens because Mac OS X keeps careful track of which users are owners of certain folders or files, and which of those items can't be altered or deleted by other users. If you encounter such a file and you feel you need to be able to delete or change it, see Chapter 21 for a discussion of privileges.*

Retrieve Items from the Trash

Remember, just because an item has been thrown in the Trash doesn't mean it's been deleted. If you have something in the Trash that you need to get back, just single-click the Trash icon in the Dock. This opens the Trash window, allowing you to see everything that's been thrown away. When you find what you need, you can drag it back out of the Trash onto the desktop or into another Finder window.

> **NOTE** *Documents and applications can't be launched from the Trash—they must be dragged out to a Finder window or the desktop before they can be used.*

Empty the Trash

The step that really gets rid of the items in the Trash is the process of emptying the Trash. Once it's been emptied, you can't get those items back. (Unfortunately, there's no "Mac Dumpster" to go rooting through.)

> **CAUTION** *Think carefully before emptying the Trash. If you delete something accidentally, you'll probably have to buy a special utility program, like Norton Utilities, to get the item back.*

If you're sure you want to get rid of the items in the Trash and reclaim the storage space that they're taking up, choose Finder | Empty Trash. You'll see an alert box that tells you the Trash is about to be emptied. If that's what you really want to do, click OK. Once you click OK, the files are gone forever (at least, without a special recovery utility program). Say "Bye, bye!"

Want to skip the alert box that tells you how much stuff will be thrown away? Hold down the OPTION *key as you choose Special | Empty Trash. The Trash is emptied immediately. (Choose Finder | Preferences and click Advanced to turn off the option Show Warning Before Emptying the Trash.)*

What do you do if you didn't want to delete a file and you've emptied the Trash? Well, it may require a special purchase. There's a chance it can be recovered, especially if you stop using the Mac immediately, and run out to get a copy of Norton Utilities. (See Chapter 24 for more on disk fixing utilities.)

Mac OS X 10.3 and higher have another special command, called Finder | Secure Empty Trash. That causes the file(s) to be deleted and overwritten with meaningless characters so that the files can't be recovered even by a special utility application.

Finder Grad School: Search for Files

Aside from digging around in Finder windows and through folders for your files, the Finder gives you another way to locate them—you can search. This is handy when you can't remember where a particular file is, but it's also useful when you want to see all occurrences of a particular file, or

How to ... Get Info on Files

Another unique Finder capability is the Info window, which allows you to learn more about files in the Finder. The Info window can be used to tell you how much storage space an item takes up, who created the item, and any comments that have been stored about that item. You can also view the Info window on disks and folders to learn more about them.

To get info, select the item in the Finder and choose File | Get Info. The Info window appears, offering you information about the selected file. (Note that the Info window's title bar name changes for the individual item you're getting info on.)

In the Info window you'll see information based on the type of file selected—that is, an alias offers different information from a folder, which is different from an application. You may also see a special pull-down menu, which you can use to switch between General Information about the file and other options, including Ownership & Permissions and others. The Info window is discussed in other chapters, including Chapter 21.

To close the Info window, click its close button.

you want to see a number of files that have something in common—like a similar filename, or they were created on the same day.

Search from the Finder Window

The Finder also gives you two ways to search. For a basic search by filename, you simply begin typing in the search box at the top of any Finder window. By default, that will cause all local disks (and hard disks or removables that are directly connected to your Mac) to be searched for a particular filename. The search begins immediately after you type the first letter and responds as you continue typing by honing the results. (Note that you don't have to type just the beginning of a name; the Finder will locate what you type anywhere within filenames.) The results appear in the Finder window, which is reconfigured slightly, as shown in Figure 3-4.

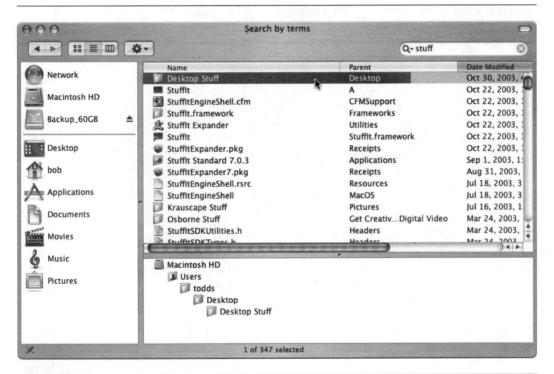

FIGURE 3-4   After typing a few letters in the search box, the Finder window reconfigures to show search results.

In the top part of the results window that the Finder window has become, you can select an item to see more about it. When you do, you'll see the results that are also shown in Figure 3-4—that's a path of folders and subfolders that lead to where that item is located.

If you find the file you want to work with, you can double-click it in the top pane of the results window to launch it, or you can drag it out of that window to the desktop, to another Finder window, or to one of the folder icons in the Sidebar if you'd like to move or copy it to that folder.

Done with the results list? To get back to a regular Finder window, you can either click the Back button or the small "X" icon in the Search entry box. You can also click an item in the Sidebar, which will cause that item to appear in the Finder window and replace the search results.

Search Using File | Find

The Finder window will work for the majority of quick searches you attempt. But if you need to toss in some additional criteria, you can use Find by choosing File | Find or pressing ⌘-F in the Finder. When you do, you'll see the Find window.

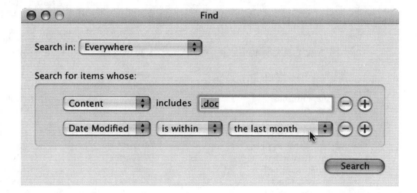

In this Find window you can build the criteria for your search. First, from the Search In menu, choose where you'd like to search—your Home folder, on Local Disks, Everywhere, or you can choose Specific Places. This changes the window so that you can place check marks next to the disk and volumes you'd like to search. (You can also add folders or volumes to this list by clicking the Add button.)

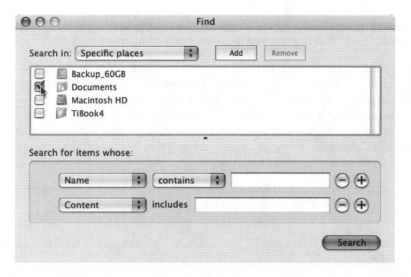

Once you've made that decision, you can start building criteria. Simply select from the menus and other options to build phrases that represent how you'd like to search. You can search based on one criterion (for instance, filename) or multiple criteria. You can add criteria by clicking the plus (+) sign next to one of the criterion lines. You can delete a particular criterion line by clicking its minus (–) sign. Change the criterion by choosing from its first menu, then build the phrase:

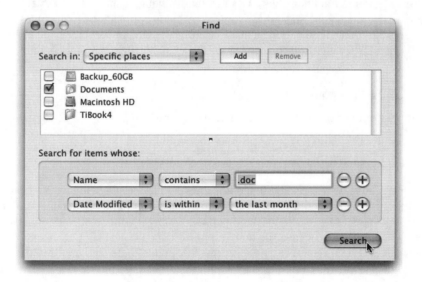

NOTE *If you have multiple criteria in your search phrase, imagine that there's an "and" between each one. Every criterion you add will limit the search further.*

When you've built your phrase, click the Search button. After a few seconds, you'll see the found files in a results window that's very similar to the results window created when you search within a Finder window. (The look of the window is less metallic, but that's all.) Scroll through the list and click once on each result to see exactly where the file is located. The path to the file will appear in the bottom pane (the information area) of the Find results window. Then, as before, you can double-click an item to launch it, or you can drag that item out of the results list to the desktop or a Finder window to copy it elsewhere.

CAUTION *Be aware that you could accidentally delete important files by moving them to the Trash using the Find window. Don't delete anything you aren't familiar with.*

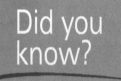

Search Inside Files

What if you could just search the insides of files to find what you're looking for? The Content search option in Find helps you with just that, although content searches are only useful for searching document files—files you've created in applications like AppleWorks, web documents built in an application such as Macromedia Dreamweaver, or documents in Microsoft Word, PDF, or TextEdit format—since those are all file types that contain text. Here's how:

1. Launch the Find window.
2. Choose Contents from the first menu on a criterion line.
3. In the entry box, enter the text you want to search for.
4. Click the Search button and you're off to the races.

When Find is done, you'll see the found documents in the results window. You can work with those files just as you would work with found documents after a regular file search.

In order for Content searches to work properly, your target volume or folder needs to be indexed. So, if Find doesn't locate a file that you think it should, you should check to make sure the disk has been indexed recently. Select the disk in the Finder and choose File | Get Info. Click the disclosure triangle next to Content Index. There you'll see if it's been updated recently; if not, click the Index Now button. It can take a while, but once it's done, you'll be able to search inside files.

Chapter 4

Master Your Workspace

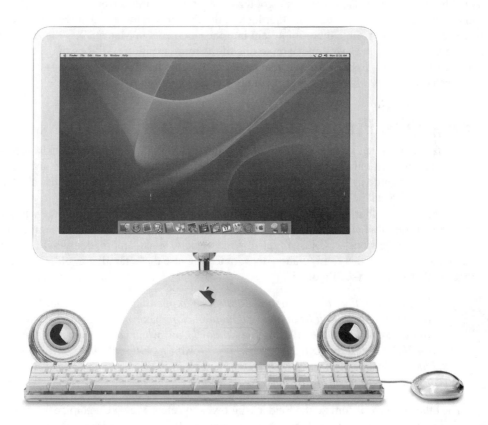

How to...

- Customize your Finder window
- Dig into the Apple menu
- Use the Dock
- Customize folders and icons
- Customize the Dock
- Use Exposé to manage open windows
- Change system preferences

Mac OS X is an exciting operating system—not just because it's powerful and reasonably bulletproof, but also because it's got tons of features. In this chapter I'd like to show you some of those features, including another look at the Finder window (so that we can customize it) and a discussion of some other important interface elements in Mac OS X—the Apple menu and the Dock. After that, we'll move on to one of the more exciting additions to the Mac OS that version 10.3 brings—Exposé window management. Finally, we'll look at system-level settings and touch on the way Mac OS X user accounts work, along with related settings.

Customize the Finder Window Toolbar

As you read in Chapter 3, the Finder window's toolbar is not only handy for quickly accessing common commands, but you can customize it to do your bidding, if desired. The first way to customize it is to hide it. When you do, your Finder window not only no longer has a toolbar, but its "brushed metal" characteristics and the Sidebar disappear as well (see Figure 4-1).

You hide the toolbar by clicking the small toolbar control at the top right of the window. (It looks like a little Tic-Tac candy.) As a result, the window reverts to a look that's familiar to users of older Mac OS versions—it's just a typical window now. What's more, double-clicking a folder when the window is in this configuration does something else that's familiar to older Mac users—it opens another window (see Figure 4-1).

> **TIP** *If you're partial to this "tunneling" approach to opening folders and windows, you can make it the default behavior by double-clicking your main hard drive, clicking the toolbar control, and then closing the window. Now, when you next open the hard drive, you'll see the plain-vanilla window. If you want to "tunnel" but continue using the Finder window, open Finder | Preferences and, in the General preferences, turn on the option Always Open Folders in a New Window.*

The other way to customize the Finder window is to select View | Customize Toolbar from the Finder menu. A large dialog sheet pops out from the frontmost Finder window. You'll see a

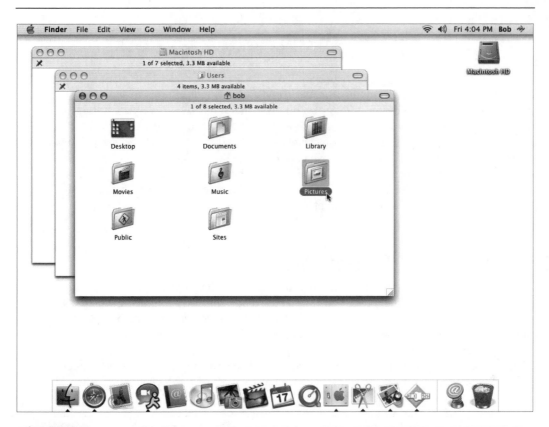

FIGURE 4-1   When the toolbar and Sidebar are hidden, double-clicking a folder icon opens a new window for that folder.

number of different tools and items that you simply drag up to the toolbar, including commands such as Eject (for removable media and CDs) and Path, which you can use to see a pop-up menu of enclosing folders (as shown at left).

You can drag items around all you like on the toolbar, and you can use the Show menu at the bottom of the dialog sheet to select whether you'd like to see icons, text, or both in the toolbar. (And note the Use Small Size option, which is handy for squeezing extra items on the toolbar.) To remove an item from the toolbar, simply drag it off and release the mouse button. To return to the default set, drag the entire default set box from the bottom of the dialog sheet up to the toolbar. When you're done making changes, click Done.

The Go Menu

Mac OS X offers another difference from earlier Mac OS versions in the form of the Go menu, which appears in the middle of the Finder's menu bar. The Go menu is mostly redundant; it allows you to quickly visit some of the same folders that you can click by using the Finder window's Sidebar. You can also use Go | iDisk to quickly access your own iDisk or that of others. You'll find a convenient Recent Folders menu, which you can use to visit folders you've been to recently in the Finder. And, you'll find the Connect to Server command in the Go menu, which enables you to access remote server volumes over the Internet. (It's discussed briefly in Chapter 21.)

Understand the OS X Apple Menu

Click the Apple icon in the top-left corner of your screen and the Apple menu appears, as shown in Figure 4-2. At the top of the menu, you'll find the About This Mac command, which you can choose if you'd like to see the exact version of Mac OS X that you're running, the amount of memory you have installed, and the type of processor your Mac has. To close the About This Mac window, click its close button.

The next command you'll see is the Software Update command, which gives you quick access to Mac OS X's built-in upgrading system. (See Chapter 24 for details on Software

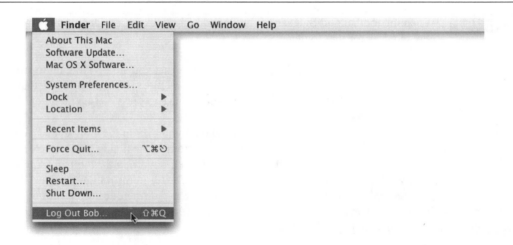

FIGURE 4-2   The Apple menu in Mac OS X

Update.) After that is the Mac OS X Software command, which is something of a marketing ploy. It launches, in your web browser, Apple's Mac OS X Downloads page, where you'll find updates to Apple's software, additional drivers, Dock Extras, along with commercial, shareware, and freeware programs from third parties. If your Internet connection isn't designed to connect automatically, you'll need to connect before issuing this command.

The System Preferences command can be used to quickly launch the System Preferences application, where you can choose settings and preferences for the Mac OS X environment. System Preferences is discussed in detail later in this chapter and in many others later in this book. Likewise, the Dock menu commands are discussed later in the section "Set Dock Preferences."

The Location menu is used to change the preset location for your network settings—see Chapter 21 for details.

Launch Recently Used Items

The Recent Items menu tracks the most recent ten documents that you've worked with and the ten applications that you've launched. By selecting this menu, then selecting one of the documents or applications, you can quickly relaunch that item. If you tend to work with the same small set of applications or documents, you'll find that the Recent Items menu is a handy way to launch them without having to open the Applications folder.

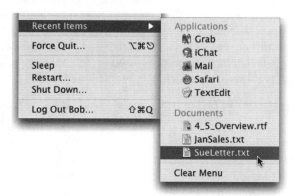

The Recent Items menu has another command, Clear Menu, which you can select to clear the Recent Items menu of its remembered applications and documents. (You can make some changes to how this works in the Appearance pane that's discussed later in this chapter in the section "Set Appearance.")

Force Applications to Quit

The Force Quit command is used as a troubleshooting tool. If you encounter an application that is no longer responding to input, and you've waited more than a few minutes to see if it has an internal problem it's recovering from, you can force that application to quit. This causes the application to quit without saving any changed data—the Mac OS is *killing* the application's processes, forcing it to go away without giving the application any opportunity to respond. That means it's a last resort, but one that you'll occasionally need to implement. If you want to force an application to quit, select the Force Quit command. The Force Quit Applications window will appear.

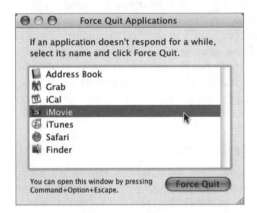

Select the application that you'd like to force quit, then click the Force Quit button. That application should quit—it will disappear from the Dock and the Force Quit Applications window. Click the Force Quit Applications window's close button to close the window. In most cases, you can now continue to work. With Mac OS X, there is generally no need to restart your Mac after an application has frozen or crashed, unless you notice other odd or problematic behavior with your applications. If you do, that may mean you need to do some troubleshooting. See Chapter 24 for more on dealing with problem applications and trouble with the Mac OS.

TIP *You can also press ⌘-OPTION-ESC to bring up the Force Quit Applications window.*

Issue System Commands

The final four commands in the Apple menu are the system-level commands that directly affect the Mac OS and the iMac. The first three—Sleep, Restart, and Shutdown—are discussed in Chapter 1.

Select the Log Out command to quit all active applications, close your user account, and display the Login window so that another user can access his or her unique user account. If you've set up multiple users (see Chapter 21), you'll definitely get used to using the Log Out command. But even if you're the only user of your iMac, logging out is one way to secure your files and applications from interference from others.

Master the Dock

The Dock is used primarily to launch applications and, once they're launched and running, to switch between multiple applications. But it's also handy for a few other tasks, including managing minimized windows and quickly digging through folders, thanks to the folder pop-up feature. We'll look at all those in this section.

> *Unlike the Apple menu, the Dock in Mac OS X doesn't really update any interface element in a previous Mac OS version. Instead, it sort of combines the capabilities of Mac OS 9's Launcher, Application menu, and even the older Apple menu into a single interface element that is otherwise completely unique.*

Launch and Switch Between Applications

You'll notice immediately that the Dock has some default icons on it—most Mac users will see the same icons, with an exception or two. The usual suspects include the Finder, Mail, Safari (web browser), iMovie, iTunes, iPhoto, System Preferences, and others. You'll notice also that the Dock is divided into two different sections by a dividing line. On the left are application icons (shown below), and on the right are document icons.

To launch an item on the Dock, click its icon once. If that item is an application, you'll see the icon "bounce" up and down to indicate that the application is being launched. You'll also see a small triangle appear beneath that application's icon. The triangle is the *running indicator*, which tells you that the application is currently launched and running. Here you'll notice that the Finder and Safari both have running indicators:

The Dock is the heart of Mac OS X's ability to *multitask*, or run more than one application simultaneously. Using the running indicators, you can see immediately which applications have been launched and are running. You can then click any of those applications in the Dock to switch quickly to it.

But what about applications that aren't on the Dock? When you launch an application from the Applications folder or elsewhere, that item will add an icon to the Dock while that application is active. When you quit the application, its icon will disappear.

Document icons that appear on the right side of the Dock work the same way—click them once and they'll be launched in their associated application. (If that application isn't already on the Dock, an icon and running indicator will appear for that application.) The only difference is that the document doesn't bounce, and a running indicator doesn't appear beneath it—running indicators are reserved for applications.

Minimize Windows to the Dock

The right side of the Dock can be used to create shortcuts to your favorite documents, but you'll probably use it more often for *minimized* windows. When you click the minimize button in a Finder window or in an application's document window, that window is minimized to the Dock,

Switch Between Running Applications

You can cycle quickly through your running applications by pressing ⌘-TAB. When you do, a special window appears in the center of the screen enabling you to choose from an open application by pressing TAB repeatedly. (This also works with ⌘-SHIFT-TAB, which simply scrolls through items in the opposite direction.)

Actually, ⌘-TAB works in another interesting and handy way: it allows you to switch back and forth between two particular applications as you're working. For instance, say you're working in AppleWorks and you want to switch to your web browser, Safari. If Safari is running, you can use ⌘-TAB once to switch to it. Now, when you're ready to switch back to the most recent application (in this example, AppleWorks), press ⌘-TAB again—just once. You'll switch immediately back to AppleWorks. Work for a bit, and, if you need to, you can switch back to Safari quickly by, again, pressing ⌘-TAB once. It keeps working that way until you break the chain by switching to a different application.

where it will appear on the document side of the dividing line. That's a convenient way to get open windows off the screen, while one click of the window's tile in the Dock will return it to full screen. Plus, the windows, when minimized, are actually miniature versions of themselves, making them (hopefully) easy to identify and return to.

If you're not sure what a particular window represents, simply point to it with the mouse (but don't click the button). The *mouse-over name* (as shown in the preceding illustration) will appear just above the Dock to show you what the window's title is. In fact, this works for any type of icon in the Dock, including applications, documents, and minimized windows.

Add Items to the Dock

Of course, you can add icons to the Dock yourself to make it quite a bit more useful as a launcher. You'll probably find that you have applications and documents to which you'd like quick access. That's easy enough to accomplish. All you have to do is drag any application or document from the desktop or a Finder window down to the Dock. If you drag it to the correct side (applications to the left of the dividing line, documents and folders to the right), a space will open up on the Dock where you can drop that item.

When you drag an item to the Dock, nothing happens to the original application or document—it stays right where it is on your hard drive (or on whatever storage device it's located). Instead, a special alias is created in order to make the new Dock icon possible. That also means that removing items from the Dock has no effect on the original item. If you remove a Dock icon, the original application or document is still safely saved on your hard disk.

So how do you remove a Dock icon? Simply use the mouse pointer to drag the icon away to anywhere above the Dock. When you release the mouse or trackpad button, the Dock icon will disappear in an animated poof of smoke. Remember—only the Dock icon has been deleted. The original item is fine.

You can also move items around on the Dock in the same way: simply drag-and-drop the Dock icon from one location to a new location. As you move the icon around on the Dock, space will open up between two other icons, as long as you don't cross the dividing line.

TIP *Want to resize the Dock? You can do it as easily as you move items around on it. Place the mouse pointer on the dividing line in the Dock, and you'll see the pointer change into a two-sided arrow. Now, hold down your mouse or trackpad button and drag the mouse up the screen to make the Dock (and each icon on it) bigger, or drag it down the screen to make the entire Dock smaller.*

Use Pop-up Menus

The Dock has another trick we haven't looked at until now. Click and hold the mouse button on a Dock icon, and you'll see a small pop-up menu appear.

Each pop-up menu will vary in what it enables you to do. A running application's menu will show you a list of its open windows and a Quit command, while an inactive Dock icon's menu will generally give you just the option Show in Finder, which you can select to reveal that icon's original item in a Finder window.

TIP *A running application's menu will have the command Keep in Dock if it's not already on the Dock permanently. Select that command if you'd like quick access to this application even when it's not running.*

The pop-up menu technology makes another special case possible—pop-up folder navigation. If you drag a folder icon from a Finder window to (the right side of) the Dock, a new folder tile is added. (It could be your Documents folder, for example, or any personal folder that you like to be able to access frequently.) Click and hold the mouse button on that folder icon and a pop-up menu appears—with the contents of that folder! If there's a subfolder inside that folder, the subfolder appears as a hierarchical menu—select it and that subfolder's contents appear. You can dig down five folders deep to quickly find the document, application, or folder you want to open and use. (In this example, I've dragged my home folder to the Dock, and I'm accessing it via this menu trick.)

And don't forget that you can define the term "folder" pretty loosely. You can even drag a disk icon—your hard disk or an attached USB or FireWire disk, for instance—to create a Dock icon for it, as well.

Interestingly, you can't drag an item directly from the Sidebar in a Finder window to the Dock (or for that matter, to a folder or the desktop), because those Sidebar items are already shortcuts. You'll need to locate the actual folder you want to place in the Dock and then drag its icon from a Finder window.

Set Dock Preferences

I mentioned earlier that you can quickly change some Dock options using the Dock menu in the Apple menu. You can also fine-tune those options in the Dock pane of the System Preferences application. To launch the Dock Preferences, choose Dock | Dock Preferences from the Apple menu.

In the Apple menu, you can choose Dock | Turn Hiding On to activate hiding; in Dock Preferences, turn on the option Automatically Hide and Show the Dock. When hiding is turned on, the Dock disappears below the bottom of your screen and only reappears when you point your mouse at the bottom few pixels of the screen to reveal it. This is done to give your applications a little more "screen real estate" so that your application's windows can be maximized without portions of them hiding behind the Dock.

With magnification turned on (either by selecting Dock | Turn Magnification On in the Apple menu or by turning on the Magnification option in the Dock Preferences pane), individual icons

Change Folder Icons

One problem comes up when you add a few folder icons to your Dock—they all look kind of the same, making it difficult to tell which is which. The solution to that is to alter the folder's icon before you drag it to the Dock. Once the folder's icon is customized, the Dock icon will be as well.

You'll need to begin by actually creating the custom icon. You can do this in a painting program (such as AppleWorks' Paint module or Macromedia Freehand) or a third-party application specifically designed to create icons. (Icons are 128 pixels by 128 pixels in Mac OS X.) Then, to change a folder's icon, select the drawn icon in your editing application and choose Edit | Copy. Now, locate the folder in a Finder window, select it, and choose File | Get Info. In the General section of the Info window, highlight the folder's icon and choose Edit | Paste in the Finder. If you have the correct file permissions to alter that folder, you should see the new folder icon appear in place of the original.

To return to a standard folder icon, select the icon again in the Info window and select Edit | Cut to remove the new icon.

on the Dock will become larger as you pass the mouse pointer over them. The Dock Preferences slider can be used to choose exactly how large magnified items will become. Magnification is particularly useful when the Dock has many different items on it and the individual icons are becoming difficult to see.

In the Dock Preferences pane, you have other options, including a slider that changes the size of the Dock and a check box that lets you turn on or off Animate Opening Applications, to determine whether or not an application icon will bounce in the Dock as its application is loading.

When you're done in the Dock Preferences pane, choose System Preferences | Quit to leave the System Preferences application.

You can move items around on the Dock by simply dragging the icons around—drop an icon in its new location and it stays there. (The only rule is that applications go on the left of the dividing line and documents or other aliases—along with minimized windows—go on the right.)

Also, you can resize the Dock easily by clicking and dragging the dividing line. Drag up to make icons on the Dock bigger (until it fills the screen) and down to make it smaller.

Manage Windows with Exposé

With your powerful Mac at your disposal, you're bound to have multiple applications open at once. The Dock offers one way to manage and switch between those applications, but Mac OS X version 10.3 introduced another one—a very *cool* one—called Exposé. This technology offers a more graphical approach, giving you a few different ways to view and manage the open windows on your screen.

Exposé is activated in one of two ways—you either press special function keys, or you move the mouse pointer to a corner of the screen to trigger it. When you do, you have three choices:

- **All Windows**   The All Windows command (F9 on the keyboard) forces Exposé to show you all of the windows you currently have open. When you mouse over a window, you'll see its name. You can then click that window to bring it to the foreground and begin working on it. (See Figure 4-3.)

- **Application Windows**   Press F10 on your keyboard, and that tells Exposé that you want to be shown all of the windows in the current application only. This works just like Figure 4-3 except that you're only seeing windows that were created by the current application. (This is great, for instance, if you have multiple web browser windows open and you need to pick a particular one.)

- **Desktop**   Press F11, and all open windows scoot out of the way, giving you access to your Mac's desktop. You can open Finder windows, move things to the Trash, copy and move—even launch—applications. Your other windows stay hidden (you can see them on the edge of the screen) until you either press F11 again, press another Exposé function key, or you switch away from the Finder.

See what I mean by cool? Not only can you visually switch between windows and applications, but the F9 feature even allows you to do things like quickly check your Mail Inbox. Because the windows are actually live versions of the real thing, you may find that you can learn what you need to simply by glancing at a window quickly via Exposé.

Not keen on the function keys? Launch the System Preferences application (choose Apple | System Preferences) and choose Exposé. In the Active Screen Corners section, you can choose a behavior for each corner on your screen, such as All Windows for the top-left corner.

Close System Preferences, and that preference is set. Now, if you move the mouse pointer up to the top left corner of your screen and leave it there for a second, the assigned Exposé mode

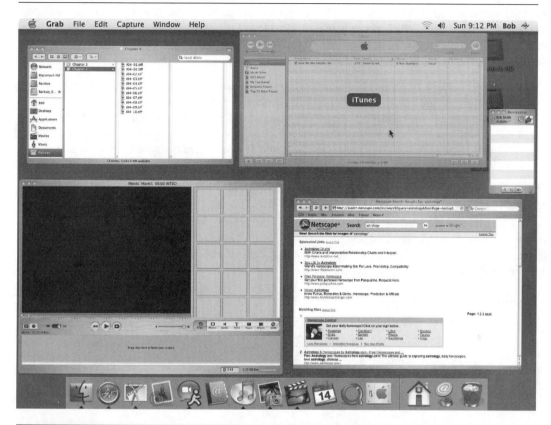

FIGURE 4-3 Press F9 and Exposé will show you all open windows so that you can pick the one you want to work with using the mouse pointer. (F10 is similar, but you see only the windows for the current application.)

will kick in. To get out of that Exposé mode, simply click on the menu bar, the desktop, or on the window you want to select.

We have limited room here, but you should dig into Mac Help (in the Finder, choose Help | Mac Help) and learn some of the neat features of Exposé, including the ability to drag-and-drop items using it.

Personalize Your Settings

Ready to start customizing your Mac workspace? From settings for your display to the appearance of your desktop, you can make personal choices about your Mac in the System Preferences application. Select Apple | System Preferences or click the System Preferences icon in the Dock to launch the application. Then, click one of the preference icons to load the *preference pane* that corresponds to that item. When your changes are made in the pane, you can click the Show All icon to see all available icons, or click one of the icons at the top of the System Preferences window to switch to a different pane.

You can drag icons from the main portion of the System Preferences window up to the toolbar in that window to add them for quick access. Note also that some settings require an administrator's password to change. If you're not using an administrator's account, you'll find that there's a padlock icon on some screens and you can't alter some settings on the iMac, such as Date and Time and Energy Saver settings. See Chapter 21 for details on administrator accounts.

Adjust Your Mac's Monitor

As you may have noticed, your Mac—whether an iMac, iBook, or eMac—doesn't have any knobs on its front or side for adjusting the display. That's because all of the controls are in software, accessible via the Displays pane in System Preferences. On that pane you'll see a few different tabs, depending on your model (see Figure 4-4).

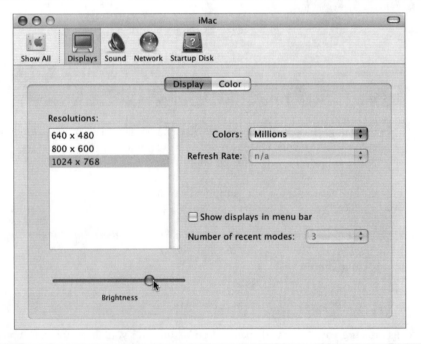

FIGURE 4-4   The Displays pane of System Preferences is where you can change settings for your Mac's screen (shown are the options for a flat-panel iMac G4).

Display

On the Display tab you'll set the color depth, refresh rate, resolution, and brightness/contrast. Not all models offer all of these options, but you'll see a combination of them that's appropriate to your Mac's type of display. Here's a quick rundown:

- **Colors**   Your Mac can display a range of colors from 256, to thousands, to millions according to the *color depth* you choose—the number of distinct colors that could potentially be shown on the screen. The more colors that appear on screen, the more photo-realistic the images on your screen are. A JPEG photo file displayed at 256 colors will offer less detail than one rendered at millions of colors. In most cases, choosing Thousands or Millions of colors from the Color menu is appropriate.

- **Resolution**   The iMac supports three different screen resolutions: 640 × 480, 800 × 600, and 1024 × 768. The significance of resolution is threefold. First, the more pixels on the screen, the more information you can see. At 1024 × 768, you can see a lot more of a given word processing page, for instance, than at 800 × 600. Second, the more pixels on the screen, the smaller each pixel. In order to see more of the page on your Mac's screen, the elements on the screen will have to get smaller—meaning you may have to squint more—since the size of your monitor stays the same. Third, with LCD displays (those on the iMac G4 and iBook), the display is designed for an optimal resolution, which it defaults to. If you pick a different one, the result is a bit fuzzier or muddier than the optimum setting.

NOTE   *On most any LCD-based Mac model (iMacs and iBooks), you can't set the Refresh Rate—it's unselectable. That option is for the eMac and earlier CRT-based iMacs; those models have three default refresh rate options, and each is available at a particular resolution. The higher the refresh rate, the better the image quality, with less shimmering.*

- **Brightness (and Contrast)**   These options are relatively self-explanatory. You can use the sliders to change the brightness (and contrast, if you're using a CRT-based eMac or iMac) shown on your screen. There are two considerations. First, you should never set any CRT monitor to its highest brightness setting, since that can wear out the monitor more quickly, causing it to dim prematurely. (LCD displays are OK at a high brightness setting.) If you need the monitor very bright, make sure you've tried different contrast settings before setting brightness all the way up.

    Second, changing brightness (and contrast) may affect how the screen looks compared to printed documents, especially color documents. You'll learn how to calibrate the display to correct for lighting conditions and to create optimum color output shortly, in the section "Color and Calibration." You might want to calibrate before going nuts with the brightness and contrast.

On some Mac models, you can press F1 *and* F2 *to change brightness settings.*

Geometry (CRT-Based Macs)

The Mac's software settings include the ability to fine-tune the screen characteristics of a CRT (cathode-ray tube) display like the one in the eMac and early iMacs so that you get a perfectly square image with all the right proportions—assuming that's your desire. For most people, Murphy's Law of Vertical Hold takes effect—the more you mess with any of these controls, whatever your intent, ability, or skill level, the worse the picture looks. Maybe you'll have better luck. You get to these controls by clicking the Geometry tab in the Displays pane.

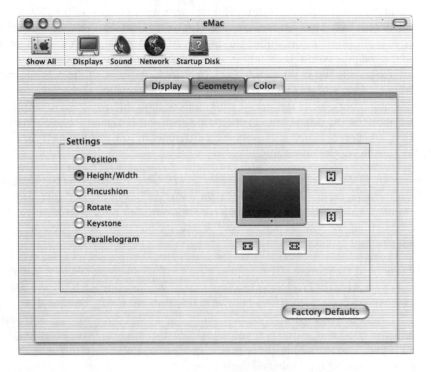

Now, you can go about changing many, many different settings regarding the size and dimensions of your monitor's picture. Here's what each does:

- **Position**   With this setting, you can change the vertical and horizontal placement of the screen image so that it's centered as much as possible.

- **Height/Width**   This setting allows you to change the size of the screen's image. You may notice that your screen, by default, doesn't fill the available space. That may be a good thing, since the very edges of a monitor tend to distort the picture somewhat. But you might also be able to tweak out a slightly larger picture using these controls.

- **Pincushion**   If your screen appears to bow in or out at the middle or edges (giving it a pear or an hourglass shape), you can use Pincushion controls to take it back to a rectangular shape.

- **Rotate**   The screen may appear slightly higher in one top corner than the other. If that's the case, you can rotate the image to bring it level again.

- **Keystone**   If the top or bottom of the screen is bowed in or out, you can change that with the Keystone setting.

- **Parallelogram**   If the screen rectangle slants in one direction or the other, you can shift it back with this control.

To change a setting, just click the radio button next to the setting you want to alter, and the controls on the right side of the window will change to reflect that. Click the little control buttons that appear around the image of an iMac screen to make your changes. You should see the screen react immediately.

If you mess it up beyond recognition, click the Factory Defaults button. This will reset the picture to the way it was calibrated back at the Apple assembly line.

Color and Calibration

Built into the Mac OS is a technology, called ColorSync, that makes it possible for you to fine-tune the color, brightness, and other characteristics of your Mac's monitor. This is useful for two reasons—first, it allows you to calibrate the display for different lighting conditions. Secondly, ColorSync allows you to create a color profile for your monitor, so that it can compare that color profile to the profile for your printer. The more accurate the color on your display, the closer it will be to the final, printed product if you have a color printer that also supports ColorSync.

To begin calibrating, choose the Color tab in the Displays pane. You can calibrate in one of two ways. The easy way is to simply make sure that the appropriate profile for your Mac is chosen in the Display Profile list. This will give you a decent approximation that should cause your display screen to look fine in average indoor lighting conditions.

The second method takes a little more work. Begin by selecting your Mac's entry, then click the Calibrate button. Now the Display Calibrator Assistant appears and guides you through the calibration process.

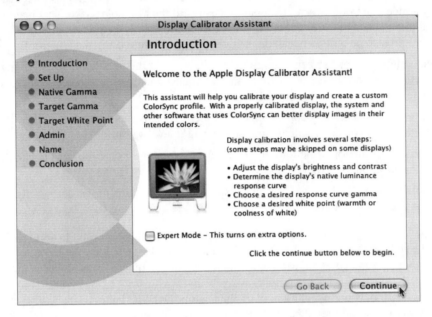

NOTE *You may have trouble with the assistant if you have red-green or similar color vision impairments.*

Walk through the steps of the assistant, following its instructions. When you're done with the assistant, you'll have a newly calibrated display, and perhaps even a more richly colored screen. In the last step of the assistant you give your settings a unique name—that name is added to the ColorSync Profile list. For instance, you might have two different color settings named Bright Day and Night. Now, whenever you want to change calibrations, you can quickly select different profiles from the ColorSync Profile list.

Change Sound Settings

In the Sound settings pane of System Preferences you can make some sound adjustments such as choosing an alert sound, changing volume, and choosing the input and output that your Mac should use for recording and playback. Select the Sound pane in System Preferences and you'll see, at the top of the pane, three tabs—Sound Effects, Output, and Input.

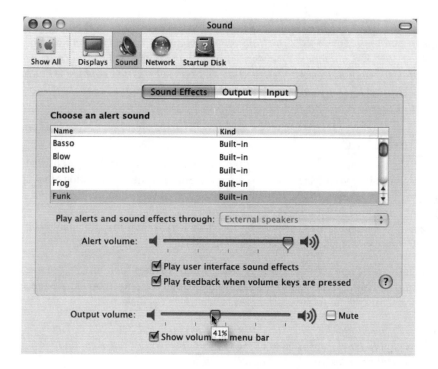

On the Sound Effects tab, you can select an alert sound in the scrolling list, and if you have more than one potential output, you can choose the sound output that you want to use for the alert sound from the Play Alerts and Sound Effects Through menu. You'll also find check box options where you can decide when the alert sounds (and other user interface sounds) will play. Below that, you'll find sliders for the volume of the alerts, which you can set separately from the Output volume that's controlled at the bottom of the screen. Next to that Output volume you'll also see a Mute check box, which you can select to turn the volume off immediately.

On the Output tab you choose the connected device that you'd like to use to play back computer audio. By default that's probably External speakers on an iMac G4, or Built-in speakers on other all-in-one (eMac and earlier iMac) and portable models. If you have other types of output connected to your Mac, you can select them here. (Note that headphones aren't a preference—plugging in headphones automatically works with an External or Built-in speaker setting.) The Output tab also gives you a Balance slider for balancing the signal between left and right.

On the Input tab you can choose the device that your Mac should use for recording. All models we're discussing have an Internal or Built-in microphone, but if you attach a different type of device—another microphone, a USB audio port, or something similar—you'll want to select that device here. You can also set the input volume for the device you select using this screen.

NOTE *Most of the latest Apple consumer models—iMac, eMac, and iBook—don't have an external input for an RCA or "line-in" style device. Instead, if you want to connect a stereo component or external microphone for recording, you may need a USB device that makes that connection possible, such as the popular iMic (**http:// www.griffintechnology.com/products/imic/**), made by Griffin Technologies, or a similar device.*

Set Date and Time

Another of the basic settings for your iMac is the time and date. You probably set these when you first plugged in, turned on your Mac, and answered the Setup Assistant questions that appeared. But you may have some reason to revisit them, including a move to another time zone or perhaps recognition that something is set incorrectly.

The Date and Time pane offers controls on four tabs across the top of the pane. Here's a look at the different things you can set regarding the date and time:

■ **Edit Date and Time** In the Current Date (Today's Date) section, click in the Date entry box and either type or use the arrows to change the date. You can do the same thing for setting Time in the Current Time section.

NOTE *If you can't edit the date and time, it's either because the Set Date & Time Automatically function has been chosen or because you're not signed into an administrator's account. (See Chapter 21 for more.)*

■ **Use a Time Server** If it isn't already turned on, you can turn on the option Set Date & Time Automatically to use an Internet-based time server, which is a great idea if you regularly access the Internet, as it keeps your Mac's clock accurate to "official" Internet time governed by atomic clocks. You can choose Apple's time server from the pull-down menu, or you can enter a different address.

■ **Set the Time Zone** Click the Time Zone tab, then select your approximate time zone on the map, followed by a more exact time zone in the pop-up menu.

■ **Turn Clock On or Off** Click the Clock tab, then turn on the Show the Date and Time option, followed by where and how you'd like to view it by choosing from the radio buttons and check boxes. You can even turn on the Announce the Time option if you'd like your Mac to speak the time aloud every so often (choose that interval from the menu).

Set Appearance

Open the Appearance pane of System Preferences, and you'll see options to choose the appearance and highlight color for your Mac's interface. The Appearance setting can be important; graphic artists tend to opt for the Graphite appearance, which is less colorful and distracts less from the colors used in photos and other graphical documents.

Other options lower on the screen govern how scroll bars react when you click on them. Choose either Jump to Next Page to quickly page through documents or Scroll to Here to move directly to the selected spot in the document, as well as whether or not the Mac should use Smooth Scrolling, which is a special effect that scrolls a window when you click a new location in the scroll bar. (By default, the page "jumps" to a new location, instead of scrolling, when you click in the scroll bar.)

Toward the bottom of the screen you can also choose how many items appear in the Recent Applications and Recent Documents menus (from the Apple menu). At the very bottom of the screen you can adjust font smoothing (which makes fonts appear smooth—as if printed on paper—when viewed on screen, but can make small text hard to read) and decide at what size font smoothing should be turned off.

Set Desktop and Screen Saver

In the Desktop and Screen Saver pane you can choose what your Mac's desktop pattern or image will be, and you can set the screen saver's characteristics. Each has its own tab. On the Desktop tab, choose first from the list of types of images or colors, and then make your exact selection in the area to the right.

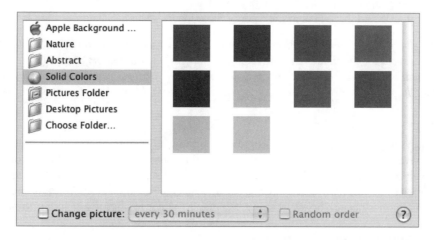

Also, notice the Change Picture option, which can be used to automatically change the desktop image you see every so often. (You can set it to change images up to every five seconds, which makes for a very active desktop.)

On the Screen Saver tab, you can choose the screen saver you want to use on the left side of the screen, and a sample appears on the right side. Actually, your Mac doesn't need a screen saver. Years ago CRT monitors could "burn in" an image after days or months of displaying the same screen image—you may have seen this on older ATM machines. Today, that doesn't happen, so the screen saver is either for show or for password protection. (If the latter, then you'll need to set that in the Security pane of System Preferences, where you can turn on the option Require Password to Wake This Computer from Sleep or Screen Saver.)

Once you've selected a screen saver (there's also a Use Random Screen Saver option), you can click the Options button to set some animation options for that screen saver and then use the slider to determine how long your Mac should be inactive (without your pressing a key or moving the mouse pointer) before the screen saver kicks in. Finally, you can click the Hot Corners button if you'd like to choose a corner of the screen for starting and/or disabling the screen saver. With a *hot corner*, you place your mouse pointer in that corner, and after about a second, the command kicks in. (Disabling the screen saver means it won't turn on even after the specified amount of inactivity. That's a handy hot corner command for when you don't want your Mac to sleep for some reason.)

Save Energy Automatically

The Energy Saver pane allows you to do some interesting things—you can actually schedule your Mac to sleep or to shut down and start up automatically. You can also cause it to dim the monitor and even go to sleep after a period of inactivity. When your Mac sleeps, the processor, hard disk, and monitor all consume much less energy, but the power stays on and applications and documents stay open. Tap a key on the keyboard, and the Mac springs back to life. To set these options, you'll find three tabs in the Energy Saver pane—Sleep, Schedule, and Options.

The Energy Saver pane requires an administrator's account in order to make changes. If you see a locked padlock in the pane, you may not be able to make setting choices without clicking the padlock and entering an administrator's user name and password. See Chapter 21 for details on creating accounts and a discussion of permission issues.

Sleep Timers

To set how quickly your system goes to sleep during periods of inactivity, locate the "Put system to sleep whenever it's inactive for" slider. Then, move the slider to the amount of time you want the Mac to wait before it puts itself to sleep. You'll also see a separate slider for the display, as well as an option to put the hard disk to sleep. If you want to set separate sleep times for the display or hard disk, click those check boxes, then use the display slider to choose a length of time.

Schedule Sleep (or Shutdown)

You can schedule your iMac to automatically sleep, start up, and shut down, if you'd like. To do that, click the Schedule tab. Now, place a check mark next to the option you'd like to automate—this works in an interesting sort of way. If you want the computer to start up on its own at certain times, place a check mark next to Start Up the Computer. Now, just finish the sentence that determines the setting, as in "Start up the computer Weekdays at 8:13 AM." You use the first menu to choose what days it should start up the computer and then set the time at the end of the sentence:

The second entry enables you to determine whether the Mac shuts itself down or simply goes to sleep at a certain time. (You can also leave it turned off completely if you want to manage the end of the day manually.) If you turn the option on, choose either Sleep or Shut Down from the first menu, and then the options are the same as the first setting.

Set Options for Energy Management

Finally, you've got some options to set for energy management. For most Macs you'll see Wake Options and Other Options. Place a check mark next to any options that you think should be active. For instance, Restart Automatically After a Power Failure can be handy for a computer that's also used in your home for network access, to share iTunes music (see Chapter 14), and so on.

Your Account

The last options I want to cover in this chapter are those that relate to your user account. As we discussed in Chapter 1, you may already find that you log into and out of your Mac. But whether you log in manually or your Mac logs you in automatically, the truth is that you have a user account and that account offers some options.

For one, your user account is responsible for managing your home folder and keeping track of your personal settings and preferences—that's how more than one person on a Mac can use it and have their own desktop pattern, folders, e-mail accounts, and so on. Mac OS X is a multiuser operating system, meaning it can allow users to have their own workspace and "look and feel." Most of those personal settings issues are tracked as you make changes in System Preferences and in the options that the individual applications offer you. (If you're curious, those preferences are usually stored inside your home folder in your personal Library folder, in a subfolder called Preferences. More on that in Chapter 24.)

But what about preferences that govern your actual user account? Those are found in the Accounts pane of System Preferences (see Figure 4-5). On the pane you'll find four tabs— Password, Picture, Security, and Startup Items.

This Accounts pane is actually used whenever you want to alter account settings, whether for you or for anyone else on your Mac. If you have administrative capabilities, you can create and manage other people's accounts, as discussed in Chapter 21. For now, though, we're focused on

FIGURE 4-5   The Accounts pane is where you set preferences about your user account.

your own account. Select it in the list on the left, and you can change settings on the right. Here are some of the things you can accomplish:

- *Change your password.* You do that on the Password tab by simply retyping a password in both the Password and Verify entry boxes. In the Password Hint entry box, you can enter a hint that helps you remember this password. That hint is displayed in the Login window after three failed attempts. (Make sure it's something that only jogs your memory and not someone else's imagination.)

NOTE   *Whenever you attempt to change your password, you're asked to authenticate (with your old password) every time, regardless of whether the padlock icon is locked or unlocked.*

- *Change your picture.* You have a personal picture in the Login window, which you can change in the Picture tab. Select from Apple's list of standard images, or click Edit to add an image. (If you have an Apple iSight camera, you can click the Take Video Shapshot button to take a picture of yourself.)

- *Encrypt your home folder.* You can *encrypt* (secure your data by scrambling it in such a way that it can't be read without a password) on the Security tab. This one is worth some discussion, so I'm saving it for Chapter 22.

- *Add startup items.* Click the Startup Items tab and you'll see the screen that lets you manage startup items. It's here that you can cause applications or utilities to launch automatically and immediately after you log into your account. For instance, if you always want Mail to launch itself when you log into your Mac, you can drag the Mail application icon into the window and drop it. When you do, it's added to the list. (Note that you'll need to drag the application from the desktop or a Finder window, not from the Dock.)

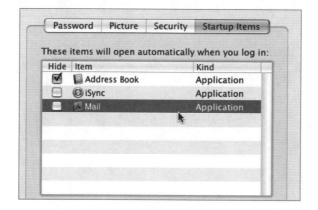

Once you have items on the list, you can drag them around to reorder them, or select one and press the DELETE key to remove it from the list. (The original file isn't affected on your hard disk.) You can drag documents and aliases into the list, as well, if you always want a certain document—or even an Internet shortcut (see Chapter 18)—to load.

TIP *You can cause an item to load automatically but remain hidden—in the sense that the window doesn't appear. (Application icons still appear on the Dock.) To do that, click the Hide check box next to the startup item.*

That's it. When you're done making choices, close the System Preferences application, and those options are now in force.

Chapter 5

Get a Quick Start on the Internet

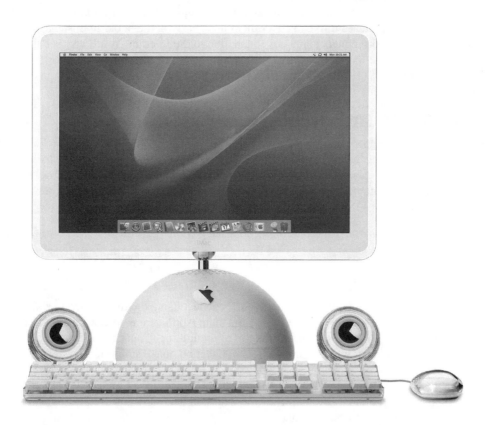

How to...

■ Sign onto the Internet

■ Get your mail

■ Browse the Web

■ Manage your bookmarks and history on the Web

■ Use Internet shortcuts

■ Search the Internet

Clearly the Internet is a big part of the iMac and iBook experience—after all, it's what the "i" in iMac stands for. (The "e" in eMac stands for "education," but it's pretty much an iMac in spirit, so the same Internet focus applies!)

Getting signed onto the Internet and walking through the basics of e-mail and web browsing are important enough that I'd like to cover them here, early in the book. In this chapter you'll see how to connect and disconnect a modem connection to the Internet. You'll also see the basics of reading and sending e-mail messages as well as surfing—and searching—the World Wide Web. Then, in later chapters (18–20), we'll dig deeper into the Mac's Internet strengths and capabilities.

Connect to the Internet

If you've already stepped through the instructions for plugging in your modem and creating your Internet account in the Setup Assistant discussed in Chapter 1, then you're ready to connect to the Internet via your iMac's modem. All you need to do is launch the Mac's Internet *dialer* application, called Internet Connect. Then, you tell the dialer to connect, and it goes through the process of dialing your ISP and beginning the Internet session.

 If you have another type of connection, see Chapter 22 first, and then proceed with this chapter.

Sign On (and Off)

With a modem connection to the Internet, you'll connect using the Internet Connect application, which is located in the Utilities folder inside the main Applications folder. Launch Internet Connect by double-clicking its icon. At the top of the Internet Connect window, you'll see a few different buttons in the toolbar—for a modem connection, make sure Internal Modem is selected. Now, all you have to do is make sure nobody else is using the phone line (just yell really loud there in your home or office, if necessary) and click Connect. The Connect button immediately changes to a Cancel button, and you'll see messages on the Status line, indicating whether the connection is being completed or not.

```
●●●                    Internal Modem                    ⬭
  [Summary]  [Internal Modem]  [AirPort]  [VPN]

        Configuration:  [ Main Number              ⬍ ]
     Telephone Number:  [ 1-719-457-0008            ]
         Account Name:  [ todds                     ]
             Password:  [ ●●●●●●●●●●                ]
                        ☐ Show modem status in menu bar

  Status:  Establishing Connection...        ( Cancel )
```

> **TIP**
>
> *In the Internet Connect window you can turn on the option Show Modem Status in Menu Bar to see a modem menu bar icon. You can then use that icon's menu to connect and disconnect.*

Once the connection is open, the Internet Connect application will display your current connection status, including how long you've been connected, whether data is being sent and received, and what your IP (Internet Protocol) address is currently.

At this point, you're ready to fire up your e-mail application or web browser and start enjoying the Internet. While you're connected to the Internet and Internet Connect is active, the Internet Connect icon in the Dock shows a small lightning bolt. When you're ready to disconnect, click the Disconnect button.

> **NOTE**
>
> *You can actually quit Internet Connect and your Internet connection will remain active as long as you're using the Internet. Eventually, it may "time out" and disconnect after a period of inactivity, according to the settings discussed in Chapter 22. To sign off manually, launch Internet Connect again or select Disconnect from the modem menu bar icon.*

Get, Read, and Reply to E-mail

If you're not already partial to some other e-mail program, you'll probably opt to use Apple Mail for your e-mail needs. It's a great program, particularly in Panther, and Apple has designed it to work well with other built-in applications such as the Address Book and iChat. We'll discuss Mail quickly in this section and then make a longer examination in Chapter 18.

Get Your Mail

If you've used the Setup Assistant to create an Internet account, Mail may already have all the information it needs for you to get started. Once your Internet connection is active, launch Mail (click its icon on the Dock).

When you open Mail, you'll be greeted by one of two things. If your e-mail account hasn't been configured, you'll see a Welcome to Mail screen. On that screen you're asked to enter the information that's necessary for accessing your e-mail account. If you don't know what that is, flip over to Chapter 18 for some of the details.

After setting up an account (or if your account is already set up), you may be asked if you'd like to import mail from another application. Click Yes if you have e-mail stored on your Mac in another e-mail application. Then you can choose that application from the list and click Import. Otherwise, click No.

Next, you'll see the main viewer window shown in Figure 5-1. Mail should check automatically for your e-mail; you can check manually by clicking the Get Mail icon in Mail's toolbar.

Once your mail has been downloaded, the messages will appear in the message list. If you don't see any new messages, but you think some mail has been sent to you, the first step is to check and make sure you have the inbox selected. Click the In icon in Mail's Mailboxes drawer to view your inbox, where new messages are routed automatically. Now you're ready to read messages.

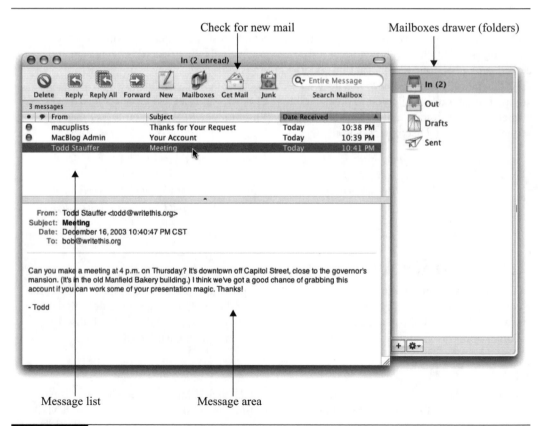

FIGURE 5-1 Mail's main viewer window

Did you know?

E-mail Addresses

The key to sending and receiving e-mail is the e-mail address. In order to receive e-mail, you have to tell others your e-mail address, and to send messages to others, you'll need to know their addresses. The e-mail address can be broken up into three or four parts:

- **Account name**   The name that identifies you or your e-mail account (if more than one person is using it) is unique among the accounts on your ISP's e-mail server computer. That's the "myusername" part of *myusername@myisp.net*.

- **Server computer**   Some, but not all, e-mail addresses will include the actual name of the e-mail server computer in the address. An example might be *todd@mail.mycompany.com* where "mail" is the actual e-mail server computer.

- **Domain name**   This is a name given to a group of computers at a particular organization. If you work for Apple, for instance, your address might be *todd@apple.com*. The "apple" part suggests the domain for that company.

- **Domain name extension**   This part of the address suggests the type of organization you're dealing with. A commercial entity gets a .com, while an ISP (like Earthlink) generally gets a .net extension, as in earthlink.net. Other extensions include .edu (educational), .mil (military), .org (organization), and country codes like .uk (United Kingdom), .fr (France), and .au (Australia).

It's not terribly important to remember what each part of an e-mail address is intended to signify. What's more important is remembering that whenever you enter an e-mail address, you need to enter the entire address as you've been given it, so that it can reach its destination account.

NOTE   *If you don't see the Mailboxes drawer in Mail, click the Mailbox icon in the toolbar to reveal the Mailboxes drawer.*

Read Your Mail

Messages you haven't yet read appear in the Mail message list with an aqua-colored dot in the left column of the list. (A green dot in the second column indicates that your message is from someone who is in your Address Book and is a .Mac subscriber who is online in iChat—see Chapter 18.) To read a message, just click once on its topic—the message text appears in the message area, where you can scroll to read it. If you prefer, you can also double-click a message subject, which causes the message to appear in a new window. Once a message has been read, it stays in the inbox message list, but the small dot disappears to indicate that it's already been read. (Also, once all the messages in your inbox are read, the inbox will no longer be bolded in the mailbox list.)

Sort Your E-mail

Want to switch the view around a bit? Each message in the message list takes up a full row—the columns represent the read or unread status (the small dot in the far-left column), From, Subject, the date the message was received, and other information. If you figured that these columns work a little like the columns in Finder window List view, you're right. You can click the column heading in each case to change the organization of the inbox.

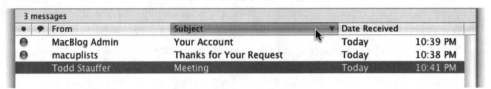

Once you have the message list sorted according to one of the column headings, you'll notice that it's in either ascending or descending order. You can change that order by clicking the heading *again*. The little triangle flips sides to indicate that you've switched from ascending to descending order or vice versa.

You can turn on and off some additional columns. Choose View | Columns | Number to see a serial number assigned to each message as it appears in the inbox, or choose View | Columns | Size to see the size, in kilobytes, of each message. And that's just a sample—the View | Columns menu has a number of options.

Search Your Mail

Have quite a bit of e-mail in your inbox? You can search through the inbox or any other folder so that the list shows only messages that are *focused* on a particular person or topic.

In Mail's toolbar, open the Search Mailbox menu, which looks like a small magnifying glass. In that menu, select the part of the messages you'd like to focus on: Entire Message, From, To, or Subject. Then, enter a keyword in the Search Mailbox entry box, such as the name of the sender (if you've chosen From) or part of the subject (if you've chosen Subject). As you type, you'll notice that the message list gets smaller. It's focusing on messages that match your keyword.

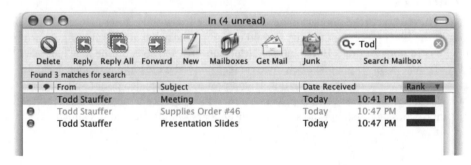

In fact, you don't have to type the whole keyword at all—often typing just a few letters will work. Once you've found the message or messages you're interested in, you can read, reply to, file in another folder, or delete the message(s). When you're done working with the filtered messages, delete the text from the search entry box and you'll remove the filter, once again revealing all your e-mail. (You can also click the small "X" icon in the Search Mailbox entry box itself.)

> **TIP**   *Filtering e-mail works in any folder or mailbox that you select, not just the inbox—see Chapter 18 for details on creating and using additional folders for storing messages.*

Reply to a Message

If a message that you're reading deserves a reply, click the Reply button in the toolbar (or select Message | Reply), and a new window appears, ready for your reply.

You should see that the original message has already been "quoted" for you. That just means that the original message has been included in your reply so that the person you're replying to can have his or her memory jogged about what, exactly, you're replying to. Now you can just begin typing, creating a message that probably looks something like the one shown in Figure 5-2.

Notice in Figure 5-2 that the quoted part appears at the bottom of the message window, with the new reply (the part I wrote) at the top of the message. This is Mail's default treatment of quotes, although you're free to move your insertion point to an area below the quoted text if you prefer it there. You can tell the quoted text by the fact that it appears in a different color. (In fact, each "level" of quoted text appears in a different color, so you can easily follow an entire back-and-forth of a conversation.)

When you're done composing the reply, you're ready to click buttons in the Reply window:

- **Send**   This button sends the message immediately if you're still online. If you're not connected, Mail will display a dialog sheet asking if you'd like to save the message for later delivery. If you choose OK, the message is stored in the outbox. It's then delivered the next time you successfully send another reply or new message.

- **Save as Draft**   Select this button and the message isn't sent at all—it's saved in the Drafts folder. Drafts are just that—rough versions of e-mail messages you don't yet want to send. You can select the Drafts folder to view those saved messages, then double-click a draft to reedit it, and, if desired, send it at that point.

> **TIP**   *Don't forget to check every once in a while so you don't leave a message languishing, unsent, because you still need to edit it. (I do it all the time, then I kick myself for not sending an important message.)*

- **Attach**   Click this button to send a file or files (such as an image file or word processing document) as *attachment(s)* to this message. (You can also simply drag the icon of most any file into the composition window to add it as an attachment. Attachments are discussed in Chapter 18.)

FIGURE 5-2
A reply, complete with the "quoted" message so that you can respond

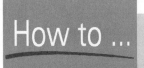

How to ... Reply to All Senders

This is a special case: if you're reading a message that was sent to more people than just you, you can send your reply to *all* recipients. If Mindy sends a message to you, Jack, and Tina, the question is whether or not you want to send a reply only to Mindy, or if you want everyone to see the reply. If you want to send it just to the original sender, select the message in the main viewer window and click Reply; if you want to send it to all recipients to keep the group conversation alive, click Reply All.

If you've already clicked Reply and you're viewing the composition window, you still have another chance to add those additional recipients. Click the Reply All button in the toolbar of the composition window.

Note that you can always remove one or more recipients by deleting their names from the To: or Cc: text boxes; you can also add another person by typing his or her e-mail address in those boxes.

Delete a Message

You can highlight a message in the message window and click the Delete button in the toolbar to delete it from the message list (or you can press the DELETE key on your keyboard). It's not gone forever, though; it's simply moved to the Deleted Messages mailbox.

If you'd like to immediately delete all messages in your Deleted Messages mailbox, choose Mailbox | Erase Deleted Messages. (You can also CONTROL-click on a mailbox and select Erase Deleted Messages.) You'll see an alert box confirming your decision—click OK to delete those messages.

You can set Mail to empty the Deleted Items folder when you quit the program or to delete messages after a certain number of days in the Deleted Messages mailbox. To alter this setting, choose Mail | Preferences and click the Viewing button. In the Erase Deleted Mail When menu, choose how long Mail should wait before permanently deleting a message after it's been moved to the Deleted Messages mailbox.

5

> **TIP** *Mail responds well to the Undo command, which you can access by choosing Edit | Undo or pressing ⌘-Z. This even works if you've moved or deleted a message—but before you've erased it. Invoke Undo and an accidentally deleted message should reappear.*

Compose a New Message

If you're interested in sending a new message, it's even a little easier to do than replying. The only difference is that you need to know the e-mail address of the person you want to send the message to, and you'll need to enter a subject for the message.

> **SHORTCUT** *By default, Mail checks the spelling of your message as you type and lets you know when it thinks a word is suspect by underlining that word. Hold down the CONTROL key and click that word to reveal a pop-up menu that includes suggested spellings. If you see the correct spelling, select it; if you believe the word is correctly spelled, you can choose Ignore Spelling to get rid of the underlining, or Learn Spelling to add that word to your dictionary.*

Here's how to compose a new message in Mail:

1. Click the New button in the toolbar, select File | New Message, or press ⌘-N.

2. In the New Message window, enter an e-mail address for the To: box. If you have more than one To: recipient in Mail, you can type a comma (,) between each e-mail address. (You can also click the Address button to open your Address Book and add addresses from it.)

3. Now, press TAB to move to the Cc: entry box and type an e-mail address if you'd like to send a "courtesy copy" to anyone.

4. Next, press TAB to move to the Subject line. Enter a subject that's informative without being terribly long. Press TAB.

If you want to send a Bcc (Blind courtesy copy), select View | Bcc Header from the menu. A blind courtesy copy is sent to the specified recipient without the other recipients' knowledge. Choose View | Reply-To Header to add a line that enables you to type the e-mail address where you'd like your recipients to send their replies.

5. Type your message in the body of the message window, and then select a signature from the Signature menu if you're set up to add a signature to your messages (discussed in Chapter 18).

NOTE   *If you have more than one e-mail account, a small menu appears above the message body. Here you can choose the account from which you want to send your message.*

After you've typed the body of your message, it's pretty much like a reply—click the Send or the Save as Draft button in the toolbar.

Web Browser Basics

The World Wide Web is really a group of computers that use a certain *protocol*—a set of computer codes for transmitting information—more than it is a place or program. While it may seem that you're connecting to some monolithic mechanism that broadcasts information like a TV network, the fact is that web server computers are distributed all over the Internet and, therefore, all over the world. Since each individual server has its own address and each one

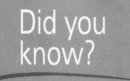

E-mail Formats

By default, Mail sends messages formatted in Rich Text Format, which enables you to add different font effects, styles, and colors to messages using the controls in the composition window. This works great when you're sending to and from other Mac OS X users, but can fall down a bit when sent to other computer users and platforms.

If you find that your recipients are complaining of odd character codes in your messages, you should instead send them plain text messages: when you're composing a message in Mail, you can choose Format | Make Plain Text to send a particular message without codes and formatting. To make Plain Text the permanent default, select Mail | Preferences, and then click the Composing icon. In the Default Message Format menu, choose Plain Text.

If you do send Rich Text e-mail, and you opt to use special fonts in your e-mail messages, note that they should be very common fonts—Arial, Helvetica, Times New Roman—particularly if you're sending this message to users of non–Mac OS X computers. The message will be more likely to look the way you intended.

speaks the same HyperText Transport Protocol (HTTP), it's possible for you to connect to and read documents from computers all over the globe.

You may be surprised to learn that the web browser is a fairly simple program. It's designed to read web documents and format them to fit on your screen. The documents have instructions—things like "make this text bold" and "place an image document here on the page"—that the web browser interprets. Those instructions are in the HyperText Markup Language (HTML), which is actually simple to learn.

Your web browser translates those commands into a coherent page, while offering you built-in features that help you organize, search, and approach the Web in a structured way. We'll take a look at some of those basic features here, while more advanced web browsing topics are covered in Chapter 19.

This chapter focuses on Safari, the Apple-branded web browser included with Mac OS X. Currently, Mac OS X also ships with Microsoft Internet Explorer (IE), but Microsoft has stopped developing IE for Mac, so I won't go into its special features in any detail.

The Internet Address

The basis of locating pages on the Web is the Uniform Resource Locator (URL), which serves as the primary mechanism for addresses on the Web. (URL, by the way, is often pronounced like the name "Earl," and this chapter makes more sense if you read it with that in mind.) The idea of the URL is simple—every web document has its own address on the Internet. That way, if you want to view a particular document on a particular computer in a particular country, you simply enter the address.

Consider these sample URLs:

```
http://www.apple.com/
http://www.macblog.com/imac_book/index.html
```

URLs are made up of three basic components—the protocol, the web server address, and the path to the document. The protocol tells the browser what sort of Internet server you're trying to access. Enter `http://` for web servers, `https://` for web servers that have a security certificate and encryption enabled, and `ftp://` if you're accessing a File Transfer Protocol (FTP) server (FTP allows you to download files).

The server computer's address is simply the address to a particular computer or group of computers running a web server application. Note that this can sometimes be a numbered address like *206.100.129.49* instead of a named address like *www.csindy.com*. (In fact, as far as the Internet is concerned, all computer addresses are numbers, not names. The names are just for human convenience.)

The path statement tells the server computer what folders and subfolders a particular document is stored in on the web server computer. Something like */imac_book/index.html* tells the server computer to "look in the *imac_book* folder and get me the *index.html* file." The server computer complies and sends a copy of that document, which is then displayed in your web browser.

Most browsers allow you to enter web addresses without the full URL. If you prefer, type www.apple.com *or* 206.100.129.49 *without the protocol. It's a little quicker.*

Surf the Web

It's called "surfing" because, just like riding waves in the ocean, you never know exactly how you're going to get somewhere or how far down the beach you'll end up. In a web browser, though, you surf by clicking a hyperlink (see Figure 5-3).

Edit your bookmarks   Address box   Click a hypertext link   Bookmarks Bar

Back — Forward

Images and buttons can also be links

FIGURE 5-3   The main browser window in Safari

What you'll most often do on the Internet is read documents and click links to new documents. Sometimes you'll do other things, such as filling in forms and downloading files, which we'll discuss in depth in Chapter 19.

If you want to get a quick start, though, here are the basics:

■ A *hyperlink* is text that appears underlined and in blue. (Images and buttons on the page can also be hyperlinks.) Click a hyperlink once with the mouse to open a new web page. Hyperlinks are the basic method for "browsing" on the Web—click a link you think is interesting to see the associated document.

TIP *When you pass over a hyperlink using Safari, your pointer icon turns into a hand with an index finger sticking up—that means the pointer is over a hyperlink that can be clicked. To select it, just click the mouse once.*

■ The *Back* and *Forward* buttons are used to move to a previous page, then forward again (if desired). If you click a hyperlink, for instance, read the page, and then decide to go back to the previous page, click the Back button.

■ The *address box* is used to directly enter URLs, as discussed in the previous section. You type the URL (like `http://www.apple.com/`), then press return to visit that address. You should enter addresses as precisely as possible, including all the dots (.) and slashes (/).

To quit Safari, choose Safari | Quit from the menu. Once you've quit the browser, you might also want to sign off of the Internet via Internet Connect so you don't keep the phone line tied up.

NOTE *Don't be surprised if some links open a new web document in your window. There's a special code that web authors use to make a link open a new window. It's harmless enough, but if you don't like it, click the close box or button in the new window. In fact, you can do it yourself by holding down the ⌘ key whenever you click a link; the resulting page will open in a new window.*

Manage Bookmarks, History, and Shortcuts

Eventually you'll come across a site that's worth remembering, and at that point you'll want to create what most other browsers, including Safari, call a *bookmark*. (Internet Explorer calls them "Favorites.") Bookmarks do one thing—save an URL for future reference. To set a bookmark, open the page in the browser window. In Safari, choose Bookmarks | Add Bookmark. A small dialog sheet appears:

Enter a name for the bookmark and choose where you'd like to store it from the menu. (The Bookmarks Bar is actually underneath the toolbar in Safari; the other locations are predefined—they correspond to menu items in the Bookmarks menu.) Click Add and the new bookmark is added.

Use and Edit Bookmarks

In Safari, you access and edit bookmarks in an interesting way: click the small bookmark icon in the toolbar (it looks like an open book), or choose Bookmarks | Show All Bookmarks. When you do, you'll see the Bookmarks interface within Safari (see Figure 5-4).

To use a bookmark, you'll locate it in this interface and then double-click it to launch it. You may need to remember the folder you stored it in, which is accessed by selecting the folder's name on the left side of the interface.

Beyond letting you access your bookmarks, this interface gives you free reign to manage your bookmarks. You can drag a bookmark from one folder to another, for instance, and you can delete bookmarks. You'll notice that the window is divided into two "panes"—Collections and the main listing pane. The Collections pane is where the main folders for the Bookmarks menu appear. You can drag them around to rearrange them, select them to see their contents in the main listing pane, and you can even delete them. (To do so, select a folder and press the DELETE key on your keyboard.)

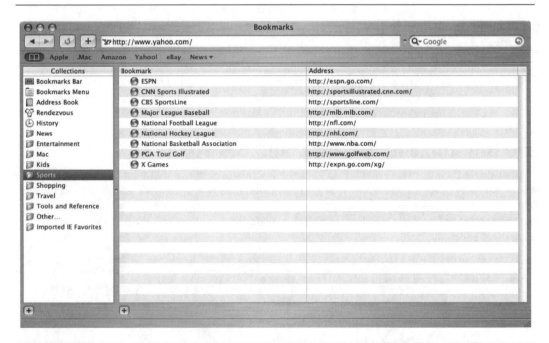

FIGURE 5-4   The Bookmarks interface enables you to create folders and move bookmarks to those folders to organize them.

You can also create a new folder by clicking the plus (+) button at the bottom of the Collections pane of the window. An untitled folder appears, enabling you to edit the name. You can also create subfolders within one of the folders in the Collections pane. Select a folder and click the second plus (+) button that's below the main listings pane. A new subfolder is created that you can edit.

The Collections pane is interesting—not only does it show you the main folders that will appear as menus in the Bookmarks menu, but it also gives you access to some other items, such as the Bookmarks Bar (so that you can add items to the bookmarks that appear below the toolbar in Safari), to your history (discussed next), and even to URLs found in your Address Book.

> **TIP** *You can add subfolders to your Bookmarks Bar, which is very handy. Within those subfolders you can put tons of links that you use often. Those links are then available by selecting the name of the subfolder as if it were a menu, and then clicking the bookmark. In other words, you can use subfolders to add one, two, five, or more submenus full of bookmarks to your Bookmarks Bar for easy access.*

5

Follow Your History

All browsers, including Safari, maintain a *history* of the sites that have been visited. How they maintain that history varies. Safari tends to remember every site that you've visited in the past five days or so; Internet Explorer is similar. Some other browsers (notably, versions of Netscape Navigator) only remember the sites that have been visited during a given browsing session. The history is simply a list of recently visited URLs that you can revisit by selecting the History menu and then selecting the page you want to visit. (If the page was visited on a previous day, you'll select that day's menu first, then the page.)

> **TIP** *In Safari, you can open a new window by selecting File | New Window. In fact, you can browse simultaneously in two, three, four, or more browser windows. Safari tracks them all and remembers visited sites, even if you subsequently close those windows and open others.*

You can edit the history in Safari if you'd like to delete items or if, perhaps, you'd like to drag-and-drop between your history listing and your bookmark collections. Click the Bookmark button on the toolbar and you'll see History in the list of collections. Click History and you'll gain access to that same history listed in the History menu. In the bookmark interface's main listing pane, you can access history items, move them to other collection folders, or delete them by highlighting and pressing DELETE on your keyboard.

> **NOTE** *You can delete your entire stored history by selecting History | Clear History.*

Use Shortcuts

One final, convenient way to store links to important sites is to create shortcuts to them. Shortcuts are actually small files that you can store in the Finder that point to Internet resources—sort of like aliases for the Web. And they're fun to create—you simply drag-and-drop.

The question is *what* to drag-and-drop. In Safari, you have a few different options. The easiest way to create a shortcut is to open the page in question in Safari and then click and hold on the URL in the toolbar. As you drag away, you'll see that the URL comes along with the mouse pointer. Drag it to a Finder window or the desktop, and when you release, you'll see an Internet shortcut like this one:

This works with hyperlinks as well. Click and drag a hyperlink and you'll see it turn into a graphical representation—it looks a little like a comic book dialogue circle. Drag that to the desktop or a Finder window, release the button, and you've got a shortcut.

 *Put your favorite shortcuts in a folder and put that folder on the Dock. Now you've got quick access to important web sites that you can launch regardless of whether or not Safari is running.*

Search the Internet

Need to find something important on the Internet? Safari offers quick access to Google.com searches, which are easily among the Web's most popular. To search Google without first visiting Google.com, simply type keywords in the Google entry box at the top-right of the Safari window.

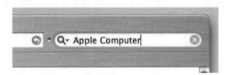

Press RETURN and Safari will show you a Google results page.

The Google search box can respond to the same keywords and codes that a Google search uses, so you can add to the effectiveness of the search using quotation marks, plus and minus symbols, and some other tricks. Here's how:

- *Find a phrase.* Using quotation marks, you can search for words that must appear together in pages that result from a Google search. For instance, searching for `Apple Computer` will find pages that are relevant to both the company and to other Apple-related or computer-related topics. By contrast, searching for `"Apple Computer"` forces Google to find results that have those two words as a phrase.

- *Force a keyword.* If you want to make sure the search results include a particular keyword, you can use a plus symbol (+) to make that clear. For instance, if you'd like to search for a guy named Steve Jobs, who is a resident of Dallas and happens to have the same name as a famous technology CEO, you could use the phrase `"Steve Jobs" +Dallas` to force Google to prioritize results that include Dallas in the document. (The plus sign is also handy when you want to require Google to search for a common word such as "an" or "a" or "and.")

■ *Avoid a keyword.* The opposite can be done with a minus (–) symbol, so that you can ignore entries that include a particular keyword, such as `"Steve Jobs" -Pixar`, which would deprioritize results that include the keyword Pixar in the document.

■ *Add synonyms to the search.* Google can look not only for a keyword but also for synonyms of that keyword if you put a tilde (~) in front of the keyword, as in `writer ~discussion` to search for sites that would include writer chats, questions, forums, and so on.

■ *Search a site.* Finally, a great little trick enables you to search for keywords only on a particular site by using an URL, as in something like `iBook site:www.apple.com`, which would focus on results exclusively from Google's archive of Apple's site.

5

TIP	*You can click the magnifying glass in the Google search box to see a list of searches that you've done recently.*

Chapter 6

How Mac Applications and Documents Work

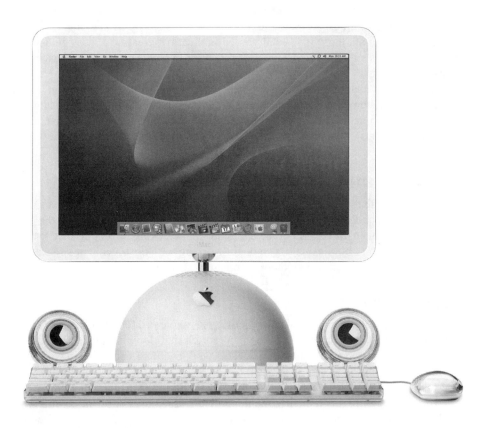

How to...

- Launch documents
- Create, open, and save documents
- Manage your permissions
- Use commands to perform basic tasks like selecting text, cutting, copying, and pasting
- Undo mistakes, close documents, and quit applications
- Dig into the preferences settings of your applications
- Customize application toolbars
- Use the Services menu

In the first part of this book you've seen the tools that the Finder makes available for launching and managing applications. At the same time, those tools can be used to manage documents that you create—after all, those icons that you're duplicating, creating aliases of, and, sometimes, throwing away represent your documents. But you need to create some documents before you can manage them, right?

That's what this chapter is about—opening, saving, and invoking common application commands within documents. Fortunately, you'll find that most Macintosh applications have a lot of things in common, including the commands discussed in this chapter. If you haven't used Macintosh applications in the past, get ready to learn a little bit about all of them.

Launch, Open, and Create Documents

You've already seen that there are myriad ways to launch an application to begin using it—double-clicking an application icon in the Finder, choosing the application from the Recent menu in the Apple menu, or launching the application by clicking its icon in the Dock. In this section, let's move on to how, exactly, you begin working with documents in applications. You can launch documents directly, open them, or create new documents.

Launch a Document

If you want to work with an existing document that you've created (or one that's been downloaded or copied from a CD or another disk), you can launch that document directly. That causes the document's associated application to launch as well, enabling you to begin working with the document immediately.

The easy way to launch a document is simply to double-click its icon in a Finder window or on the desktop. Doing this launches the document's associated application and tells the application to load the document you double-clicked. This works great when you're loading a document that has been saved by that same application previously. For instance, when you double-click an AppleWorks document, the AppleWorks application will be launched. Note that the document's icon can be a clue that tells you what application it's associated with.

6

TIP   *You can also launch a document by selecting it in the Recent Items menu in the Apple menu or by single-clicking a document icon on the Dock.*

The other way to launch a document is to drag-and-drop the document onto an application's icon—whether that application icon is on the desktop, in another Finder window, or on the Dock. This method is particularly effective when you're trying to launch a document that was not originally saved by the application. In many cases, the application will launch and attempt to translate the document if necessary, so that you can work with it.

NOTE   *You can also select an icon and choose File | Open in most applications, or you can* CONTROL-*click an icon and choose Open from the contextual menu that appears.*

Startup Trouble

If you double-click a document that your Mac hasn't properly associated with an application (maybe you copied the document over the Internet or over a network connection), you'll see an alert box. In Mac OS X, the alert warns you that an application isn't associated with this document.

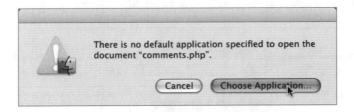

When you see this, click the Choose Application button. In the Choose Application window that appears, you can locate an application to use with this document, highlight that application, then click Open.

If you don't see an application that you know could open the document in the Choose Application dialog box, choose All Applications from the Show menu. Then you'll see nearly every application on your iMac—hopefully, the one you want will show up now.

NOTE   *Another way to get a document to open in a particular application is to* CONTROL-*click the document icon and then choose Get Info. In the Info window, click the disclosure triangle next to Open With and then an application from the menu that appears.*

Create a New Document

When you first launch an application, sometimes it will create a blank document for you as it opens. Other times, it just launches and sits there. If that's the case (or if you're already working in the application and you want a new document), you can create a new document by choosing File | New. This works in *any* application that creates documents.

What happens next can vary. In some cases, a document window just pops up. (That's what happens in a program like TextEdit.) In other cases, you may be greeted by a dialog box that requires you to make choices as to what sort of document you want to create, whether or not you want special help creating the document, and so on.

You can also use ⌘-N to create a new document in nearly all applications. Sometimes, you can click a running application's icon in the Dock, and as you switch to it, you'll often open a new document.

Open a Document

If you've already created a document you want to work on, the first thing you'll do after the application has started up is head to the File menu and choose Open. That brings up the Open dialog box, which may look something like Figure 6-1 for a native Mac OS X application. If you're working with a Classic application, the Open dialog box may look more like Figure 6-2. If it still doesn't look like either of these, you're probably working with a much older Mac application.

You'll probably notice that the Open dialog box looks familiar. In some ways it's like a small version of the Finder window in Columns view, complete with the Sidebar. You'll generally open to your home folder, although some applications work slightly differently. To open folders, select

FIGURE 6-1   The Mac OS X Open dialog box appears in applications that have been updated to use it.

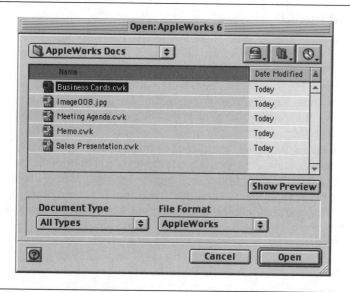

FIGURE 6-2   The older Open dialog box still shows up in applications you run in Mac OS 9 or the Classic environment.

them once in the first column, and their contents appear in the second column. To move back, use the scroll bar at the bottom of the columns. (You can also use the menu at the top of the Open dialog box to change the folder you want to view.) Once you find the document you want to open, select it and click Open, or simply double-click the item.

Not all programs' Open dialog boxes have a File Format or Document Type menu, but when they do, you can use those menus to narrow down the number of files you'll see in the dialog box. The application will offer suggestions like "AppleWorks Document" or "HTML" that you can choose if that's the sort of file you're looking for. If you choose something other than "All Documents" or "All Readable Documents," be aware that you're not seeing every file in the folder. You're seeing a subset that matches the Document Type menu criteria.

In the Classic Open dialog box, things work a little differently. In this one, you dig into subfolders by selecting a folder and clicking Open, or by double-clicking a folder. If you need to move "up" in the folder hierarchy, do that using the menu at the top of the dialog box. When you see the document you want to open, highlight it and click the Open button.

NOTE   *Unlike native Open dialog boxes, Classic dialog boxes aren't quite as aware of the home folder structure of Mac OS X, so they may open automatically to some odd folders. Remember, if you're using Mac OS X, your home folder is located inside the Users folder (on the main level of your hard disk). If you're using Mac OS 9 exclusively, you can probably just save your files in the Documents folder on the main level of the hard disk.*

Save Your Document

Save quickly and save often. This is some of the best advice I can give you. When I'm writing a typical book chapter, I save that document just about every three sentences or so. That's right—every three *sentences.* Why? Because I don't want to type them again.

Whenever you're working in an application, there's always a chance that the application could run into an error, something could go wrong in the Mac OS, or something could go wrong with your Mac. Whatever happens, losing a lot of data because you forgot to save regularly is no fun. So, learn to save.

The first time you save a document, you'll need to find a place to put it and you'll need to name it. To do that, become acquainted with another dialog box. Choose File | Save to bring up the Save dialog box and start the saving process. Figure 6-3 shows the Save dialog *sheet* that appears in native Mac OS X applications—it actually pops out from under the title bar in your document's window. This can be helpful because it lets you know exactly which document is to be saved.

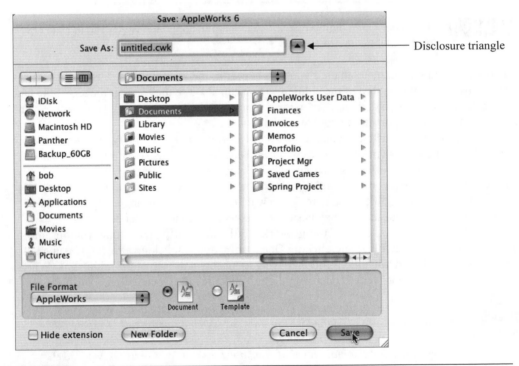

FIGURE 6-3 The native Save dialog sheet is similar to the Open dialog box, except it pops out from under the document's title bar.

Most of the time, the Save dialog sheet will be a bit simpler than is shown in Figure 6-3. By default, you'll just see the top part of that dialog.

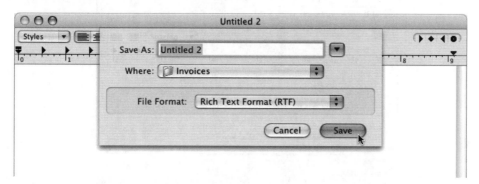

Using the menu at the top, you can quickly select a folder, if it appears. If it doesn't, though, you'll want to click the disclosure triangle at the top right of the dialog sheet. That will reveal the full Columns-style interface. Here's how to save:

1. Select the folder you want to use to save the file. You can create a new folder for the file by clicking the New Folder button if you need to.

You can quickly select the Desktop folder (so that you can save items on your desktop) in a Save dialog by pressing ⌘-D.

2. Type a name for the file in the Save As entry box, then choose a format for the document from the File Format (or sometimes File Type) menu.

3. Click Save. The document is saved and you're returned to the document to continue working.

The Classic Save dialog box (see Figure 6-4) works in a similar way. The only difference is the absence of the Columns interface; instead, you'll select a folder and click the Open button to dig through subfolders until you find the folder you want to use for saving.

Once you have the document saved, you can choose File | Save to save any changes to that same document. You won't see the Save dialog box, since the application already knows where to save the file and what to call it. In fact, for even faster saving you can just press ⌘-S to instantly save what you're working on. (That's what I do every three sentences.)

What if you want to save this file in a new place and/or with a new name? In that case, you use the Save As command in the File menu. That brings the Save dialog box (or dialog sheet) back up, allowing you to save the document (and any changes you've made since your last Save operation) to a new document located in a new folder. This is sort of like invoking the Duplicate command in the Finder—you create an entirely new copy of the document, which you can give a different name and put in a different folder, if you like.

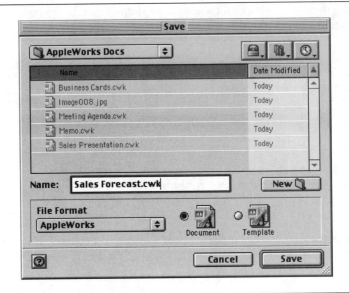

FIGURE 6-4 The Classic Save dialog box

Plus, after you've invoked the Save As command, the document file on your screen is the new document you just created. This can be useful if you want to keep the original file as it was but want to alter a copy of it to use for some other reason. Perhaps you're creating an invoice: you open last month's invoice, choose File | Save As to create a new copy with a new name, then edit the new copy for this month's invoice.

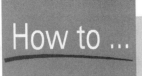 ## Get a Handle on Permissions

You can't always save where you want. No, that's not a Rolling Stones song—it's just a Mac truism. Mac OS X uses concepts called *ownership* and *permissions* to govern access to folders stored on your hard disk. If you own a folder, you can alter it or delete it; if you have permission to access a folder, you may be able to launch and save files found in that folder. And if you have neither ownership nor permission, you may not be able to access the folder at all.

This ownership and permissions approach is why it's handy to save your personal documents inside your home folder. You own your home folder, and, hence, you have ownership of and permission to access any subfolders within your home folder, including any subfolders that you create in your Documents or Music folder and so on. You can see the permissions setting for a particular folder by selecting the folder in the Finder and choosing File | Get Info or pressing ⌘-I. In the Get Info window, click the disclosure triangle next to Ownership & Permissions.

Another interesting folder is the Shared folder, found inside the Users folder from the root level of your hard disk. You don't own the Shared folder, but you do have permission to read and write files in that folder. You can't delete files in that folder that you didn't create, however, because you don't have ownership of them.

Elsewhere on your Mac you'll run into circumstances where you can't save a file—that may be because you don't have the proper permissions or ownership. For instance, you can't read or write to files inside the folders of other users on your Mac, except for the Public folder. But you can read files in other users' Public folders, and you can write files to the Drop Box folders in other users' Public folders.

So what do you do if you can't save a file to a particular folder? You may just not have the correct permissions—try a different folder. If, however, you feel certain that you *should* have permissions, you may need to troubleshoot for a permissions issue—see Chapter 24 for details.

Basic Application Commands

Now that you've seen how to create, open, or save documents, you're ready to actually do something within those documents. Obviously, what you do depends somewhat on the application in question (I wouldn't try writing a novel in iCal calendar software, for instance), but there are some common commands that you'll find in nearly every application you encounter. Let's look at some of them.

Select and Select All

You're familiar with selecting icons in the Finder with the mouse. Selecting text (or objects like spreadsheet numbers or graphical images) in a document is similar, although it can vary a bit. For instance, if you're typing text in a text editor or word processor, you can't just point and click the mouse once to select a word in that document. You can, however, point and *double-click* to select a word.

To select more than one word, hold down the mouse button and drag the mouse pointer across the words you want to select. The words (or parts of words) become highlighted, just as if you were selecting multiple icons in the Finder. You can drag the mouse pointer (which will look like a capital letter "I") from left to right and/or up/down the page to select multiple words or lines of text.

Can you make a meeting at 4 p.m. on Thursday? It's downtown off Capitol Street, close to the governor's mansion. (It's in the old Manfield Bakery building.) I think we've got a good chance of grabbing this account if you can work some of your presentation magic. Thanks!

\- Todd

There are a couple of tricks, too. In most text programs, triple-clicking will select an entire paragraph or a continuous line of text. In applications where triple-clicking doesn't select the entire paragraph, try clicking four times rapidly.

> **TIP** *Another trick is to place the cursor at the beginning of the text that you want to select, then hold down the* SHIFT *key and click at the end of the text that you want to highlight.*

If you'd like to select everything in a given document, there's a command for that, too. From the Edit menu, choose Select All. All the text (or objects) in the document will be highlighted. You can also invoke this command from the keyboard by pressing ⌘-A in nearly any application, including the Finder.

Cut, Copy, and Paste

These three commands are present in nearly every application ever written. The Cut, Copy, and Paste commands allow you to move text and objects around within documents or from one document to another. In fact, you can cut and paste between applications in most cases.

The Cut and Copy commands are similar. Highlight text or objects in your document and select the Edit menu. Choose Cut if you'd like to delete the text or objects from the current document or current spot in the document; if you just want to copy the selection to use elsewhere, choose Copy. You can also use the keyboard: ⌘-C invokes Copy and ⌘-X invokes Cut.

Your selection is moved to something called the Clipboard—it's a file that's stored in the System folder on your iMac's hard disk. Now, the contents of the Clipboard can be pasted into another section of the document or another document altogether.

> **NOTE** *You can switch to the Finder and choose Edit | Show Clipboard to see the contents of the Clipboard at any time.*

To paste, place the insertion point in the document where you'd like the text or objects to appear. (In some documents you don't place the insertion point; you just click the document window to make sure it's active.) Then, pull down the Edit menu and choose Paste. (Or, press ⌘-V on the keyboard.) The text or objects will appear in the document.

Want to do it another way? In many applications you can drag-and-drop text to different parts of the document, to a new document, or even to the Finder. Try this:

1. Using the mouse pointer, highlight some text you've typed into a document—for instance, an AppleWorks document.

2. Now, point the mouse pointer at the highlighted text, click the mouse/trackpad button, and hold it.

3. Drag the text to another part of the document or to another document entirely.

4. Release the button.

When you're finished, you've effectively cut and pasted the text, even though you didn't use the commands. (Also, using drag-and-drop means you didn't replace the contents of the Clipboard, just in case you have something that you've stored with the Edit | Cut or Edit | Copy command that you still want to be able to paste with Edit | Paste.)

> **TIP** *Also, as a neat trick, some applications will let you drag text or images from the document to your desktop, creating a "clipping" file. That file can then be used to store the text or to drag it into another document at a later date.*

You can copy and paste much more than just text and objects like drawings and images. If you can select it in an application, there's a good chance you'll be able to copy and paste it. When in doubt, try the commands and see if they work.

Undo

Here's another perennial favorite of application programmers—the Undo command. This command is designed to immediately countermand the most recent action or command you've performed. For instance, if you just deleted an entire paragraph in AppleWorks, choose Edit | Undo to get that paragraph back. It usually works for formatting text or objects, pasting, deleting, typing, and so on. Most any activity can be taken back. You can usually undo immediately by pressing ⌘-Z on the keyboard.

Many programs will also have a Redo or similar command that is designed to undo an Undo command. If you undo something you didn't actually want to undo, head back to the Edit menu and look for the Redo command.

> **NOTE** *Some applications, such as Microsoft Word or Apple's iMovie, have multiple undo capabilities. Basically, that means you can undo more than one command: keep choosing the Undo command and the program will keep working backward through your most recent actions.*

Quit the Application

About done with that application? All applications have a Quit command that closes the application, hands the RAM space back to the Mac OS, and cleans up any open files. In a native Mac OS X application, that command is in the application menu (the one named for the application, such as TextEdit or AppleWorks) under Quit. You can also press ⌘-Q in almost any Mac application to quit. In Classic applications, you'll find Quit in the File menu.

TIP   *I recommend that you save changes first before quitting. It's always possible that quitting the application could trigger a crash or error that would cause you to lose data. If you save first, you are assured of having your data intact.*

When you quit a program, it should ask you to save any unsaved documents and may ask you to make other decisions—like hanging up the modem or waiting until a particular activity is finished. Of course, it depends on the program.

NOTE   *Most of the time, closing a document window in a program does not actually quit the program. Many beginning Mac users make the mistake of closing a document window and believing the application is also closed. You can close a window by clicking its close box or button, choosing File | Close Window, or pressing ⌘-W. But that rarely quits the program—it just closes the current window or document. You need to invoke the Quit command in applications; otherwise, they remain open, take up RAM, and make it more difficult for you to run other programs.*

Did you know?

The Application Menu

All Mac OS X native applications have a special menu, called the "application menu," that appears just to the right of the Apple menu when the application is active. You can tell it's the application menu, because it's named after the application! For instance, if you're working in TextEdit, you'll see the TextEdit menu; if you're working in AppleWorks, you'll see the AppleWorks menu.

The application menu is basically designed to do two things. First, it reminds you instantly of what application you're working in, which can come in handy if you're having a long, hard day. Second, it holds application-specific commands, such as Quit and Preferences. While Classic applications often have these commands in the File menu, Apple's Mac OS X engineers decided that didn't make much sense—you're not quitting the file, you're quitting the *application*. Thus, the application menu was born.

Set Preferences

Most applications offer a dialog box that allows you to set your preferences for how the program behaves, what values it defaults to, and so on. The preferences are completely up to the individual application. There really isn't too much in the way of standardization, except for the location of the Preferences command. I discussed the Finder Preferences in Chapter 4; I'll talk about the preference settings in AppleWorks, iMovie, Mail, Safari, and your other bundled applications throughout the book.

To open the Preferences dialog box, you'll generally invoke a Preferences command. In most native Mac OS X applications it's under the application menu, such as AppleWorks | Preferences or TextEdit | Preferences. In Classic applications, you'll often find it under Edit | Preferences. If you don't find it there, look under the File menu.

Click Buttons, Check Boxes, and Sliders

You'll find that many preferences settings, dialog boxes, and other components that make up applications—and many parts of Mac OS X—rely on some typical controls to help you make decisions. You've already seen some of these, but let me go ahead and define them formally. Here's what they do:

- ■ **Radio buttons**   This type of control allows you to make one selection among two or more choices per option. Click the button next to the item you want to choose.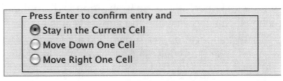

- ■ **Check boxes**   A check box allows you to choose each item individually. If you want the item active, you'll click in the box next to the item and a check mark (sometimes it's an "x") will appear in the box.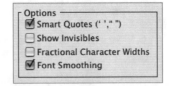

- ■ **Sliders**   A slider bar allows you to choose from a range of values from low to high just as you might for a volume control on a home stereo system. In fact, slider bars are used most often for changing the volume level, brightness level, and so on. The menu bar icon volume control (discussed in Chapter 2) is a slider control. You just drag the slider up and down on the control to change the value.

Use Toolbars

While not required of Macintosh applications, toolbars are a popular addition. Toolbars put small *iconic* buttons in a special bar below the menu bar in an application, giving you quick access to the most popular commands in that program. An example is the following illustration, which shows the toolbar from AppleWorks.

Many such toolbars allow you to quickly access fonts, font styling, and many other commands that you might use frequently in the program. But often, at least for me, the little icon buttons on toolbars make no sense whatsoever. In that case, the solution is usually to point at an icon with the mouse pointer and wait a few seconds. Most applications have a little pop-up window or other way of showing you what a particular icon is for.

 *More and more native Mac OS X applications offer a* window *toolbar (as opposed to AppleWorks'* application *toolbar) that's similar to the Finder window's toolbar, which can often be customized in the same way. Look for a Customize Toolbar command in such applications, which enables you to drag icons to and from the toolbar easily.*

Check Out the About Box

Want to know more about an application? All applications are required to have an About box, which you can access while the application is active. If you're currently working with a Mac OS X native application, pull down that application's named menu (such as TextEdit, AppleWorks, and so on). You'll see that the first menu item is About... followed by the name of the application.

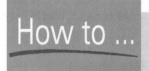 **Get Help in Applications**

Many Apple-written applications use the standard Help Viewer discussed in Chapter 2, while others use the other Classic and Mac OS 9 Help systems discussed in the appendix. If you encounter an application that doesn't offer either, that doesn't necessarily mean you're out of luck. Choose the Help options on the Help menu, and start by looking for hyperlinks to click, topics to explore, or a search box that lets you enter keywords. You'll find that most alternative help systems will likely offer something along the lines of hypertext links within explanatory documents. Most of them will be similar enough to the Apple Help system that you should be able to figure them out with relative ease. If your application doesn't have a help system, look in the application's original folder for a Users Guide or a Read Me file, which may give you some indication as to how to use it. Many such files are in PDF format, meaning they can be viewed in the Preview application (in your main Applications folder in Mac OS X) or Adobe Acrobat Reader, which is installed on all iMacs.

(In a Classic application, you'll find About… in the Apple menu.) Choose that item and you'll see a little something about the application. Some applications will place help, tips, and other buttons in the About window that will, occasionally, give you help when using the application.

Explore the Services Menu

The last feature I'd like to cover quickly is the Services menu, which is a commonly found menu command in Mac OS X native applications. What the Services menu does is enable you to access some of the features of *other* applications from within the current application. It's a neat way to enable your applications to work together.

For example, say you're browsing the Web in Safari and you see a paragraph of text that you'd like to e-mail to a friend. It's easily done if you use Apple Mail—simply highlight the text in question and choose Safari | Services. In the Services menu, choose Mail | Send Selection (see Figure 6-5). The result should be a new composition window in Mail (in fact, it'll launch Mail if it isn't already running) that you can then use to send the highlighted text to someone else.

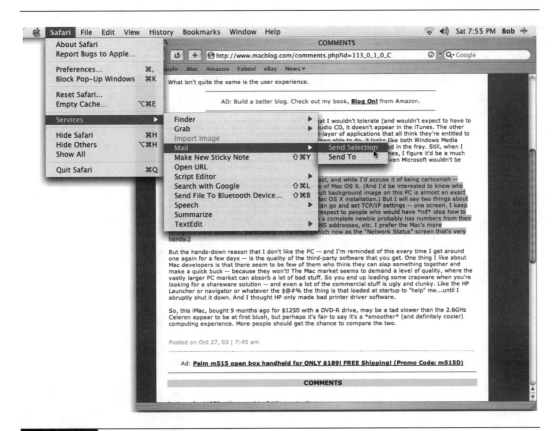

FIGURE 6-5   Using the Services menu

Generally you'll find that items in the Services menu work best when you've highlighted or selected something in the current application; if not, you'll find that most of the commands in your Services menu are grayed out. Also, the Services menu has its limits. In most applications it works best with highlighted text, and some commands that seem as if they should work don't always work. But, when the Services commands do work, they offer some great shortcuts.

Part II

Get Your Work Done

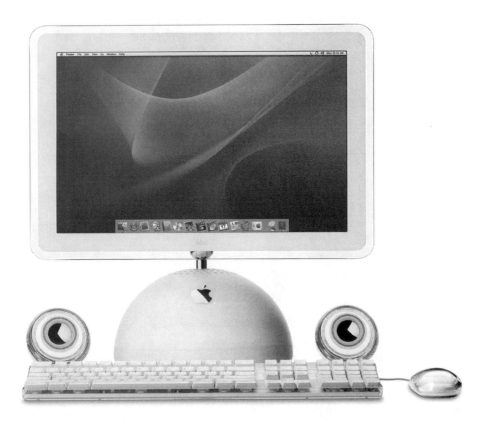

Chapter 7

Type and Format Documents in AppleWorks

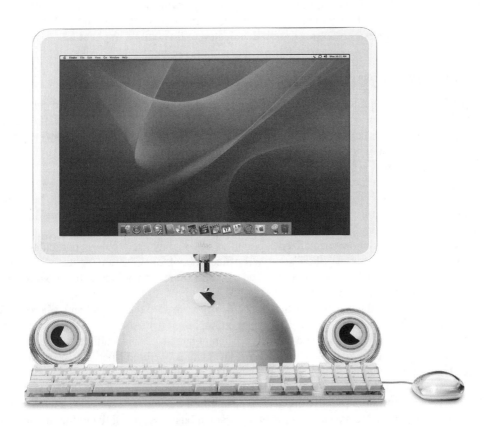

How to...

- Create a word processing document
- Type your document and format the text
- Format paragraphs, align elements, and create headers and footers
- Format the entire document, including margins, sections, and tabs
- Spell-check and find and replace automatically
- Create and use paragraph styles
- Use prebuilt templates and create your own document templates

In this chapter you'll get a brief introduction to AppleWorks, the Mac's built-in productivity application. As you'll see, AppleWorks is great for creating written documents, offering all the tricks that a computer brings to bear on the task. And AppleWorks is so much more, as well, which is why Chapters 7 through 11 are all dedicated to this unique application.

Get to Know AppleWorks

AppleWorks is what's referred to as a "works" application, because it's designed to perform more than one major document-creation function. While a program like Microsoft Word is designed solely for word processing, AppleWorks offers a number of different modules, allowing you to create word processing documents, spreadsheets, databases, images, drawings, and other types of documents. So why would you choose anything else?

In most cases you probably won't have to. AppleWorks is a very good program that allows you to do some rather unique things—including putting its parts together to create layouts that feature word processing, images, spreadsheet tables, and database data in the same documents. In that respect, it's a very powerful and very enjoyable program to work with.

But you may need more specialized capabilities or you may need to use a particular program—like Microsoft Word—because the rest of your office, school, organization, or secret-handshake society requires it. That's okay, but you'll need to spend some money to buy that program, and then you'll need to install and learn it.

In exchange, you'll get a program that's specifically tailored to the task at hand. Microsoft Word, for instance, offers a lot of tools for collaborating on important word processing documents— you can embed comments, track changes, and even give different human editors a different color to use within the document so it's easy to see who is making what changes. We used Microsoft Word to create this book, for instance, largely because of its collaborative capabilities.

So, you'll want to use a tool that's designed for the job. Sometimes that's Microsoft Word, but AppleWorks is truly an impressive application, and you'll be able to accomplish a lot with it. If your tasks are personal, educational, or even for a small business, you'll likely find it completely adequate for your needs.

But even if it doesn't fit all of your needs, in nearly all cases, documents created in AppleWorks can be translated into documents that can be read by other applications like Word, Excel, QuarkXPress, and others when the time comes. So, feel free to try things in AppleWorks first, then move on to something else if you need more power.

NOTE   *AppleWorks 6.1 and higher now has Microsoft Word (and Excel) translators built into it, so you can actually load and save documents in Word's .doc format.*

Write with Your Mac

A word processor—such as the word processing module within AppleWorks—is designed to do a number of things. It's designed to accept text and images that you type or add through menu commands, then allow you to format the text and images in many different ways. It's worth saying that word processors are designed to help you format entire documents—from memos and letters to longer documents like reports, pamphlets, and books. Word processors allow you to do many things to long and short documents:

■ Change the document size, margins, and spacing

■ Insert headers and footnotes

■ Change the font, style, and formatting of text

■ Create documents in outline form

■ Format text in tabular form

■ Format text with bullets, numbers, or special tabs and indents

■ Check spelling

■ Change formatting for paragraphs, sections, or the entire document

In most cases, however, a word processor is not designed for creating a particular *page*. That's what layout applications like QuarkXPress and Adobe PageMaker are designed for. Such applications have highly sophisticated tools that allow a page designer to drop text, images, effects, lines, and shapes onto a page and manipulate them freely to create the most stunning advertisement, pamphlet, or publication.

So, word processing really is a little closer to the typewriter than it is to the layout table. But there is a difference between a typewriter—even most electronic, computerized typewriters—and a word processing application. Word processing applications allow you to change your mind. You can experiment with documents after the fact. That means you can create the document first, then worry about how it will be formatted.

Start Your Document

To begin, launch AppleWorks or choose File | New if AppleWorks is already open. The Starting Points window appears, allowing you to choose the type of document you'd like to begin.

In AppleWorks, the type of document you choose helps determine what sort of tools and menu commands you see. In this case, you're interested in creating a word processing document, so leave that selection highlighted and click OK. Now you'll see the word processing commands and a blank document window.

Next step: start typing. There are actually a couple of rules you should follow when typing in a word processor, especially if you're used to a typewriter. Some of these rules are

- *Don't press TAB to indent the first line of a paragraph.* You can format paragraphs so that they are indented automatically, either before or after you've typed them.

- *Don't press RETURN at the end of a line.* You only need to press RETURN at the end of a paragraph. Whenever you type to the right margin of the page, the next thing you type will automatically *wrap* to the next line.

- *Don't put two spaces after a period.* Many typists get used to pressing the SPACEBAR twice after the end of a sentence, but that throws off the automatic spacing capabilities of a word processing program, and it just looks bad with many standard Mac fonts.

- *Don't worry about double-spacing while you type.* You'll be able to set line spacing for your document at 1.5, double-, or triple-space after you've typed it (or, as you'll see, before you begin).

- *Don't press RETURN many times to get to a new page.* You can easily insert a page break if you're done on one page and want to begin on another one.

- *Don't enter asterisks, dashes, or numbers for lists.* You can add bulleted list items automatically. If you need to create a list like the one you're reading right now, you can do that with commands: just enter each line and press RETURN. You'll be able to go back and format the bulleted or numbered list later.

- *Don't do anything with tabs or spaces to change the margins.* You don't need to insert many spaces, add tabs, or press RETURN in order to create special margin spacing— for instance, if you want to have a block of quoted text that's squeezed onto the page. Again, you can do that with special document formatting commands, covered later in this chapter. For now, just type the paragraph normally.

■ *Don't use spaces to create columns or table layouts.* At the very least, you should use tabs and the document ruler to set up the spacing in your document. That's covered later in this chapter, too.

Most of these issues are addressed in the section "Format Your Document," which appears later in this chapter. You'll find that what you need to do while typing is pretty simple:

1. Type words.

2. When you get to the end of a sentence, type a period, then press the SPACEBAR once.

3. When you get to the end of a paragraph, press RETURN.

That's all you do while you're typing your document. Remember, you'll be able to change just about anything once you have the words on the page. For now, typing is the primary goal.

Fonts, Styles, and Sizes

Aside from the typing basics, there are two other precepts for the accomplished word processing typist. (That's you.) The first is to *save often,* which is covered in an upcoming section. The second is to format your text as you're typing. It's not mandatory, but learning to format as you type makes creating your documents easier.

By text formatting I mean three things: the font, the style, and the size of the text. These things can be changed easily before or while you're typing a line of text, so I'll include them here while you're getting started with your word processor.

Fonts

The word "font" is used in most Macintosh applications to mean "typeface," which is defined as a general design for a set of characters. Popular typefaces are Courier, Times New Roman, Helvetica, and so forth.

If you'd like your typed text to appear in something other than the default font, you can head up to the Font menu, choose a new font, and begin typing. Your text appears in that new font.

Similarly, you can select existing text and change it to a new font. Select text by moving the mouse pointer to the left of the first word you want to highlight, press the mouse button, and drag the mouse pointer to the right of the last word you want to choose, then release the mouse button. If you want to choose all the words in your document, choose Edit | Select All. Then select Text | Font and click the font you want to use for the highlighted text. Your text should change immediately (see Figure 7-1).

You can also select a font from the Font menu that appears at the top of the document window in the ruler area.

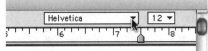

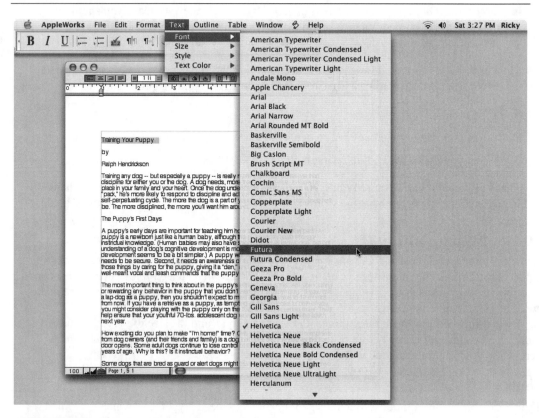

Highlight some text and choose a new font from the Font menu, and you'll see it in your document.

TIP *You can opt to have the Font menu in AppleWorks show you the shape and style of the fonts as you select them. (It slows down the menu's rendering, but it's pretty useful.) Select AppleWorks | Preferences | General. In the Preferences dialog box, choose General from the Topic menu. Then, turn on the Font Menus in Actual Fonts option and click OK to close the dialog box. Now whenever you select the Font menu, you'll see actual examples of the fonts instead of just their names.*

Styles

The text styles represent different effects you apply to the fonts for emphasis—things like italics and boldfacing. You can change the style of your text in either of the two ways that you change the font—either before you type, or by selecting text that's already been typed.

To change the style, select the Text | Style menu in AppleWorks, then click on the style you want to use. Begin typing and your text appears in that style.

To change the style of text that already appears, select that text in the document window and then pull down the Style menu. Choose the style you want to use, and the highlighted text changes immediately to that style. Note that you can also select styles from the default button bar that appears above your document window. "B" is for bold, "I" for italics, and "U" for underline. (For plain text, make sure all three are deselected.)

Often you'll want a more convenient way to change styles, especially with the four major styles: Plain, Italic, Bold, and Underlined. In these special cases, you'll find it's most efficient to learn the keyboard commands for changing text styles. Except for the Plain command, these commands are common not just in AppleWorks, but in almost any application where you can style text:

⌘-B	Boldface	⌘-U	Underline
⌘-I	Italic	⌘-T	Plain, unstyled text

Now you can quickly switch styles while typing. Press ⌘-I, type a word in italics, then press ⌘-T to return to plain text. (You can also press ⌘-I to turn italics off again—you'll find that some applications don't support ⌘-T.) Press ⌘-U and ⌘-B and you'll be typing bold, underlined text; press ⌘-T and you're back to plain text again.

Most fonts also include a few special characters that you might want to enter as you're typing. OPTION-*8, for instance, will type a bulleted point character;* OPTION-DASH *(the "-" sign) will create an en dash;* OPTION-SHIFT-DASH *will create an em dash.*

Sizes

You can change the size of text in your document by highlighting the text and using the Text | Size menu to choose the point size. *Points* are a traditional way of sizing fonts in publishing terms—72 points equals about one inch, so 12 points equals about one-sixth of an inch in height. Traditionally, 72-point text was reserved for newspaper headlines that declared war or the surprise winner of a presidential election; these days the biggest headline on the front page on any given morning is probably about 72 points.

Readable body type is typically about 12 points; 14 points looks like "big" type you find in some of those movie novelizations. Try 18 points for a subhead in your report—24 or so can look good for the title of your report. As with fonts, you can also use the special Size pop-up menu that appears in the document window's ruler area.

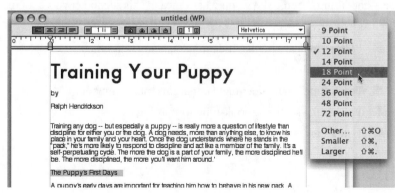

You can also change text sizes as you type. Pull down the Text | Size menu and choose the new size from the menu, then type in that new size. If you want to use the keyboard commands for changing font sizes, they might take some memorizing: ⌘-SHIFT-< makes text smaller, and ⌘-SHIFT-> makes it bigger. (Note, by the way, that these are specific AppleWorks keyboard commands and don't work in all applications.)

Save Often

If you've been following so far, you might see from the figures in this chapter something terribly wrong is going on. The document I'm working on is still untitled, which means it hasn't been saved!

My rule: save every three sentences. It usually doesn't take long for each save (once the initial save is complete), and it'll sure make you happy if and when your Mac or your application crashes. (It does happen. That fashionable Mac encourages you to put it in high-traffic areas where you're bound to trip over the power cord.) Having saved very recently, you won't be as upset when you only have to retype a few sentences to catch up. If you have to retype an entire page or two, you won't be nearly as pleased.

To save the document the first time, choose File | Save once you've typed something. Use the Save dialog box to find the folder where you want to store the file, and then give it a name and click Save. From then on, you can just press ⌘-S to save as you're typing. Every three sentences, remember? (For more on saving, see Chapter 6.)

AppleWorks 6 includes an Auto-Save function that automatically saves your document every few minutes. Choose AppleWorks | Preferences | General, then choose Files from the Topic menu. If it isn't already checked, check the box next to Auto-Save. You can also use the entry box to enter the number of minutes (or hours or seconds) you want AppleWorks to wait between saves. Click OK to put your preference into action.

Format Your Document

I know it seems that creating a document should be so much more complicated than the "just type it" mantra I've repeated so far. And it's true that you can do some complicated things in a word processing document—the sort of stuff that would make a Ph.D. thesis advisor proud. But "just type it" is still great advice, because it's easier to format the document before or after you type—not during. Let me show you what I mean. This section covers a lot of stuff in a little space, including:

- Formatting paragraphs: indenting, spacing, alignment
- Inserting elements: page breaks, headers, footers
- Formatting whole documents: margins, page numbers
- Formatting sections: book-type formatting
- Using tabs and the ruler: making changes visually

Whether you're writing reports, documentation, thesis papers, research, legislation, contracts, or books, you'll find you're able to get pretty deep into document formatting without filling too much of the space in your head.

Format Paragraphs

There are four basic formatting tasks you'll be managing when it comes to your paragraphs—indenting, line spacing, bullets, and alignment—and all four are controlled from within the Paragraph dialog box. To start formatting a paragraph, place the insertion point in that paragraph (you don't have to highlight the whole paragraph, but you can if you like). To format more than one paragraph at once, highlight all of them. (Remember that quadruple-clicking usually selects paragraphs.) With that out of the way, choose Format | Paragraph. That causes the Paragraph dialog box to appear.

Indenting

Now, in the Paragraph dialog box, you can make some choices about how that paragraph is going to look. On the left side of the dialog box, you have three margin choices. All three are entered in the entry boxes in inches—a standard indent is about 0.5 inches. You can indent the left, right, or both margins (both is usually for block quotes, programming code listings, or movie script dialog), or you can indent just the first line of the paragraph.

Click in the entry box next to Left Indent, First Line, or Right Indent, then type the number of inches you want for the indent. You can press TAB to move to the next box or press RETURN to accept the value and close the dialog box. If you'd like to see how your settings look before you close the dialog box, click the Apply button. That makes your changes but leaves the dialog box open for further changes or experimentation. (You can also drag this dialog box around if it's hiding the paragraph you need to see after the change is applied.)

TIP   *You don't need to type the "in" for inches when entering your own number—just the number will suffice.*

Line Spacing

In the Line Spacing entry box, enter a number, then choose the units for that number in the little pull-down menu next to it. If you want to double-space, you can just keep the units set at "lines."

You can also fine-tune your spacing to give yourself more or less space between lines as necessary. For instance, you'll sometimes want a document to look like it's double-spaced, but it's actually squeezed a bit less than double to fit more words on a page. (For instance, you might do this in the unlikely event that you actually wrote too *much* for your term paper.) In that case, you should choose Points as the units for Line Spacing and select a point size that's a little less than twice the point size of your text. If your text is 12 points, for instance, you could choose 20 points to get a slightly squeezed double-spacing effect.

 *You'd think you could just choose 1.75 lines for the Line Spacing, but AppleWorks rounds it up to 2 lines. It will only accept whole and half values, so 1.5 is acceptable, but 1.25 gets rounded up to 1.5.*

The other spacing options allow you to add additional space above and below a paragraph—this can often be useful if you choose a more contemporary style for your document in which you don't indent the first line of your paragraphs. In that case, a little extra space before and after a paragraph will make it clear where one ends and the next paragraph begins.

Make a List

When you type a list in AppleWorks, you simply type each item or sentence, then press RETURN after each item. So, technically, you're creating a number of different paragraphs, even if they're really short. In order to turn them into a list, you can select each item and give it a label in the Paragraph dialog box. The labels vary from bulleted points, to numbers, to Roman numerals.

There's a slightly more efficient way to make a list:

1. In the document window, type each list item and press RETURN after each.

2. Drag the mouse pointer to select every item in the list.

3. Select Format | Paragraph.

4. Choose the Label menu from the Paragraph dialog box and select Bullet.

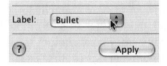

5. Click Apply or OK.

That's it—the list is created. Every item you've highlighted becomes its own list item. If you clicked Apply and you're still in the Paragraph dialog box, you can change the item's left and right indent as desired—sometimes you'll want a list indented from the left margin to help it stand out.

If you want to change a bulleted paragraph back to a regular paragraph, select it and choose None from the Label menu in the Paragraph dialog box. That will return the paragraph to normal, nonbullet mode.

Alignment

The last little task for the Paragraph dialog box is aligning the paragraph. You can align the paragraph in four different ways:

- **Left**   Paragraph is flush with the left margin and ragged on the right margin.
- **Right**   Paragraph is ragged on the left margin and flush with the right margin.
- **Center** Both left and right margins are ragged, but the entire paragraph is balanced toward the center.

■ **Justify**   The paragraph is spaced so that the text is flush with both the left and right margins, like most columns of text in a newspaper.

To choose one of the alignments, just pull down the Alignment menu and make your choice. Click Apply and you'll see the paragraph's alignment change.

Format Multiple Paragraphs

Clearly, it could get a bit tedious to format every paragraph of a document manually like this. Fortunately, that's not mandatory. If you like, you can select as many paragraphs as you like— or even choose Edit | Select All (⌘-A) to highlight the entire document—and perform the same Paragraph dialog box changes to them all at once.

You can also copy one paragraph's traits and apply them to another paragraph. To do that, place the insertion point in the paragraph you want to use as a model, then choose Format | Rulers | Copy Ruler (⌘-SHIFT-C). This copies the paragraph settings. Now, place the cursor in the paragraph you want to change to the copied settings (or highlight multiple paragraphs). Choose Format | Rulers | Apply Ruler (⌘-SHIFT-V). The selected paragraph(s) change to reflect the model paragraph's settings.

Why are these commands called Copy Ruler and Apply Ruler? Because the ruler in the document window reflects all of the settings you can make in the Paragraph dialog box. See the next section for information about using it to quickly format paragraphs.

Shortcut: Use the Ruler

For some of the paragraph formatting options, you don't have to go to the Paragraph dialog box. Instead, you can access them (along with font and font size commands) right in the document window, in the ruler. (If you don't see the ruler area, choose Format | Rulers | Show Rulers. To hide rulers, choose Format | Rulers | Hide Rulers.)

For instance, if you'd like to align a paragraph, place the insertion point somewhere in that paragraph and click one of the alignment buttons in the ruler. You can tell by looking at the buttons how they align—left, center, right, and justify (see the following illustration). If you don't like how the paragraph looks, click another alignment button. The changes are made instantly.

Alignment (Left,
Center, Right, Justified)   Line spacing   Tabs   Columns

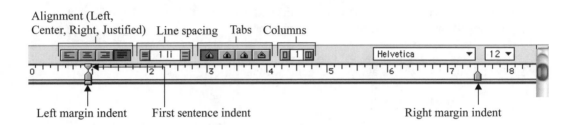

Left margin indent   First sentence indent   Right margin indent

For line spacing, the button on the left pushes lines together, while the button on the right spreads them apart. Select the paragraph(s) you want to alter the line spacing of, then click on the line spacing button of your choice.

 *Here's a cool trick—if you double-click the line-spacing number box where it says something like "1 li" or "2 li," you'll immediately open the Paragraph dialog box.*

The ruler can also be used to quickly format the indenting of paragraphs. Select the paragraph(s) you want to indent, then drag the little indent sliders. (Point at a slider with the mouse pointer, hold down the button, and drag it to the right or left. Let go of the mouse button to place the slider.)

The sliders determine how things are indented—on the left side, the top slider determines the first-line indent and the bottom slider determines the left-side indent of the rest of the paragraph. Notice what this lets you do: if you indent *only* the bottom slider, you'll end up with a paragraph whose first line is flush with the left margin and the rest of the lines are indented, just like in academic bibliography entries.

The right margin indent slider just controls the right-side indent of the entire paragraph. Using a combination of the three you can quickly and visually accomplish anything you can do with indents in the Paragraph dialog box. Of course, you'll have to eyeball the measurements—in the control panel you can be exact to a fraction of an inch.

Insert Elements

Once you have your paragraphs nice and neat, you may start to get the feeling that there are still some things missing—elements you'll usually find at the edges of your document. Here are some of the special elements you can insert into your document:

- **Headers**   Need something at the top of every page? Add a header and it'll automatically be put at the top of all your pages.

- **Footers**   Create a footer and the same thing appears at the bottom of your pages.

- **Page numbers**   Add page numbers that automatically count for you.

- **Date and time**   Choose a quick menu item to add these to your documents in the header, footer, or wherever you like.

- **Section breaks**   Dividing your document into sections—for new chapters, for instance—makes it easier to renumber and manage things.

- ■ **Page breaks**   When you're ready for a new page, but not finished with the last one, you can break immediately and start a fresh page.

- ■ **Footnotes**   Writing a scientific, academic, or commercial report that needs footnotes? You've got 'em.

Headers and Footers

These small sections appear at the top and bottom of the page and allow you to add your name, the document's name, a page number, the date and time, or just about anything else required.

To create a header, select Format | Insert Header. A small section appears at the top of the current page in your document window. Now, you can type anything you need in that section—you can even adjust what you type using the paragraph formatting tools.

Footers work the same way—choose Format | Insert Footer and a small section appears at the bottom of the page. While editing a header or footer, you can press RETURN to add additional lines. Doing so will take away space from the document, not from the margins, which will always stay the same as their setting in the Document dialog box (discussed in the section "Format the Whole Document," later in this chapter).

Now all you need is something to put in the header and footer.

Page Number, Date, and Time

Over in the Edit menu, AppleWorks makes it easy to add the page number, current date, and current time to your document. You can add them anywhere, but the best plan is to put them in the header or footer of your document. And the best part is that the date, time, and page numbers will be updated automatically. The Date and Time commands are a great way to get an automatic record of when documents are modified.

To insert a date, time, or page number, place the insertion point in the header or footer where you want the date to appear. (Note that you can type your own text as well, such as "Modified:" and "Page Number:".) Then, choose the appropriate Insert command from the Edit menu, as in Edit | Insert Date | Auto-Updating, or Edit | Insert Page #. Whatever element you're inserting appears, as shown here:

```
First Draft, Last Modified: 1/10/04                              Page:  1
```

> TIP   *Want to enter a date, time, or page number that never changes automatically? Choose the Fixed option, as in Edit | Insert Time | Fixed.*

When you select the Insert Page Number command, you'll get a small dialog box that allows you to choose which page-related number you want to enter. Here's the breakdown:

- **Page Number**   Inserts the current page number for that page in the document or section.
- **Section Number**   Inserts the current section's number. You can create different sections of a document—for instance, for chapters—and number them. (We'll cover the "sections" concept next in this chapter.)
- **Section Page Count**   Enters the number of total pages in the current section. (See the next section, "Section Breaks.")
- **Document Page Count**   Enters the total number of pages in the document. This would be useful for something at the top of the page that said "Page 4 of 15"—you'd get the "15" to automatically update by inserting the Document Page Count command.

Beyond these, there's a Representation menu you can use to choose how the page numbers will be shown. If you want something that says "Section C, Page 4," you can have those numbers automatically updated, too.

The point of having all of these different page numbering options is to give you the opportunity to choose different combinations of page numbering schemes and have them automatically updated. Plus, you can add your own text in the header to help explain your scheme.

Section Breaks

While we're on the topic of all this numbering, let's quickly look into section breaks. You can create a section break anywhere in your document: a section is simply an internal label for a part of your AppleWorks document. Sections allow you to divide a large document into chapters, lessons, segments or, well, sections. You can then number the sections separately, start over with new page numbering, and so on, as discussed earlier.

To create a section break, place the insertion point where you'd like the new section to begin within your document, then select Format | Insert Section Break. Now, a line appears dividing the two sections of the document. (This line will not print in the final document.) If you've used the automatic section numbers with the Insert Page Number command, the section numbers on subsequent pages will reflect the new section. And you can do a whole lot more with sections, formatting those sections individually, if desired, using the Format | Section dialog box. (That's a little outside the scope of this chapter, but many of the choices will be familiar or self-explanatory.)

Page Breaks

If you're typing along in your document and you decide you want a new page, you can choose Format | Insert Page Break. That automatically moves you to the top of a new page. Plus, new text below a page break will always appear at the top of a fresh page when printed, even if you add text before the page break occurs. If you were to press RETURN a bunch of times to get to a fresh page, you'd have to go back and fix the Returns every time you reformatted, added text, or otherwise messed with the text in the document.

Footnotes and Endnotes

If you need footnotes in your document, they're pretty easy to add. Place the insertion point at the end of the word or sentence you want to footnote. Then choose Format | Insert Blank Footnote. A superscript footnote number appears next to the selected word, and you are magically transported to the bottom of the page (or the end of the document) where you can type the footnote text.

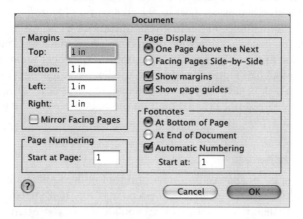

There's nothing like coming home after work to be greeted by your new, sweet, lovable puppy. But remember the Pavlovian way in which dogs learn. If you walk through the door, squeal with delight, toss aside the groceries and rush over to chase, cuddle or toss the

¹ "Basic Dog Psychology," Dog Universe Journal, vol. 4, issue 3, p. 45

You can choose where footnotes are added—at the bottom of the page or the end of the document—using the Document dialog box, which is covered in the next section. If you're currently set up to place footnotes at the end of your document, the command will be Insert Endnote instead of Insert Blank Footnote.

To get rid of a footnote, delete the footnote number in the body of the document. The footnote itself will automatically disappear.

Format the Whole Document

After you're done formatting individual paragraphs, you may have reason to make choices of a more global scale. In that case, you'll want to get into the Document formatting preferences. Select Format | Document and the Document dialog box appears.

Here's a look at the different options in this dialog box:

- ■ **Margins**   Your first Document options focus on the margins for your document. You can select the top, left, right, and bottom margins for the entire document from this dialog box. Just enter the value for each margin, in inches. The larger the margin numbers, the more white space will appear around the text in your document.

- **Page Numbering**   In the entry box you can enter a number other than 1 if this document should start its page numbering from a different value.

- **Page Display**   In this section you can choose how pages are displayed on screen (discussed next) as well as whether or not margins and page guides (lines around the text that show margins) are displayed on the screen.

- **Footnotes**   The last little section in the Document dialog box allows you to choose how footnotes will appear—if space is left for them at the bottom of every page or if they all appear, as endnotes, at the end of the document. You can also have footnotes automatically numbered, if you desire. Just check the check box and enter the number the footnotes should start with in the entry box.

So what's this "facing pages" concept? Think about a typical letter or memo—usually, pages come right after one another and no one really expects you to print on the back side of pages. When you finish one page you move it out of the way and read the next page.

If you're writing a book, report, pamphlet, or similar document, though, you may be creating *facing pages*. That is, readers expect to turn the page in a book and read the backside of that same page, then move over to the right side page and read that one. Those are facing pages, and you can set up AppleWorks to create facing pages in the Document dialog box.

While working with the margin numbers, you can select the Mirror Facing Pages check box in order to change the margin options slightly. The Left and Right margin options change to Outside and Inside margins. Why? Because once you have pages set up to face one another, you can adjust the inside margins together to provide a uniform look. This is important if you plan to bind and distribute your documents in a booklet, pamphlet, or newsletter form. You'll want facing pages to have mirror-image margins when placed next to one another (see Figure 7-2).

Of course, if you'll be formatting and printing your documents as facing pages, you'll probably want to view them as facing pages, so select the radio button next to Facing Pages Side-by-Side in the Page Display section of the Document dialog box. Now the pages are moved so that the document window looks more like Figure 7-2. (Likewise, click the button next to One Page Above the Next to return to the default behavior.) You can also make choices as to whether or not margins and page guides—the light gray lines that show you the boundaries of the page—should be displayed.

Tabs and the Ruler

The TAB key on your Mac keyboard can be a powerful tool in the fight against chaos in your documents. By default, a standard document offers tab points every half-inch or so. But you might want more specialized tabs than that—tabs that help you align text, for instance.

There are four different types of tabs you can add to your document: left-aligned, right-aligned, centered, and aligned to a particular character, usually a decimal. What these tabs do, in most cases, is give you the freedom to align things for impromptu tables and arrangements of columns of text in your documents.

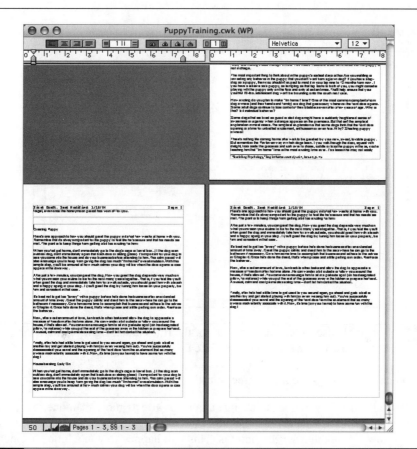

FIGURE 7-2   Facing pages need mirror-image margins to look right once they're in book or booklet form. (The pages are being viewed at 50 percent magnification using the view controller at the bottom-left corner of the document window.)

Say, for instance, that you wanted to create a table of contents. In that case you'll need two things: a right-aligned column of chapter descriptions and a second column that's aligned to punctuation. In this case, it's the dash that separates a document's section and page number. It would look something like Figure 7-3.

How does this work? Before you type any text, click the button that corresponds to the type of tab you want to create. Now, click on the ruler itself to place that tab on the ruler. You can then drag it back and forth to get it lined up exactly how you want it.

If you want a right-aligned column to end on the two-inch mark, drag it there. If you want to align a column of currency figures, put the decimal-aligned tab on the six-inch mark, and that's where the dollars will line up.

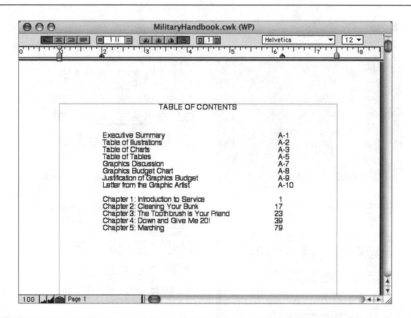

FIGURE 7-3 This table uses a left-justified tab for the titles and a right-justified tab (centered on the dash) so that the numbers line up nicely.

Need to switch some things around? Three rules:

■ *Highlight* all *rows.* If you need to change a tab that affects more than one row of text, select *every* row first, then change the tab in the ruler. Otherwise, you'll only change it for the row where the insertion point is. This will happen to you a lot by accident, so be wary.

■ *Double-click the tab.* If you need to change a tab that you've already dragged to the ruler, double-click it. The Tab dialog box appears, allowing you to make changes. For instance, you can change the alignment of the tab, add a fill (automatically fill in behind the tab with dots or dashes, which nicely completes the Table of Contents effect), or tweak the location of the tab by entering the inch mark where it should appear.

■ *Drag the tab off the ruler to remove.* To get rid of a tab, select *all* rows that are affected by the tab—they all need to be highlighted—then pick up the tab and drag it back up to the top of the ruler. It'll disappear.

NOTE *It's worth emphasizing that if you can't find a tab, if a tab is still there even though you moved it, or if only part of your document is lined up to tabs correctly, there's a good reason. It's because you didn't select every line in your document affected by that tab. Go back, select all the lines, and make your change once more.*

Spell, Find, Change, and Count

You've finally gotten through most of your document creation. You've formatted the text, cleaned it up with tabs, and saved after every three lines. Now that you've seen what a computer can do to help you format an important report or document, how about seeing what it can do to help you clean up and edit the words themselves? Here's where some of that computerized speed and savvy comes into play.

Check Spelling

By brute force your word processor can jump quickly through a document and check every word against an internal dictionary. If it finds one it's not familiar with, it suggests other words that seem to be similarly spelled. If you see the word you meant to type, you can choose it from the list. Otherwise, you can either add the word that AppleWorks doesn't recognize, type the correct spelling yourself, or just skip the suggestion.

Here's how it works:

1. When you're ready to check spelling, select Edit | Writing Tools | Check Document Spelling.

2. AppleWorks begins checking. When it finds a word it doesn't like, a dialog box pops up like the one shown to the right.

3. If AppleWorks offers the correct spelling, select it in the box and click Replace (or press the keyboard command ⌘-*number* where *number* is the number of the suggestion in the list). If you don't see the correct spelling, you can type it into the entry box. If you type something you want to check against AppleWorks' dictionary, click the Check button. If the word is spelled correctly, click Learn so that AppleWorks won't flag it again in the future. If the word isn't worth worrying about (it's an odd abbreviation or something), then click Skip.

4. AppleWorks moves on to the next word it finds misspelled.

If you don't need to check the entire document, you can check just a selection of text. Highlight the text you want to check, then select Edit | Writing Tools | Check Selection Spelling.

Find and Change

The Find and Change features use some of the same technology as spell-checking, but instead of checking the document against an internal dictionary, the file is checked against whatever text you enter in the Find dialog box. It can then change the found text to whatever text you choose.

Need an example? In earlier editions of this book the discussion in this chapter centered on ClarisWorks, which was the original name for AppleWorks up until late 1998 or so. So, in subsequent editions, I've been able to use the Find dialog box to hunt down occurrences of "ClarisWorks" and automatically change them to "AppleWorks." Likewise, a find and replace can be additive, as in searching for "iMac" and changing every instance to "iMac and eMac."

Here's how to do a find and change:

1. Select Edit | Find/Change. In the submenu that comes up, select the Find/Change command.

2. In the Find/Change dialog box, enter a word you'd like to search for in the Find entry box. If you plan to replace that word with something else, enter it in the Change entry box.

3. Click the Find Next button. The first instance of the word is found (if there are any instances of that word).

4. If you want to change this instance of the word, click Change. You can also click Change, Find, if you want to change the word and move instantly to the next instance of the word. If you don't want to change this instance, click Find Next.

5. Rinse and repeat. If you want to stop finding, click the close box on the Find window.

If you just want AppleWorks to find and change every instance of a word, you can click the Change All button instead of going through the entire document by hand. Think carefully before doing that, though, since you could accidentally change words you don't mean to change. Consider my example, where I've used Find to change nearly every instance of ClarisWorks in this chapter to AppleWorks. If I'd performed a Change All during that Find search, I would have changed the sentence right before this one you're reading. The sentence would then read: "Consider my example, where I've used Find to change nearly every instance of AppleWorks in this chapter to AppleWorks."

In the Find/Change window you'll find two check box options:

■ **Find Whole Word**   Check this option to find instances where the word in the Find entry box matches only a whole word in the document. If you search for the word pup without this option checked, it will find the letters pup within the word puppy. If you check the Find Whole Word check box, it will only find the word pup, not parts of words that include the letters pup.

■ **Case Sensitive**   Check this option and Find will pay attention to the upper- and lowercase letters you type in the Find entry box. If you search for Puppy with the Case Sensitive option checked, Find will not stop on the words puppy or puppY.

You can change words to simple spaces or nothing at all. That's a great way to delete every instance of a particular word. You can also find just about anything that you can cut and paste into the Find entry box, including spaces and line returns. Get creative— use ⌘-V to paste things into the Find entry box for more advanced searches.

Standardize with the Styles Palette

If you're serious about word processing, you should get to know the Styles palette window. What does it do? When you create a paragraph style you really like, you can give it a name and save it. Then, you can invoke that style anytime by simply selecting it in the Styles palette. Instant high-end formatting—perfect if you do a lot of the same sort of documents and you want to stop reinventing the wheel.

To open the Styles window, select Format | Show Styles. The Styles palette appears, as shown at right.

To select a style, just click it once in the Styles palette and click the Apply button. (You can also double-click the style in the Styles palette to apply it.) The currently selected paragraph in your document will instantly change to that style. If you select more than one paragraph and then select a style in the Styles palette and click Apply, all of the paragraphs will change to that paragraph style. If you don't like the style you've changed it to, click the Unapply button.

To add your own style, format a paragraph just the way you want it. Make sure the insertion point is in that paragraph. Then, in the Styles palette, click the New button. In the New Style dialog box, give your style a name and choose the Paragraph radio button. Make sure the Inherit Document Selection Format option is turned on, then click OK. The style is created. You can now double-click the new style in the Styles palette to format other paragraphs.

The Styles can be used for other types of formatting, too, including table and outline styles.

Use Templates for Automatic Documents

Templates in AppleWorks are preformatted, often by professional designers, to make you look good. When you create a new document using a template, you get a new document that already has some attractive elements created for you. Then, you enter your own information to finish the document. In the Teacher Letterhead templates, for instance, you can select the sections of the document that are currently generic looking and change them into something you can use. For example, you can change the name section, the address, or other information to your own, as shown here:

Create a Document from Templates

To use a template, you'll begin by creating a new document by selecting File | Show Starting Points or pressing ⌘-1. (Or, if you are just starting up AppleWorks, the Starting Points window will automatically appear.) In the New dialog box, click the Templates tab. The icons in the window change to reflect the templates you can use. Scroll through the window until you see the template you'd like to use. When you see an interesting one, click it. AppleWorks creates a new, styled document in the template's image.

You'll find that some templates are more involved than others. Some feature special styles, for instance, that allow you to continue to format the paragraphs according to the template's theme. In any case, all you have to do to work with the template is start editing, adding your own text, images, and other objects, as desired.

At some point you'll want to save the document—just save it like any other document using the File | Save command. This doesn't alter the original template. You can always go back to the Templates tab in the Starting Points window to create another document that looks like it.

TIP
If you have Internet access, you can click the Web tab in the Starting Points window. Now, click the Templates icon to launch a special AppleWorks document with web links. Now you can click through the available templates, then click the Download link next to an interesting looking template to retrieve the template to AppleWorks and work with it.

Save a Document as a Template

If you have a particular document design that you like a lot, you can save it as a template of your own, adding it to the Templates tab in the Starting Points window. That way you can use it to automatically create new documents that look like it.

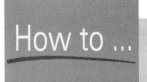

How to ... Customize the Button Bar

The Button Bar that appears by default above your documents offers quick access to some common style commands (when you're working in a word processing document) as well as quick access to buttons that let you create other types of documents. But you can also customize the Button Bar with your own command buttons, if you like. Hold down the CONTROL key and click the Button Bar, then choose Customize Button Bar from the pop-up menu. In the Customize Button Bar dialog box, scroll through the list to find the command you want to add. (Note that Word Processing has a whole subtopic about halfway down the list.) When you see a csommand you want to add, just drag that command from the list up to the Button Bar. It's added as a new button.

When you're finished customizing, click Done. To delete a button you've added, CONTROL-click that button and select Remove Button from the contextual menu.

With the document created, choose File | Save As. Give your template a name, then click the Template icon down in the corner of the Save As dialog box in the File Format section. You'll be automatically transported to AppleWorks' Templates folder in the Save dialog box's Where menu. Click the Save button and your template is saved. Now, the next time you want to create a document in that style, you can choose your template from the Templates tab in the Starting Points window.

NOTE   *If you've created a document that you need to save as an actual document, do that first. Then you may want to clear out parts of the document—like the salutation and the body, if you're creating a letterhead template—that are specific to that document so you have a more generic document to use as a template.*

7

Chapter 8

Work with Numbers, Build Charts

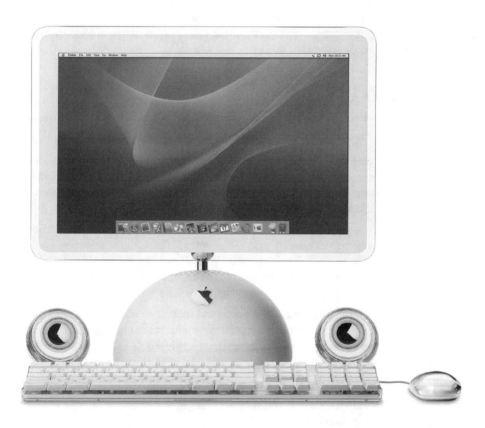

How to...

- Recognize when to use spreadsheets
- See the basics of spreadsheets
- Enter and format text and numbers in your spreadsheet
- Cut, copy, paste, and sort your data
- Build formulas that work with your data
- Use advanced formulas for what-if scenarios
- Chart your data to see how it looks

A spreadsheet application—such as the Spreadsheet module in AppleWorks—is one that allows you to create what amounts to a digital ledger book. Ebenezer Scrooge, for instance, might have tracked his accounts in one of those cool-looking, lined, leather-bound ledger books. But times have changed. These days, we have electronic spreadsheets instead of ledger books. And it's your Mac that looks cool.

Decide When to Use a Spreadsheet

So, this is like a ledger book, but better. Why? A spreadsheet allows you to do three major things well:

- **Math** You can concoct all sorts of formulas and impose them upon the numbers you've entered into your spreadsheet. Do loan calculations, find the average or standard deviation, figure the net present value—tons of things that no human should try without computerized help. By getting your numbers into the spreadsheet—where every cell has a name—you can perform many different mathematical functions.

- **What-if** Once you have a spreadsheet full of data and calculations, the spreadsheet allows you to change numbers quickly and see how that affects the whole. Say you've laid out an entire budget for the next six months. What if you decide to take a job that pays less but allows you to perform that invaluable human service (not to mention the ego boost)? Edit up that income number in your budget and see how things shake out.

- **Charts** Once you have the data entered and represented the way you like it, you can create graphics from the numbers that allow you to more clearly make your case at the next board, team, faculty, or family meeting. AppleWorks is capable of creating all sorts of charts, including exciting 3-D charts that will wow them for weeks.

So, all you have to do is enter the data, format it correctly, then get working on your calculations, what-if scenarios, and charts. Before you do that, though, you're going to have to know how to enter the data into the spreadsheet.

The building block of any spreadsheet document is the *cell*—the conjunction of a column and a row that is given a unique name in the two dimensions of a spreadsheet. In that cell you can put text, numbers, formulas—even images, although there's less reason to do that. As shown next, those cells, because they're uniquely named (with names like "A2" and "F18"), can be added together, subtracted from one another, even cosined and tangented, if those are words.

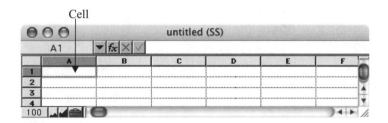

Cell

In working with spreadsheets, you'll need to get to know cell notation—the cell's name acts as a *variable* in formulas you build to work with the numbers in those cells. It's basic algebra—you'll create a formula that says "add C3 to C4," which tells the spreadsheet to sum the values it finds in cells C3 and C4. So how does it know which cells those are?

In the typical spreadsheet (AppleWorks included) the columns are lettered from left to right across the top of the document, and the rows are numbered from top to bottom. So, the first cell at the top-left corner is A1. The cell C3, then, is the cell at the conjunction of column C and row 3.

Sound exciting yet? Let's run through how to create your own spreadsheets, doctor them up, and make them look nice.

> **NOTE**   *By default, a spreadsheet in AppleWorks is 40 columns wide (reaching cell "AN") and 500 rows long. You can add to them both—the limit is 256 columns and 16,384 rows.*

Get the Spreadsheet Started

Spreadsheet documents start the same way any other documents begin—with the New command. In AppleWorks, choose File | New | Spreadsheet. Or, if you have the Starting Points window showing, select the Spreadsheet icon on the Basic tab.

> **TIP**   *Want to password-protect your spreadsheet? Actually, this works for any AppleWorks application. Choose File | Properties, and then click the Set Password button. Enter a password and click OK. Now, any time you attempt to open this document in the future, a password dialog box will appear, and you'll have to know the password to access the document.*

Move in the Spreadsheet

The first thing you'll want to do is learn how to get around. It's pretty basic. You'll start out in the top-left cell, but you can click anywhere on a cell and instantly be transported there. Once you have a cell selected, you can enter something in that cell by simply typing. Notice, when you start typing, that nothing actually appears in the cell.

You edit in the Entry Bar at the top of the document window. You won't see the results in the cell until you move on from the cell—you do *that* by pressing TAB or RETURN.

Table 8-1 shows you how to move around in a spreadsheet document.

Press This	To Do This
RETURN, DOWN ARROW	Move down one cell
TAB, RIGHT ARROW	Move right one cell
SHIFT-RETURN, UP ARROW	Move up one cell
SHIFT-TAB, LEFT ARROW	Move left one cell
ENTER (under number pad)	Accept data in cell without moving to a new cell

TABLE 8-1 Moving Around in a Spreadsheet Document

It won't take too long before these keys will become second nature to you. You just need to remember that if you want to edit something that's already in a cell, move to that cell (with the keys or the mouse) and edit it in the Entry Bar, not in the cell itself (the program won't let you edit in the cell).

> **NOTE** *The arrow keys don't allow you to leave a cell if you're currently editing data in that cell, because then you can't use those keys to move the insertion point around in the Entry Bar. If you'd prefer that arrow keys allow you to immediately leave a cell, select AppleWorks | Preferences | General. From the pull-down menu, choose Spreadsheet, if it isn't already selected. Now, select Always Selects Another Cell in the Pressing Arrow Keys section. Notice you can also change the behavior of the* ENTER *key in this dialog box. Click OK to exit Preferences.*

You can enter either text or numbers in a spreadsheet, although it's best to have a plan before you jump in and start entering things randomly. In general, you'll want series of numbers—budget numbers for every month of the year, for instance—to be in a row or a column, unbroken by other text or numbers. Figure 8-1 shows an example of a nice, neat spreadsheet that will be easy to deal with when it comes to building formulas and creating what-if scenarios.

Select Cells

There are three basic ways to select cells in the spreadsheet window:

- If you're selecting a single cell, click it once. Its frame becomes outlined.
- To select more than one cell, click and hold the mouse button on the first cell you want to select, then drag the mouse across the other cells you'd like to select. When you've highlighted all the cells you need, release the mouse button. (Note that the first cell in your selection will not be highlighted—the frame will be outlined. It's still selected, though.)
- To select an entire row or column, click its letter or number once. In the F column, for instance, you can click the "F" at the top of the screen to highlight the entire column. If you want to select more than one column or row at a time, hold down the SHIFT key and click once for each column or row that you want to add. Notice that multiple columns or rows must be adjacent in order to be selected, and you can't select both rows and columns at once.

	January	February	March	April	May	June	July	August	September
Annual Household Budget									
Work Income	3000	3000	3000	3000	3000	3000	3000	3000	3000
Investment Income	200	200	200	200	200	200	200	200	200
Savings Interest	25	25	25	25	25	25	25	25	25
Other Income	0	0	350	0	0	350	0	0	350
Total Income	3225	3225	3575	3225	3225	3575	3225	3225	3575
Rent	800	800	800	800	800	800	800	800	800
Car	225	225	225	225	225	225	225	225	225
Insurance	75	75	75	75	75	75	75	75	75
Medical Policy	200	200	200	200	200	200	200	200	200
Groceries	250	250	250	250	250	250	250	250	250
Dining	200	200	200	200	200	200	200	200	200
Entertainment	250	250	250	250	250	250	250	250	250
Clothing	500	100	100	100	100	500	100	100	100
Household	150	150	150	150	150	150	150	150	150
Misc.	75	75	75	75	75	75	75	75	75
Cash Expenses	2725	2325	2325	2325	2325	2725	2325	2325	2325
Mastercard	60	60	60	60	60	60	60	60	60
Discover	75	75	75	75	75	75	75	75	75
Amex	100	100	100	100	100	100	100	100	100
Credit Expenses	235	235	235	235	235	235	235	235	235
Savings	265	665	1015	665	665	615	665	665	1015

FIGURE 8-1   The best spreadsheets are arranged logically in a table format.

Save the Spreadsheet

To save a spreadsheet, just select File | Save, or File | Save As. The Save As dialog box appears, allowing you to name the document and find a folder to save it in. When you've made those choices, click Save. From there on, you can quickly save the spreadsheet every few minutes by selecting the Save command again or pressing ⌘-S on your keyboard.

Enter and Format Data

In most spreadsheets that you create, you'll probably enter text to label the rows and columns that will be filled with numbers. With both the text and the numbers, it's possible to do some rather intricate formatting, including the basics like font, size, style, and alignment. You'll also find some formatting options that are different from those in word processing—options like formatting numbers as currency, dates, or times.

TIP   *Actually, it's possible to perform calculations on text as well. You can do a number of things with text, including comparing word length, changing the case of text, sorting the text, adding text strings together (*concatenating *them), and so on. I'll discuss some of that later in the section "Add Formulas to the Spreadsheet."*

Format Text and Cells

Let's begin with text, since you'll likely begin with text in your spreadsheet. (You'll need to create labels for the columns and rows of numbers you plan to enter.) You might want to begin by typing a title into the first cell of the spreadsheet—cell A1. You can type text that's longer than the cell, and all of the text will actually appear just fine—as long as you haven't typed text into the adjoining cells. If you're creating the title line for your spreadsheet, that should be no problem.

TIP *Want text to wrap within the cell instead of continuing off the edge? Highlight the cell and choose Format | Alignment | Wrap. Now text will wrap within the cell.*

You can also format text using the same settings that you use in a word processor—font, size, styles, and alignment. The major difference is that for spreadsheets in AppleWorks, all of those commands appear in the Format menu. You can't format selected text differently within the same cell—formatting for text in the cell applies to all text in that cell.

Here's how to format:

1. Select the cell(s) that have text you want to format.

2. Select the Format menu and point the mouse at the type of formatting you'd like to change—Font, Size, Style, Font Color, or Alignment.

3. In the menu that appears to the right, make your formatting selection.

All the text in the cell will be affected, although the cell itself won't change. That can be a problem if you've changed the size of the text in the cell, for instance, and can no longer read it clearly. The solution: resize the cell.

Actually, you can't really change the size of an *individual* cell—you either change the size of its row or its column. To change the size of a row, point the mouse all the way over at the numbers that label each row. If you place the mouse pointer on the line that appears between any two rows, the mouse pointer changes to a pair of arrows. That's your cue that holding down the mouse button and dragging will change the size of the row, as shown in the following illustration. A column can be resized in the same way—just drag the line between the numbers.

	A	B	C
1	Annual Household B		
2		January	February
3			
4	Work Income		
5	Investment Income		
6	Savings Interest		
7	Other Income		

Text is important in most spreadsheets, especially if you want other people to understand what the heck your spreadsheet is for. Text is also very useful for charting data, which we'll get into later in this chapter. AppleWorks likes to find text on the top and left borders of your numbers; it can use that text for labels in charts, for instance. So, think in terms of labeling your data in rows and columns; the more structured the data now, the more easily it will be viewed and manipulated later.

One special case is alignment. You'll probably want to format your columns and rows so the values in them line up together nicely. Select an entire range of cells or an entire column or row and use the Format | Alignment menu command to align every cell in the range to the left, right, centered, or justified. You may also find it helps the readability of your spreadsheet to choose the row or column where your "label" cells are, then format them as bold, larger text, or what-have-you to make them stand out.

Want to delete text? Just select the cell and press DELETE. (You can also choose Edit | Clear to delete cell contents.) Likewise, you can highlight more than one cell and press DELETE to clear many cells of text (or numbers and formulas, for that matter) at once.

Enter and Format Numbers

AppleWorks automatically recognizes a number as a number (not as text) when you type a number into a cell. In fact, in order to type a number as text, if you need to, you must enter a sort of mini-function that looks like this: `="5467"`. Using this formula, the number is treated as a *string* of text characters. This might be useful if you needed to label a column or row with a number—for instance, if you wanted your columns to represent years. If you enter 2004, that's seen as two thousand and four. Enter ="2004" and it's treated as text, so you can use it as a label representing the year.

Otherwise, numbers are numbers. If you need to enter a negative number, enter a minus sign (−) before it, such as −5467. And, as is true with text, you can copy and paste numbers from one cell into another if you like.

Number Formats

Numbers can be formatted in the same way as text—font, size, style, color, and alignment—by selecting the cell or cells and using the Format menu. Numbers also have their own formatting schemes that can be used specifically to make them more meaningful, easier to read, or both. Those formatting options appear when you select a cell or group of cells, then choose Format | Number. You can also access the Format Number, Date, and Time dialog box (shown in Figure 8-2) by double-clicking a cell.

8

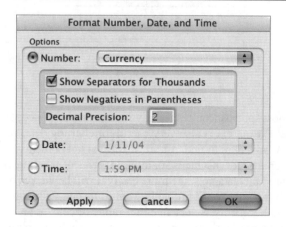

FIGURE 8-2   Format numbers using this dialog box.

In the dialog box, you start by selecting the radio button next to the type of number (Number, Date, or Time) you want in that cell or range of cells. Then select further choices from the pop-up menus:

- **Number** In the Number pop-up menu, you can make choices that allow you to change the appearance of your numbers. They can be regular numbers, currency, percentages, scientific notation, or fixed decimal numbers (with a certain number of decimal places shown). Using the check boxes, you can also decide if there will be a separator for thousands and whether or not negative values will appear in parentheses, which is common in accounting and financial notation. In the Decimal Precision entry box, enter the number of decimal places you want to show for the numbers.

- **Date** Choose one of the date formats from the pop-up menu.

- **Time** Choose one of the time formats from the pop-up menu.

You'll probably often want to format an entire row or column with a certain type of number formatting—Currency, for instance. Go ahead and select an entire range of cells or even a complete column or row. In fact, you can select an entire column or row that already has text labels in it and the text won't be affected by what you do with the number formatting, only the numbers will.

Cut, Paste, Fill

In spreadsheets, you can cut and paste either text or numbers very easily. In the sample budget document I've created for this chapter's figures, a lot of numbers repeat. It's possible to select an entire range of numbers—part of a column, for instance—then copy and paste it into the next column.

Another way to quickly enter numbers is to use the Fill Right or Fill Down commands in the Calculate menu. Enter a value for one cell, then highlight that cell and a number of cells to the right or down from that cell. Now, choose the appropriate command—Calculate | Fill Right (⌘-R) or Calculate | Fill Down (⌘-D)—and all those cells are filled with the first cell's value.

Add Formulas to the Spreadsheet

Here's where the real power of the spreadsheet shines through—creating formulas that allow you to manipulate the data. So far, you've entered text that labels data, and you've entered numbers that represent data. Now it's time to put some of that algebraic knowledge swimming around in your head to the task of creating formulas that work with your data. In this section I'll show you the anatomy of a formula, then we'll move on to some of the formulas included in AppleWorks.

Anatomy of a Formula

You've already seen that by simply typing text and numbers into the cell, AppleWorks can differentiate between the two for formatting purposes. It can immediately tell the difference between a number and text.

It can't, however, tell the difference between the cell reference "A3" and the text "A3." In order to differentiate a formula, AppleWorks needs a little code. That code comes in the form of an equals (=) sign. If you begin your typing in a cell with an equals sign, AppleWorks will interpret what follows that sign as a formula.

NOTE *After you exit the cell, if you've typed the formula correctly, you won't see the formula again in the cell. Instead, you'll see the result of that formula. (If you highlight the cell, you'll again see the formula up in the Entry Bar.)*

8

Formula Types

Beyond the equals sign, there are two basic types of formulas you'll create. The first is a straight mathematical formula with addition (+), subtraction (–), multiplication (*), division (/), or exponential (^) operators. A typical mathematical formula could easily be =34+45 or =34^2, although that would be pretty useless in a spreadsheet (you'll see why in a moment).

The other type of formula uses a built-in function from AppleWorks. These functions range from financial, to trigonometric, to logical. An example might be =AVERAGE (34, 45, 56), which would return the average of those three numbers.

As you might guess, it's also possible to use these two types of formulas together in the same cell, so that =34+45+(AVERAGE (34, 45, 56)) is an acceptable formula, too. Notice, by the way, that parentheses are used pretty liberally in these formulas to separate one operation from another. Again, it's like algebra—functions and math inside parentheses get done first, then the result of that parenthetical equation gets entered into the larger equation.

Build with Cell Addresses

What's missing in this discussion of formulas, of course, is the cell address. By using cell addresses as *variables*, you're suddenly able to do amazing things with formulas. For instance, while =34+45 isn't terribly useful in a spreadsheet (since you could just enter 79 and be done with it), the formula =B3+B4 could be very useful. Why? Because if you change the value in B3 or in B4—or in both—the result changes as well. And getting results is what spreadsheets are all about.

Now you're able to create a cell whose value is based on values in other cells. You could take this even further. How about a cell whose value is the sum of many different cells—something along the lines of =B5+B6+B7+B8? That's shown in Figure 8-3.

B9	▼	fx	×	√	=B5+B6+B7+B8		

AnnualBudget.cwk (SS)

	A	B	C	D	E
1					
2	**Annual Household Budget**				
3		January	February	March	April
4					
5	Work Income	3000	3000	3000	3(
6	Investment Income	200	200	200	2
7	Savings Interest	25	25	25	
8	Other Income	0	0	350	
9	**Total Income**	**3225**	**3225**	**3575**	32

FIGURE 8-3   A basic formula for adding cell values together

Notice that the cell addresses are starting to get a little out of hand, even with just four—what if you were adding together four hundred? In your spreadsheet you can use a special notation to denote a range of cells to be acted on. The range is separated by two periods, as in =SUM(B5..B8), which gives the same result as =B5+B6+B7+B8.

> **TIP**   *Once a formula is evaluated, you can use that formula's cell address in another formula. If you put =SUM(B5..B8) in cell B10, you can type B10 in another formula, where it will represent the result of that sum.*

Relative vs. Absolute

The cell addresses we've been talking about are called *relative addresses*. What does that mean? Say you wanted to use the Copy and Paste or Fill Right/Fill Down commands with a formula you've created. With relative addressing, the addresses within that formula will change relative to the cell you paste it into. For example, if cell B29 had the formula =SUM(B10..B27) in it, you could copy that formula from cell B29 and paste it into cell C29. The formula in C29 is changed slightly, though, to =SUM(C10..C27). AppleWorks is just assuming that's how you want it.

You can circumvent this by creating an absolute address using dollar signs ($). The address $B$10 is an *absolute address* that always points to cell B10. If I create a formula in cell B29 that looks like =$B$10+B11, then copy that formula to cell C29, the result will be =$B$10+C11. Since the second address was relative, it changed. But the first address is still B10, because the $ symbol makes it an absolute address.

> **NOTE**   *You should be aware that absolute addresses aren't updated automatically if you add rows or columns to your spreadsheet. In the preceding example, if I add a row between A and B (which I would do by selecting an entire row and then choosing Format | Insert Cells), I'll need to change all the absolute references to $B$10 so that they read $C$10. Otherwise, the values will be incorrect.*

More Operators

Want a little more confusion? In dealing with cell addresses, you can use two additional operators to change the way numbers are evaluated—the percent operator (%) turns a number into a decimal percentage (for example, =C3%) while the minus sign (–) can be used in front of a cell address to make it negative (for example, =-C3).

Other operators besides the numeric ones can be used in your formulas—they're called relational and text operators. The relational operators offer comparisons between two values. They are

=	Equal to
<>	Not equal to
>	Greater than
>=	Greater than or equal to
<	Less than
<=	Less than or equal to

Using a formula like =A3>A4 will return a value of either True or False, which will appear in the cell. If you don't find this useful, you'll likely want to use these operators within logical functions like the IF function. (IF is discussed later in this chapter, with examples.)

There's also one text operator, the ampersand (&), which allows you to concatenate text. The formula =B5&" "&B6 would create one long string of text with a space between the two cells' text entries.

NOTE *What happens when you concatenate numbers? They're turned into text. It works fine, but you won't be able to perform any math on the text-ified numbers until you turn them back into numbers with the TEXTTONUM function, which is discussed in AppleWorks Help.*

Operator Precedence

Before you can build formulas, you need to know one last little thing about them—operator precedence. We used to call this "order of operations" back in algebra class. Say you have the formula =40+10*3. What's the answer? It depends on what you do first. If you evaluate from left to right, then 40 plus 10 is 50; 50 times 3 is 150. If you evaluate the multiplication first, then 10 times 3 is 30 and 40 plus 30 is 70. You get two different answers.

One way to manage this is to rely on parentheses. Since operations inside parentheses are always evaluated first, you could create the formula =(40+10)*3 to get 150, or =40+(10*3) to get 70.

Or, you could rely on the operator precedence. In this case, multiplication has higher precedence than addition. Without parentheses, the formula =40+10*3, by rule of precedence, equals 70. Multiplication is done first, then addition. Table 8-2 shows the order of precedence for all operators— the higher in the table, the sooner the operation is performed.

Whenever a precedence level is the same for two operations, the formula is evaluated from left to right. So, if a subtraction is further left than an addition, the subtraction is done first.

8

Operator	Description
( )	Parentheses (done first)
%	Percentages
^	Exponentials
+, −	Positive or negative numbers (sign is before a cell address)
*, /	Multiply, divide
+, −	Add, subtract
&	Concatenate text
=, >, <, >=, <=, <>	All comparisons (done last)

TABLE 8-2   Order of Precedence for Spreadsheet Formulas

TIP   *When in doubt, use parentheses. That way you'll be able to decide exactly how a formula is evaluated.*

Add Functions to Your Formulas

You'll soon come up with a reason to do more than just basic mathematics between a few different cells. You've already seen that the SUM function can be used with a range of cells to add them all together and get a total. But what if you need to do something more sophisticated in your formulas? In that case, it's time to call in a function. Here's how you add one:

1. Select the cell where you want the function to appear.

2. Next to the Entry Bar on your spreadsheet document window is the Function (Fx) button. Click it and the Insert Function dialog box appears (see Figure 8-4).

3. Choose one of those functions and it's added to the Entry Bar, where you can edit it. (Note that you can filter the type of functions shown in the dialog box by selecting a category from the Category pop-up menu. The categories are discussed below.)

4. Edit the function to taste (usually, you'll add cell addresses and values) and exit the cell.

AppleWorks offers a number of different categories of functions:

■ **Business and Financial**   These are functions like PV (present value), NPV (net present value), RATE (tells you the interest rate of a payment schedule), and PMT (figures the payment required to satisfy a particular type of loan or payment scheme).

■ **Date and Time**   These functions allow you to perform various calculations regarding time. The date, day of the week, and time can all be stored as numeric values, allowing you to easily do math using them.

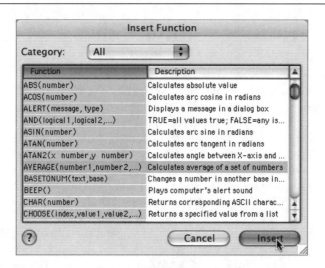

FIGURE 8-4   The Insert Function dialog box helps you enter functions into your spreadsheet.

■ **Information**   These functions are used to send information, such as alert boxes and error tones, to your user.

■ **Logical**   These programming-like functions can be used to determine if a number of values are true (AND) or if any values are true (OR), or it can evaluate values and perform other calculations based on whether they're true or not (IF). Other functions determine whether a value is present or if there's an error.

■ **Numeric**   These functions allow you to work with numbers and ranges of numbers. They include SUM (sum of numbers), RAND (generates a random number), ROUND (rounds a number), and SQRT (returns the square root of the number).

■ **Statistical**   These functions take the MEAN, find the MODE, determine standard deviation, and more.

■ **Text**   Text operators allow you to find certain words programmatically, change words to upper- or lowercase, get the length of a word, and perform similar functions.

■ **Trigonometric**   Here are those crazy functions all about angles. You can figure the cosine, sine, and tangent and convert between radians and degrees, among other things.

Some Cool Functions

Okay, I'm well over my allotted pages for this chapter, but I just had to show you some cool functions available for your spreadsheet. I'll try to get through these very quickly so you can get back to your regularly scheduled tutorial.

Tracking Antique Sales

I own an antiques business that I operate out of my home. When I make a sale at a weekend show, I remove my price sticker (which includes the item number) and paste it on a piece of notebook paper along with a notation about the actual sale price. (Selling antiques involves a fair amount of bargaining, so I usually don't get my original asking price.) I update the online inventory in the AppleWorks spreadsheet module after I get home. It's not as high-tech as I'd like to be, but it works for me. If I get a laptop I definitely will carry it with me, and I have found the program nimble enough to search in real time if I ever need to. When I first got into the business I thought I would be using the database part of AppleWorks, but, quite frankly, the calculations that are possible in the spreadsheet cells allow me to add these into the same line as they are sold, rather than taking up a separate line (which would equal a database record) for each one. It's simple, but it works great!

Mary Bischoff, Mom's Memories Antiques, West Plains, Missouri

Autosum

This is a shortcut from the AppleWorks Button Bar. It allows you to quickly generate a SUM formula in a spreadsheet of numbers like a budget or financials. I used it for the sample budget shown in this chapter. Here's how it works:

1. Highlight the range of numbers you want to total *plus* an additional cell at the end of the list.

2. Click the Autosum button.

That's it. The sum automatically appears in that blank cell (see Figure 8-5).

Now you can do it again for the next row, or just use the Fill Right command for all the other total cells in that row of your budget. Since the Autosum button creates a SUM function with relative addresses, the function will copy just fine for the rest of the row.

Although they all don't have their own "auto" buttons on the Button Bar, some other formulas work just like SUM. They include AVERAGE, MIN, and MAX, all of which can accept a range of cells, such as =AVERAGE (B2..B10).

IF Function

Here's a great one for all sorts of analysis. IF accepts a logical expression, followed by what it should do if an expression is true and what it should do if an expression is false. For instance, let's say that the value of cell B27 in my budget spreadsheet represents my over/under value for the month. If I come out more than $400 ahead on my budget for that month, then I'll put half of it in my retirement account. If I have less than $400, then I'll put $0 in my retirement account.

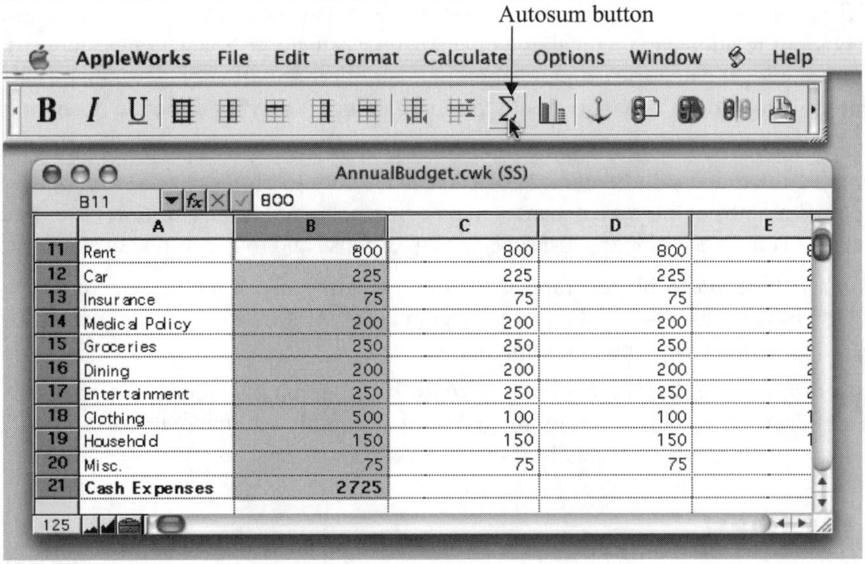

Autosum button

FIGURE 8-5   Quickly create a total of an entire selection of cells.

So, with that in mind, I can create an IF function that checks out my over/under balance and decides what to do. It will look like this: `=IF (B28>400, (B28/2), 0)`. That is, if B28 is greater than 400, return B28 divided by 2 as the value. If B28 isn't greater than 400, return 0. Here it is in action:

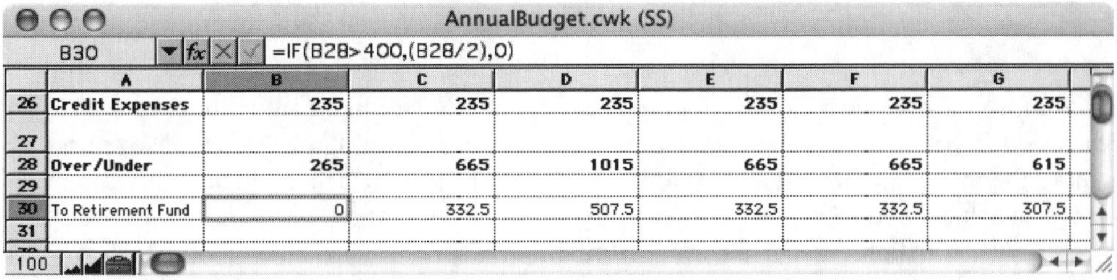

Chart Your Data

Once you've got the data in your spreadsheet arranged, calculated, and accounted for, you may find the best way to communicate the data is to create a chart. Charts go a long way toward making numbers in rows and columns much more bearable; plus, it's possible to see the relationships between data more clearly when you're looking at a chart. Here are a few suggestions about charts.

8

■ *Make sure your data is chart-able.* You should have data sets in your spreadsheet that have an obvious relationship that makes a comparison worthwhile. Sales figures among different regions, budget categories, and demographic numbers are all very chart-able. (Since your rent probably doesn't change month to month, it won't be very effective in a graph.)

■ *Charts should convey one comparison.* If I take all of my expenses and chart them over six months, the graph will be unreadable. Instead, I should either chart *one* expense over *multiple* months or *multiple* expenses in *one* month, but not both. (In some cases you might convey two related comparisons, such as total expense and total revenue over six months.)

■ *Don't include totals.* If you graph all of your expenses in one month—including the *total* of all those expenses—you'll throw your graph way off. Make sure you're not accidentally including totals when you're comparing data.

■ *Totals (by themselves!) look great in graphs.* If you graph *only* totals, that's another story. In a budget, for instance, you might graph total monthly income over six months. That makes a great graph—especially if income has been going up.

Create the Chart

Creating a chart is more about choosing the right data than it is about using odd commands. In fact, you may need to replicate your data in another part of the spreadsheet before you can chart it. When necessary, you can always re-create a part of your chart somewhere else on the sheet. You can simply

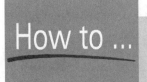

How to ... **Make the Chart Look Great**

Need to move the chart around? It's a graphical object—it's not in a cell or attached to the spreadsheet. If you like, just click somewhere in the chart and hold down the mouse button, then drag the mouse to move the chart to another part of the spreadsheet document window. In fact, you can even move it into a different AppleWorks document if you'd like, to add it to a slide show or word processing document, for instance.

Want to make it prettier? You can double-click the chart to revisit the Chart Options; make changes and click OK to update the chart instantly. You can use the Show Tools command in the Window menu to view the drawing tools, which allow you to change the way the chart looks with new colors, backgrounds, text, and other elements. We'll talk more about using the drawing tools in Chapter 10.

have formulas that point to another cell (for instance, you could type =B20 in the cell B34) to allow you to copy a new table of values to a part of your document that you can chart more easily:

	A	B	C	D	E	F	G
31							
32	TOTALS SECTION						
33		January	February	March	April	May	June
34	Total Income	3225	3225	3575	3225	3225	3575
35	Total Expenses	2960	2560	2560	2560	2560	2960
36							
37							
38							

AnnualBudget.cwk (SS) — A33

Here's how to create your chart:

1. Choose a range of data you want to chart, including (in most cases) the labels you've typed for the columns and rows.

2. Select Options | Make Chart. The Chart Options dialog box appears:

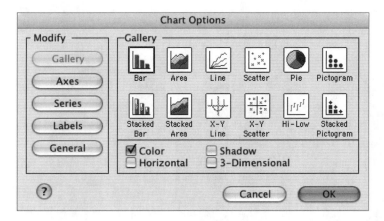

3. In the Gallery, choose the type of chart you want to use. Use the check boxes at the bottom of the window to add options.

4. Click the Axes button. Here's where you label each axis of the chart, if desired. Choose the X-Axis radio button, enter a label in the Axis Label entry box, then make other choices for how you want the axis to appear in the final chart. (If you don't customize the tick marks, min/max values, and step values, they'll be done automatically.) Choose the Y-Axis value and make the same choices.

8

5. Click the Series button. Most of this you won't need to worry about. You can, however, click the Label Data check box, and then place the label, if you'd like each individual part of the chart (each column, pie piece, and so on) to include a label that gives the exact data amount it represents.

6. Click the Labels button. Here you can decide if you're going to have a title (click the Title check box) and what that title will be. You can also decide if you'll have a legend (check or uncheck the Legend check box) and how it will be arranged.

7. Click the General button. Now you get to choose the series that is listed in the legend. You can change this by clicking the Rows or Columns radio button. This is significant—the series you choose is what each colored bar or area will represent. (If your chart comes out backward from what you expected, create another one and change the series you graph.)

8. Click OK. A chart appears in the document window (see Figure 8-6).

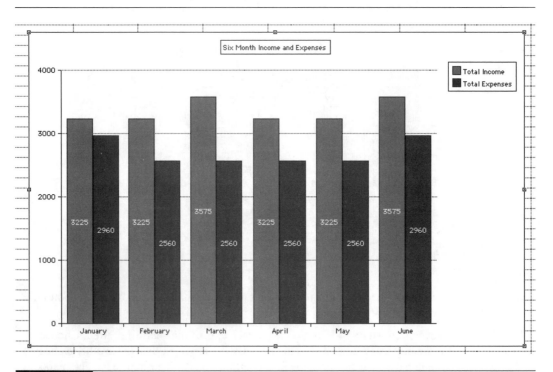

FIGURE 8-6   The final chart—looks pretty spiffy.

Chapter 9

Manage Information and Ideas with Databases

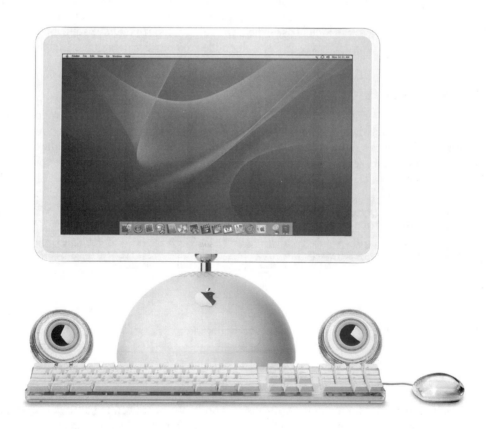

How to...

- Learn about databases
- Create the fields for your database
- Enter data in Browse mode
- Sort the database
- Create a new layout
- Build a quick report

The database module in AppleWorks is probably the most misunderstood of the components. So many people instantly associate the idea of a database with, well, computer programming or something. It seems like too much work to create a database, too much effort to be *that* organized.

But the fact is, the database module in AppleWorks is very easy to work with, and there are a lot of things you can track in a database. The basic rule is this: if you have something you need to store, sort, or search through, it's probably a good idea to consider creating a database.

What's a Database?

A database is a document that stores many different *records,* each of which is composed of several *fields* in which data is stored. Databases and spreadsheets have a lot in common—in fact, you can view databases in rows and columns just like you can spreadsheets (see the following illustration). But databases are really designed to do something quite different from spreadsheets—they're designed to track data and help you create reports based on that data.

Name	Address	City	State	Zip	Phone	Fax	E-mail
Rachel Wise	16890 49th Street	New York	NY	10032	212-555-6075	646-555-3142	rachelw@
Wes Wills	463 E. 94th Street	New York	NY	10023	212-555-6743	212-555-3633	wes@ho
Roger Smith	345 W. 12th Street	New York	NY	10012	212-555-4567	212-555-2564	roger@m
Mike Richards	425 E. 59th Street	New York	NY	10023	646-555-6743	646-324-6789	mike@pl
Anthony Tikes	345 Marblefalls Lane	Woodstock	NY	12040	845-555-4552	845-555-4556	tonyt@a

The best metaphor for a computer database is probably a card catalog at the local library. Each record in your database is like a card in the card file; each field in the database is like a line item on one of those cards. The author's name is a field, the title of the book is a field, even whether the book is currently on loan is a field. As you know, electronic databases of books are popular these days in libraries. A well-made library database offers many advantages, including reports on loaned books, searches based on authors' names, searches based on titles, and so on.

How Databases Work

You'll begin by creating a database file and defining the fields that will be used by the database to create each record. Once the fields are defined, you're ready to create your first record. It's shown to you using a default *layout*—the data entry screen. If desired, you can edit this layout, or you can create other layouts for your database.

Different layouts can be composed of different fields, if you desire, allowing you to look at the same record in different ways. Or you can use alternate layouts for different methods of data entry and/or searching. We'll cover creating different layouts later in this chapter.

Layouts allow you to create different reports based on the data, too. For instance, you could create a layout that shows all of the books in your classroom that haven't been returned (and who checked them out) or all of the invoices in your small business that are 30 days past due. Layouts can be very complex, if desired, since you're offered most of the same drawing and formatting tools you'll find in AppleWorks' drawing module (see Chapter 10 to learn about the drawing tools).

And a big part of using a database is generating useful reports. The fact that the database layouts in AppleWorks support the drawing tools also means you can create reports that will look good (and be useful) when printed.

Create Your Database

Creating your database is really pretty simple. In AppleWorks choose File | New, then choose to create a Database document and click OK in the New dialog box. (From the Starting Points window, click the Database icon.) Things get complicated in a hurry, though. Immediately, you're confronted with a dialog box that asks you to create fields for your database. And in order to do that, you'll need to think a little about your database.

Plan Your Database

With AppleWorks you'll begin by creating a new database file into which you will eventually store records. After you've launched the new document, you're asked to create fields for that database—each record will be composed of these fields. It's important to know ahead of time what sort of data you'll be tracking, since you need to define your fields before you can begin to use the database.

The key to planning your database is getting a good feel for what information you'd like to store in each record. Begin with what will be unique about each record—if you had to give each record a title, what would it be? Would it be a customer, student, or contact ID number? Would it be an invoice number? Would it be a recipe name, a CD title, the name of the photographer, or a room in your house? Once you know why each record will be unique, you may have a better idea of what you'll want to store in that record and what fields will be necessary.

For instance, I might have a database that stores information about my students in a particular class I teach. Before the semester begins, I'll want to seriously consider all of the information about each student that needs to be recorded over the next four or five months. I'll want names, addresses, phone numbers, and other contact information. I also know I'll be giving 5 major tests and 20 graded homework assignments. I'll need to have fields available to record all of that information, too.

But what about teacher conferences? Should I include parental contact information and a check box to show that each of the three conferences has been completed? How about a special section for storing notes so I can remember what to discuss with the parents?

Field Types

AppleWorks offers a number of different types of fields you can define for your database. Some are general in purpose—text fields are designed to hold pretty much any combination of text and number characters like addresses or zip codes; number fields are designed to hold numbers you plan to use in calculations. Other fields hold more specific types of formatted numbers, such as dates and times.

Still others do very specific, techie kinds of things like offer you a pull-down menu of options or allow you to click a radio button or check box. Table 9-1 shows you all the different fields.

By the way, the fact that there are a lot of field types doesn't mean that database building is hard. It can be a little intimidating, but usually only in the beginning. Once you have the correct fields set up, you'll definitely like having the database available when you need to find, search, or sort something important.

Type of Field	What It Can Contain	Examples
Text	Any combination of letters, numbers, and symbols up to 1,000 characters	Courtesy titles, personal titles, addresses, notes, phone numbers, product names, product numbers, customer ID codes, ZIP codes, social security numbers
Number	A negative or positive integer or decimal up to 255 characters	Dollar amounts, student grade percentages, number of children, quantity of purchased items
Date	Date, month, and year (offers different formats)	Current date, shipping date, date order received, date of birth, wedding date, party date
Time	Hours, minutes, and seconds (in 12- or 24-hour formats)	Current time, time of order, time shipped, time of birth
Name	Full, proper names	People's names, company names, organization names

TABLE 9-1 Database Fields

Type of Field	What It Can Contain	Examples
Pop-up menu	A menu of values; use anytime you want a limited response from many options	Compass direction, city names, U.S. states, demographic groups
Radio buttons	Multiple choice; similar to a pop-up menu but designed for fewer choices	People's titles (Mr., Ms.), name suffixes (Jr., III), computing platform (Mac, Windows, Unix), housing payments (rent, own), marital status (single, divorced, married, widowed)
Check box	Yes or no answer	U.S. citizen? Self-employed? Product shipped? Checked ZIP code? Turned in form? Talked to parents?
Serial number	AppleWorks assigns a new, ordered number for each record; good for giving each record a unique value	Customer ID, product ID, invoice ID
Value list	Choose from a list of values or enter your own	Local restaurants, election candidates, favorite computer games, magazines subscribed to
Multimedia	An image or movie file	Photo of employee, photo of household item, movie walkthrough of property for sale
Record info	Time, date, or name of person who created/ modified data	Record creation date, date/time modified, name of entry clerk
Calculation	Result from a formula using other fields	Total of invoice, sales tax, final student grade, days since shipped
Summary	Calculation from fields in this and other records	Total receivables, total of unshipped items, class average, number of items due

TABLE 9-1 Database Fields *(continued)*

Most of the fields you create will be text fields—they're the catchall for personal and small-business databases. You're more likely to use menus, radio buttons, and check boxes—fields called *controls*—if you're designing a database for someone else to do the data entry. (Controls are a good way of limiting typos by offering multiple choices.) You'll also likely use name and date fields in most any database you create, especially for business, organizational, or social databases.

Other fields that are very interesting are serial fields (where numbers are incremented automatically, which is important for invoices and inventory), calculation fields, and record info fields. All of these can be used to automate your database in a way that can make it much more valuable to use. Later in the chapter, you'll see how calculations can be used to automate important database functions.

Add Your Fields

Once you know the field types, you can add them to your database. The process for that is simple. If you've already chosen File | New | Database to create a new database document, you're presented with the Define Database Fields dialog box.

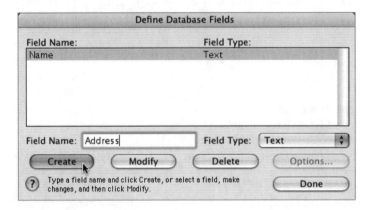

Here's the process for creating a new field:

1. In the Field Name entry box, enter a unique name for your field. It should be reasonably short and avoid additional nontext characters, especially if you think you might one day export this database to another database program.

You should definitely avoid naming your fields with formula keywords (see the discussion "Calculation Fields" later in this section) or mathematical signs, as they can make it difficult to perform calculations on data stored in your database.

2. In the Field Type menu, choose the type of field you want to create.

3. Click the Create button to create the field.

4. If desired, you can now select that field and click the Options button to make specific choices about the field's behavior. The Options dialog box allows you to make basic choices and set data-entry limitations about your field, such as setting default values, a range of accepted values, and so on. (I encourage you to explore them.)

5. Done with all your fields? When you're ready to create your first record, click Done in the Define Database Fields dialog box. (Don't worry, you can still add fields later if necessary.) The dialog box disappears and you're presented with the entry screen for your database. Enjoy!

You can always add fields to your database later by selecting Layout | Define Fields to pop up the Define Database Fields dialog box and add fields. Note that when you add fields after you've created some records, you'll have a new blank field on each existing record (in Browse mode) that you may want to go back and fill in. Also, you may need to add the field to any custom layouts that you've created.

Control Fields

Certain control fields—menus, radio buttons, value lists, and record info fields—will require additional information from you before the field can be added to the database. If the field contains radio buttons, a value list, or a menu, you'll need to enter values for those lists. A dialog box will appear right after you click the Create or Modify button in the Define Database Fields dialog box.

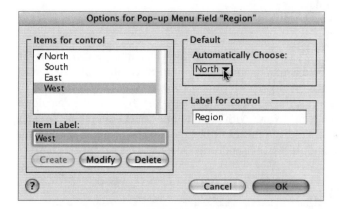

Here's what you can do in this dialog box:

- To enter a value, type a name in the Item Label entry box and click the Create button (or press RETURN).

- To create another value, type a different name and click the Create button.

- To modify an existing value, highlight the value in the Items for Control list, then type a new name for it and click the Modify button.

- To choose the default value for the control, pull down the menu in the Default section of the dialog box and choose the default value. This is the value that the control will be set to until the user changes it. (With some field types, such as a value list, you'll need to type the default value instead of choosing it from a list.)

Click OK when you're done creating the control. If you've chosen to create a record info field, you'll see a different dialog box.

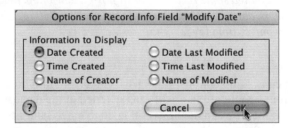

This one is more straightforward—just click the corresponding radio button to create the field you want in your database.

Calculation Fields

Here's another instance where you won't get away with a quick swipe of the Create or Modify button. A *calculation* field is one that requires you to enter a formula, somewhat akin to a formula in a spreadsheet.

If you're creating a calculation field, you'll be asked to create the calculation before the field is complete. To do that, you'll work with the Enter Formula dialog box, which appears when you first create a calculation field. (In this example, the field is designed to show the total cost of two different services (Quantity1 * Cost1 added to Quantity2 * Cost2).

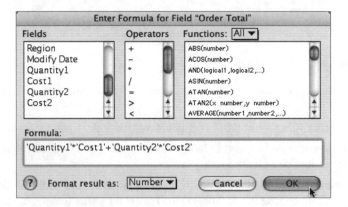

If you read Chapter 8 closely, you might notice something familiar here in the Enter Formula dialog box—the functions. In fact, most of them are exactly the same as those functions found in the spreadsheet module, although some are more limited in the database module. Still, you'll find that many of the same calculations are possible. (Refer to Chapter 8 to learn about some of the special ones.)

In database formulas, you'll find that field names are your variables—they replace the cell names in a spreadsheet when you create mathematical formulas or build functions. Most of the time you'll want to use number fields in your calculations, although you can use the built-in text functions to work with text fields, if necessary, and the date and time functions to deal with date, time, or record info fields.

There are a couple of different ways to create a formula:

- To create a basic formula, you can click a field name, click an operator, and then click another field name (perfect for adding together the cost of each item in an invoice, for instance).

- If you want to use a function, you'll usually choose the function first, then choose the field name(s) it should operate on.

- Just type it—if you already know the exact field names, operators, and/or functions you want to use.

At the bottom of the Enter Formula dialog box, choose how the result should be formatted from the Format Result As menu. (Remember, when you're entering data, this field will show the *result* of the calculation in each record, not the calculation. So, you've got to decide what sort of value that's going to be, just as with other fields.)

Then, click OK to save your formula. If AppleWorks thinks you've formatted things correctly, the dialog box goes away and the field appears in your field list. If not, you'll see an alert box telling you something is wrong. Fix the problem and click OK again.

9

Computerizing the Congregation

AppleWorks databases are at the hub of our church information systems. A Worship database keeps the pastor, office, music director, and Sunday School coordinator constantly updated on plans for Sundays. Member addresses and information are also kept in an AppleWorks database, and the surprisingly sophisticated calculation fields allow us to personalize mailings. We have older folks, for example, who want to be called "Mr. and Mrs.," while younger families are more informal and expect a "Dear Sue" greeting.

We're now experimenting for the first time with adding pictures to our member database. Photo directories are expensive and time consuming to produce. Usually by the time they're delivered, they are out of date. We're using a digital camera and iPhoto to create our own pictures and a database layout in AppleWorks to make our own.

Rev. Jim Eaton
United Congregational Church
Norwich, CT
http://www.unitedcongregational.org

Since a calculation field stores the result according to the field type you specify in the Format Result As menu, you can use the field name as a variable in other calculations. For instance, you can have a calculation field called Total, then a calculation field called Sales Tax (which might be Total * .075), and a Final Total calculation field that calculates Total + Sales Tax. Just make sure all the results are formatted as numbers if you're going to be adding and multiplying them together.

Enter and Find Records

Once you've defined your fields, you're ready to enter your first record. AppleWorks immediately drops you into Browse mode, the mode used to create records and move between them manually (see Figure 9-1). The mode is chosen from the Layout menu in the menu bar.

In Browse mode, you can click near a field name to begin entering data in that record. Press TAB to move to the next field after you've entered data; press SHIFT-TAB if you need to move back up to a previous field. Once you've entered all the data you need to enter, you can quickly choose File | Save or press ⌘-S to save.

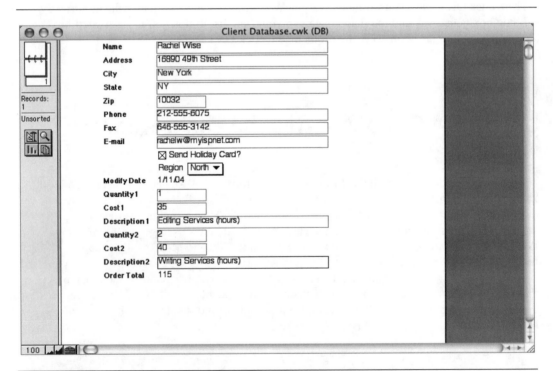

FIGURE 9-1 Browse mode is where you move through records and enter new data.

Create and Delete Records

Ready to create a new record? Choose Edit | New Record or press ⌘-R to begin entering a new record. You can also duplicate an existing record if you don't have much in it that you need to change—choose Edit | Duplicate Record or press ⌘-D. And, to delete a record while it's selected for browsing, choose Edit | Delete Record.

List View

If you prefer, you can also do your data entry in List view, which makes it a little easier to see more than one record at a time. If you have many fields, though, the window will need to scroll quite a bit. To switch to List view, choose Layout | List. (The List view was shown earlier in the section "What's a Database?")

TIP *You can drag the line that separates columns to make them wider or narrower, just as in the spreadsheet module.*

Find Records

If you only have a few records in your database, it won't be that tough to click around in Browse mode and find a particular one. But if you have quite a few records, or you're interested in looking at only certain ones, then you need to instigate a Find.

It's actually really easy to find records. Just follow these steps:

1. Choose Layout | Find (or press ⌘-F).

2. You'll see a blank version of the Browse screen. Enter data in one or more of the fields that you'd like to match with your Find.

3. Click the Find button in the left margin.

4. If any records are found, they'll be displayed. The found records are now a subset of the total database. You can scroll back and forth through the records and see only the found records.

5. Choose Organize | Show All Records when you're ready to deal with the entire database again.

By the way, it might be helpful to know that number fields in the Find layout (and calculated fields with number results) can accept basic comparisons. For instance, if you have a field that calculates a testing average, you can enter <65 to see every record that has an average under 65. The same goes for a number field that's holding a dollar amount—use <, >, <>, <, >=, or = to see which records match up. And it's the same for dates and times. You can enter <10/10/04 in a date field to find records with dates before October 10, 2004, for instance.

Save Your Search

Want to create a Find that lasts for a while? You can do it with the Search button that appears on the Tools palette in the left margin of the database window. The Search button is the magnifying glass; you can click the button to see its menu. Choose New Search and you can name the search before you enter criteria in the Find layout view.

Now, when you want to perform that search again, it appears right there on the Search button menu. Just click the button to see all your named searches.

Print Records

If you choose Print while viewing records in your database, the Print command automatically defaults to printing *all* visible records. (This doesn't mean the records you can see—it means records that are visible within the database after a Find command has been done. If you want to print records numbered 1–5, for instance, perform a Find to find records with record numbers less than 6.)

If you just want to print one record, you'll do that from the Print dialog box. Locate the untitled pull-down menu in the Print dialog box that defaults to Copies & Pages, select it, and choose AppleWorks. Now you'll see the Print Current Record option.

Give It a New Layout

Whenever you create a new database, AppleWorks designs a very basic layout, called Layout 1, which offers only the rudiments of design. Fortunately, you can do something about that by editing the layout.

Layouts are used for more than just the data entry screen—they're also used for creating and printing reports. As you'll see, a report is simply a sorted, searched database that uses a particular layout to make it look good. A layout doesn't even have to include every field in your database, so you'll often create different layouts to correspond to different reports you want to build (see Figure 9-2).

Because a database can have more than one layout, you might decide it's best to have different layouts for data entry and reports. It's up to you, but even if you don't, you can jazz up your layout so that it looks good for both a report and data entry.

Choose a Layout or Start a New One

To begin, you should figure out which layout you're currently using. Click the Layout menu to open it and look toward the bottom. The current layout is the entry with a check mark next to its name. If you want to use a different layout (assuming you have others), choose it in the Layout menu. If you want to create a new layout, choose Layout | New Layout.

If you choose to create a new layout, you'll see the New Layout dialog box. Give the layout a meaningful name, then choose whether you want the standard layout (like Layout 1), a duplicate of an existing layout, or a blank layout. You can also choose a Columnar Report, which helps

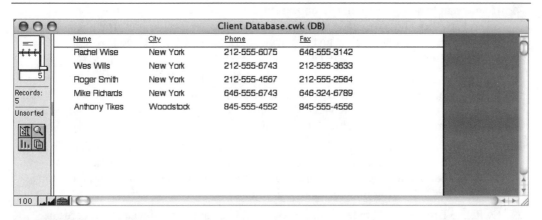

FIGURE 9-2	Here's a report layout (using the Columnar Report option) I've created specifically to show basic contact information. Notice that it uses very few of the fields in my inventory database.

you build a simple report layout that will place information about each record on its own line, as shown in Figure 9-2.

The New Layout dialog box also has a Labels option, which you can use to create a layout suitable for printing to a variety of different Avery-compatible label sheets for inkjet or laser printers. Select Labels, then choose the corresponding Avery code from the pop-up menu.

Edit the Layout

The fun is just beginning, because you can edit as you please. You edit in Layout mode. To get into Layout mode, pull down the Layout menu and choose the layout to edit. Now, go back to the Layout menu and choose the Layout command.

What can you do? You can move your text and fields around, you can draw boxes around parts of your layout, or you can add graphics and text. For the most part, the drawing and painting tools are the same ones used in the drawing and painting modules, so I'll point you to Chapter 10 to learn things like drawing and moving shapes around. But there are a few things specific to the database layout process you should know:

- Don't forget the SHIFT key. You can click a database field, then click the field's label while holding down SHIFT. Now you can click and drag one field, and the other will follow along.

- You can also use the SHIFT key to select all of the field labels at once, then you can use the Format menu to change the font, size, style, or color of the field labels.

■ If you want to add something that appears at the top of every record, choose Layout | Insert Part, then choose to add a Header. You can drag the Header line around on the layout to resize it, then add the text or image above the Header line and it will appear at the top of every page in your layout.

■ If you want more than one record on a page, you'll need to edit the layout so that more than one will fit, then drag the Body line up under the abbreviated layout. If you only have a few fields and want each record to appear on one page, do the opposite and drag the Body line down to the bottom of the page.

■ To change the appearance of a field, you can select it (or more than one field) and use the text formatting options in the Format menu. For both text and number fields, you can also double-click the field to quickly format it. (This includes things like formatting for currency and setting the precision of decimals.)

■ Switch to Browse mode to test things (assuming you have more than a few records in your database). That'll give you a good idea how things look. You can switch back to Layout mode to keep editing.

After a while you'll have a nice, edited layout designed for data entry or for a report, depending on your needs. Figure 9-3 shows the report in Layout mode; Figure 9-4 shows that same report in Browse mode. (To get the exact results shown in Figure 9-4, you may need to choose Layout | Show Multiple; otherwise you'll see only one record on the screen at a time.)

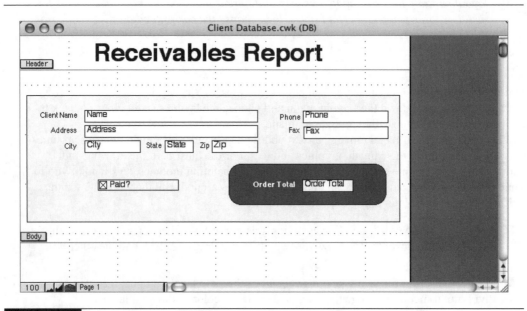

FIGURE 9-3   A new layout, still in Layout mode

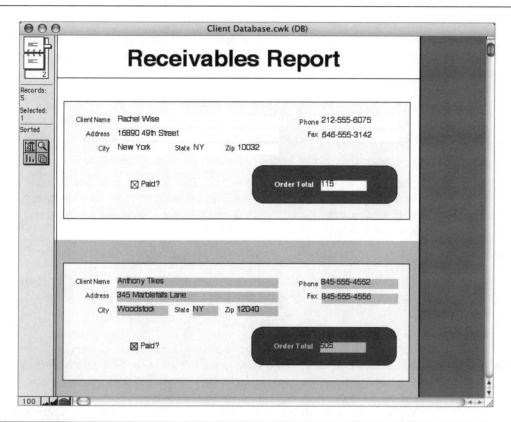

FIGURE 9-4   Here's how the new layout looks in Browse mode.

Sort and Report

The slash-and-burn report works like this—create the layout that you want to use for the report. Perform a Find and create a subset of matching records you want to report on. Switch to the report layout in the Layout menu, then change to Browse mode, if necessary. If the report looks good, print it.

You can even get more sophisticated. If you're going to be creating the same report over and over again, you can go ahead and save the whole thing—the search, the sort, and so on. You might also want to perform a quick sort before you run the report. That way you can find whose grades in the database are below 65, for example, and you can organize the report alphabetically or based on some other criteria.

Sort

Once you get a number of records in your layout, you may find, for many different reasons, that it's useful to have them sorted. This isn't always a priority while you're entering data, but it can be important when you're ready to generate a report.

Here's how to sort:

1. To begin a sort, choose Organize | Sort Records.

2. In the Sort dialog box, select the Field name you want to sort, then click the Move button.

3. Click the Ascending or Descending button in the bottom-right corner of the dialog box.

4. Next, choose the secondary field you want to sort on. This is the "sort-within-the-sort" field. If your first-level sort is on the State field, for instance, and you have more than one record within a given state, then the records could be secondarily sorted based on, say, the Phone Number field.

5. Continue until you have enough sort fields, then click OK. Your database is now sorted.

So, things are sorted. If you add records and want to sort them again, just choose Organize | Sort Records again. The criteria should still be there in the dialog box and you can just click OK again.

Save a Sort

Want to save a sort for posterity? You might find reason to work with more than one sort. If that's the case, you'll need to head down to the Sort button on the Tools palette in the left margin of the database window. Select the Sort button (it's the one with the three bars) and choose New Sort.

You'll get the same dialog box as with a regular sort, except there's an entry box at the bottom to name the sort. Do so, then set up the sort criteria. Click OK and the sort is created. Now you can return to the Sort button to perform the sort or edit it. Any new sorts you create show up on the Sort button's menu.

Build a Report

I'm not trying to rhyme the titles of these last two sections, I promise. It's appropriate, though, because the processes are so similar. If you're ready, it's time to head to the Report button and create a new report. The Report button is the one with an image of two sheets of paper on it.

Pull down the Report button menu and choose New Report. The New Report dialog box appears. Here's the crazy part—all you do is give the report a name, then choose a saved Layout, a saved Search, and a saved Sort from the menus in the New Report dialog box. If you want the report automatically printed when you choose the item in the Report button menu, check the Print the Report check box.

That's all it takes—you've just built and saved a report. Pretty easy, huh?

Chapter 10

Paint and Draw

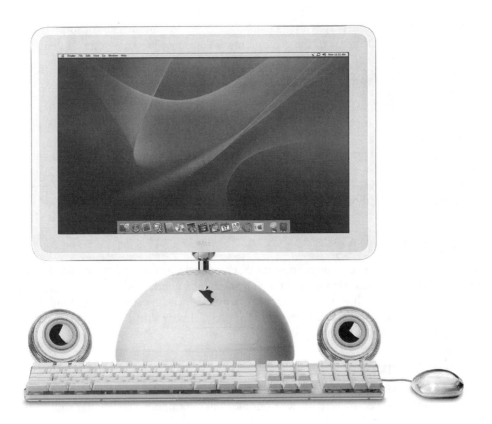

How to...

- ■ Decide whether to create a painting or a drawing
- ■ Create a painting
- ■ Add text to your painting
- ■ Save the painting
- ■ Create a drawing
- ■ Add AppleWorks elements (charts, paintings, text) to your drawing
- ■ Create objects within your drawing
- ■ Manipulate objects
- ■ Wrap text around objects

People seem to love to play with the painting and drawing modules in AppleWorks, which allow you to create some of the great graphics that Macs are known for. If you're quite the artist, especially with a computer mouse, you'll want to head directly for the painting module, which puts both your free-form and shape-driven ideas on a virtual canvas.

If your needs are a little less abstract, you'll prefer the drawing tools, which can be used to create diagrams, drawings, signs, labels, and even desktop layouts with precision. Drawing documents are about creating straight lines, curves, boxes, circles, and shapes, and adding text when necessary.

As you'll see, the tools for both drawings and paintings overlap somewhat, enabling you to create shapes, lines, colors, text, and objects from other AppleWorks modules. In Chapter 11, you'll see how these tools make it possible to extend AppleWorks into other realms, too—presentations, for instance. For now, though, it's all about getting something on your virtual canvas.

Start Your Painting

To create a new painting document in AppleWorks, select File | New, then choose to start a painting document. (If you're already viewing the Starting Points window, simply click the Painting icon on the Basic tab.) Your untouched document "canvas" appears on screen along with the tools you'll need to get started. If you'd like to save immediately, choose File | Save As to give this document a name and find a folder to store it in.

Set the Document Size

Depending on your reason for creating this painting, the first thing you might want to do is create a document that's a certain size. If, for example, you're building a newsletter page or a page on

How to ... Decide on Painting vs. Drawing

You may be wondering why AppleWorks offers two different modules—drawing and painting—for what seem to be very related tasks. The answer is simple: *objects*. The drawing tools in AppleWorks allow you to create objects—shapes, lines, text—that can be moved around, grouped together, and placed relative to one another on the drawing document. This is different from the painting module, which treats the document window more like an actual artist's canvas. Once you put a shape, line, brush stroke, or text on the canvas, that's it—it can't be moved again as an individual shape.

You *can* cut and paste portions of a painting document, and you can erase parts of it, too, but you can't pick up an individual shape or text object and drag it around. You can only cut, copy, paste, or erase sections of the canvas. The difference is a little like watercolor painting versus collage art. In a collage, you can lay down elements on your canvas, then pick them up and move them around. In watercolor painting, once you paint something onto the canvas, you either have to wipe it off (if you can) or paint over it to change it. But once you've blended colors and shapes together, you can't move them again.

Of course, the AppleWorks painting tools offer a little more freedom than that. After all, you can select square chunks of your painting document and drag them around. And the Magic Wand can be used to grab shapes from within the painting and drag them around. But, if you want to create boxes and lines that can be moved around and organized on the page, you're better off using the drawing module.

10

the Web, you may want to create a painting that's less than the standard document size. You can then place it in the larger document, wrap text around it, and create an interesting layout.

Choose Format | Document and you can determine exactly how many pixels wide and long you want your document to be. In the Document dialog box, use the entry boxes under Size to determine the width and height of your painting in pixels. (*Pixels* are "picture elements," or individual dots on the screen.) When you close the Document dialog box, your canvas will change to reflect your sizing.

Size	
Pixels Across:	640
Pixels Down:	480

This is another distinction between the painting and drawing modules—the painting tools *can be used for editing individual pixels if you zoom in close enough. The drawing tools can't be used on individual pixels.*

Use the Painting Tools

With document size set, you're ready to begin work with the painting tools. There are quite a few of them, but they fall into three basic categories: shapes, selection tools, and brushes. Before you can see any of them, though, you may need to make sure that Window | Show Tools has been chosen. (If you see Hide Tools when you choose the Window menu that means that the tools are currently being shown. See 'em?)

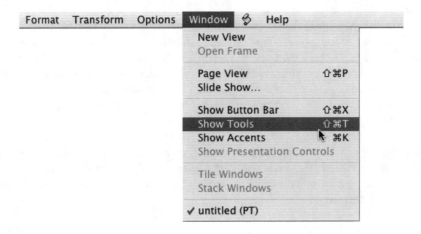

Shape Tools

If you want to create a shape, simply select a shape tool by clicking it in the toolbar. Then, move the mouse pointer to the window and choose a starting place for your shape. Now, click and hold the mouse button, then drag out to create the shape. When you release the mouse button, the shape is committed to the document canvas.

TIP
Double-click the Rounded Rectangle, Arc, or Triangle tools' icons to change some options that govern how the shapes look.

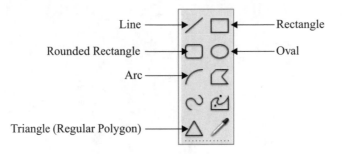

Six of the shape tools—Line, Rectangle, Rounded Rectangle, Oval, Arc, and Triangle (Regular Polygon)—all work in the same way: just select the tools, then drag to place that shape in your painting. Be aware that many of the tools have options that you can see by double-clicking the tool. For instance, the Triangle tool can be used to create other-sided polygons by double-clicking the tool in the Tools palette and entering a number in the dialog box that appears.

The other three shape tools work a little differently. Each requires extra input before you can draw the shapes. Here's how to use each of them:

- **Freehand tool**   Select this tool, then click and hold down the mouse button in the document window. Drag around the screen to create a curvy shape. When you release the mouse button, a line is drawn straight back to the starting point and the shape is filled in. (If you're trying to create a particular shape, draw it so that you end up as close to the starting point as possible.)

- **Bezier tool**   Choose the tool, click the mouse button in the document window, then move to the next place you want to create a point. Click the mouse button to create the point. To close the shape, double-click the mouse on your last point or click very close to the original point to end the shape.

- **Irregular Polygon tool**   Choose this tool, then click once in the document to begin your polygon. Move the mouse to the next point in the shape and click again. Continue to click for each point on the shape until the next to last one—you can double-click that point to automatically draw a line back to the original point. (The lines of your polygon can be curved, if you like—just hold down the OPTION key while you move the mouse.)

Selection Tools

The next set of tools, the selection tools, allow you to select different parts of your painting in order to copy, paste, clear, or drag the part to some other section of the canvas. Here's how they work:

- **Eyedropper**   This tool does one thing—picks up the color that's under it when you click the mouse button. Choose the Eyedropper, point at a particular color, and click the mouse button. That color then becomes the Pen color and/or the Fill color. (You'll see the colors change in the colors section of the toolbar as well as in the Accents window, which is discussed later in the section "Color Tools.")

- **Selection Rectangle tool**   This tool is designed to select a rectangular section of the document. Choose the tool, then click and hold the mouse button in the top-left corner of the part of the document you want to select. Now, drag down toward the bottom-right corner of the portion you want to select. Let go of the mouse button and your selection is highlighted. (Double-clicking the tool's icon selects the entire window.)

10

■ **Lasso**   The Lasso allows you to be a little more cavalier in your selection. Select the Lasso's icon, then click and hold the mouse button in the document window while you draw, freehand, the shape you want to select. Release the mouse button and your selection is highlighted.

■ **Magic Wand**   With this tool, you won't need to drag and release—the Magic Wand is designed to "magically" select shapes in the document window. Select the tool, then head over to a shape and click it. All or part of the shape will be highlighted. If you don't get what you want, try clicking a different part of the shape. (You can also hold down the SHIFT key while selecting in order to select more of a shape or more shapes.)

What do you do once something is selected? Press the DELETE key and everything in the selection area will disappear. Or pull down the Edit menu and choose any of those commands—Cut, Copy, Paste, Duplicate—to perform such functions on the selection.

Brushes

With all of the brush tools, you hold down the mouse button and move around in the document window when you want to draw or paint. When you don't want to draw or paint, release the mouse button. Brushes come in different shapes and have different purposes:

■ **Paint Brush**   Use this tool to paint brush strokes of color onto your document. You can change the shape and size of the brush by double-clicking the Paint Brush icon. Select a new size and/or shape and click OK. Also, notice the Effects menu, which allows you to change the way the Paint Brush works, offering more sophisticated special effects like blending and tinting.

■ **Pencil**   Use this tool to draw thin lines or to fill in a drawing at the pixel level. The Pencil can be used at high magnification to fill in individual pixels with color. Double-click the Pencil icon in the Tools palette to switch instantly to 800 percent magnification.

■ **Paint Bucket**   This is the fill tool—choose the Paint Bucket, click in your document, and any shape or form is filled in with color. You can draw a closed shape, then fill it with this tool, or click outside of a closed shape to fill the entire screen with color.

■ **Spray Can**   The Spray Can creates a spray-painting effect, making it look as if some paint is scattered on your electronic canvas. The more you spray on one particular area, the thicker the coverage of paint in that area. Double-click the Spray Can to change the size of the dots and the amount of coverage the Spray Can shows. You can also test the settings in the testing area in this window.

■ **Eraser**   The last brush tool is actually an "anti-brush" of sorts—the Eraser. It erases all layers of shapes and color on your document, taking it back to the original white background.

Options for most of these brushes can be found in the Options menu, where you'll also find options to change the Paint mode from the standard Opaque to Transparent Pattern, and Tint, which mixes your paint color with any colors you paint over.

Color Tools

Want to change the colors? To see the color tools, you'll need to select Window | Show Accents if the Accents window isn't already on your screen. Now you'll see the Accents window, shown in Figure 10-1. This is a powerful little window that's chock-full of controls, which I'll try to cover here quickly. In essence, you can select the characteristics for three different tools: the Fill color, the Pen color, and the Text color.

> **NOTE** *The Accents window's color tools are duplicated at the bottom of the Tools toolbar in AppleWorks version 6.1 and later. The color tools in the toolbar are a bit confusing at first blush, but once you get used to the options presented in the Accents window, you can quickly make most of those same choices on the toolbar without opening the Accents window.*

Here's how the Accents palette works in a nutshell. Select the tool—Fill, Pen, or Text—that you need to alter. Then, click the tab that corresponds to the characteristics you want to alter. For instance, if you'd like to change the Fill color—the color that fills a particular shape, for instance—

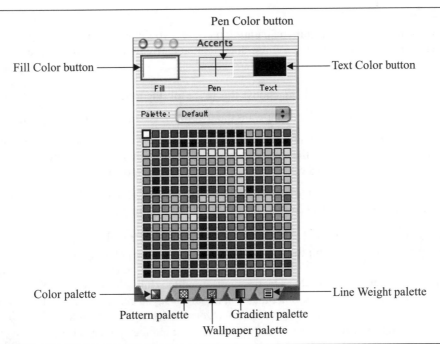

FIGURE 10-1   The Accents palette window is where you'll find all your color and line controls.

click the Fill Color button at the top of the Accents palette, then click the Color palette tab at the bottom. Now you'll see a window full of color options. Click one of the colors to make it the Fill color. (Note also that you can select options in the Palette menu to change the colors that are shown in the window.) You can change the Pen (for the outline of shapes and lines) or Text color in the same way: click the Pen Color or Text Color button at the top, click a palette tab at the bottom, then make your selection. If you want the Pen tool to have a pattern, for instance, you can select the Pen Color button at the top of the window, click the Pattern palette tab, then select a pattern.

You'll get used to the Accents palette window after some practice. Be aware that not every tool is active when you click a particular palette tab—for instance, the gradients and patterns only work with the Fill tool, not Pen or Text. The Line Weight options (which include options for shaping the ends of lines, too) only work with the Pen tool, not with the others. (Inactive tools are "grayed out" and can't be clicked.) Once you've selected your color, pattern, weight, or other options, return to the drawing and enjoy the new settings!

TIP *Want my limited artistic tips? When painting an object or landscape, remember your light source. Figure out where the light is coming from, then use darker versions of your colors on the farther side and use lighter versions of your colors on the side closer to the light. Also, a nicely placed shadow goes a long way to making a painting look more realistic, if that's your goal. You can use the Tint and Transparency options (Options | Paint Mode) to create distance and perspective effects, too.*

Add Text

Here's the last thing I'll show you in the painting module—you're going to have to figure out the artistic part yourself. Adding text to a Paint document actually involves switching to the word processing tools and creating a text frame. Here's how:

1. At the top of the Tools palette, choose the Text tool (the letter "A").

2. Click in the document where you want the text to be. An insertion point appears.

3. Head up to the menu bar and format the text (using the cleverly named Text menu) just as you would format text in the word processing module. You may also want to use the Text Color tools in the Accents window or at the bottom of the toolbar to change the text color.

4. Type the text you want. If you need to change formatting, quickly type ⌘-A to invoke the Select All command, then format the text using the Text menu.

When you're done entering and editing the text, click the Pointer tool just above the shape tools in the toolbar to switch back from the word processing tools to the painting tools.

Once you've placed the text, it's there for good. It can't be moved (unless you also move the background behind the text using the selection tool) or edited. It has become part of the painting, just like a brush stroke or a shape. (Sometimes, but not always, you can manage to select text with the Magic Wand, especially if you zoom in close. To zoom, click at the bottom left of the document window on the number—probably 100—and choose another number, which is the percentage size you want for the window. Zoom way in with 800 percent to see fine detail; 25 percent is zoomed out so you see more of the document at once and smaller.)

TIP *Fonts in Paint documents don't always print as well as fonts in Draw documents. If you want smooth printed fonts, you should select your Paint image, choose Edit | Copy, then use Edit | Paste to add the image to a Draw document. Now, create your text with the drawing tools (discussed later in this chapter) and print from there for best results.*

Save Your Image

You know that File | Save allows you to save your Paint image in AppleWorks' document format. But if you'd like to use the Paint image in other programs—to use the image in an iMovie or add it to a professional layout or web page, for instance—you'll need to save it as a more common file format. To do so, you can choose File | Save As. In the dialog box, give the file a name, then choose the file type from the File Format pop-up menu. There you'll find options such as JPEG, PICT, TIFF, and other common image formats. (If you're not sure which to use, choose TIFF for working with other graphics applications and JPEG if you plan to use the image on the Web or as an e-mail attachment.)

If you plan to use the document in an earlier version of AppleWorks, called ClarisWorks, or in ClarisWorks for Kids, select one of those options. Once you've chosen how to save it, click OK to save the file.

NOTE *Need to know more about image file types? They're discussed in Chapter 15.*

10

Draw Objects and Text

The drawing tools can be used much the same way the painting tools are used—for fun, for artistic creation, or for logos and images you'll use elsewhere. The drawing module can be used for more businesslike reasons than the painting module. As I've said, the drawing tools are a good

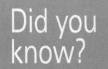
Did you know?   Draw in Databases and Spreadsheets

By the way, the drawing tools are also found elsewhere in the AppleWorks suite, including the database module and the spreadsheet module when you're dealing with charts. You'll notice that a lot of the object-manipulation commands (as well as some of the drawing tools) are found in those parts. If you're trying to create a database layout or improve the appearance of a chart, what you'll learn in this section on the drawing tools will help.

way to present information graphically. Using these tools, you'll be able to create signs, posters, certificates, and more.

Create Objects

To begin, open a drawing document by choosing File | New, then select Drawing and click OK. (From the Starting Points window, simply click the Drawing icon on the Basics tab.) A new drawing document appears.

You can place text, graphics, shapes, other multimedia objects, and even spreadsheet objects in your drawing document. When you're in the drawing module, everything is an object, meaning that everything you add to your drawing document remains its own entity. You can pick objects up, move them around, and even stack objects on top of one another (see Figure 10-2).

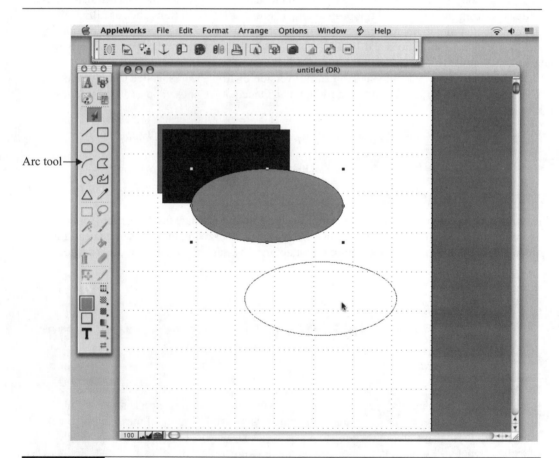

Arc tool

FIGURE 10-2 In the drawing module, you create objects that can be moved around.

There are three basic types of objects you'll create in the drawing module: shapes, text, and objects from other modules. That includes spreadsheet objects, charts, painted images, scanned photos, QuickTime movies, and other multimedia objects you can bring in from other applications.

Shapes

The shapes you find in the drawing module are a subset of those found in the painting module, and they work pretty much the same. One important thing to remember is that most objects in the drawing module can easily be reshaped or resized after they've been created, so your dimensions don't have to be as perfect as they do in the painting module.

Here are the tools you can use to draw different shapes:

- **Line tool**   Click the Line tool, and then click once in the document window. Move the mouse pointer and click again to create a line between the original point and the final location.

- **Rectangle tool**   Choose the Rectangle tool, then click and hold the mouse button in the document window. Drag the mouse to create your rectangle, then release the mouse button when the rectangle is the size and shape you want it.

- **Rounded Rectangle tool**   Choose this tool, then click and drag in the document window to create the shape. Release the mouse button when you've got it the right size. To shape the corners of the rounded rectangle, make sure the tool is selected, then choose Edit | Corner Info.

- **Oval tool**   Select the Oval tool in the toolbar, then click and drag to create the oval. Release the mouse button when the oval is the correct dimensions and circumference.

- **Free-Form tool**   Select the tool, then click and drag in the document window. Drag out the shape you want to create, ending as close to the starting point as possible. In the drawing module, this shape isn't forced closed—it can just be a squiggly line, if you prefer.

- **Bezier tool**   Select this tool, then click in the document to create the first point. Now, move the mouse and click to create additional points for the shape. End as near the first point as possible, then double-click to complete the shape.

- **Triangle (Regular Polygon) tool**   Select this tool, then click and drag in the document window to create a triangle (by default). To change the number of sides, make sure the tool is selected, then choose Edit | Polygon Sides. In the Number of Sides dialog box, you can enter as many sides as you'd like the polygon to have.

- **Polygon tool**   Select the Polygon tool, then click in the document window to place the first point. Move the mouse pointer and click to place a second point; repeat until all the points for the shape have been laid out, then double-click to draw a line between the last point and the first point, closing the polygon.

- **Arc tool**   Select the Arc tool (shown in Figure 10-2), then click and drag in the document window until the arc is the correct size. To change the arc's characteristics, make sure the Arc tool is selected, then choose Edit | Arc Info.

10

TIP *The* SHIFT *key can be used to constrain many of these tools. Hold down the* SHIFT *key while you draw a line (or draw the side of a shape) and the line will be perfectly straight. Hold it while using the Rectangle tool to draw a square. Hold it down while using the Oval tool to draw a circle. Hold it down while drawing an arc to keep the arc symmetrical.*

The drawing module also includes an Eyedropper tool and the same color tools (in the Accents palette) described in the earlier section about the painting tools. The Accents tools work slightly differently, though. To change colors and textures in a drawing, first select a shape that's already been created. Then choose a color, texture, or pattern from the Accents palette. Same with lines—even if they've already been created, just select them in the document window and choose a new color, pattern, or size, or add arrows. You can always change them back later, if desired.

TIP *To change the Polygon tool's behavior, choose Edit | Preferences | General and make sure the Topic menu shows Graphics. Now, click to change the shape-closing behavior in the Polygon Closing section. With the Manual option, you need to click to place the last point pretty much right on top of the first point in a shape.*

Text

To create a text object, click the Text tool in the top of the Tools palette. It's the tool that looks like a capital "A"; it allows you to click and drag in the document window to create a text box.

This is similar to working with the painting tools. You've actually created a word processing *frame* within the drawing document here—it's like opening up a little window into the word processing module. Watch carefully and you'll notice that the Button Bar and menus change when you're editing inside the text box. The insertion point appears and you're ready to type.

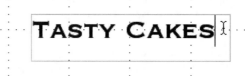

Type your text, then format it using the menus. When you're pleased with your text, click the Pointer tool in the Tools palette or click outside the text box to switch back to the drawing tools.

Unlike the painting tools, you can edit text that you create in the drawing module. If you want to edit the text, just double-click it if the Pointer tool is selected, or select the Text tool and single-click the text. The text box appears, the menus change, and you're ready to edit the text.

Other Frames

I want to touch on the idea of frames here. You can create spreadsheet and painting frame objects right here within the drawing module. Just as you can create a text frame that switches around your menus and Button Bars, you can create spreadsheet and paint frames that let you use the tools from those modules.

To add frames from other modules, click one of the frame tools at the top of the toolbar—you'll see icons that represent word processing, spreadsheet data, painting, and a table frame. To add a spreadsheet frame, select the Spreadsheet icon (it looks like a small spreadsheet with numbers on it), then click and drag in your document window to create the spreadsheet object. A table of cells appears and the insertion point is ready to edit. Now you can type away to add spreadsheet data in your drawing document. You can enter anything you might enter in a typical AppleWorks spreadsheet.

You can even create a chart. Enter spreadsheet data that works for a chart, then choose Options | Make Chart. (If you don't see that option, double-click the spreadsheet to make sure it's selected for editing.) Now, create a chart as discussed in Chapter 8. When you click OK, the chart appears in your document. Best of all—it's an object, just like everything else (see Figure 10-3).

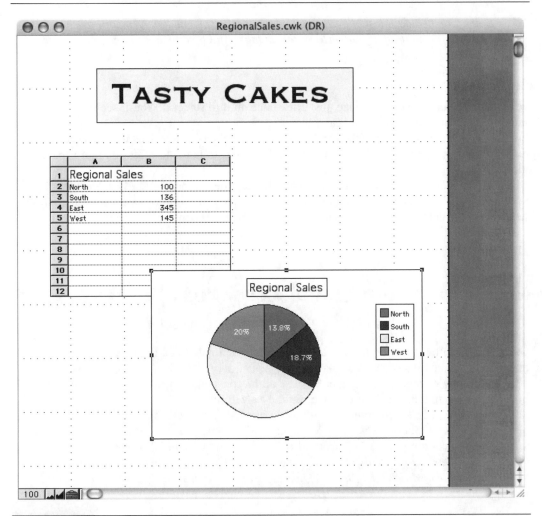

FIGURE 10-3   A chart from spreadsheet data can easily be added to your drawing document.

Creating a paint frame within your drawing document is a similar process. Select the Painting icon (it looks like a painter's palette), then drag out a paint object in the document window. You'll notice that the tools and menu commands change to those of the painting module. Paint all you want inside the paint object, then click outside it when you're done.

Manipulate Objects

Once you've got your objects created, you're ready to arrange them. The key is to figure out how to select and drag them around—that part's pretty easy. With the Pointer tool selected in the toolbar, point to an object, then click and hold down the mouse button while you drag the object around the screen. Drop the object when you're done moving it by releasing the mouse button.

 *Don't forget Undo! Most of these manipulations can be immediately undone by choosing Edit | Undo right after you perform the change. And if you want to undo your undo, choose Edit | Redo.*

Select Objects

If you want to change an object's size, just click once on it to select it. You'll see the *resizing handles*—little black rectangles—appear.

You can click and drag one of the handles to make the object larger. This includes text boxes, spreadsheet objects, and paint objects, all of which can be stretched to offer you more space to work in.

But that's not all you can do. With an object selected, you can press DELETE to delete it from the document, or choose any of the Edit menu commands like Cut, Copy, or Paste. You can paste an object from any AppleWorks module into any other module. (The major exception is the painting

 **Professional-Level Possibilities**

Using AppleWorks' draw module, I have created and maintained an important wiring diagram for the audio system of a small cable TV station, which would have been very difficult to draw with pencil and paper because of the constant erasures. It was easy to do in AppleWorks, and the results are very clear and easy to follow.

There are 73 wires numbered on each end connecting three terminals and nine pieces of equipment for output on two cable TV channels. I could have done it in color, but I wanted to be able to make it reproducible on a black-and-white photocopier. I therefore selected a different dashed line for each wire so that they would be easy to follow.

Richard T. White, former chairman, Cable Commission of Grosse Ile, Michigan

module, which will accept the Paste command, but won't store the object as an object—it just turns it into dots, or pixels, that become part of the painting document. That's even true of spreadsheet objects, which can be painted right into a painting document.)

Arrange Objects Front and Back

Sometimes you'll find you have one object that's "on top of " another object—it's obscuring part of the second object. This often happens, for instance, if you decide to create the background for a text object after you've created the text object. Drag the background to the text and it obscures the text.

If you really want that background in the, well, background, then make sure it's selected and choose Arrange | Move Backward, or go for the gold and choose Arrange | Move to Back. In either case, the selected object is moved behind other objects. The Arrange | Move Backward command is designed to move objects back one layer at a time (just in case you have three or four objects stacked on one another). Move to Back immediately moves the selected object to the back of all objects on the screen.

As you might guess, you can bring objects to the foreground just as easily. Select an object, then choose Arrange | Move Forward or Arrange | Move to Front.

Align Objects

There are two different ways to align objects. You can select a particular object and choose Arrange | Align to Grid. This only does something if you've previously selected the Options | Turn Autogrid Off command. Autogrid is what forces objects to "snap" to a particular position on the page whenever you drop them. It keeps you from making precise little movements, but helps you by aligning everything to the grid. If you've turned it off, but you now want an object aligned to the grid again, choose the Align to Grid command.

The Align Objects command is even cooler. Select two or more objects that you want to align relative to one another. Now, choose the Arrange | Align Objects command. You'll see the Align Objects dialog box.

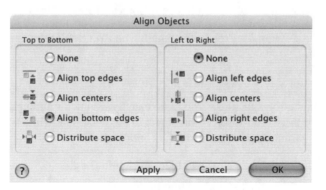

See the options? Decide how you want objects aligned, asking yourself some questions like:

■ If your objects are in a vertical column, do you want them aligned on the right or left edge? Should the vertical distance between the objects be distributed evenly?

■ If it's a horizontal row of objects, should the bottom or top be aligned? Should the horizontal distance between the objects be distributed evenly?

■ In either case, should the centers of the objects be aligned?

Make your choices and click OK.

Reshape Objects

As mentioned, objects in Draw are unique because they can be changed and reworked after they've been created. One way to do that is to change the way the shape is made with the Reshape command. This works with objects created using the Arc, Polygon, Freehand, Bezier, and Regular Polygon tools. Choose Arrange | Reshape and you'll see resize handles that let you change the shape of the object.

After you've changed the shape, you'll still be in Reshape mode until you select Arrange | Reshape again. So, click another object and reshape again. Or choose the menu command to return to normalcy.

Free Rotate

The Free Rotate command works much the same way as the Reshape command:

1. Choose Arrange | Free Rotate from the menu and you're in Free Rotate mode.

2. In the document window, select an object to rotate.

3. Now, click and grab one of the image's handles, then move the mouse. You'll see the object rotate along with your mouse movement.

4. Release the mouse button when you have the object where you want it.

Don't forget to choose Arrange | Free Rotate again when you're done rotating to leave Free Rotate mode.

Flip and Rotate

These are more precise controls that allow you to do exactly as much rotation and flipping of an object as you'd like. For these, you'll select the object in the document window first, then choose the command from the Arrange menu. Here are the commands:

■ **Flip Horizontally**   Quickly flips an object from left to right.

■ **Flip Vertically**   Flips the top and bottom of an object.

■ **Rotate**   Brings up a dialog box that allows you to enter how many degrees the object should rotate. Rotation works counterclockwise (entering 9 0 causes the object to rotate counterclockwise 90 degrees), but you can enter a negative number to rotate clockwise. (Note that –90 and 270 give the same results, since rotation covers the total 360 degrees in a circle.)

■ **Scale by Percent**   Brings up a dialog box that allows you to reduce or enlarge your object vertically or horizontally. Enter a percentage for each to stretch or enlarge the object.

Group and Lock

With the Lock command, you fix an object so that it can't be moved, reshaped, or rotated. Locking is simple—just select the object and select Arrange | Lock from the menu. The object becomes locked—it can't be moved or shaped. (You can edit text and make changes in spreadsheets and similar objects, though.) To unlock the object, select it and choose Arrange | Unlock.

The Group command allows you to take two or more objects and cause them to function as a group—move one and you'll move them all. They become, in essence, one object. To group objects, select them all (hold down the SHIFT key as you click additional objects in order to select more than one). Choose Arrange | Group ⌘-G) and the different objects become one object. You'll notice that the object handles change so that the entire group can be selected, moved, resized, shaped, or rotated as one object.

To ungroup, select the object and choose Arrange | Ungroup (SHIFT-⌘-G). Once you've created a grouping, you can also group that grouping with other objects (and so on, and so on), although that can get a touch complicated.

Obviously, it's best to group related elements, especially things that always need to be together as one object or together but a certain distance apart. (It can be annoying to get everything set up correctly and then accidentally move one of the related objects. Just group them and that can't happen.) It's also easy and recommended that you group objects temporarily when you want to move them, together, across the screen. Select, group, move, ungroup—you can do it very quickly and it keeps all those objects the same relative distance from one another

10

Chapter 11

Create AppleWorks Presentations

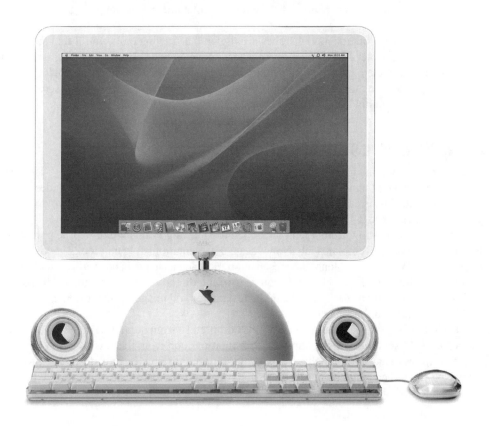

How to...

- Create the presentation
- Build master slides
- Create and edit slides
- Arrange and organize slides
- Present the show

AppleWorks 6 includes a module that's specifically designed to help you create presentations, although you'll find that the tools are very similar to the drawing tools. In essence, the tools enable you to create a number of *slides* (often based on a template), which are really just 640 × 480 drawing documents that can then be displayed, full screen, one at a time. You can use the special slide show controls to automatically advance the presentation, or you can press a key to move from one slide to the next.

Because the presentation module relies heavily on the drawing tools, you'll find the discussion of those tools in Chapter 10 helpful. Then, you can move on to creating and editing slides, placing transitions between them, and even adding information from other AppleWorks modules or imported items like QuickTime movies and sounds. Finally, you'll display the image, full screen, so others can witness your handiwork.

Creating the Presentation

You've got two options for building a slide show—the easy way and the hard way. The easy way is to use a preexisting template to create your slides, complete with a few sample slides and a full-fledged design. This is easier because, with such a template, all you really need to do is focus on your text and bulleted-point ideas, not on how the overall slide will look.

To build a slide show from a template, open the Starting Points window (File | Show Starting Points) and click the Templates tab. Now, locate a presentation style that looks good to you and click its icon. When you're done, the presentation module has loaded and you'll be looking at your first sample slide (see Figure 11-1). If you're working directly from the template, all you have to do is create new slides as desired and edit the text and/or add images or other frames, all of which we'll discuss later in this chapter.

The other way to create a presentation is completely from scratch. You begin by selecting File | New | Presentation or selecting the Presentation icon from the Basics tab in the Starting Points window. That will launch a blank presentation with no elements designed into it. From there, you'll build and edit the master slides for your presentation. First, you'll need to access those master slides using the Controls window, discussed next.

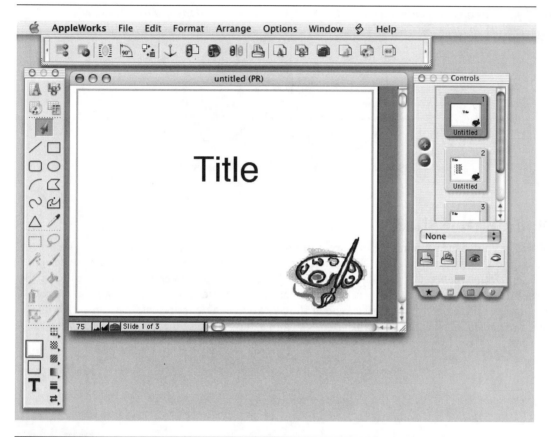

FIGURE 11-1   After selecting a Presentation template, you can immediately begin editing your slides.

The Controls Window

To create or edit your presentation, you'll dig into the Controls window, which appears whenever you launch a new presentation or presentation template. (If you don't see the controls, select Window | Show Presentation Controls.) The Controls window includes four tabs across the bottom— Master, Slides, Organize, and Slide Show. You'll work through each of the tabs as you're editing both the look and the content of your presentation until, finally, you're displaying your presentation onscreen.

 *You can click and drag on the Drag lines at the bottom of the Controls window if you'd like to make the Controls window larger and reveal more slides or other items.*

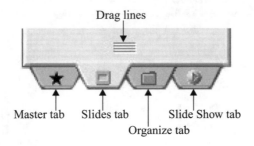

Drag lines

Master tab   Slides tab   Slide Show tab

Organize tab

Build Master Slides

Whether you've used a template or started from scratch, the first step you may want to take is editing your *master slides*. These slides aren't actually used in your presentation—they're design masters, from which all of your other slides will be created. You can create hundreds of master slides if you like, although you'll probably find that you don't need more than between three and five master slides, one for each basic type of slide you'd like in your presentation. To work with your master slides, click the Master tab (the star icon) at the bottom of the Controls palette window.

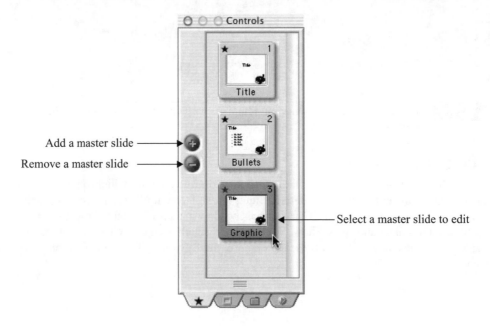

Add a master slide

Remove a master slide

Select a master slide to edit

If you're creating a presentation from scratch, you'll note that you have only one untitled master slide to start with. You might want to create a few more at the outset, depending on your presentation. For instance, you may want one master slide for section titles, another for slides that are primarily bulleted-point slides, and another master for slides that include a special area for images or QuickTime movies, and so on.

TIP *You can click the name of a master slide once to highlight it, then type to give the master slide a more unique name, such as "Title slide" or "Bullets slide," or something to remind you of its purpose. Also, the bullet character—which you may find useful when creating your slides—is typed by pressing* OPTION-8 *in most fonts.*

Now, whether or not you're working from a template, you can select a master slide in the Controls window and edit its general appearance in the main presentation window (see Figure 11-2).

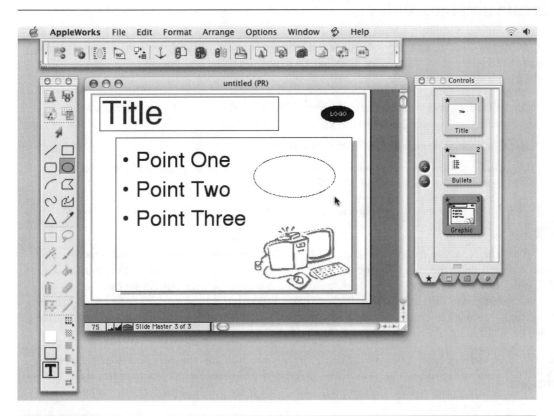

FIGURE 11-2   Editing a master slide from scratch

You can use all of the drawing tools to create the slide—lines, shapes, colors, and even text. In fact, you'll particularly want to work with text, because you'll need to create the places on your master slide where you'll later be able to edit the text for each individual slide of your presentation. Note, however, that once you're editing the actual slide, you won't be forced to use every text area or bulleted point that you create—you'll have full control over each individual slide. The master slides are simply starting points.

NOTE   *When you're editing an existing master slide from a template, you may find it handy to choose Options | Edit Background if you want to gain access to the slide's background images or shapes.*

Once you have your master slides edited to taste, you can move on to creating and editing the actual slides for your presentation.

Create and Edit Slides

The next step in building your presentation is to create some slides. You can begin by creating all the slides you think you'll need for your presentation at once, or you can create them one at a time, go in and add the text and images for that slide, then move on to the next one. In either case, actually creating the slide is simple:

1. In the Controls window, make sure the Master tab is selected, then click once on the master slide you'd like to use to create your new slide.

2. Click the Slides tab in the Controls window.

3. Click the Add button (+) on the Slides tab. The new slide is added and automatically appears in the main window for editing.

TIP   *If you select an existing slide first, the new slide will be added immediately after the selected slide.*

That's it. Now you can edit the slide itself, changing its title, bulleted text, and whatever else you'd like to do to the slide. As noted earlier, you can actually edit directly on each individual slide itself, if you think it needs to deviate from the master slide's design. Simply use the drawing tools to change the slide as much as desired. Then, repeat the preceding steps for each additional slide that you want to create, noting that you don't need to switch back to select a master slide every time if you'd like to use the same master slide for multiple new slides.

TIP   *Remember when attempting to edit text on the new slide, you may first need to select the text (word processing) tool at the top left of the toolbar. Then, click the text on the slide that you want to edit. This is particularly true if the text is part of a grouped (Arrange | Group) object.*

Remember that slides can be more than simply text and drawn shapes. You can select one of the frame tools, as described in the "Draw Objects and Text" section of Chapter 10, if you'd like to add data or images from another AppleWorks module. This enables you to add spreadsheet data, graphs, painting frames, tables, or other frames, using the tools from other AppleWorks modules.

If you have a QuickTime movie, an external image file, or some other external file that you'd like to add to a slide, you can do that, too. Select File | Insert, then locate the multimedia file you'd like to add in the Insert dialog box. (For more on the Insert command, see the section "Add Graphic Frames" in Chapter 10.)

NOTE   *AppleWorks can import AIFF, MP3, and even tracks directly off audio CDs. It can also import QuickTime movies, Macromedia Flash animations, and a variety of others. As you'll see later in the section "Present the Show," AppleWorks has special options that enable you to play back audio and video files automatically on each slide.*

As you're adding and editing your slides, you can also arrange and rearrange them on the Slides tab of the Controls window. Each slide is an icon that you can drag and drop before or after other slides. Click and drag one slide and you'll see a blue line appear in between slides. Release the mouse button when the line appears in the new location where you'd like the slide, and the slide will be placed there, as well as renumbered.

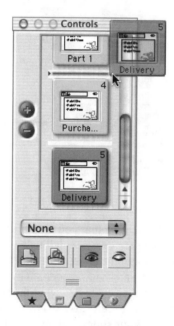

At the bottom of the Controls window, you'll find a menu and some buttons that help you make choices about each slide. Select a slide and use the pop-up menu to select a *transition* for that slide. Each transition represents a special effect that is used to transition from the previous slide into this slide. (That is, the transition that you select for the slide will be used when the slide *appears* on screen, not when it's leaving the screen.) Special transition effects are a fun way to spice up the presentation and make it a bit more professional—as long as you don't go overboard. I suggest you pick a few basic transition types and stick to them.

You can also select a slide and click one of the four buttons along the bottom of the Controls window to determine whether the slide should be printed and whether it should be shown as part of a slide show. If you'd like to leave a slide in your presentation, but not print it, select that slide and click the printer icon with the circle and a line through it. If you'd like the slide to be in the presentation, but not show the next time you display the slide show, select that slide and click the closed-eye icon.

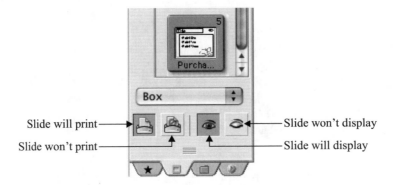

Slide will print

Slide won't print

Slide won't display

Slide will display

Add Notes to Slides

The presentation module has a neat little feature that you may find useful if you're serious about your presentations—the Notes view. In Notes view, a small text area appears beneath each slide, where you can type a little information about the slide, such as notes to yourself, a script of what to say about that slide, and so on. To enter Notes view, choose Window | Notes View. You'll see the main Presentation window change to show you a small view of the slide and a text area underneath where you can begin typing your notes (see Figure 11-3).

Once you have notes associated with your slides, you may find it handy to print those notes separately, perhaps to use while you're actually giving the presentation. To print your notes, choose File | Print. In the Print dialog box, choose AppleWorks from the pull-down menu. Now you'll see a radio button that enables you to print the notes instead of the slides. Turn on that option and click Print to begin printing.

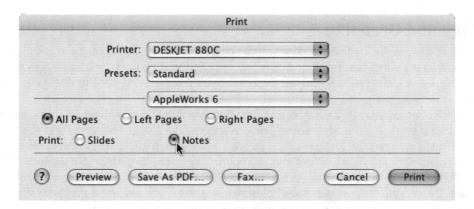

What comes out of your printer are pages that include a representation of the slide at the top of the page and the notes below them, making it easy for you to see, at a glance, which notes are related to which slides.

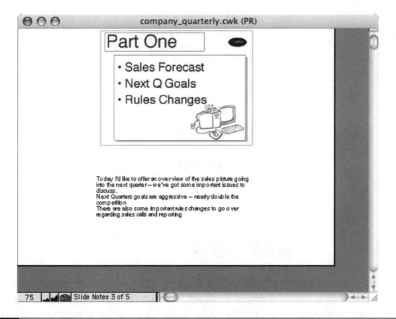

FIGURE 11-3   In Notes view, you'll find a small area below the slide for typing your notes.

Arrange and Organize

On the Organize tab of the Controls window, you can drag slides around more quickly than dragging slides around on the Slides tab. You'll find, however, that the Organize tab is best used when you've already named your slides on the Slides tab. Otherwise, you'll see a listing of "Untitled" slides that are impossible to do much with.

If you have named your slides, you can use the Organize tab to drag individual slides around and change their position in the slide show. You can also use the Add (+) button to add a folder, which you can then name. The folders you create are for your benefit only—they won't affect the order, presentation, or the visual look of slides. You can, however, drag slides into the folders to create different logical breaks in your presentation, which may help you see and organize the presentation better. You can then click the disclosure triangles to hide and reveal the slides in each folder, making it a bit easier to work on a section of your presentation at a time.

Note that the Organize tab gives you one other interesting capability. When you select a folder and click the Delete (–) button, you'll delete not only that folder, but also the slides in that folder. This is an easy way to quickly delete slides, but be careful—it's also an easy way to delete slides you didn't mean to delete, thus ruining an afternoon's worth of work!

Present the Show

Once you've created and arranged your slides, you're ready to present the show. To begin, you should set the options for how the slide show will be presented by clicking the Slide Show tab in the Controls window. There you'll see a number of settings you can select and alter to determine whether the show will run automatically, whether the cursor will be visible, and how movies and sounds will be played.

Here are the options:

- Under Slide Options, you can turn on the Auto-Advance Every option to have the slide show run on its own. In the Seconds entry box, enter the number of seconds each slide should appear on the screen. You can also enable the Play Show Continuously option if you'd like the show to loop on screen.

- Turn on or off the Show Cursor option depending on whether you'd like to be able to move the mouse cursor around on the screen while the slide show is being displayed.

- Under Movies & Sounds, turn on the Show Controls option if you'd like the QuickTime player controls to appear. This will enable someone watching a self-running presentation to stop and start playback of the QuickTime movies or sound.

- Select Play Automatically if you'd like any inserted QuickTime movies or sounds to play; select Finish Before Advancing to Next Slide if you'd like the slide show to wait until the movie or sound has fully played before going to the next slide.

11

■ Select Play All Movies and Sounds in a Slide at Once if you'd like all multimedia to play simultaneously in slides that have more than one movie and/or sound inserted.

Once you've made your selections, you can click the large Play button (with the right-pointing triangle) to play the slide show on screen. (You can also select Window | Slide Show to begin the show at any time.) Once the slide show is playing (if it isn't set to advance automatically), you can either press the SPACEBAR or the RETURN key, or click the mouse button, to advance to the next slide. To stop the presentation and return to AppleWorks, press ESC.

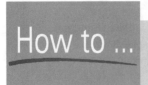

As noted in Chapter 23, most Macs have a video-out port that can be used to display your presentation on a larger monitor or on a compatible presentation system—sometimes even a TV screen. Hook your Mac up to an external display, and you can use AppleWorks for presentations to large groups!

How to ... Create a Self-Running Presentation

You may have noticed that the AppleWorks presentation module gives you all the tools you need to create a self-running presentation, good for a "kiosk" presentation or a multimedia brochure for your company or organization. The key to a successful self-running presentation, though, is to create QuickTime audio files and/or video movies that accompany each slide. (See Chapters 14 and 15 for hints on how to create audio and video files.) For each slide, you'll want to record some narration or display a QuickTime movie, which you add to the slide using the File | Insert command. Then, you use the Slide Show tab in the Controls window to set the show to auto-advance, play continuously, and to play movies and sounds automatically so that the media files finish before advancing to the next slide.

The result: as people watch the slide show, each slide will advance automatically either after a set number of seconds, or after the narration audio (or video) is finished. Your viewers can then concentrate on watching as much of the show as they want—it will continue to loop. What's this good for? How about setting up a Mac in the front of your real estate office, chamber of commerce, school, organization, or company and have that Mac play back a presentation complete with audio and video of your group's highlights, sales materials, or interesting educational tidbits?

Chapter 12

Print Your Documents and Send Faxes

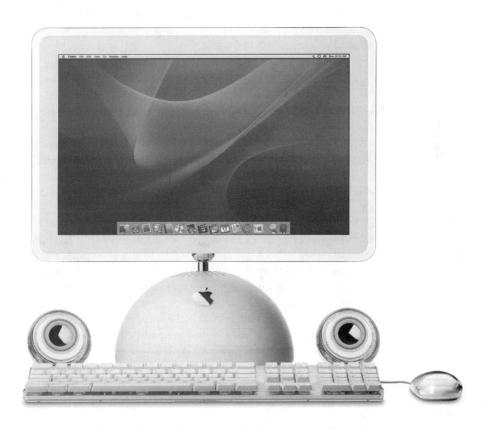

How to...

- Choose your printer
- Get your printer and Mac talking to one another
- Print documents and manage print jobs
- Understand and add fonts to your Mac
- Send and receive faxes from your Mac
- Receive faxes online

You probably want to print stuff. Whether you already have a printer or you're still in the shopping phase, let's take a look at your needs and figure out how to get you up and printing. It's actually pretty easy with an iMac, eMac, or iBook, especially if you can buy a USB printer.

To begin, let's talk about the different types of printers you can get and what the advantages are of each. Then, we'll take a look at how you set up a printer and print to it. Later we'll discuss fonts, as well as how to send and receive faxes.

Buy a Printer

Two major types of printers are used in the home, home office, or most businesses and organizations: laser and inkjet.

Inkjet printers tend to be less expensive, they generally print in color, and, depending on the model, they offer good-to-exceptional print quality. Inkjets can be slightly easier to set up than laser printers, but they rely strongly on their own software drivers, whereas some higher-end laser printers—particularly higher-end workgroup printers that use the PostScript language—use a driver written by Apple that integrates well with the Mac OS.

Laser printers are often faster and quieter than inkjets. Most inexpensive lasers don't print in color, and laser printers tend to be more expensive at the outset. But many laser printers will connect to your Mac using Ethernet technology, making it easy to share the printer with a number of different Macs or other computers. Laser printers tend to have more professional-level options— paper trays and envelope feeders, for instance. And laser printers that use the PostScript printer language are preferred for professional-level printing.

If you're trying to decide between the two, probably the most important considerations are your volume of printing, the need for color, and the desired quality of black-and-white printing. If you expect to print hundreds or thousands of pages a month—or if you'll be in situations where you need to quickly print 20- to 100-page documents and send them somewhere—then you'll likely want a laser printer. You'll also want a laser printer for a lower cost-per-page over the long term. And you'll want a laser if you print many important documents that are mostly text and require no color.

Inkjet technology has improved remarkably over the years, and you can get a good color printer for less than $100. Inkjet printers are great if you run a small business and plan to print brochures, signs, menus, thank you notes, invitations, overhead slides, and so forth. While not always workhorses for hundreds of pages per month, an inkjet printer provides flexible printing with a variety of options. Look for an inkjet that accepts a number of different types of paper and transparencies, especially if you plan to make full use of color on business cards, overhead slides, and photos. And inkjet printers are more likely to be offered as *multifunction devices*, which can print, scan, copy, and sometimes fax documents, as discussed in the sidebar.

NOTE   *If there's a downside to inkjet printers it's that their pages tend to smudge a little more easily than laser-printed pages, particularly immediately after they've been printed or if they get a little wet.*

If you want to share one printer between two or more computers, a laser or high-end inkjet printer with an Ethernet connection is best, as it allows the printer to be an independent entity on your local network. (It also tends to make the printer much more expensive.) Most USB printers, however, can be shared between Macs using Apple's USB Printer Sharing technology, the downside being that the Mac connected to the printer must be left on and a user must be logged into the Mac in order for others to access it.

Did you know?

Multifunction Printers

Once virtually nonexistent in the Mac market, "all-in-one," or multifunction, printers (that include scanning, copying, and often fax capabilities) now abound from manufacturers such as Canon, Epson, HP, and Lexmark. Usually for less than a scanner and a printer separately, you can get a single box that performs all those tasks for your home or small office.

So should you? Keeping in mind the adage "jack of all trades, master of none," a multifunction printer can be a good investment, if you consider a few caveats. First, these devices are highly dependent on driver software, meaning they'll need software drivers specifically written for Mac OS X. Second, some multifunction devices offer fewer features for Macs than for PCs, so read the box (and Mac magazine reviews) carefully. Finally, the very cheapest multifunction printers sometimes don't allow you to copy or fax unless the Mac is powered on—I recommend moving up to a device that has "standalone" copying and faxing capabilities, as software-based copying and faxing can be less convenient and more problematic.

Your best bet is to read up on the printer in question in your favorite Mac magazines or web site reviews before buying an all-in-one to ensure that all of the printer's features are activated for Macs and that the driver and other software for the printer is reliable.

12

Understand Printer Connections

Printers also offer a variety of ways that they can be connected to your Mac. There are two ways to directly connect to a modern Mac—USB and by a network (either Ethernet or wireless). In the case of USB (version 1.1), you should be able to connect the printer directly to an available USB port on your Mac using an "A-to-B" USB cable. You can do this while your Mac is turned on, and when you do, it may be recognized by your Mac. (In many cases you'll need to go through a setup process, discussed later in the section "Set Up Your Printer and Mac.") USB is common for most inkjet printers and many personal and small-business laser printers.

At the time of writing there aren't many USB 2.0 printers on the market, but that may change in the future. If so, be aware that you may need an adapter to connect a USB 2.0 printer to a consumer eMac, iBook, or an older iMac that doesn't support USB 2.0 connections.

Workgroup-style laser printers (those designed for a network) will usually connect via Ethernet, although how you're connecting dictates the type of Ethernet cable you need. If you're only connecting the laser printer to your Mac, you may need an Ethernet *crossover* cable, which is designed to allow two Ethernet devices to talk to one other. Connect the cable to your Mac's Ethernet port and to the Ethernet port on the printer. (Macs that have Gigabit Ethernet—which currently means the latest iMac G4 models—don't require a crossover cable; others do.)

You'll need an Ethernet hub if you plan to use the network-ready laser printer with more than one computer. You can do that easily with all the devices plugged into the hub; all the computers (especially if they're Macs and compatible with the printer) will locate and recognize the printer when you set them up.

If you want to use your network printer with a wireless network (using an AirPort card that's installed in your Mac), you may need an add-on of some kind if your printer isn't wireless-capable on its own. The easiest way to add such a printer to a network is to connect it via Ethernet to your wireless *router*, which might be an AirPort Base Station or a similar device. Most wireless routers include multiple Ethernet ports so you can connect wired and wireless devices on the same network. You can also add printers by connecting them to special adapters, called wireless printer servers, which make it possible for your wireless Macs to connect to typical printers using the printer server as a go-between. (See Table 12-1 for some examples, and see Chapter 22 for more details on wireless networking.)

TIP   *Actually, you can connect a USB printer to an AirPort Extreme Base Station, which has a special USB port for that purpose. Doing so allows your entire network to access that USB printer.*

Choose a Printer's Language

There's one more topic to cover before we get to the setup process—printer languages. Printers can use different languages for describing a page—that's the data that's sent from the Mac to the printer to tell it what the page should look like. Professional publishing types tend to use printers that use the PostScript language. A PostScript-language printer includes a special processor, its

Company	Product(s)	Web Site
Epson	Wireless printers Wireless printer servers	**http://www.epson.com/**
Hewlett-Packard	Wireless printers JetDirect wireless printer servers (for use with HP printers)	**http://www.hp.com/**
D-Link	Wireless printer servers Wireless routers/printer combos	**http://www.d-link.com/**
LinkSys	Wireless printer servers	**http://www.linksys.com/**
Troy Group	Wireless printer server	**http://www.troygroup.com/**

TABLE 12-1   Sources for Wireless Printers and Printer Servers

own RAM, and some PostScript fonts built into the printer itself. (Fonts can also be uploaded from the Mac to the printer.) In this case, a program that wants to print to the printer simply sends a series of PostScript commands to tell the printer how the document should be printed. Then, the printer does all the work using its own processor to create the printed page.

Many inkjet printers use a different language, the Printer Control Language (PCL), a standard originated by Hewlett-Packard Corporation. In this case, the printer requires a special driver so that your Mac can speak PCL, create the page, and send it to the printer in the proper format. Mac does all of the processing, which is why inkjet printing can be slower than laser printing; it's also why most inkjet printers are cheaper, since they don't have their own processor, RAM, and so on—they rely on the Mac for all that.

This situation is also why inkjet printers (and many USB-based laser printers) need to have special driver software written for them, while PostScript-language printers, even if they aren't specifically designed to be Mac compatible, often work just fine using the built-in LaserWriter driver discussed later in this chapter.

NOTE   *Earlier non-PostScript printers were made specifically for Macs using the QuickDraw printer language. For instance, HP's DeskWriter series, although nearly identical to the DeskJet series, used QuickDraw instead of PCL for the Mac version. QuickDraw isn't compatible with Mac OS X, which shouldn't be a problem since modern Macs also don't have the same ports as those older printers. If you can't hook it up, you definitely can't use it with your Mac.*

Set Up Your Printer and Mac

We've discussed different ways to attach a printer to a Mac, including wired and wireless approaches. In most of those cases, you'll either connect the printer directly to a USB port on your Mac, or you'll connect the printer via Ethernet.

The next step is to tell your Mac about the printer and assign it a printer driver. If you have a USB printer, a wireless inkjet printer, or a laser printer that uses the PCL language, you'll likely use an individual printer driver from the manufacturer. (If your printer came with a CD-ROM, run that CD's installation program first to install the software driver—better yet, check the manufacturer's web site to make sure there isn't an update available. Some drivers from common inkjet printers are included with Mac OS X.) If you have a PostScript laser printer that's connected via Ethernet, you'll likely use the LaserWriter driver that's built into Mac OS X. To choose that driver and otherwise set up the printer, you'll need to launch the Printer Setup Utility, which is located in the Utilities folder inside the main Applications folder.

Set Up a USB Printer

In Mac OS X, you'll need to add the printer in the Printer Setup Utility (which was called Print Center in versions of Mac OS X prior to version 10.3). If the Add Printer dialog sheet appears automatically, select Printers | Add Printer or click the Add button in the toolbar. Use the pop-up menu at the top of the dialog sheet to select USB. Now, you should see a list of any USB printers that are attached to your Mac.

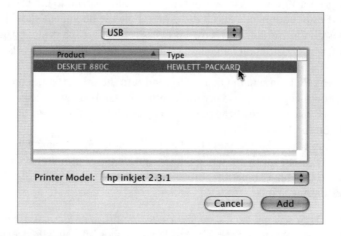

If a driver is detected for the printer, you'll see it listed in the Printer Model text box; if not, you can open the Printer Model menu and choose a manufacturer, then dig to find a specific driver. If you don't see a good match, you'll need to cancel this process, locate (on a disc or the Internet) or download a Mac OS X native driver, and install it so that it will show up in this list.

If the printer is recognized, simply select it in the sheet and click Add. Now you can close the printer list or quit the Printer Setup Utility.

NOTE   *Mac OS X has basic drivers for Canon, HP, Lexmark, Epson, and a few other brands of inkjets built in. For more features and better printing, you may need to check the manufacturer for an updated, full-function driver for your printer, depending on the model.*

Choose a Network Printer

If your printer is connected via Ethernet, either using a crossover cable or plugged directly into an Ethernet hub, or if the printer is connected to a network that you access via AirPort, setting up the printer is usually very simple.

In Mac OS X, you connect to the network printer in the Printer Setup Utility. Once launched, select Printers | Add Printer or click the Add button in the toolbar. In the dialog sheet, you'll need to choose the networking protocols that are used to reach the printer. You've got three choices:

- Choose AppleTalk from the pop-up menu if you're attempting to connect to an AppleTalk printer. (AppleTalk printers tend to be specifically designed to support Macs, but remember that the printer needs to be configured for AppleTalk; and the networking port that you're using—either Ethernet or AirPort—needs to have AppleTalk enabled in the Network pane of System Preferences.)

- Choose IP Printing if you're using an IP-capable Ethernet printer. This is becoming more common for small workgroups and home networks, particularly with non-PostScript laser printers and in cross-platform (Windows, Mac, Linux) settings.

- Choose Windows Printing if you want to connect to a laser printer that's been configured for a Microsoft Windows–based workgroup or home network.

AppleTalk

If you choose AppleTalk, your next step will be to select the printer and open the Printer Model menu if you'd like to choose a driver for the printer.

NOTE   *If you don't see your printer, you may need to launch the Network pane of System Preferences and turn on AppleTalk for the port—either Built-in Ethernet or AirPort—that you're using for the connection to this printer.*

IP Printing

If you choose to configure an IP-based printer, you'll need to know the IP address for the printer. (If you're not sure about this number, ask your system administrator or whoever set up the printer.) Enter it in the Line Printer's Address entry box, and then choose a PPD for the printer from the Printer Model pop-up menu. Click Add to add the printer.

Windows Printing

If you choose Windows Printing, you'll then choose a Workgroup from the second pop-up menu. (Sometimes you'll need to choose Network Neighborhood and then select a workgroup; other times you'll simply see the correct workgroup in the menu.) When you see the Windows PC that you'd like to connect to for the printer connection, select it and click Choose; now you'll see a dialog box that asks you to log into the computer. Enter a user name and password. Once you've logged in successfully, you'll see the printers that are available for sharing.

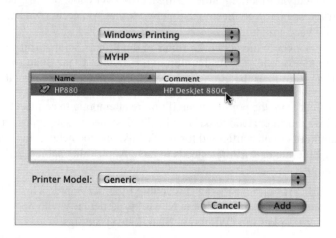

Select a printer and then select a driver for the printer from the Printer Model menu. When you've made that choice, click Add. The printer should be added to the list in your Printer Setup Utility.

If you have trouble accessing printers that are on a Windows network, you should launch the Directory Access applications in your Mac's Utilities folder (inside the Applications folder) and make sure SMB services have been activated.

Show Info

Once you have a printer in the printer list, you can still access vital info and change the driver software if necessary—simply select the printer in the list and click the Show Info button in the toolbar. The Info window appears. Using the menu at the top of the window, choose Printer Model to see a screen that allows you to change the current printer driver. You can also use the menu to access the Name & Location of the printer (which can help you get a sense of how it's configured if it's a remote printer), and you can access Installable Options, which is where you can determine, for some printers (particularly workgroup laser printers), what options will be made available in the Print dialog box.

When you're done in the Show Info window, click the Apply Changes button to put your changes into action. (You can click the close button at the top of the window if you want to exit without applying your changes.)

Print Stuff and Manage Print Jobs

Once you have your printer set up, you're ready to print. Before you send the page to the printer, though, you may want to check the options in Page Setup before printing, so that you know everything is set up correctly. Then, after you've invoked the Print command and sent the print job to the printer, it's passed to the print queue, which is responsible for managing your print jobs as they travel from your Mac to the printer. We'll look at all of those elements in this section.

Page Setup

When you've created a document and you're ready to print it, begin by choosing File | Page Setup. That brings up the Page Setup dialog sheet, shown in Figure 12-1.

You don't need to visit this dialog sheet every time you plan to print—only when you need to change a major option for your printer and sometimes when you've recently changed printers (while the application was open) and you need to make choices about the paper size and orientation of your document. But it's also where you set some important options. At the top of the sheet you'll find the Settings menu, where you'll choose, in most cases, Page Attributes, so that you can set up the printer and the paper size that you want to use for printing.

In the Format For menu, you'll choose the printer for which you want to make a setting change. (The Page Setup window gives you the ability to set up multiple printers, if you have them, because you can pick from among those printers the specific printer that you want to send jobs to in the Print dialog box.) In other words, this window is totally about configuration—it

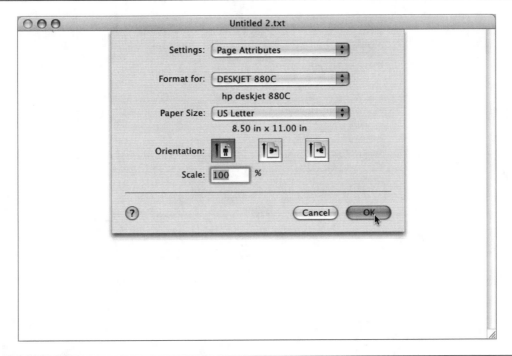

12

| FIGURE 12-1 | The Page Setup dialog sheet will be similar to this in most of your Mac OS X applications.

doesn't dictate which printer you're printing to, but just what type of paper and orientation will be used when you do opt to send a job to this printer.

Now you'll have some additional options in the dialog sheet to think about:

- **Page (or Paper) Size**   Choose what size paper the application should plan on printing to. (The default is 8.5 ×11-inch paper.)

- **Orientation**   Choose whether the document should be printed in Portrait mode (regular orientation on the page) or in Landscape mode (lengthwise, as with ledger sheets).

- **Scaling or Scale**   Enter a percentage if you'd like the document to be printed at anything other than 100 percent.

When you've finished making changes, click OK in the Page Setup dialog sheet.

Select Print

Once you've made your Page Setup choices, you're ready to print. In Mac OS X, the printer dialog sheets are fairly uniform from application to application. Some of them offer slightly different options and layouts, but most will look pretty similar to Figure 12-2. (The differences are usually pretty basic and mostly found in Microsoft products!)

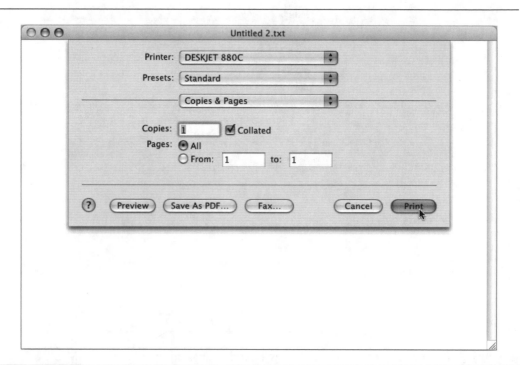

FIGURE 12-2   Mac OS X's standard Print dialog sheet

The Print dialog sheet tends to have three menus—a Printer menu, Presets menu, and an untitled menu that enables you to choose different options for a particular setting. In the Printer menu you select the printer to which you want to send the document you're about to print. Any printers that have been set up previously should work fine, although an exclamation point icon (!) next to a printer in the list tells you that there's currently an issue with that printer that needs to be resolved. To do that, you switch to the printer's queue window and see what the problem is. (More on the queue window in the next section.)

The Presets menu is used to quickly access stored settings, making it possible for you to store multiple sets of preferences and switch between them. Once you've got some settings defined, you can use this menu to quickly switch between stored presets:

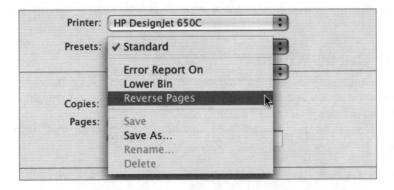

To create presets, you'll first change some settings (described next), then choose Save As from the Presets menu, and, in the dialog box that appears, give those settings a name. They're added to the menu (such as "Lower Bin" and "Reverse Pages" in the example) so they can be selected in the future.

It's in the untitled menu that you'll make most of your choices. Here's a look at some of those options:

- ■ **Copies & Pages**   Here you can enter the number of copies you want to print and choose the range of pages that you want printed. (Remember that the number is inclusive, so printing from page 2 to 4 will include both page 2 and page 4.)

- ■ **Print or Quality modes**   Many inkjet printers will enable you to choose different quality settings depending on how quickly you want to print and how laserlike in quality you want the final output.

- ■ **Color**   Choose whether or not you want a color document printed in color and whether you want a color matching system to be used.

- ■ **Application specific**   You'll often find a category of options that are specific to the application you're printing from, enabling you to make different decisions based on that application's document types and capabilities.

12

■ **Printer specific**   You'll find some categories that are special to your printer—anything from output pins and resolution settings to error handling and ColorSync. Some of those are common for PostScript printers, for instance. Some printers will have a menu called Printer Features or named for the printer. In any case, experiment with these if you need to perform some sort of printerly magic that your model makes possible.

When you're done making all of your printing selections, click Print. The job is sent to the printer and you've nothing left to do but monitor its progress and await the output.

In the System Preferences application choose Print & Fax and you can set certain options on the Printing tab, including whether you want a default printer to appear in the Print dialog box and whether you want to share your printer with others on a network.

The Printer Queue Window

In native Mac OS X applications, you can monitor current print jobs using the printer queue application. When you print a document, the printer queue window is automatically launched and its icon appears on the Dock. Select that icon and you'll see a window named for your printer. In that window, you'll see the status of current jobs, as well as the current job that's printing, shown at the top of the window.

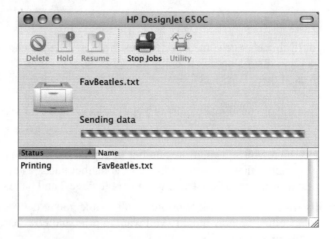

To hold a job (so that it drops out of the line and doesn't print, but stays in the queue), select it and click Hold; other jobs will continue printing. To release that particular document, select it again and click Resume. To delete a job (so that document won't print), select it and click Delete. To stop the entire queue, click Stop Jobs or choose Queue | Stop Queue from the menu; to start it again, click Start Jobs or select Queue | Start Queue.

You can't drag items around in the queue to rearrange them—unfortunately. You can, however, drag some types of documents to a printer queue window to add them to the list, as

How to ... **Create a PDF**

Mac OS X has the native capability to create a PDF (Portable Document Format) file from nearly any application. With a PDF, others can see not only the text of your document, but the images and formatting, even if they don't have the same application that you used to create the document. (Note that PDFs are for *viewing* documents; without special programs, your recipients won't be able to edit a PDF document.) You'll find that some programs have a Save As PDF command in the File menu; if not, you can still create a PDF from the Print dialog box. Choose File | Print in your application. In the Print dialog box, instead of choosing the Print button, choose the Save As PDF button. That brings up a Save dialog box where you can enter a name for the file and choose a location, then click Save. When you do, you've created a PDF that you can store, review, print, or send to colleagues or friends.

shown in Figure 12-3, and have them print without requiring that you first launch the application and choose Print. That can come in handy. (You can also drag items to the printer queue icon in the Dock or to a desktop printer icon, as discussed in the next sidebar.)

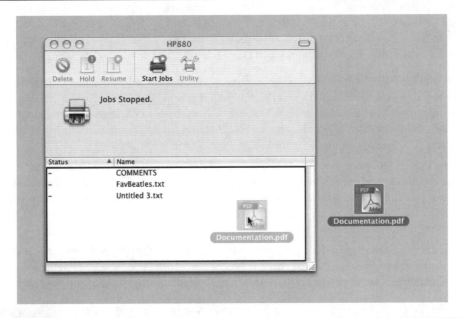

FIGURE 12-3   You can drag certain types of common text and image documents to add them directly to the print queue.

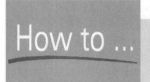

How to ... Create a Desktop Printer Icon

Want quick access to your printer(s)? You can add a desktop printer icon for any printer that's configured in the Printer Setup Utility. The desktop printer icon is basically an alias to your printer queue, but it enables you to launch it quickly and it can serve as a drag-and-drop target for items you'd like to print.

To create the desktop icon, open the Printer Setup Utility and display the printer list; now, click on a printer, hold down the button, and drag out to your Mac's desktop (or the Dock). Release the button and you've got an alias to your printer queue; you can double-click it to view activity in the queue at any time.

Understand and Add Fonts to Your Mac

A *font* is a collection of letters, numbers, and punctuation marks with a particular typeface, weight (bold or not bold), and size in plain or italic. However, the word "font" is also frequently used to mean a typeface with a particular design, such as Courier or Arial. I'll use the term font loosely.

When you select a font, the application passes that information to the Mac OS, which helps the application render that font. The font files serve two purposes. First, font files tell your printer how printed text should appear. Second, they tell your Mac how to display text on the screen.

Fonts can come in a number of different formats—Mac OS X is compatible with three types of fonts called PostScript, TrueType, and OpenType. Each has its uses and advantages:

- **PostScript** The original professional type of font, developed by Adobe, used to be somewhat more complicated to work with than it is now. PostScript fonts are designed for printing, not screen display, but Mac OS X has a built-in *rasterizer* that makes PostScript fonts display properly on screen. PostScript fonts come in Type 1 and Type 3 varieties—Type 1 is more compatible and Type 3 more sophisticated.

- **TrueType** Developed by Apple and Adobe, TrueType is the original all-in-one font that can be used both for screen display and for printing. TrueType makes *scalable* fonts (those that can appear at nearly any point size, like PostScript) available for consumers at a relatively low cost. TrueType fonts are still not as sophisticated as PostScript fonts, but they work well for day-to-day tasks.

- **OpenType** Developed jointly by Microsoft and Adobe, OpenType fonts are sort of a next-generation hybrid of TrueType and PostScript. OpenType fonts are useful for any application and are easy to work with—they're cross-platform, modern, and very capable.

These days, you can buy pretty much any font and it works well in Mac OS X. If you want cheap or free fonts online, they'll likely be TrueType. If you print to an older laser or proofing printer, you might want to stick with PostScript; if you're looking for the flexible and most modern standard, you can pick OpenType.

> **TIP** *OpenType fonts can contain either PostScript- or TrueType-style data. PostScript-based fonts have an .otf filename extension and TrueType-based fonts have a .ttf filename extension.*

Add Fonts

You can buy TrueType, OpenType, and PostScript fonts from computer stores or online font stores—any such fonts should work fine with your Mac. In Mac OS X, fonts can be stored in a number of different places. If you'd like to add fonts that everyone can use, copy the font files to the Fonts folder inside the main Library folder on your hard disk. If you'd like to install fonts for your own personal use, install them in the Fonts folder that's inside the Library folder inside your home folder. Ideally, Mac OS X applications are updated instantly with font changes, but in practice some applications may need to be restarted.

> **TIP** *If you work with Classic Mac applications (see the Appendix), you'll need to store imported fonts in the Fonts folder inside the System Folder that you use for your Classic environment. Fortunately, fonts in the Classic System Folder are also recognized and made available in native Mac OS X applications. So if you intend to use fonts (aside from bitmapped fonts, which aren't recognized in Mac OS X) in both environments, you can install them in the Mac OS 9 Fonts folder.*

Delete Fonts

To delete a font, just open the Fonts folder and drag the font to the Trash.

It's a good idea to think carefully before deleting a font file, because you can't always anticipate when an application or document might need that particular font. If you want to simply deactivate a font, drag it to a folder outside of the System Folder or the Library folder where it's been stored. (Create a "Disabled Fonts" folder on your hard disk, for instance.) Now that font won't appear in the Font menu of any of your applications. If you get error messages requiring the use of a disabled font, you can still drag the font back into the Fonts folder if it's needed.

Manage with Font Book

Mac OS X version 10.3 includes a new utility program, called Font Book, which can be used to manage your fonts (as well as to simply get to know them better). To launch Font Book, find it in the main Applications folder and double-click its icon. Figure 12-4 shows the Font Book window.

The first trick to Font Book is that it enables you to view a font quickly to get a sense of what it looks like. You can quickly click around and see which font you'd like to use in a document, for instance.

The second trick you can accomplish with Font Book is you can create collections of fonts. You'll see that Apple has started some already—Classic, Fixed Width, Fun, and so on. Those are

12

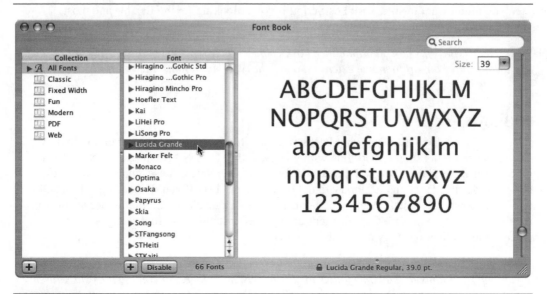

FIGURE 12-4   Font Book lets you see and manage groups of fonts.

collections of fonts that will appear in your Font panel when you're selecting fonts in your applications. (Choose Format | Font | Show Fonts in TextEdit, for instance, to see the Font panel.) These collections can be enabled and disabled to de-clutter your Font panel. To create a collection, simply click the plus (+) symbol at the bottom of the Collection column, then type a name for the collection. Now, drag fonts from the Font column to that collection name to add them. To remove fonts from a collection, select the collection and then highlight the font you want to remove. Press DELETE and the font is removed from the collection (it's still available as a font, however).

Thirdly, you can use Font Book to disable particular fonts. If you have a font that's giving you trouble or that you simply don't want to see in your applications for some reason (maybe just to cut down on clutter), select that font and choose Disable at the bottom of the Font column. Now the word "Off" appears next to the font. To reenable it, select the font and click the Enable button at the bottom of the Font column.

TIP   *Would you like it if disabling a collection also disabled the fonts in that collection? That's not how it works by default, but it can be handy for manipulating tons and tons of fonts. To make Font Book work that way, open Font Book | Preferences and turn on the option All Fonts in the Collection under the section Disabling a Collection Turns Off. Now it will work that way.*

Finally, you can use Font Book to install and remove fonts if you don't want to do it the manual way. With Font Book active, choose File | Add Fonts. An open dialog sheet appears—locate the font that you want to install and click Open. The font will be added to your Mac and made available for you to use with your applications.

NOTE *In Font Book Preferences you can change the default method that Font Book uses for adding fonts so that the fonts are available to Classic applications or for all users on your Mac. See Font Book | Preferences for the options. Also notice that you can turn on the preference Always Copy Font Files When Installing if you'd like Font Book to move the font files around on your Mac.*

When you're done with Font Book, choose Font Book | Quit to close it. Now your selections should be reflected in your applications' Font menus and Font panel interface.

Fax with Your Mac

Mac OS X 10.3 has the built-in ability to send a fax from your Mac's modem. To send a fax requires relatively little setup—you can send faxes straight from the Print dialog box in many applications. Receiving a fax is easy, too—it just requires a little setup time.

Send a Fax

To send a fax you'll use the Fax command in the Print dialog box. Here's how:

1. To send a document by fax, first make sure that you have a phone line plugged into your modem and that the phone line isn't already in use.

2. Now, in the application where you've created the document that you want to fax, choose File | Print.

3. In the Print dialog box, locate the Fax button and click it.

4. The dialog sheet will reconfigure and you'll have an interface that lets you make some decisions about the fax:

   ■ In the To section, enter the fax number to which you want to send the fax. You can also click the small icon that has a person's silhouette to open the Address Book and select someone that way, although you'll need to be careful and make sure that person has a fax number set up in Address Book.

   ■ On the Subject line, enter a subject for this fax.

   ■ Use the Dialing Prefix box to enter anything that needs to be dialed before the phone number you've entered.

   ■ If you'd like a cover page for your fax, click in the text entry box and type the cover sheet message; the Cover Page check box will be checked automatically.

12

5. Now, if necessary, you can choose some options from the unnamed pop-up menu. For instance, choose Modem and you can set some basic dialing preferences. Choose Scheduler and you can choose when you'd like the fax sent—immediately, at a particular time, or you can send it to its queue "on hold" so that it doesn't print until you specifically release the queue.

6. When you've made the necessary selections, click Fax. That sends the fax to the fax queue and launches the application called Internet Modem. A window pops up to show you the fax in progress.

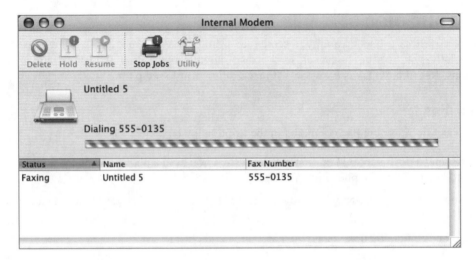

You should hear the modem dial and, if all goes well, a fax pick up on the other end, give its initial tone, and then the speaker will go silent as the fax is sent.

You'll notice that you can manage the Internal Modem window as if it were a printer—it's based on the same interface and concept, enabling you to delete, hold, resume, and stop jobs. When you're done with the Internal Modem window, choose Internal Modem | Quit to leave it.

Receive a Fax

To set up your Mac to receive faxes, first make sure the modem is connected to the phone line that you want to use. (A household line probably isn't the best solution unless it's a dedicated fax/modem line—otherwise your Mac will be picking up the phone when calls are incoming.)

Also, if your modem is turned off in the Network pane of System Preferences, you'll need to turn it back on. You do that by choosing Network Port Configurations from the Show menu and then placing a check mark in the On column next to the Internal Modem entry.

To set up the Mac to answer calls, launch System Preferences (Apple | System Preferences) and click the Print & Fax icon. Choose the Faxing tab at the top of that window. Now you'll see the options for receiving faxes (see Figure 12-5).

Turn on the option Receive Faxes on This Computer if that's what you want to do. Now, you can enter the fax number (which it reports to the caller when it's receiving and to the receiver when you're sending a fax) and choose the number of rings the Mac should wait before answering. You can also choose up to three options for received faxes: you can have them saved to a folder as a PDF file, e-mailed to a particular e-mail account, or printed on a default printer. Make your choices (place a check mark next to each) and then enter the required information—e-mail address, printer choices, and so on—so that each action can be completed.

That's it. Close System Preferences and your Mac is ready to receive faxes.

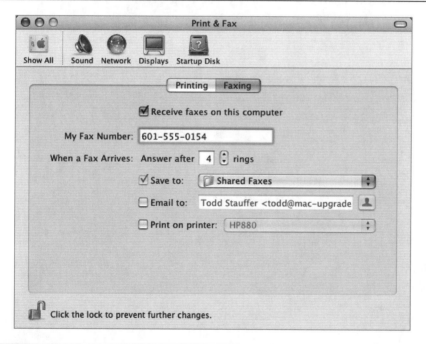

FIGURE 12-5   Options for receiving faxes

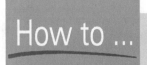 **Receive Faxes Online**

Don't have a free phone line for receiving faxes? eFax (**www.efax.com**) is a web-based service that enables you to receive faxes as e-mail attachments. When you sign up, the service assigns you a phone number, which you can give out to friends and colleagues or clients. (Often you'll pay a premium to get a phone number in your area code or a toll-free number.) When someone sends a fax to that number, the fax is turned into an image file and sent to you via e-mail. You can then double-click the image and view the fax in the special eFax viewer software that you download from the service. (You can also enable TIFF format in the eFax online preferences, which makes it possible to view your faxes in Preview or a similar graphics application.) It's a handy way to receive and manage faxes, as they're stored as digital files on your hard disk—you can place them in folders, rename them, and so on.

Chapter 13

Track Your Schedule and Contacts

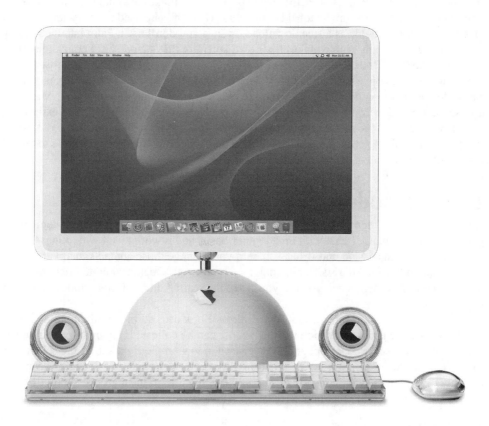

How to...

- Get to know Address Book
- Manage contacts
- Work with iCal
- Add appointments and notes
- Fill your To Do list
- Sync up with a Palm PDA or iPod
- Use iSync and .Mac together

In previous editions of this book I've covered Palm Desktop in this chapter—Palm Desktop is the software that PalmOne (**http://www.palm.com/**) makes available to Mac users for synchronizing data with Palm handheld computers. That software used to ship with new consumer Macs and is still available as a free download, even if you don't use a Palm handheld computer.

These days, though, Apple makes their own software that's largely the equivalent of Palm Desktop—Address Book and iCal. Those two applications can be used for a one-two punch of managing your contacts and managing your schedule, respectively. Then, if you do have a handheld computer, an iPod, or even a mobile phone that's compatible with your Mac, you can use Apple's iSync software to synchronize your contacts and schedule with that external device. Plus, if you've got .Mac service, you can use iSync for even more synchronizing duties, such as making your bookmarks available to you online and synchronizing your schedule to an online version of your calendar.

Get to Know Address Book

Address Book isn't a terribly complicated program, but it's handy for tracking people who you call, write, e-mail, or chat with on a regular basis, and it works well with other Apple applications—such as Mail and iChat—to help you manage those contacts in any number of contexts. To launch Address Book, click its icon on your Dock or double-click its icon in the Applications folder. When you do, you'll see the main Address Book window shown in Figure 13-1.

As with many Apple applications, the Address Book uses a Finder columns-like interface. On the left are the groups in which various people can be collected; the middle column shows individuals in the selected group, and the viewer window on the right shows the selected person's (or entity's, in the case of Apple) information. As you'll see later in this section, it can be handy not only to have all of your contacts organized here, but also to have groups set up that you can use for bulk e-mails and other neat tricks.

Add and Edit Contacts

The first thing you may want to do in Address Book is select your own entry and fix it up a bit. To update your own info, make sure All is selected as the Group, then select your name in the

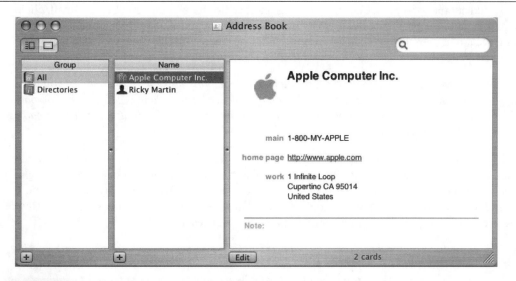

FIGURE 13-1   Here's the Address Book soon after its first launching.

Name list and you'll see, in the viewer window, the "card" that represents the information that Address Book knows about you so far. (In case you're wondering, it got your name from your Mac OS X user account entry.)

Edit a Card

To edit your (or any) card, click the Edit button. Now, you'll notice that the entries on that screen can be edited. Click in an entry and change it to whatever you need it to be. Likewise, notice that most of the entry labels can be changed. Click on "work" for instance, and you can change it to "home" or "main" or something else.

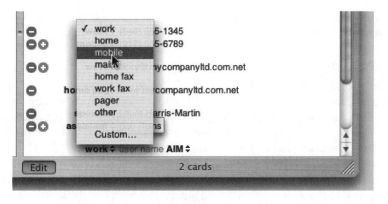

To add another of a particular item, such as another slot for a phone number or e-mail, click the plus symbol (+) that's on one of those lines. (For instance, on the last line of phone entries, you'll see a plus sign that you can click to add another phone entry line.) If you add a line you don't need, click the minus symbol (–) for that line and it's deleted.

TIP *You can decide that a card is for a particular company, instead of a person, if you like. Click the Company check box at the top of the card's screen and you'll see the company name change places with the individual name on the card. You'll also see the company's name in the Name column instead of the person's name.*

You've got some other options as well. If you don't see a field that you'd like to have for this card, choose Card | Add Field and then choose the field that interests you. For instance, you might want to add Job Title or Department for a corporate contact, or perhaps Birthday or Nickname for your friends. To customize the template for new cards once and for all, choose Address Book | Preferences, then click the Template button in the Preferences dialog box.

TIP *You can also customize the name of existing labels. If "Work" or "Home" isn't working for you, choose Custom from that label's pop-up menu. You'll see a dialog sheet that enables you to type in your own label. And, you can customize the format for phone entries by choosing Address Book | Preferences and clicking on the Phone button.*

And what about the image? It can be handy to have a picture for a person in your Address Book; and it can be doubly handy to have a picture of yourself (or an image that represents you), as this image is the one that's used by iChat AV and Mac OS X to represent you when necessary. To change the image, double-click in the image area next to your name. A window appears that you'll use to set the image. You have some choices:

- Drag an image file into that window.
- Click the Take Video Snapshot button to take a snapshot of yourself (or something else in the room) using your iSight camera or your digital camcorder, if it's recognized.
- Click the Choose button and use the Open dialog box to locate an appropriate image.

When you're done editing the card, click the Edit button again and you'll see that it no longer looks "pressed down"; the card is now in a viewing—instead of editing—mode.

Add a Card (or vCard)

When you're ready to add a new person to Address Book, you can do that by clicking the plus (+) icon that appears under the Name column in the main Address Book window; you can also add a person by choosing File | New Card. When you do that, you get a totally blank card to start customizing and filling in. When you're done, either choose to create a new card or click the Edit button to finish the current card and move on to other tasks.

Another way to add a card to your address book is to drag a vCard onto Address Book. *vCard* is a standard format for addresses, which many contact-management applications recognize, including Address Book. If you receive an e-mail attachment with a .vcf filename extension,

SarahRogers.vcf

that's likely a vCard. You can drag it onto the Address Book window and drop it pretty much any way you want to, and it will be added to the Address Book without requiring you to enter any information.

If you receive the card from a Mac user or if you have preferences set not to show filename extensions, you can be pretty sure that any item with the icon shown in the illustration is a vCard. Drag it to Address Book or choose File | Import | vCards in Address Book.

TIP *Using the menu command has an added advantage—it creates a new group called Last Import, which you can consult to see what addresses were added.*

NOTE *Address Book can also import contacts in LDIF (Lightweight Directory Interchange Format), which might be handy if you're transferring data from another contact application or database to Address Book. You may be able to export from that other application into either vCard or LDIF and then import in Address Book.*

One other easy way of adding people to your Address Book is worth pointing out. If you use Apple Mail for receiving e-mail, you'll find that you can pretty easily add the name of someone who has sent you e-mail to your Address Book. (You won't get much more than a name and e-mail address, but it's a start.) To do that, select the e-mail in Mail and choose Message | Add Sender to Address Book from Mail's menu, or press ⌘-Y. That adds a card for that person to your Address Book, although, as mentioned, it will be a little sparse.

TIP *The Address Book has some special AppleScript scripts that can be used to import addresses from some popular applications. Choose the AppleScript menu (it looks like a little curly scroll of paper between the Window and Help menus) and choose Import Addresses. You'll see a dialog box where you can choose the application from which you want to import, and then you'll be walked through the process by the script.*

Export Addresses

Address Book can help you create your own vCard, too—simply select your own entry in Address Book and choose File | Export as vCard, or drag your entry out of the Address Book to a Finder window or the desktop. Now you can send that vCard to anyone you would like to have your contact information. (You can also create vCards of other people's information and give them to people you know—colleagues, friends, coworkers—if you want to easily share information about people already in your Address Book.)

If you're interested in moving more than one vCard to another copy of Address Book, you can do that too: select multiple people in Address Book and choose File | Export vCards (note the slight change in the command). In the dialog box that appears, give the vCard a name, and Address Book creates a *single* vCard that includes all of those addresses. You can now send that group of addresses to whoever needs them—even if it's another computer of your own.

Create Groups

Groups are handy for sending e-mails to everyone at one time. In fact, Mail relies on Address Book if you plan to create a group that you want to be able to e-mail repeatedly. Creating groups is also handy just for making your Address Book a little easier to deal with. You can create groups for simply organizing and whittling down your cards when necessary—groups that separate family from friends or friends from business contacts and so on.

> **TIP** *Groups are also handy when it comes to synchronizing data with devices such as mobile phones, because iSync (discussed later in the chapter) allows you to limit the contacts you sync to certain groups.*

To create a new group, simply click the plus symbol beneath the Group column (you can also select File | New Group). A new group appears in the list, with the name highlighted so that you can begin typing to create the group. Once you've named it, you can populate that group by dragging names from the Name list to that group's name and dropping them there. (It's called "name dropping." Get it?)

Another way to create a group is to highlight a number of names in the Name list (remember that you can hold down the ⌘ key and click items to select noncontiguous items) and then choose File | New Group from Selection. Name the group, and that's it—you've got a group and it's already populated.

> **TIP** *Plan to send e-mail to one or more of your groups? If that's the case, you might find it handy to select the group and choose Edit | Edit Distribution List. That brings up a window that you can use to select the appropriate e-mail address for each person. You'll sometimes have more than one e-mail per person, so you may need to make some decisions about how they'll receive a group e-mail. You can do that by selecting an address for each person as appropriate. When you're done with the window, click OK.*

Use Your Contacts

So once you've got your contacts in Address Book, what do you do with them? The most obvious thing is to refer to them when you need to know someone's address and phone number. A handy way to get that information quickly is to use the search entry box at the top right of the window. As you begin to type the first few letters that you're searching for, the list dwindles in the Name column; eventually, you'll get down to a single entry.

One other handy addition is the Note field that appears on each person's card by default. If you'd like to use vCard to help you remember things about individuals you're keeping track of, you can do that using the Note field, which is active even when the card is not currently being edited. Simply click in the Note area of the screen and begin typing to make a note about that person.

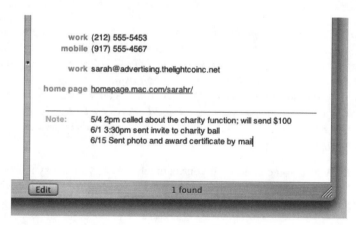

TIP   *Apple mentions in its Help pages for Address Book that the Note field is searched along with other fields, so, if you like, you can use it to add keywords that can be useful for searches. (For instance, if you were using Address Book to track sales leads, you might type the keyword* nails *to track people who buy nails from you, or* hammers *for people who buy hammers—something along those lines.)*

Aside from tracking the folks you know, Address Book is probably most handy for its integration with Apple Mail. Once you've got cards for all of the people you need to reach, you've taken a step to being a bit more organized and automated in Mail. When you're composing a message, you'll find that simply typing a few characters in the To field of a new message will bring up either that individual or even that group, if that's what you're typing.

You can also use the Address command on the composition window toolbar to add folks in an interesting way. The Addresses window shows you the various groups that you've created and gives you quick access to the people in your Address Book. You can highlight either an individual e-mail address or entire groups and click the To: or Cc: button to add those people to the message you're composing.

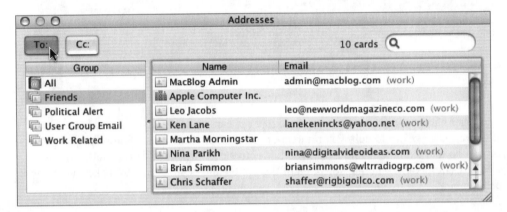

If you want to send a message to a group but you don't want all of the group members to see one another's e-mail addresses, you should add the group to the BCC line of your e-mail instead of To or CC. (You'll need at least one "To" recipient, but that can be yourself or someone else who has a public e-mail as far as the group is concerned.) Putting people's e-mail addresses on the BCC line is generally considered proper "netiquette" because it keeps everyone's e-mail address private. (This is particularly important for PR and business e-mail, but can apply to hobbyist and enthusiast group e-mails as well.)

So is there anything else you can do with your contacts? Well, you can synchronize them with either external hardware devices or via the .Mac service on the Web. We'll cover both of those later in the section about iSync.

Work with iCal

To complement Address Book, Apple ships iCal for free with every Mac as well. iCal is Apple's calendaring application, handy for managing events, appointments, projects, and To Do lists. iCal integrates with Address Book so that you can link people to particular events or appointments; it also works with .Mac or other Internet options to publish iCal calendars online.

What is perhaps most unique about iCal is that it take a multiple-calendar approach. Instead of just one calendar with all sorts of events in it, iCal encourages you to create multiple calendars and give them each a category. For instance, you might create a Work calendar and a Home calendar. (In fact, those are the first two defaults created for you.) If your work is more project oriented, like mine is, you might create calendars for each project so you can see how they overlap and what your scheduling responsibilities and conflicts are.

Other Mac users out there have taken it to another level, creating calendars for all sorts of interesting things like professional and college sports schedules, government and religious holidays, film festivals, music concert schedules and tours, episode calendars for TV shows. And the way iCal works, you can layer those calendars, or turn them on and off quickly, so you can check for conflicts or de-clutter your calendar, according to your mood or need (see Figure 13-2).

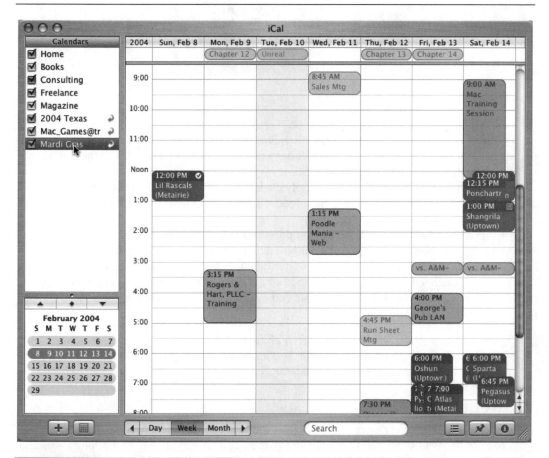

FIGURE 13-2   iCal can be used with multiple color-coded calendars that you can turn on and off to help visualize your schedule.

13

Create (and Customize) a Calendar

Actually the first thing you need to do might not be creating a new calendar, since two are created automatically—Home and Work. You can, however, customize those immediately if you like. Select one of them in the Calendars list and choose Window | Show Info or click the "i" icon that appears at the very bottom-right corner of the iCal window. When you do, you'll see the Info window, which is handy to have open for all kinds of things. Right now, with calendars, it allows you to change the name, the color that's assigned to this calendar (note the Custom option which you can use to broaden the palette), and you can add a description.

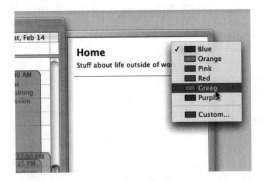

To create a new calendar, simply double-click the Calendar list and a new one appears—you can immediately begin typing to give that calendar a name. Then, head back over to the Info area to give it a description and choose a color.

To change the visibility of a calendar, simply click the check box next to its name in the Calendars list. If the check box is filled, the calendar's items are displayed; if the check box is empty, the calendar's items are not displayed.

To delete a calendar, select it in the list and press DELETE. You'll be asked if you're sure, which is a good question—deleting a calendar will delete all associated appointments, events, and To Do items. You'll want to be sure that's your intent before you delete an entire calendar. If you're sure, though, click Delete in the dialog box. The calendar disappears along with all of the aforementioned items associated with it. (If you need to, you can quickly select Edit | Undo to bring a calendar back from deletion.)

You can change the way you view the calendar by clicking the Day, Week, or Month button at the bottom of the window or by choosing from the View | Day View, View | Week View, or View | Month View commands.

Add Events

Events can be of two basic varieties in iCal—either they have a start and end time, or they're considered *all-day* events that don't really have a particular time assigned. Back in Figure 13-2, you can see both: regular events (more like appointments, really) appear in the middle of the calendar at their appointed times on the grid, while all-day events appear at the top of each day. In the Figure 13-2 example, those all-day events are mostly chapters (Chapter 12, Chapter 13) that I need to get written.

To create an event, you first want to select the calendar, in the Calendars list, to which this event will be assigned. Then, you can click on a general spot on the calendar (if it will be a time-assigned event) and choose File | New Event. The event will appear on the screen near the last place that you clicked with the pointer. Simply begin typing to give the event a description. Once you've described it, you can set its time more accurately by dragging the top bar of the appointment to a particular time, as well as by dragging the bottom edge of the appointment to give it the right length.

If you'd like to change the event to an all-day event, reveal the Info drawer (Window | Show Info or ⌘-I) and click the All-Day check box. That will send the event to the top of the calendar listing (in weekly or daily view).

> **TIP**   *You can double-click on the calendar to create an event at about the time where you're clicking; you can also double-click in the all-day event area at the top of a daily or weekly view to create an all-day event without accessing the Info drawer.*

The Info drawer is handy for a few other things. Aside from enabling you to select the exact time (and date) for a particular event, you can also use the Info drawer to set the status of an event, whether the event should repeat, and whether it should have an alarm. You can also choose which calendar it should belong to if it happened to have been created under the wrong calendar color. Let's look at some of these changes:

- ■ **Status**   Use the menu to choose from Tentative, Confirmed, Cancelled, or None for the status of this event.

- ■ **Repeat**   You can choose how often you'd like this event to repeat, or select Custom to display a dialog sheet that enables you to set your own schedule for the event.

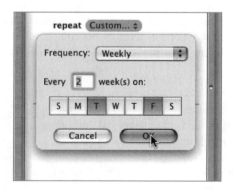

- ■ **Alarm**   Click the Alarm option and a menu appears. You have the option of having no alarm (none), a dialog-box message, a message with a sound, an e-mail sent to your main e-mail address, or you can have iCal automatically open a file. Make your selection from the menu and then make any other choice as prompted.

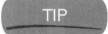

If you don't like the e-mail address that iCal is using, make sure the correct card is set as your personal card in Address Book. (You can select a card and choose Card | Make This My Card if the current selection is incorrect.) If the card is correct but the e-mail address is the wrong one (out of multiple addresses), choose Edit | Edit Distribution List and choose the correct e-mail account for your card.

You may have noticed that there's another entry in the Info drawer—the Attendees entry. You can add attendees to an event by dragging them from the Address Book application or the Show People window (Window | Show People) to a particular event. When you do, they're attached to the event and shown in the Info window. You can choose your attendees from the Attendees menu in the Info drawer, and when you click one of them, you get the option of removing or editing the attendee or sending him or her an e-mail. Or, click the Attendees label itself and you'll get the option of sending invitations to them. If you select Send Invitations, they're sent immediately and automatically. Those people can then reply to your invitation via their copy of iCal, and when their response is received, you can click it to find out if the invitation is accepted or not.

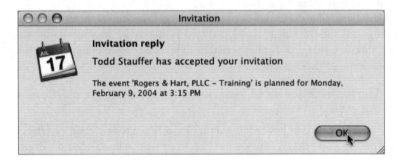

If you don't want to use the invite feature, you can still use your attendee listings to send e-mail to each, if desired. Just click on one of their names in the Info drawer and choose Send Mail from the menu. That will open a new message in Mail so you can write to them.

Add To Do's

Along with your events you can create and track To Do items, which are a bit simpler and not as focused on start and end times. To create a new To Do item, first choose the calendar you want it associated with, then choose File | New To Do or press ⌘-K. When you do, the To Do pane will appear and the new To Do item will be listed, ready for you to type a description.

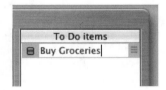

Once it's typed, you can click the three small lines next to the description to set a priority level—three darkened lines is top priority. The box to the left of the To Do item is the check box that you click when the item has been completed.

To go into a little more detail with your To Do item, you'll need to reopen the Info drawer if it's been closed: click the "i" icon at the bottom of the window. (Notice, right next to it, the push-pin icon, which is used to hide and display the To Do list.) In the Info drawer, you can use a menu to set the priority, you can choose a different calendar, and you can click the Due Date check box if you'd like to set a date for this To Do. If you do opt for a date, then you get the additional option of setting an alarm for the To Do item. The alarm options are the same as they are for events.

Publish and Subscribe to Calendars

If you have a calendar that you'd like to share with others, you can publish it on the Internet. The easiest way to do this is to publish it to your .Mac account. But that's not the only option— iCal can publish a calendar directly to a WebDAV-compatible web server. You can also export a calendar to an ICS file, which can be used with other applications or sent to others who have iCal. (To do this, choose the calendar, then choose File | Export. In the dialog box, give the calendar a name and click Export—the file is immediately exported in ICS format.)

Once an iCal is published, it's not just viewable; it can also be *subscribed* to by others, so that they actually see the calendar in their copy of iCal. On the flip side of that, you can subscribe to the calendars of others as well, including some that Apple links to and some others you'll find either on your friends' sites or on iCal-devoted web sites.

Publish a Calendar

This feature of publishing calendars is really something to think about, particularly for remote workers, nonprofits, and so on, as it's a great way to quickly make your schedule known to others. It can just plain be handy (even for parents to post for their kids to see and vice versa).

Publishing a calendar is really pretty easy to do—all you need to know is where you want to put the calendar. You have two choices: First, you can publish to .Mac space if you've subscribed to the .Mac service. Second, you can publish to a WebDAV server, which is a special type of web server that allows you to log in and transfer files over the Web's HTTP protocols. (With non-WebDAV servers, you have to log in using FTP protocols, which usually means using an FTP client application.) Here's how to make that all work:

1. Select the calendar in the Calendars list that you'd like to publish.

2. Choose Calendar | Publish.

13

3. In the dialog sheet that appears, enter a name for the calendar that will be used for the published version (you might want to elaborate a bit on the current name so others will understand its purpose).

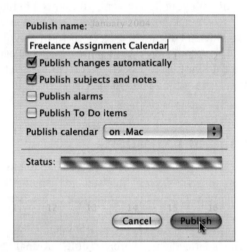

4. Then, you make changes using the check boxes, turning on or off the various options. Some of these, such as publishing changes automatically and publishing subjects and notes, will affect the appearance of the calendar online. Others, such as alarms, aren't published in the sense that they show up on the Web, but rather that they're part of the calendar that can be subscribed to.

5. Finally, choose your destination from the Publish Calendar menu. If you choose .Mac, iCal will automatically use the login information that you have set in the .Mac pane of System Preferences. If you choose WebDAV, you're asked to enter the URL of the server and the user name and password for accessing it.

TIP *You can use a program called iCal FTP (**www.drewfindley.com/findleydesigns/ products.html**) if you'd like to publish an iCal on a web site that doesn't support the WebDAV protocols.*

6. With all those settings made, click Publish.

If the publishing process is successful, you'll be told where you can visit your new online calendar, as well as what URL to access in order to subscribe to the calendar.

NOTE *When you're viewing a published calendar, you can choose the Preferences button on the page to make some decisions about how things will look on screen.*

Once you've published a calendar, you may want to tell people about it. Choose Calendar | Send Publish Email in iCal to launch Mail and automatically generate an e-mail that has the links necessary to access your published calendar. Personalize the e-mail, add some recipients, and send it off—they can now access your schedule at will, or even subscribe to it and see it in their own copy of iCal.

Need to "unpublish" a calendar that you no longer want on the Web? Highlight it in the Calendars list and choose Calendar | Unpublish. In the dialog box, choose Unpublish again if that's what you want to do.

Subscribe to Calendars

As mentioned earlier, subscribing to calendars can be a great way to keep up with what other iCal users are doing or a fun way to easily add entertaining items to your own iCal. In that second case, you'll find some public calendars you can subscribe to at places like Apple's **http://www.apple.com/ical/library/** or **http://icalshare.com/** on the Web. Access those places and you'll find links that you can click in your web browser to automatically subscribe iCal to those calendars.

If someone else has posted a calendar that you want to subscribe to, that's easy, too. If you know the URL (which starts with **webcal://**), you can choose Calendar | Subscribe and enter that URL in the dialog sheet that appears, along with some options regarding how it's updated and whether or not alarms and To Dos should be removed from the calendar.

The other way to subscribe to a calendar is to simply locate and click the Subscribe link that's posted on that calendar.

Click that link and the Add Calendar URL dialog sheet appears with the URL already entered for you. Make your choices and click Subscribe.

To unsubscribe from a calendar, choose it in the Calendars list and press the DELETE key.

Use iSync

I mentioned Palm Desktop at the start of this chapter—obviously one of its main reasons for being was its ability to synchronize data with Palm OS devices. It's still great for that, and it offers a more complete Personal Information Manager (PIM) solution than do iCal and Address Book. (Although Apple's tools are good, and they offer some features that Palm Desktop doesn't, they're designed for slightly different tasks.) Without some sort of syncing capability, it would be tough for iCal and Address Book to work as a replacement for a Palm Desktop for those who like the Palm—so, Apple offers iSync.

13

iSync actually does more than just synchronize data with a Palm OS device; it also synchronizes such data with an iPod and certain mobile phones via a cable connection or wireless Bluetooth technology. And, beyond all that, iSync will also synchronize data with Apple's .Mac server, giving you online access to contacts, calendars, and even browser bookmarks. It's kinda cool.

Sync with Hardware

Once you've got some data in Address Book and iCal, you're ready to launch iSync and explore your synchronization options—assuming you've got something to which you want to sync data. You can check Apple's site for compatibility (**http://www.apple.com/isync/devices.html**) to see if you have anything (or have a sudden need to buy anything) that qualifies.

Add Devices

If you've got a device that appears to be compatible, begin by connecting it to your Mac. In the case of devices that have USB or FireWire cables, that shouldn't be too hard—just plug them into the appropriate ports.

NOTE *If you have a Bluetooth device—and your Mac supports Bluetooth either out of the box or using a Bluetooth wireless adapter—you may first need to "pair" the device with your Mac. To do that, launch the Bluetooth Setup Assistant, which is found in the Utilities folder inside the main Applications folder, and follow the on-screen instructions. For more on Bluetooth and Macs, visit **www.apple.com/Bluetooth/** on Apple's web site.*

Once the device is plugged in, here's how you can add the device in iSync:

1. First, launch iSync, which is found in the Applications folder.
2. Then, choose Devices | Add Device in iSync.
3. In the Add Device dialog box, you'll see everything that you've plugged into your Mac that iSync recognizes. If you don't see the device you're looking for (and it's not a Palm OS device), click Scan.

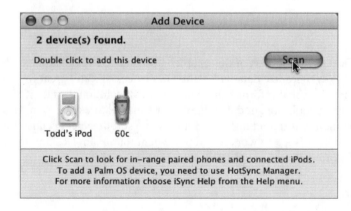

4. To add a device to iSync, double-click it in the Add Device window.

To remove a device, select it in iSync and choose Devices | Remove Device.

Palm OS devices are a little different. Before you can add them to iSync, you first have to download and install Palm Desktop (**http://www.apple.com/downloads/macosx/productivity_tools/palmdesktop.html**) and the iSync Palm Conduit, which, at the time of this writing, is linked from Apple's iSync download page (**http://www.apple.com/isync/download/**). With those two items installed and working, you can add a Palm OS device to iSync.

iSync Help can walk you through this installation, and—once everything is installed— launch Palm's HotSync Manager, then choose HotSync | Conduit Settings. In the dialog sheet, make sure Enable iSync for This Palm Device is active. If everything works as it should, the Palm device will appear immediately in iSync.

Sync with iSync

Once the device is added, you're free to begin synchronizing it with the data you've stored on your Mac in Address Book, iCal, and so on. First, you've got to decide what you need to sync. To do that, select an item in iSync and you'll see the options for that item appear in the window (see Figure 13-3).

Each device has slightly different options, but Figure 13-3 shows you the gist. You need to select the contact and calendar items that you'd like to synchronize with and make any other choices that are particular to the device. (My mobile phone, for instance, has an option to limit the number of events that are synchronized, since it doesn't have all that much built-in memory.) You also choose which direction the synchronizing goes in—whether items on the devices should be added to Address Book and/or iCal, for instance.

With those choices made, click the Sync Now button to begin the process. As items synchronize between your Mac and your devices, you'll see progress and activity in the iSync window.

13

When it's done, you'll get a report from iSync about any problems or failures. Read the error messages and see if you can make sense of them. Sometimes a particular contact entry in Address Book has bad data that won't work well with a particular device; sometimes you lose a connection for some reason, such as a loose cable, batteries that run down, and so on. Try to reset the device (or make any changes that seem warranted) and sync again.

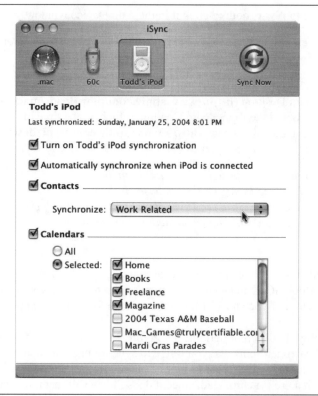

FIGURE 13-3   The iSync window lets you choose what to synchronize.

NOTE

During a sync operation, iSync will warn you whenever more than 5 percent of a database item has to change. The reason is to get you to make sure you want to proceed, just in case something is set incorrectly such that important data could be overwritten or otherwise lost.

Explore iSync and .Mac

iSync's other major synchronizing ability is with the .Mac subscription service. Using this feature, you can synchronize a number of things, including Address Book contacts, iCals, and your Safari bookmarks.

If you have a .Mac subscription and your information has been entered in the .Mac pane of System Preferences, you're ready to take iSync's .Mac capabilities for a spin. Here's how:

1. Click the .Mac button in iSync's window.

2. When the .Mac controls are revealed, you may find that you need to register before you can use the feature. Click the Register button.

3. Enter a name for this computer and click Continue. (.Mac may tell you that you need to choose another name if you've used that name previously with your .Mac account. Make your decision by clicking the appropriate button.)

4. Choose how to handle data in the For First Sync menu. If you're marrying all data from both locations, choose Merge Data on Computer and .Mac; if you're syncing one to the other, select the appropriate choice.

5. Click Sync Now. That will cause the first synchronizing operation to take place.

NOTE   *Don't see your contacts online? You may need to activate .Mac synchronizing from within the Address Book interface online in order to see your contacts. Sign into .Mac (**http://www.mac.com/**), click the Address Book icon, and then locate and click Preferences. See if you can locate your contacts.*

When synchronizing is done, you can access the .Mac controls in iSync to make further or future changes. Otherwise, you've got your data synchronized and it should be accessible from the Web. To get to it, log into **http://www.mac.com/** from any browser with your user name and password, then choose the items that you'd like to access from within the .Mac interface. You'll find buttons for your Address Book, bookmarks, and iCal among the other .Mac features (like HomePage and WebMail). Choosing Bookmarks, for instance, pops up your Safari bookmarks in a special window that you can use throughout your browser session to access your own bookmarks easily.

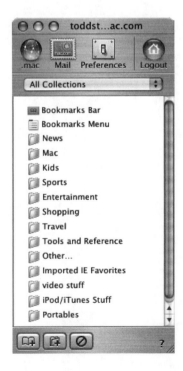

13

TIP   *Synchronizing your iCal calendars is not the same as publishing them—the point is that you can use .Mac to download those calendars to another Mac. If you want to access your calendars online, you should publish them from within iCal. Then, add their links as bookmarks in Safari. That will allow you to easily access them using your synchronized bookmarks via .Mac.*

Chapter 14

Leap into Digital Media with QuickTime and iTunes

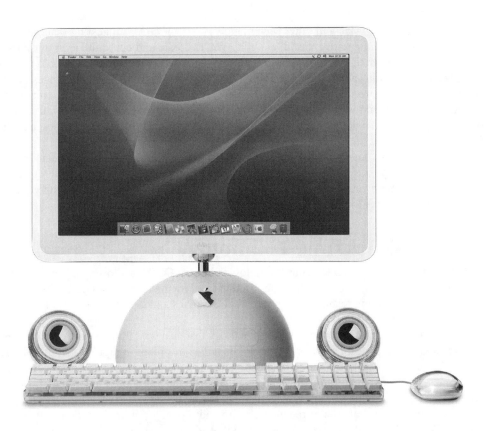

How to...

- Understand QuickTime
- View a QuickTime movie
- Use QuickTime on the Web
- Get to know iTunes
- Import and manage songs
- Buy songs online
- Create playlists and burn CDs
- Sync with iPod or MP3 Player
- Use your iPod as a hard disk

A pple markets the iMac and other Mac models as *digital hubs*, suggesting that they can be the center of your creative world, enabling you to create and edit quite a bit of digital audio and visual material. In this chapter, you'll be introduced to QuickTime, the technology behind the iMac's multimedia capabilities—the ability to integrate sound, video, and images. With both QuickTime and other technologies, you can play digital movies and movie clips, create, edit, and play digital sounds, and work with images to incorporate them more easily into your documents. In this chapter, you'll met the QuickTime Player, the iMac's image viewers, iTunes, and the DVD Player.

This chapter also covers one of Apple's main iApps—iTunes—which relies heavily on QuickTime's ability to work not only with video files, but with audio files as well. iTunes is used for importing and purchasing digital music files, which can then be played back on your Mac or synchronized with an iPod.

Understand QuickTime Technology

Just as your Mac requires underlying technologies in Mac OS X to allow it to print—you may have noticed that nearly every application offers almost identical Print dialog boxes—it also benefits from underlying technology to play digital movies and digital sound. That technology, developed by Apple, is QuickTime.

QuickTime is a rather advanced digital technology that, in a way, mimics an animation flipbook. It stores images in the form of ones and zeros, then displays them in rapid order, usually between 10 and 30 frames per second. (For comparison, a film is generally shown at 24 frames per second, while television is displayed at about 30 frames per second. Any more than about 10 frames per second gives a reasonable sensation of movement to the viewer.)

QuickTime is also capable of recording audio and layering it with the video so that it can be synchronized with the video or complementary to it. Audio can also stand alone within a QuickTime "movie" file, then be played back at any time using the QuickTime Player application or many others that support QuickTime technology.

NOTE   *QuickTime is also a translation technology. Built into it is the ability to translate between different audio, video, and image file formats. Different applications and computer platforms (like those from Microsoft, Sun Microsystems, Silicon Graphics, and other computing companies) save files in different formats. QuickTime, and applications that take advantage of QuickTime, offer the ability to translate to and from Macintosh file formats. In that way, it's easy to play or display nearly any movie, sound, or image file you find on the Internet or elsewhere.*

Want QuickTime to do more? It can. QuickTime Streaming is a technology that makes it possible to view QuickTime movies as they are transferred over a network connection—generally, this is done over the Internet. In most cases, you'll open a movie document stored on your iMac's hard drive. With streaming, it's possible to view a movie as it arrives, instantaneously, over long distances. This has many applications, not the least of which is the possibility that you can watch live events via *webcasts* or "narrowcasts." This can be a very interesting technology, especially if the event wouldn't otherwise be broadcast for television.

Finally, QuickTime is multimedia. You've probably heard that catchphrase before and wondered why it's significant. *Multimedia* is defined as the bringing together of many different media—audio, video, still imagery, text, virtual reality—to communicate ideas, educate, or entertain. Obviously, QuickTime fits the bill quite nicely.

QuickTime technology is built into Mac OS X. The manifestation of QuickTime on your Mac is the QuickTime pane of System Preferences and the QuickTime Player application that is, by default, in the Dock on your Mac and located in the main Applications folder.

At the time of writing, the latest version of QuickTime is QuickTime 6.5. If you have an earlier Mac model, you'll find it's always a good idea to keep up with the latest version of QuickTime, as each version tends to add both capabilities and efficiencies. You can download QuickTime from **http://www.apple.com/quicktime/**, or you can use the Apple | Software Update command to download and install new versions of QuickTime when they come out.

NOTE   *Plan to work a lot with movies and multimedia? Then I recommend you upgrade to QuickTime Pro. To get QuickTime Pro, you must register with Apple and pay a small fee (about $30 at the time of this writing) via the QuickTime web site. In exchange, you'll get a registration code that, when entered, upgrades the capabilities of the QuickTime Player and the QuickTime web browser plug-in.*

14

Use the QuickTime Player Application

If you have a QuickTime movie that you've downloaded over the Internet or copied from a CD-ROM, you can double-click it to launch the movie file. When you do, most likely the QuickTime Player application will launch (see Figure 14-1).

The QuickTime Player offers controls that look a lot like a cassette recorder's or a VCR's controls. When you have a digital movie file loaded, you'll find Play, Stop, and Fast Forward buttons. You'll also find a slider bar that shows the progress of the movie as it's playing. Grab the playhead on that slider and drag it back, and you can play part or all of your movie again. You'll

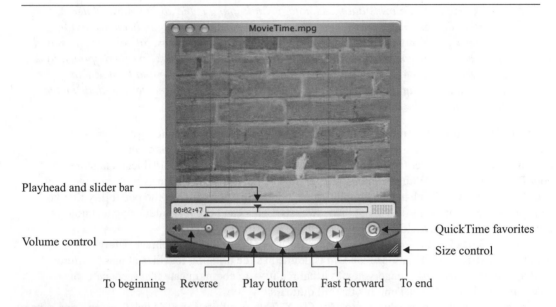

Playhead and slider bar

Volume control

To beginning   Reverse   Play button   Fast Forward   To end

QuickTime favorites

Size control

FIGURE 14-1   The QuickTime Player interface is a little like a VCR, but with a bunch of other features.

also find you have control over the volume by dragging the little volume slider back and forth with the mouse.

Select the Movie menu (from the menu bar) and you can choose the size at which your movie will display. Movies generally open at their optimum size for quality viewing. If you'd like to see the movie a little larger, you can choose Movie | Double Size. The quality of the video won't be as good (it will most likely appear more "pixelated" or jagged), but it will be larger. The farther back you sit from your monitor, the better it will look.

You can also get some information about the movie—choose Movie | Get Movie Properties to see the Properties window. Here, you can find out about the different audio and video tracks in the movie and view other relevant information.

NOTE   *A QuickTime movie can have three kinds of tracks: video, audio, and text. Each track is a separate line of data in the movie document that is synchronized with the others. The digital data stored in the video and audio tracks is compressed because video and audio, without compression, require huge amounts of storage. These compression schemes are called codecs, which stands for "compressor/decompressor." The better the codecs, the better the quality of a QuickTime movie file and the smaller and more transportable the movie will be.*

The QuickTime Player has some video and sound controls, as well, that are hidden by default. Select Movie | Show Video Controls to see controls for Brightness, Color, Tint, and

Contrast; choose Movie | Hide Video Controls when you're done. For audio, select Movie | Show Sound Controls to change the balance, bass, and treble settings for QuickTime playback.

View a Streaming Movie

A streaming movie is one that is displayed in your QuickTime Viewer (or your web browser) as it is transmitted over the Internet. The most common way is to locate a streaming QuickTime *feed* somewhere on the Web using your browser application. You'll click a link or a button on a web page that begins the streaming movie. When you do that, your QuickTime Player is often automatically launched (or switched to, if it's already running) and the streaming movie appears. You might see indications of the streaming process before the movie actually starts—QuickTime Player gives you messages to show what's happening, like "Connecting," "Negotiating," and "Buffering." Those are all indications that your streaming movie is being loaded over the Internet and preparing to play.

Your streaming movie experience may be a little different from playing a regular movie from your hard disk or from a CD. First, you'll probably notice that your streaming movie is lower quality than a typical QuickTime movie you play from your hard disk or a CD-ROM. Why is that? Because the data has to be sent in real time over the Internet. *Real time* means it's played almost as it arrives, to give you a seamless viewing experience. Good-quality QuickTime movies need a lot of data to flash up a pretty picture 15 to 30 times per second, and many Internet connections can't handle that sort of demand. So, picture size and quality are compromised in order to allow you to see *something* in your QuickTime Player. The slower your Internet connection (and the slower the Internet server computer that's sending the movie data), the worse the picture quality. That's one good reason to get a cable modem or special DSL access! (See Chapter 22 for more on high-speed access.)

The second thing that's a little weird about streaming video is the way fast forward and rewind work. Usually, a QuickTime movie played from a regular hard disk, CD, or DVD allows you to flip through each frame or use the Fast Forward/Rewind buttons to shuttle through the movie just like a VCR does. With a streaming movie, though, things don't work that way. You can often go to a different section of a streaming movie, but you generally do this by moving the slider bar in the QuickTime Player. Then, the connection has to be renegotiated (you'll see those messages again) before the movie can begin playing in its new spot.

If the streaming movie you're watching is a live event or live broadcast, then you obviously can't fast forward or move to a later part of the movie, since it hasn't happened yet! (For that matter, you often can't rewind, either.) With live broadcasts you also generally can't pause the movie and return to the same spot—when you click Play again, you'll see the connection negotiated and you'll start at the current spot in the live broadcast. In other streaming movies, you can pause and play again at the same spot.

Use the QuickTime Web Browser Plug-In

Along with the QuickTime Player comes the QuickTime plug-in, an addition to web browsers that allows them to display QuickTime movies directly within the browser's document window. You'll notice that the controls are pretty much the same whether you're viewing a movie with

14

QuickTime Player (playing from your hard disk) or with a web browser (playing across the Internet).

Volume → Play/Pause   Slider and playhead   Options   Forward   Reverse

QuickTime movies must be embedded in the web page for them to appear in the browser; otherwise, they're downloaded to your iMac first, and you view them in the QuickTime Player. If they're embedded in the page with special HTML codes, the movie, QuickTime VR, or QuickTime audio movie plays from within the browser screen itself. This works great for streaming QuickTime, which allows you to watch a movie *while* it is being transmitted over the Internet.

 *If QuickTime movies aren't displaying correctly, the QuickTime plug-in may not be in the right place. In Mac OS X, it should be stored in the Internet Plug-ins folder inside the main Library folder on your hard disk.*

 *If you've upgraded to QuickTime Pro, you'll be given a few other options with the plug-in, including the ability to save movies directly from web pages. Click and hold the mouse button on an embedded QuickTime movie (or CONTROL-click the movie) and a pop-up menu appears. Choose Save as QuickTime Movie to save the movie to your iMac's hard drive. Then you're free to view it in the QuickTime Player.*

Manage and Play Your Digital Music with iTunes

iTunes is a great little application that enables you to work with CDs and digital audio files, including those in the AAC (Advanced Audio Codec) and MPEG-3 (*MP3*, or Motion Picture Experts Group Level 3). These digital audio files are special high-quality music files that are generally only a few megabytes in size, meaning they can be easily transported over the Internet. They're small, but when they're played back, they sound close to CD quality. (That's what all the Napster hype was about a little while back.)

With iTunes, you can turn CD audio into digital audio files and store that music on your hard disk. And, you can create your own playlists, then use those playlists to burn CDs using the built-in CD-RW (or DVD-RW) drive that many Macs feature.

On new Macs, you'll find iTunes in the main Applications folder for the Mac OS X version. (In fact, you should see it on your Dock for quick launching.) If you don't have iTunes, it's a free download from **http://www.apple.com/itunes/** on the Web. When iTunes is launched, you'll see the main interface, shown in Figure 14-2.

NOTE   *The first time you launch iTunes, you'll be greeted by the iTunes Setup Assistant. After you've answered the assistant's questions, you'll see the main iTunes screen.*

On some Mac models, you'll immediately be greeted by a list of songs—these are songs that Apple has preloaded on your Mac for you. To play one of the songs, select it in the list and click

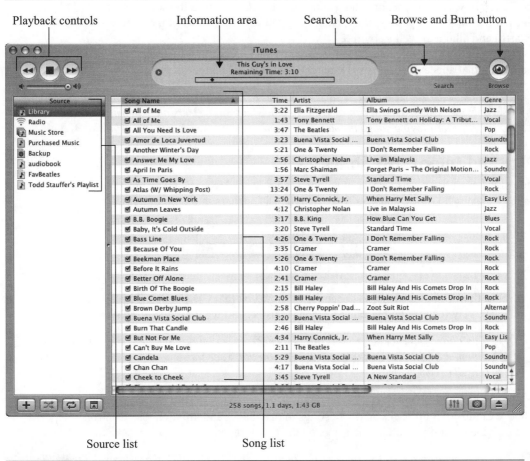

FIGURE 14-2   The iTunes interface

the Play button in the top-left corner of the iTunes window; it becomes a Stop button you can click to stop playback. The small slider bar underneath the Play button can be used to adjust volume. The Forward and Reverse buttons can be used to move between songs, while the small slider in the information area can be used to move around within a song.

 *iTunes has a special feature, called the Visualizer, which can be fun to watch while you're playing back songs. Click the eight-sided star button in the bottom right of the iTunes window, or select Visualizer | Turn Visualizer On to see this effect in action. Also, if you see the option, try Visualizer | Full Screen.*

If you look at the Source list, you'll notice that you're seeing the Library; the Library is where all your songs are stored in iTunes. To search for songs in the Library, you can begin typing in the Search box; as you type, matching songs and artists appear in the song list. If you'd like to take a different look at your Library, click the Browse button. Now you can peruse your songs by artist and album as well as by title.

Need to delete a song? Select it in the Library and press DELETE or choose Edit | Clear. In the dialog box that appears, click Yes if you really want to delete the song.

 *Click the maximize button in the iTunes window and it turns into a tiny controller that shows only the basic playback controls, the volume slider, and a truncated information window— perfect for playing songs in the background while you work, study, or surf the Web.*

Play and Import CD Songs

One of the most basic reasons you'll launch iTunes is to play audio CDs. Insert an audio CD in your Mac, launch iTunes, and you'll see that the CD appears in the Source list.

Select the CD and the song list changes to show you that CD's songs. To play a song, select it and click Play (or just double-click the song), just as you would with a digital music file.

 *If you have Internet access, iTunes can check a special database for the names of your commercial CDs and the songs on it. If you don't see those names, choose Advanced | Get CD Track Names.*

As with a home CD player, you can opt to have the songs shuffle or repeat during playback. Choose Controls | Shuffle if you'd like songs to play back randomly; choose Controls | Repeat One or Repeat All if you'd like the songs on the CD to repeat.

 *You can drag the CD's songs around in the song list if you'd like to hear the tracks in a particular order.*

The real power of iTunes, however, is the fact that it lets you import songs from your CDs into the iTunes Library. The process of importing songs turns them into AAC files (by default), which can then be played back directly off your Mac's hard disk without the CD. As you'll see, you can then place the songs on a playlist (for custom mixes of your favorite songs), and, if desired, you can burn those songs onto a recordable CD, if you have a compatible CD-RW drive. You can also sync those songs with your iPod and take them with you.

To import a song from a CD, insert the CD in your Mac's CD drive. Now, when the CD appears in the Source list, select it. Next, to import a single song, drag the song you want to import from the song list to the Library icon in the Source list. The song will be imported. You'll see a small orange icon appear next to the track number of the CD song, and "Importing" will appear in the information area. (iTunes imports songs more quickly than it plays them, so you'll see the import process end before the song stops playing.)

To import all the songs on that CD, simply click the Import button in the top-right corner of the iTunes window.

All of the songs on that CD will be imported. When it's done, you can switch back to the Library by selecting it in the Source list. The songs from the CD have been added to your song library; they can be selected and played at any time, regardless of whether the CD is in your iMac's drive.

Want to eject the CD? You can press the EJECT key on the keyboard (if you have one), press ⌘-E, or choose Controls | Eject CD.

You can change the type of music file that's created when you import songs from CDs. Choose iTunes | Preferences, and then click Importing. In the Import Using menu, choose the encoder you would like to use—AAC offers the best quality, but MP3 is more compatible with third-party external players. AIFF and WAV are best for use with audio editing applications. (And they create large files.) Note that you can also use the Setting menu on the Importing screen to change the quality level of the audio you're recording.

TIP   *The command Advanced | Convert Selection is based on this preference setting. If you'd like to change a group of songs that are already encoded as AAC to MP3 (for instance), first change the encoder preference, then highlight the songs and choose Advanced | Convert Selection to MP3. Note that you can't convert every song; some AAC songs are protected, including those that are downloaded from the iTunes Music Store, and they can't be reencoded in this way.*

14

Buy Songs from the iTunes Store

The big news in the last little while with iTunes has been the addition of the iTunes Music Store, which allows you to use the iTunes interface to dig into iTunes Music Store and buy individual songs, currently for 99 cents per song—entire albums are also available at reasonable prices. You can also buy audio books from iTunes Music Store. When you make your purchase, you'll have an audio file downloaded to your Mac in the form of a protected AAC file. There are some rules to exactly how that file works (we'll cover those), but it's pretty straightforward.

To jump in and begin browsing in the iTunes Music Store, click the Music Store listing in the Source list. If you've got Internet access, the iTunes window will reconfigure itself—it will actually look a little more like a web browser window—and you'll be viewing the iTunes Music Store. Click around to explore within the store, or enter a keyword (artist, song title, album, or a partial version of any of those) in the Search Music Store entry box and press RETURN. When you do, you'll get a list of results (see Figure 14-3).

FIGURE 14-3   Here's a list of songs that result from a search.

One of the cool things about the iTunes Music Store is that you can listen to a little of any song that you want to, whether you plan to buy or not. Of course, the store limits it to 30 seconds to entice you to buy the songs that seem interesting, but it's still a diverting way to spend some time. To listen to a song, you'll usually double-click it in a list or use the player controls in the top left to play the songs, control the volume, and so on.

In listings of search results you'll see small arrow icons that can be used to change what you're looking at. In a list of song titles, you can click an arrow next to an artist's name to see all of the songs by that artist, or click the arrow next to an album's name to see all of the songs on that album.

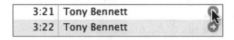

You'll get used to browsing around and checking out the features of the store. In fact, you should try clicking the Browse button that's up in the top-right corner near the search entry box. When you do, the interface reconfigures again to enable you to move very quickly through the various genres, albums, and artists that iTunes Music Store has to offer. Also, you should notice the arrow controls that appear at the top of the listing portion of the iTunes Music Store screen. They look just like the buttons on a web browser, and they have similar functions of going forward a screen, back one or more screens, or to "home."

But once you've done some browsing, the burning question becomes—how do you buy a song? To buy a song successfully, you'll need either an Apple ID or an AOL account. If you don't have one of those, you'll need to register for an Apple ID. In any of those cases, you'll start by clicking the Sign In button near the top right of the interface. When you do, you'll see a dialog box that lets you sign in.

14

If you have an AOL account, choose the radio button next to the AOL logo and enter your screen name and password in the entry boxes; if you succeed, you'll use your AOL billing information for the iTunes transactions. If you have an Apple ID (which can include a .Mac account), you can click the radio button next to the Apple logo and enter the ID and password in the entry boxes. If you don't yet have an account, click the Create New Account button and you'll be walked through the process.

Once you've logged in, you're ready to buy songs. On any listing screen in the iTunes Music Store you should see the button Buy Now next to a song. (On an album screen you'll see Buy Album, and if you're viewing AudioBooks, you'll see a link that says Buy Book.) When you click that link, one of two things happens. If you're signed in, you'll see a dialog box that confirms that you want to make the purchase, and then the song is downloaded immediately. (You can even put a check mark in that box to keep from seeing the confirmation message in the future.) You'll see the song downloading in the information area at the top of the screen.

If you aren't signed in when you click the Buy Song (or similar) button, you'll see the login window first. Then, after a successful login, you'll see the confirmation window, and if you click Buy, the song will be downloaded.

Songs that you buy are automatically added not just to your Library, but also to a special playlist called Purchased Music, which you can look at to see the songs that you've bought recently.

Have a problem with a download? If your Internet connection cuts out or you don't seem to get an entire song, relaunch iTunes (if necessary) and choose Advanced | Check for Purchased Music. That gets your copy of iTunes to check with the iTunes Music Store to see if there's a download-in-progress that needs to be completed.

Manage Songs and Burn CDs

I've mentioned playlists a few times without really defining them: a *playlist* is simply an arrangement of the songs that are in your Library. You drag songs from the Library to a playlist, arrange them, and the songs are played in that order. Playlists can be created and deleted at any time without affecting the songs on the playlist—the digital music files aren't deleted when you delete a playlist, and they aren't duplicated when you create more than one playlist. They're always there, safe in the Library, until you decide to delete them from the Library itself.

To create a playlist, choose File | New Playlist or click the plus symbol (+) button at the bottom of the Source list. Now, type a name for the playlist and press RETURN. (If you need to rename the playlist, it works just like a list item in the Finder: click once on the name and wait a second, then you'll be able to type a new name.) To add songs to the playlist, simply switch back to the Library and drag songs to that playlist's entry in the Source list.

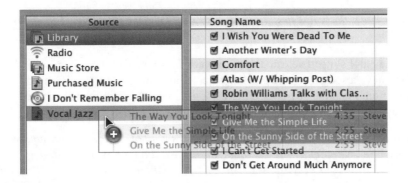

iTunes AAC Rules

Did you know?

When you buy and download a protected AAC song, there are a few things you should know about it. It doesn't work exactly like a song that you've imported from a CD. Here are a few of the differences:

- A protected AAC can only be played on a Mac that has been authorized to play songs that are associated with your Apple ID or AOL account. You can authorize up to three copies of iTunes to play songs using your ID. (You're asked to authorize when you attempt to play the song on that computer.) It's also important to *deauthorize* a computer (Advanced | Deauthorize Computer) when you're no longer going to use it or allow it to play your songs; otherwise, you'll cut down on the computers you can use with your purchased songs. (You should also deauthorize a computer before you sell it, or format its hard disk.)

- You can share your protected AAC songs (on a local network), but only if the computer that is sharing the song is authorized to play songs in your account. Otherwise, they get skipped over.

- A protected AAC can be burned to a CD, but you must change the order or make-up of the playlist that you use for that CD at least once every ten burns.

- You can't translate a protected AAC song to another format from within iTunes.

- You can sync a protected AAC song to your iPod, but like any song on your iPod, you can't copy it from your iPod to other copies of iTunes.

- You can usually tell a protected song from an unprotected one based on its filename extension—the .m4p extension is a protected AAC song, and .m4a is an unprotected AAC song.

14

SHORTCUT *You can select the songs first, in the Library, and choose File | New Playlist from Selection.*

Now, with the playlist itself selected, you can pick up songs and drag them around to change their order; to remove a song from the playlist, select it and press DELETE. (It isn't deleted from the Library, just from the playlist.) To add more songs, switch back to the Library and drag more songs to the playlist.

TIP *iTunes has a feature called Smart Playlist that's kind of cool to play around with. Choose File | New Smart Playlist and you'll see a dialog box. In the dialog box you can create rules for your playlist—rules like letters that the name of the artist contains, the size of songs, the genre of songs, and all types of criteria. When you click OK, the playlist is created and automatically populated with songs in your Library that match its criteria. You can then use those playlists to be a little more clever and varied than the playlists you simply create and drag files to.*

You'll notice that the number of songs and the amount of time those songs take up is shown at the bottom of the iTunes window when you're viewing a playlist. This is to help you if you plan to burn a CD using this playlist. Once you have all of the songs on the playlist you want to burn to CD (and the total length doesn't exceed the rated length of the CD-R, which is usually 74 minutes), you're ready to burn.

NOTE *Actually, total length can exceed the CD, if you like, but only the songs that fit will be burned onto the CD.*

Burning a CD in iTunes requires either an internal Apple CD-RW drive or a compatible third-party drive that's supported by iTunes. (See **http://www.apple.com/itunes/burn.html** for a list of compatible CD-RW drives.) If you've got that, and you've created your playlist, here's how to create the CD:

1. Select the playlist you want to use for your CD.

2. Click the Burn CD button in the top-right corner of the iTunes window. (You'll only be able to select it if a playlist has been chosen; otherwise, it's protected by a little "metal shield.")

3. You'll be prompted to insert a blank CD-R disc. Do so. (Remember that CD-R discs tend to be a little more reliable than CD-RW discs if you plan to play your CD in standard CD audio players.)

4. When iTunes has recognized the disc, you'll see "Click Burn CD to Start" in the information window, along with the number of tracks and the total time for the disc. If it all looks good, click Burn CD. (iTunes doesn't warn you if the total time for your playlist is longer than your CD can support, so do the math yourself before clicking the Burn CD button.)

NOTE *If you wait more than 30 seconds before clicking Burn CD, the Mac will eject the CD and you'll need to reinsert it.*

Now, iTunes will step through the process of burning the CD. Depending on the speed of your CD-RW mechanism, this could take quite a while—somewhere between 5 and 15 minutes. Ideally, you don't want to do much else with your Mac while the burn is taking place, just to be on the safe side and avoid a circumstance where another application slows down the Mac and causes a problem with the CD writing process. In practice, though, checking your e-mail or writing a letter shouldn't interrupt iTunes in Mac OS X.

When iTunes is finished, you should see the new CD there in the Source list, with the same name as the playlist you used to create it. Now you can play the songs directly off the CD, if desired, or you can eject the CD and take it with you to play in other CD audio equipment.

TIP *Choose iTunes | Preferences and click Burning, and, on the Burning screen, you can choose different disc formats. An MP3 CD can be used in consumer CD (and DVD) players that recognize MP3 songs. That lets you cram a lot more songs on a single CD, but it ignores AAC and other song types. A data CD or DVD can be used for backing up your songs or transporting them to another computer for playback. Make those choices and close Preferences; the next time you burn a CD, you'll do so using the new disc format type you've selected.*

Sync with an iPod

Another reason that iTunes has become the center of the universe for many Mac users is its role in managing the songs on an iPod. The iPod is Apple's portable digital music player—actually it's a small hard disk wrapped in an attractive case, complete with an interesting interface to help you play back the songs. When you plug your iPod into your Mac using a FireWire cable or a special dock, you automatically launch iTunes (or switch to it) and the iPod appears in the Source list.

By default, iTunes is set up to synchronize all of the songs in your iTunes Library and place them on the iPod. Most iPods are at least 4GB in size (that's the iPod mini) and on up to 40GB in size. So, generally it won't get filled up. But, if it does, it defaults to its second-level behavior—it switches into a manual mode that allows you to simply drag-and-drop songs on the iPod. (In manual mode you can also remove songs from the iPod by selecting them and pressing the DELETE key. They're removed from the iPod but not from your Library, assuming the song is still in your Library.)

iTunes doesn't just transfer your Library to the iPod; it transfers any playlists that you create as well. And, on the iPod's small interface screen, you can select from those playlists and play

14

only the songs on them, which is handy when you only want to play certain songs. (Maybe you have certain playlists for the morning commute that are different from the songs you listen to on your walks around the neighborhood or down at the local gym.)

NOTE *The transfer works in one direction only. The iPod won't let you synchronize music from the iPod to iTunes. This is a precaution designed to keep iPod users from pirating music, with the idea being to prevent you from moving music from one machine to another via the iPod.*

If you don't like the automatic updating approach, click the small iPod button that appears at the bottom right of the iTunes window and you'll see the iPod Preferences screen. You can choose from three modes—automatic, manual, and an interim mode that only updates certain playlists. That way you can more closely control what gets updated to your iPod, but you don't have to manually drag each and every song.

When you're ready to disconnect your iPod, you can simply unplug it or remove it from its dock once it's been automatically synchronized. If you're in manual mode, select the iPod in the Source list and click the Eject iPod button, which is in the bottom-right corner of the iTunes window. Once it's ejected, you can unplug it or remove it from its dock.

TIP *Manual mode has one other advantage—it enables you to play songs directly from your iPod using iTunes. This is handy if you're working in a version of iTunes where you can't synchronize your iPod, but you still want to hear those songs.*

How to ... Use Your iPod as a Hard Disk

You saw in this chapter that the iPod's music files can be automatically synchronized, and Chapter 13 discusses the iPod's ability to hold Address Book and iCal information. Aside from those features, the iPod can also be used as a FireWire hard disk, mounted in the Finder and accessible like any other.

To make that happen, you first mount the iPod in iTunes and use the small iPod button to open iPod Preferences. In that dialog box, locate the Enable Disk Use check box and put a check in it. When you do, the iPod appears not only in iTunes, but also in the Finder window Sidebar (and, in most cases, on the desktop). You're now free to copy files to and from your iPod (the iPod is a regular FireWire hard disk, so any files can be transferred to it). You can also access the Calendar and Contacts folders that are used for iCal and Address Book data (respectively). The only items you cannot directly access are your digital song files; they are hidden from you in the Finder.

When you're done using the iPod as a disk, select it and drag it to the Trash, choose File | Eject, or click the small Eject icon next to the iPod entry in the Sidebar. When you do, the iPod is unmounted and you're free to disconnect it from your Mac or remove it from its dock.

14

Frames: The Secret Power of AppleWorks

AppleWorks, the all-in-one office application included with consumer Macs, is a powerful program. While this book has numerous chapters (Chapters 7 through 11) dedicated to showing you how to use AppleWorks' various functions, some of the serious power in AppleWorks comes from using those functions together. One way to do that is to create *frames* of different information—each frame can hold a type of data from one of the AppleWorks modules. The result is a great deal of flexibility in terms of how you present information, and it's why AppleWorks is able to create nearly any type of document you can think of.

In this special section I'd like to focus on creating newsletters and reports. Using frames, you can place text, images, graphics, tables, and spreadsheet data all on the same page, and then format the page(s) to your liking—you can be as creative as you like while building some very informative documents in the process.

FRAMEWORTHY IDEAS

Why would you want to add a frame from one AppleWorks document to another? Here are some thoughts:

- You want to add an image or a section of spreadsheet data to a report you've created in the word processor or a presentation you're building using the presentation module.

- You want to add a text box to your spreadsheet, which you use to explain elements of the spreadsheet to the people to whom you send it. (Hint: you can give the text box a colorful background so that it stands out.)

- You want to add an image, drawing, or painting to a report page in your database.

- You want to mix text, images, and other types of data in a Draw document in order to build a newsletter, sales flyer, or other layout.

That last option is something we'll look into a little more in this special section—how to get the various modules of AppleWorks working together to build impressive layouts.

Understand Frames

I f you've read Chapter 10, you may already have an idea of how frames work, but let's go into it again briefly here. A frame is a window into another module of AppleWorks—you can add a spreadsheet frame to a word processing document, for instance, if you'd like the freedom to do a little math in your word processing document, which might make for an even more effective report or presentation, for instance (see Figure S-1). In fact, you can add frames to nearly any document you create in AppleWorks, with the exception of certain types of frames within the database module. (And even then you can add graphics and text to your reports and layouts.)

So how is this done? You add frames to a document using the frame tools, which appear at the top of the Tools palette. (If you don't see the tools, choose Window | Show Tools.) Choose one of the tools—the Text tool, the Spreadsheet tool, the Paint tool, or the Table tool—then move to your document window and click-and-drag the mouse to draw the frame. What appears inside the frame depends on the type of frame you're creating. It could be an empty text frame, a spreadsheet frame, a graphical "paint" frame, or a table. (We'll look at most of those in more detail in this project.)

Another thing that happens when you select one of these tools is that the menus change. This might seem odd at first, but it makes sense. The frames are a "window" into each module, so the menus change to reflect the commands in that module. When a spreadsheet frame is selected, you'll see the spreadsheet commands; if a paint frame is selected, you'll see the painting commands.

TIP

In the image in Figure S-1, notice that I've turned off the Column and Row headings, which you can do by selecting the frame and (in spreadsheet frame mode) choose Options | Display, then turn on or off the portions of the spreadsheet that should be displayed.

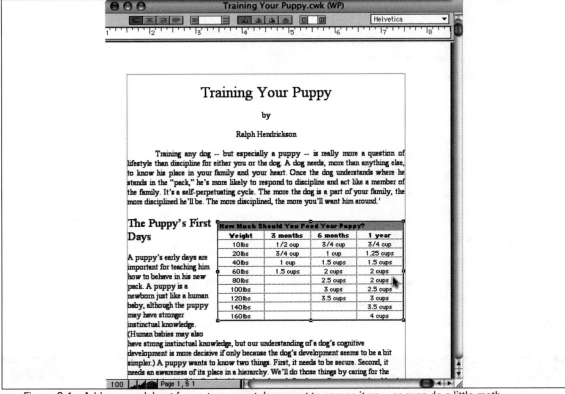

Figure S-1.   Add a spreadsheet frame to a report document to spruce it up—or even do a little math.

To select a frame that's been created, like the spreadsheet frame shown in Figure S-1, you simply double-click it. When you do, you should see the object become highlighted and the commands change.

Add Graphic Frames

As I've already mentioned, most AppleWorks documents can accept frames from other modules, and they can also display frames that contain imported graphic image files. The graphics can be from a variety of sources, including graphics you create in AppleWorks and save as TIFF, JPEG, and so on, or those that you create in other applications and save in those formats. The graphics can also be one of the many images that come with AppleWorks, which you can find by selecting File | Show Clippings. And,

you can just as easily scan graphics or digital-camera images into your computer and store them as image files. Any of these are easily added to your layout.

There are four basic ways to add graphic images to your document, such as a report or newsletter:

- **Build the graphic**   Using the tools in either the drawing module, a paint frame, or a spreadsheet frame, you can add images (or spreadsheet cells or charts) you've created in AppleWorks.

- **Insert from file**   If you don't have a frame selected and you choose File | Insert, you can search your hard drive (or connected network drives) for image files that can be added to your document as their own frames.

- **Insert clipart** AppleWorks offers libraries of *clipart*—small images, royalty free, that you can add to your documents—which can be used to augment your layout from the Clippings window.

- **Copy and paste** In most cases, you can select images or parts of other documents, then copy and paste them into your Draw document using the Edit | Copy command and Edit | Paste command. They'll show up in their own frames that can then be moved, stretched, rotated, and so on.

To add a graphic from a file, make sure no frames are selected in the document (so that AppleWorks doesn't try to add the graphic into that frame), then choose File | Insert. The Insert dialog box appears. Find the file you want to add and click OK. The graphic appears in your document in its own frame. Note that the file *format* of your graphic is important—you'll need to have it in PICT, TIFF, JPG, GIF, BMP, or a similar format. (You can see them all by pulling down the Show menu in the Insert dialog box.) Graphic file formats are discussed in detail in Chapter 15.

If you're adding from a library, choose File | Show Clippings, then select the type of clipart you'd like to look at. (The topics appear on small tabs at the bottom of the Clippings window. If you don't see any topics, you should click the Search button in the Clippings window to retrieve clippings from Apple's server computers over the Internet.)

Find the graphic you want to use by selecting the names in the bottom half of the window; the top half will change to show the graphic. Once you find the

WORKING WITH OBJECTS

Chapter 10 offers some specific details on the various things you can do with objects, which include frames of spreadsheet, table, text, or graphical data. Here are a few things you can do with objects. Flip to Chapter 10 for details.

- Arrange objects You can work with objects as if they were in layers, with some objects on top of others. To make that happen, you use the commands in the Arrange menu such as Arrange | Move Forward and Arrange | Move Back.

- Align objects You don't have to eyeball them—you can let your computer arrange objects perfectly using the Arrange | Align commands.

- Scale You can change the size of objects by percentage.

- Rotate AppleWorks offers a number of commands for rotating objects, which can appear at any angle to the original.

- Flip Many objects can be flipped so that they become mirror images (horizontally or vertically) of their original orientation.

- Wrap text One that we'll use more in this section is wrapping text around objects, which causes the text to flow around the object so that both the object and any underlying text can coexist on the same document page.

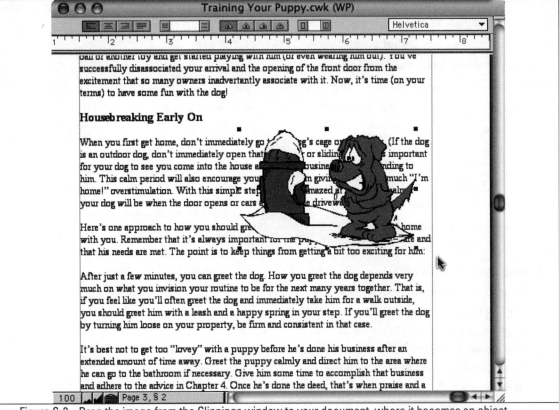

Figure S-2. Drag the image from the Clippings window to your document, where it becomes an object.

graphic you like, simply drag it from the Clippings window to your document (see Figure S-2). It becomes an object in your layout. If you're done with the Library window, click its close box.

Notice your floating graphic and your text commingling in an uncomfortable way? We'll cover that in the section "Wrap Text," coming up next.

ADD INLINE GRAPHICS

You can also add graphics in another way—as *inline* graphics (or other objects) that become embedded in the text. Instead of floating freely in their own frames, embedded images are placed at a specific point in the text. You accomplish this by inserting, pasting, or dragging an image from the Clippings window while you have the Text tool selected and the insertion point placed somewhere in the selected text frame or word processing document. The image appears as part of the text instead of in its own frame, meaning it will move around if you alter the text that comes before it. (In fact, you may notice this happening accidentally if you have the Text tool selected when you're dragging and/or pasting images into your layout.)

Wrap Text

Whether it's a text frame or a graphic, if you've created a frame that you want to float among the columns of your layout, you'll want to wrap text around it. This is a great way to add visual appeal and a hint of professionalism to your document. It's also simple to do:

1. Choose the main text frame or frames that have the text in them that you want to wrap around an image or some other text.

2. With the main text frame(s) selected, choose Options | Frame Links.

3. Now, select a frame (it can have graphics or text in it) that's currently overlapping text. It may be a little tough to select—try to make sure the underlying columns or frames of text aren't also selected. If they are, SHIFT-clicking one of the selected frames will deselect it while leaving others highlighted.

4. Choose Options | Wrap Text.

5. In the Wrap Text dialog box, choose the type of wrap you want. The Regular option wraps text around the frame, while Irregular wraps the text around the actual image or shape within the frame. No Wrap, of course, eliminates the text wrap if it was there.

6. Enter a number for the gutter, if desired. This determines the number of points to keep between the frame (Regular) or graphic (Irregular) and the wrapped text. The typical text size of typed output is 12 points, so something like 6 points might be good for each side (6 points is half an inch).

7. Click OK.

That's it, the text is wrapped either regularly or irregularly. Figure S-3 shows the image with Regular wrap.

This gives your layout a great look, although you'll still need to check it carefully to make sure everything is lined up nicely. If things aren't working out, you may need to resize the graphics frame or choose Regular instead of Irregular wrap, for instance.

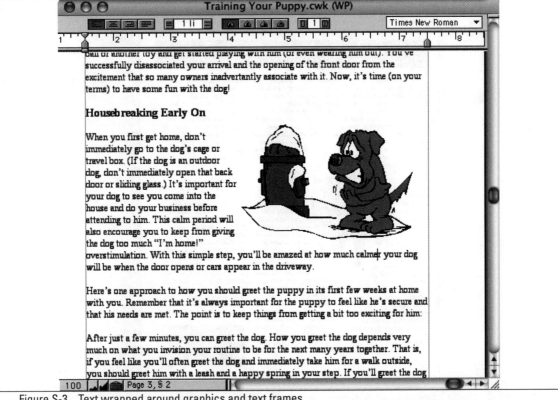

Figure S-3. Text wrapped around graphics and text frames

TIP

Want a different shape for your wrap? Draw that shape using the drawing tools, but make the shape the same color as your background (white with no outline). Now, place it behind the item you want to wrap text around (using Arrange | Move Backward), and wrap the text to that shape you just created.

The Ultimate Frames Workout: Build a Newsletter

You've seen how you can use frames in AppleWorks to add data from one AppleWorks module to another type of document. Perhaps the ultimate exercise of these muscles is a newsletter. We'll create text frames in columns, add headlines—it'll be fun (see Figure S-4). Plus, what you learn by creating a newsletter can be applied to any sort of layout, from brochures to letterhead to mail merge documents.

Create a Draw document by choosing File | New, selecting Draw, and clicking OK. (Or, select the Basics tab in the Starting Points window and double-click the Draw icon.) The first thing you need to do is make sure you're seeing all the drawing tools because they'll be important throughout this process (Window | Show Tools). You'll also probably want to view the rulers in

Figure S-4. Here's a finished layout using the techniques discussed in this section (and in Chapter 10).

the document window (Format | Rulers | Show Rulers), since you'll be lining things up and spacing them evenly.

Next, you'll probably need to set up the document's margins and pages. This works the same as with any other Draw document. Choose Format | Document, then enter numbers for the margins on the page and the number of Pages Down and Pages Across you'd like the document to have. (I prefer to place all my pages horizontally, since that just looks more like a newsletter to me. Your approach is up to you, though.) You may also want to choose Window | Page View, which enables you to scroll through the pages in this layout.

Now you're ready to create the frames that will hold the different parts of your newsletter. If you're

serious about creating a newsletter *right now*, remember that you can type your stories in the word processing module to get them nicely spell-checked and formatted, and you might want to have some graphics or images on hand to drop into the layout.

TIP

You'll find that changing the magnification is a handy thing to do when you're trying see the whole page at once and get a feel for its overall design. To change the magnification, select the percentage in the bottom-left corner of any AppleWorks document. It's actually a menu—you can simply choose the percentage to change the size of the document.

You can also type directly into the layout, as you'll see, but sometimes it's easier to write the story beforehand so it can be checked and edited.

Create Text Frames

In drawing projects, as discussed in Chapter 10, you can create a text frame, type text, and then the text will become an object. Unfortunately for our newsletter, AppleWorks, by default, collapses the text frame around the typed text so that only that text becomes the text frame, regardless of the size of the frame you draw.

That won't quite work for us in the newsletter, since we want the column to stay a fixed size. That way we can move text around within the columns and the column won't change sizes just because we don't have enough text to fill it. It can be convenient to have the frame grow around your text in certain cases. But in order to build a newsletter-type document, you'll want to create frames that are a fixed size.

CREATE A "LOOK" FOR YOUR NEWSLETTER

When you're building a newsletter or similar multipage layout, you'll probably find that there are certain elements you want on every page. You might, for instance, add a *folio* at the bottom of each page, which is magazine-industry lingo for the page number, publication name, and anything else you see at the bottom of every page. Or, you might have other design elements you want on every page, such as a certain background color or watermark-style graphical image.

What isn't any fun is adding those elements to each page. Fortunately, AppleWorks enables you to edit the *master page* in a multipage Draw document. The master page lets you design a foundation of sorts for each page in your layout—you can add background elements and folios, for instance. Then, once you've designed the master page, your actual page designs will all start with the master page's design as a foundation.

To edit the master page, choose Options | Edit Master Page. Now, create the elements that you want to place on every page of your layout. (For page numbers, first add a text frame, then choose Edit | Insert Page #, as described in Chapter 7. You can add automatic dates and times with similar commands in the Edit menu.)

When you're done, choose Options | Edit Master Page again to remove the check mark next to the command. Now you can return to editing each individual page in your layout, with the difference being that they all have the master page elements on them now. (And you can return to the master page and edit it later if necessary.)

To do that, you must create a *linked* frame (this might be a good time to drop back to 67 percent magnification, by the way).

1. With the Pointer tool selected, choose Options | Frame Links.

2. Now, select the Text tool and drag out a frame on the page.

3. Release the mouse button and the insertion point appears—you can type in the frame if you want.

4. To see the entire linked frame, click once outside of the frame. Its handles appear to show you the entire frame object.

The text frame is an object in the same way that a drawn rectangle or line is an object—it can be rotated, resized, moved, or even sent to back or sent forward (see Figure S-5).

So why create a "linked" frame? Linked frames allow text to flow from one frame to another, like text flows from column to column on a newspaper page.

> **TIP**
>
> If you already have a regular nonlinked frame of text, you can select it and choose Options | Frame Links to turn that frame into a linked frame.

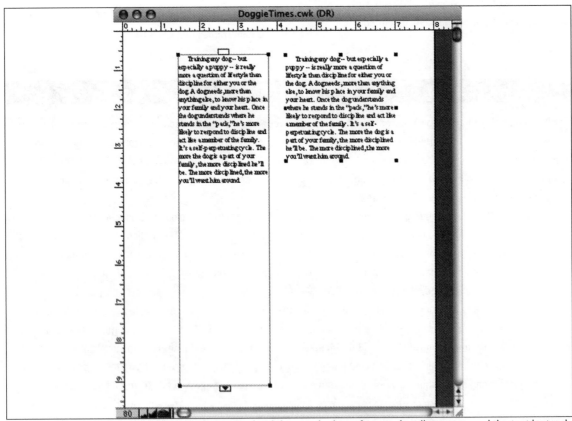

Figure S-5. On the left, a linked text frame; on the right, a typical text frame—it collapses around the text instead of maintaining its shape.

The frame borders keep disappearing after you select other objects! To see your frames at all times, select them and choose to surround them with a line (choose Hairline from the Line Width button menu in the toolbar). Just don't forget to remove the lines before you print the document.

With your frames created, you can add text by typing into the frame, copy and pasting into that frame, or you can use the File | Insert command to launch an Open dialog box where you can select a text file and import it into the frame. (AppleWorks word processing documents work great, as do RTF files, text files, and even Microsoft Word documents in the latest AppleWorks versions.)

Link Text Frames

If you've created one text frame that's overflowing with text, you can create another one to link to it so that it takes up the slack. Here's how:

1. Select the first frame to see its frame handles.

2. At the bottom of the frame, locate the continue indicator (it's the downward pointing arrow). Click it once.

3. Now you're ready to draw the linked frame. Drag to draw the frame onto your page. (Don't worry—you can resize it later.)

4. When you release the mouse button, text flows into the frame from the original frame. They're linked. When selected, the new frame will show a linked indicator (a little chain link icon) at the top, and if the story is long enough to overflow the frame, it will show a Continue indicator at the bottom, as shown in Figure S-6.

What's important to realize about linked frames is that they flow just like different pages in a word processing document flow. So, if you go back to the original frame and add or delete text, the linked frame will change to reflect the added or subtracted text. If you simply had two frames into which you'd cut and pasted text, you'd be in for quite an experience if you added text to or subtracted text from either of them, because you'd need to do some crazy cutting and pasting to make the columns look right again.

Frames don't have to be the same sizes or shapes to be linked, so you can link a narrow column of text to a large rectangle of text and it will still flow fine. In fact, you can create a linked frame on a new page, if you like.

NOTE

If you're familiar with expensive desktop publishing programs, you'll find these linked frames useful but limited. You can't reorder the links or link to an existing frame. You can only create linked frames by clicking the Continue indicator and drawing the frame. Also, cutting or copying the frame breaks the link—a pasted frame can create its own linked frames, but it's no longer linked to the original.

Link indicator

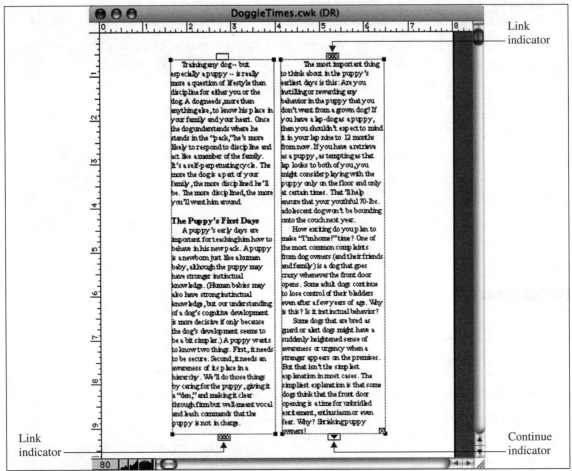

Link indicator

Continue indicator

Figure S-6. Linked frames allow text to flow from one frame to the next.

Resize Frames

Once you've got a couple of text frames on your page you'll probably realize that it's nearly impossible to get them to look like perfect columns on the page—after all, you're drawing and arranging them by hand. This can be frustrating, to say the least.

Fortunately, there are some tools to help you. The first is the Object Size window, which allows you to make some precise decisions about how each frame will appear. Choose Options | Object Size, and you'll see the window shown in S-7.

This is a great little window, because it gives you amazing precision in placing and aligning your frames as columns. From top to bottom in the left column, the measurements are

- **Left location**   The point, in inches, where the left side of the frame appears
- **Top location**   The point, in inches, where the top of the frame appears
- **Right location**   The point, in inches, where the right side of the frame appears
- **Bottom location**   The point, in inches, where the bottom of the frame appears

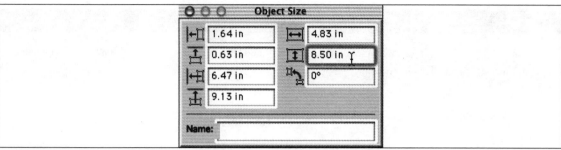

Figure S-7. Make precise choices about the size and position of your objects.

Now from top to bottom in the right column:

- **Object width**   The width, in inches, of the frame

- **Object height**   The height, in inches, of the frame

- **Rotation**   Amount of rotation, in degrees, of the frame

And, at the bottom of the Object Size window, you can give the object a name.

While you're creating your layout, you should keep in mind how useful these measurements are. For instance, if you want all of your frames to be aligned at their tops, you can choose a top location measurement and enter it for each. Similarly, you can check all your columns to make sure their bottoms align exactly. This will also help to keep the text aligned across columns so the column layout doesn't look jagged. An example of what you *don't* want is shown here:

more a question of lifestyle than discipline for either you or the dog. A dog needs, more than anything else, to know his place in your family and your heart. Once the dog understands where he stands in the "pack," he's more

earliest days is this. Are you instilling or rewarding any behavior in the puppy that you don't want from a grown dog? If you have a lap-dog as a puppy, then you shouldn't expect to mind it in your lap nine to 12 months

Probably the best tools here are column width and height—two measurements that are almost impossible to eyeball. Select one of your columns and check its width. If you've got three columns, one is probably about 2.25 inches or so wide, right? Go ahead and make it a nice, round 2.25 inches exactly. Now, select another column and make it 2.25 inches wide. Do it for the last one, and your columns will all be a uniform width.

TIP

Align the bottoms of your frames, and then give them all the same height measurement if you want them to align at the tops, too. Columns of different heights simply can't align at both the top and bottom. It goes against the laws of physics.

Align Frames

Keep repeating to yourself that frames are objects and objects can be manipulated, as you learned in Chapter 10. You're using the drawing tools, so all of the same tools for shapes can be used to manipulate frames. That includes the alignment tools.

Here's a neat trick to align frames as columns and get that gutter just perfect:

1. On your layout, place your left- and rightmost columns where you want them on the page relative to the edges.

2. Now, select all three frames by holding down the SHIFT key while you click them.

3. Choose Arrange | Align Objects.

4. In the Align Objects dialog box, choose the Distribute Space option in the Left to Right section.

5. Click Apply.

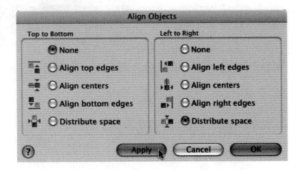

See what happened? Your columns snapped into place, distributing the remaining space equally between the two gutters. Perfect. If you like what you see, click OK to get out of the Align Objects dialog box. Or, you can use the other settings— like Align Bottom Edges under the Top to Bottom options—to change other alignment issues regarding your columns.

Lock Frames

When you've finally got your frames in place the way they need to be, go ahead and lock them down. That'll keep you from accidentally moving the columns around once they've been carefully arranged. Select the frames to lock (hold down the SHIFT key as you select more than one frame), then choose Arrange | Lock. You can still select the frames and edit text within them, but you can't move them on the page until you unlock them.

Create Floating Text

You've already seen quite a bit on adding text in frames—this really isn't much different. You may find that creating a linked frame is the best approach here, if only because a linked frame doesn't collapse around the text. You likely won't actually be linking it to anything—you just want the additional control the linked frame gives you. Here's how to create floating text:

1. Make sure Frame Links is selected (with a check mark next to it) in the Options menu.

2. Click the Text tool and drag to create a text frame on the page.

3. Enter the text (a pull-quote, headline, and so on) for this floating text frame. Format the text.

4. Click outside the text frame. The text frame should be selected, with handles showing. (If it's not, click it once to select it.)

5. Click and drag the text frame to its final destination. It's okay if the frame obscures the text beneath it—you'll fix that momentarily.

Now, wrap the text around this text frame object, as discussed in Chapter 10 for graphic objects: select the text frame and choose Options | Text Wrap. Now, in the Text Wrap dialog box, choose the style (try Regular

for headlines and Irregular for many pull-quotes or for graphics), and then enter a Gutter size and click OK. That should cause the text in the background frames to wrap around your text object.

TIP

Want images in your newsletter? Remember that your newsletter is ultimately a Draw document—consult Chapter 10 for a look at the drawing, painting, and graphics frame tools in AppleWorks. And don't forget lines—as shown back in Figure S-1, the lines between columns can help to make your layout look more professional.

Check Out Applewords Assistants

Y ou've seen how you can use AppleWorks to create a newsletter from scratch. In fact, AppleWorks is so powerful that you don't even have to create your own layouts—you can start with help from the Assistants. There are six Assistants to help you create different layouts:

- **Address List** This Assistant walks you through the process of creating an address list database, where you can track the names, addresses, phone numbers, and other information of your personal, business, or other contacts.

- **Business Cards** This Assistant walks you through adding the company name, address, title, and phone number to create a business card, which it then generates as a database document. Using the database tools, you can modify the card in Layout mode, then switch to Browse mode, which automatically fills a page with eight instances of the card. The cards can then be printed to plain paper and taken to your print shop, or printed on card stock and cut at home. You can also get perforated card stock at most office supply stores, which can be used to create business cards.

- **Calendar** Using the spreadsheet tools, this Assistant quickly creates a monthly calendar, automatically placing the dates correctly, based on the month(s) you choose. There's really only one choice—a single month per sheet of paper.

- **Certificate** This Assistant quickly tosses together a certificate, award, diploma, or something similar. The result is a Draw document that can easily be edited.

- **Envelope** This Assistant walks you through the process of setting the alignment and printing path for the envelope. Envelopes can be tough to print—you'll need to read your printer's manual carefully to figure out how to orient and feed the envelope to your printer. Then you can make an informed decision on how to set up this Assistant, which generates a word processing document that's easily edited.

- **Home Finance** This Assistant automates the process of creating a variety of different "What If" spreadsheets that you can use to decide how to manage debt, calculate net worth, and even determine how much you can afford to put into a home.

To use an Assistant, select the Assistants tab in the Starting Points window. Click one of the Assistant icons to begin. Assistants work by asking you a series of questions about your document. You enter information in the Assistant dialog box, then click the Next button to move on to the next series of questions.

When you get to the end of the Assistant, you'll see a Create button, which causes the Assistant to take all the information you've input and create the document based on that information. You can also click the Cancel button to leave the Assistant, click the Back button to go back to the previous questions, or click the Begin button to return to the beginning of the Assistant.

Chapter 15

Explore Digital Photos and iPhoto

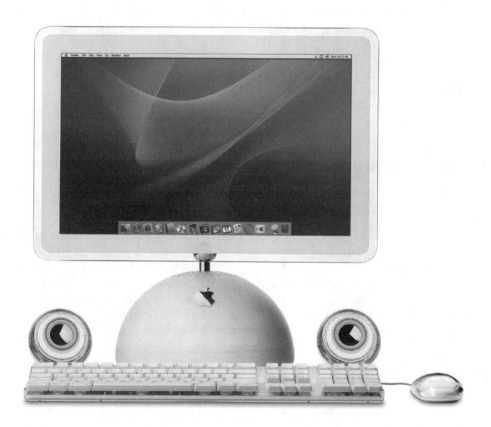

How to…

- Understand image file formats
- Import into iPhoto
- Manage your photo collection
- Edit photos
- Output your photos
- Display photos online
- Export your photos to a file
- Export photos as a web page

Another of the iApps that Apple includes with the iMac and other consumer models is iPhoto, an application that enables you to manage, store, and manipulate photos that you take with a digital still camera. Apple offers up some fun stuff that you can do with iPhoto and your camera, including displaying those photos on the Internet via .Mac, using the photos in iDVD to create a slideshow, or even creating a photo album that you can pay to have printed, bound, and shipped to you via a service that Apple offers.

In this chapter we'll also briefly cover the concept of digital image files and the file formats you'll likely encounter—the techie stuff behind the fun of a program such as iPhoto.

Understand Image Formats

If you're working with an image from a digital camera, one that's been scanned into a computer, or one that's been created in a high-end graphics application, the big question is, What format is it saved in? There is no single standard for digital images, although there are a handful of common ones.

In order for different types of applications and different types of computers to be able to read and display these image files, we need some standard formats. iPhoto and Preview—the built-in image viewer in Mac OS X—can read many popular formats, as shown in Table 15-1.

One way to identify the different sorts of images is to look at the filename's extension, especially if you've downloaded the images from the Internet or otherwise transferred them from non-Macintosh computers. Unix (including Mac OS X) and Windows both deal heavily in these filename conventions that help each program figure out what format a particular file is using.

Work with iPhoto

If you're a digital photo buff at all, you're probably going to love iPhoto. iPhoto has a number of tasks, and it manages them all pretty well for a consumer-oriented application. First, it enables you to import photos from a digital camera into a single application that makes the process fairly

Format	Extension	Description
BMP	.bmp	The Microsoft Windows "bitmap" graphics format, the native format for Windows-based computers.
GIF	.gif	Graphics Interchange Format, originally developed by CompuServe. This format is popular for nonphotographic images (like buttons, arrows, and stylized text) that are created for the Web.
JPEG	.jpg	Joint Photographic Experts Group format, developed by the group of the same name. This one is used on the Web for photographic images because it offers high-quality images with lots of color information, and it compresses into small files that don't take up a lot of storage space on hard drives.
PICT	.pic, .pict	Macintosh Picture file, the native format for Classic Mac OS, including Mac OS 9. This is the format that the Classic Mac uses for screenshots and for copy-and-paste images; Mac OS X, on the other hand, uses Adobe PDF for such images. Many graphics programs can save files to PICT format, and Appleworks still does well with PICT files.
PNG	.png	Portable Network Graphic, a file format designed to replace the GIF format for web development because GIF relies on patented technology. PNG is gaining some popularity, but GIF remains very popular.
QuickTime image	.qif	QuickTime image format, best used for editing frames within QuickTime movies.
TIFF	.tiff, .tif	Tagged Interchange File Format, used extensively in publishing. This high-quality format creates very large files that take quite a bit of storage space but maintain clean scanned and edited images.

TABLE 15-1   Popular Image Formats

straightforward and logical. Second, it enables you to organize those photos, creating virtual "photo albums" that you can name and group together. Then, iPhoto lets you edit each individual photo, if you like, with some surprisingly capable photo editing tools. Finally, it enables you to output those photos in a variety of ways, including to the Internet, as desktop images, to iDVD for a slide show, or as a special, bound book that you can order from Apple and have delivered to your home. And, yes, you can even have prints made.

15

Import into iPhoto from a Camera

You have a few different options for getting photos into iPhoto. The most obvious one is to use your digital camera—that's what iPhoto is designed for. iPhoto recognizes, primarily, cameras that are connected to your Mac via USB or FireWire connections; in fact, when you hook up many digital cameras, iPhoto launches automatically. (This is also true of many digital memory card readers, if you'd prefer to remove the memory card from your camera and insert it in a third-party reader.) Once recognized, you can import the photos from that camera easily.

Here's how to accomplish that:

1. Launch iPhoto if it isn't already running.

2. Plug your camera's USB or FireWire cable into its onboard port and then connect the other end to a USB or FireWire port (as appropriate) on your Mac.

3. When the camera is recognized by iPhoto you'll see it show up in the bottom-left corner of the iPhoto window.

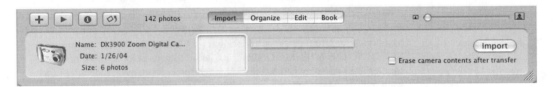

4. To import the photos on that camera, click the Import button. (Before doing so, you may want to turn on the Erase Camera Contents After Transfer option first.)

The images are imported, with progress shown in the center of that information area at the bottom of the screen. When done, you'll find those images are displayed in the iPhoto library and easily accessible by clicking the Last Roll item in the Source list.

 *Every import operation done by iPhoto is considered a "roll" as if it were a roll of film that had been developed and you'd received the prints back. That's the metaphor that Apple is going for, so when you see that you can view photos "by roll" you can mentally translate that to "by import operation." For instance, if I just created "Roll 6" by importing some photos, the next import operation I do will create Roll 7.*

Import Digital Images into iPhoto

If you already have images stored as computer files that you want to use in iPhoto, you can import those as well. Choose File | Import. In the Import Photos dialog box, locate the folder, disc, or image that you want to import, select it, and click Import. That should bring the selection into the iPhoto Library as a new roll.

 *You can also drag a folder of photos to the iPhoto library window and drop it to import them quickly.*

View the Library

Click the Photo Library icon in the Source list and you're shown all of the images in your iPhoto library. By default, they're organized by title. At least at first, though, most of your images won't have customized titles; instead they'll be named for their roll and the image number that they are on that roll, as in Roll 24 -5. Not terribly handy.

Of course, you can change the way you view your library. One approach is to organize by roll, so that you can locate images by recalling (in a general sense) when the image was imported. To do that, choose View | Film Rolls. You'll see the iPhoto window change to show you the rolls from which each photo came, as shown in Figure 15-1.

The truth is that by default the photos are always organized by roll—we're just now revealing that organization. (Before, all the images appeared in a row.) To actually change the way the images are organized, you'll dig further into the View menu by choosing View | Arrange Photos and then choosing a method, such as by date or by title. That will literally reshuffle the images as they appear in the Library. (To get them back to default behavior, choose View | Arrange Photos | by Film Roll.)

Another interesting option for limiting the images that you're forced to scroll through in the Library is to click the disclosure triangle next to Photo Library in the Source list. That reveals some special albums that you can use to view images by the year on their timestamp. Choose the

15

FIGURE 15-1   Viewing images organized by rolls in iPhoto's library

year that interests you, and, most likely, that will reduce the number of photos you see in the main viewer window.

Edit Photo Info

You can change the name and date associated with an image if you like. Choose an image in the Library and you'll see its name appear in the Title entry box that's below the Source list. (If you don't see this area, you need to click the small "i" logo info button that's at the bottom of the Source list.) To edit the title, just place your cursor in that box and start editing.

You can also change the date of an image, which can be useful if, for instance, your camera's date wasn't sent after batteries had run down and you took pictures with a timestamp that wasn't accurate.

The info area does a cute little trick—with the name and date showing, click the "i" icon again and you'll see it change so that there's a comment area. You can now type a comment (a short caption, for instance) that can be associated with the image and used later in albums and books.

TIP

iPhoto has a special command that enables you to change the info for more than one photo at a time. Select multiple photos in the Library and then choose Photos | Batch Change. In the dialog box that appears, choose the information item that you'd like to change (Title, Date, or Comments) and then enter or choose what you want to set that information item to. (For instance, you can choose to change the title to the filename, which might prove helpful under certain circumstances.) Experiment with the options.

Delete Photos

You can delete photos from the Library by selecting one or more and pressing the DELETE key on your keyboard or choosing Photos | Move to Trash. That moves photos to the Trash item that appears on the Source list, meaning they're marked for deletion, but aren't yet gone. It also doesn't mean they're in the Finder's Trash; that's a different trash can, and emptying those items from the Finder doesn't empty the Trash in iPhoto.

If you want to retrieve items from iPhoto's Trash, simply select the Trash entry on the Source list. You'll see the images in the main window, and you can drag them back to the Library icon or to another album's name.

When you really decide to do away with those photos, choose File | Empty Trash. In the dialog sheet that appears, click OK if you're sure you want to delete the files and Cancel if you decide not to.

Organize Photos into Albums

The key element in organizing your photos in iPhoto is the *album*, which is simply a grouping of photos that you can create for various reasons. Once you have some photos arranged in an album, you can use those photos for output to a variety of targets such as a web page, slide show, picture book, and so on.

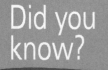

Rate Your Photos

iPhoto enables you to give each photo in your database a rating, if you like, between zero and five stars. Once the photos are rated, they can be searched and organized based on that rating. You'll find that you can create "smart" albums, for instance, that gather together only your favorite (or least favorite) images into collections.

To rate an image, highlight it in the Library and choose Photos | My Rating and the rating that you want to give the image. Note that you can also CONTROL-click an image to get a contextual menu that also includes the My Rating command, or you can highlight an image and press keyboard commands between ⌘-0 and ⌘-5 to give the photo a rating, with ⌘-5 being five stars.

If you'd like to see the star rating in the Library window itself, choose View | My Rating (if it doesn't already have a check mark next to it).

15

To create an album, choose File | New Album in iPhoto. A dialog sheet appears asking you to name the album—just begin typing to give the album a name. Press RETURN when you're done, and the new album appears in the Source list.

Now you can switch back to the Library and begin dragging photos from the Library to your new album. That's how you populate it—you can drag them one at a time, or you can drag a group of photos. To drag a group, use the ⌘ key while clicking to add to your selection, and then drag them all over to the album's name in the Source list.

TIP   *You can also create an album from a selected group of photos. Begin by highlighting the photos you want to add to a new album, then choose File | New Album from Selection. Give it a name, press RETURN, and the album is added to the Source list.*

The photos that you add to an album aren't moved or removed from the Library—they're still there. In fact, you can group the same image into multiple albums, if you like. The albums are designed as a way to easily organize images into collections that you want to see used together. And having them organized in that way makes it easier to output them using iPhoto's other features.

Create a Smart Album

As with iTunes, iPhoto offers a "smart" album choice that can be set to gather together images automatically in your Library that meet certain criteria. Here's how to create a smart album:

1. Choose File | New Smart Album.

2. In the dialog sheet that appears, type a name for the album in the Smart Album Name entry box.

3. Using the menus and entry boxes, create a criterion that will be matched against the photos in your Library.

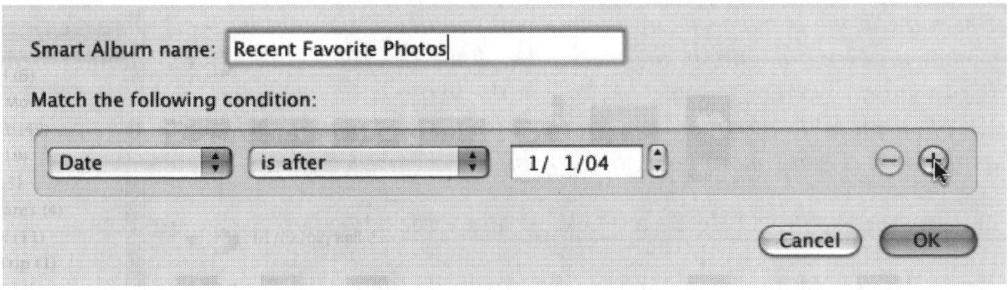

Smart Album name: | Recent Favorite Photos|

Match the following condition:

| Date ⬍ | is after ⬍ | 1/ 1/04 ⬍ | ⊖ ⊕ |

Cancel   OK

4. Now, decide if you want to add another criterion line. If so, click the plus (+) symbol that appears in the right margin of the dialog sheet and add another line of criterion logic.

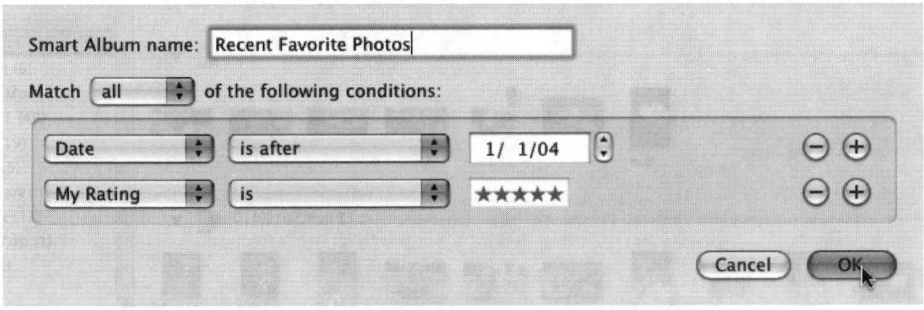

Smart Album name: | Recent Favorite Photos|

Match [all ⬍] of the following conditions:

| Date ⬍ | is after ⬍ | 1/ 1/04 ⬍ | ⊖ ⊕ |
| My Rating ⬍ | is ⬍ | ★★★★★ | ⊖ ⊕ |

Cancel   OK

5. Repeat adding lines as necessary. When you're done, click the OK button.

That creates the smart album and immediately begins populating it with images from the Library that match your criteria.

To edit the album, select it and choose File | Edit Smart Album or CONTROL-click the album's name and choose Edit Smart Album from the contextual menu. To delete the album, select it and press the DELETE key on your keyboard, then click Remove in the dialog sheet that appears.

Edit Photos

I haven't really discussed the buttons that appear below the main window in iPhoto yet because there's a sort of natural flow from importing to organizing. But you'll find as you organize and edit your photos, you may need to click the Import button when you want to return to the import interface so that you can access your camera again, and sometimes you may want to click the Organize button to get back to the full Library when you've gone to one of the other screens, such as the Edit screen.

To get into editing mode, highlight an image and click the Edit button or simply double-click an image while you're viewing the library or an album. That should give you a close-up of the image in question and give you access to the controls for editing that image.

15

TIP
You can edit the image in its own window if you like. Choose iPhoto | Preferences and choose the General icon. In the section Double-Click Photo, turn on the option Opens Photo in Edit Window if you'd like to edit the photo in its own window that appears on top of the main iPhoto interface. (Notice also the option to launch the image in another application if that's more appealing to you.)

So what are those controls? Here's a quick list and some advice on how to use them:

- **Crop**   Drag your mouse on the image and you'll create a box. The more visible portion of the image is the part that you'll keep if you click the Crop button (see Figure 15-2), which will discard the excess image. Crop can work with Constrain to crop images to a particular size.

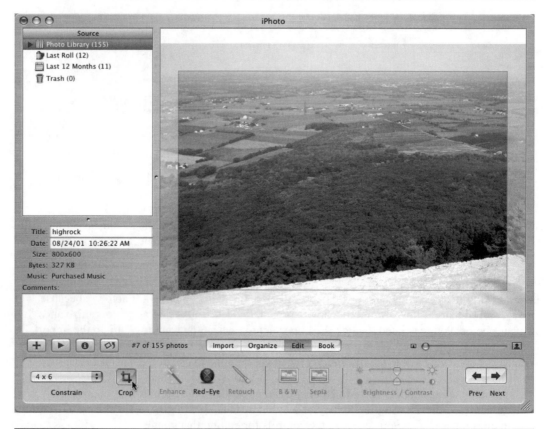

FIGURE 15-2   When you crop an image, you cut out the areas that fall outside of your selection area.

■ **Constrain** If you intend to use the image for a particular purpose—you want it to be the size of a 3 × 5 photo, or you want it to have the aspect ratio of a movie DVD, for example—you can choose that constraint from the menu. You'll see that portion of the image highlighted. Now click the Crop button if you'd like to do away with the extra portion of the image.

> **NOTE** *You don't have to crop images in order for them to fit into different situations. When you create a book or slide show, the images will be resized to fit the dimensions of the target project. That said, the Constrain feature is a good one for getting the* ratio *correct for images, so that if they are resized, they don't appear squished or distorted.*

> **TIP** *The option Constrain as Portrait allows you to use the same dimensions listed (2 × 3, 3 × 5, and so on) but in an upright orientation so that the image portion highlighted is taller than it is wide.*

■ **Enhance** Click the Enhance button to automatically "improve" the colors in your image (that's what Apple's iPhoto Help says). What it does is push the contrast and saturation on some images and makes some color correction guesses. Usually it does a good job, but sometimes you'll want to choose Edit | Undo after clicking Enhance to get the image back to its original state. You can click Enhance more than once to add to the effect (although the changes will often be increasingly subtle).

■ **Red-Eye** If you have an image of a person or animal where the eyes appear red because of the flash on the camera, you can fix that using the Red-Eye feature. Simply highlight the eye in question (by dragging a box around it in the image area) and click the Red-Eye button. That should take it back to something approaching normal.

■ **Retouch** Click the Retouch button and you'll get a small crosshair, which you can place on small blemishes in the image. Now, move the crosshair to the blemish area, click and hold down the mouse. Using small, slow strokes, wipe away the blemish area. (iPhoto sort of averages the colors around the blemish to blend everything together.) If that doesn't seem to work, you may first need to zoom in using the zoom slider (over on the right side below the image) and reposition so that you see a much more close-up view of that blemish, then click and drag to remove it. Here's the zoom slider:

> **NOTE** *When you're done retouching the image, click the Retouch icon again to get out of Retouch mode.*

15

- ■ **B&W**   Click the B&W button to turn your image to black and white.
- ■ **Sepia**   Click the Sepia button to make your image *sepiatone*, which gives it an "Old West" or aged film appearance.
- ■ **Brightness and Contrast**   Use the sliders to change the brightness and contrast of your image.

The contrast can be a bit more useful to liven up the colors in your image, particularly if you make the image bright.

When you're done editing an image, you can click one of the arrow buttons to move on to the next or previous photo, or you can click the Organize button to return to the main Library viewer. If you have the Edit window open, click the close button to close the Edit window.

Did you make mistakes with this image? Choose Photos | Revert to Original to toss out your edits and return the image to its original state.

Output Your Photos

With your images organized and edited, the next step with iPhoto is to output those images. iPhoto has lots of options in that department, which are represented by the buttons at the bottom of the iPhoto interface that you see when you're in Organize mode (see Figure 15-3). You can create a slide show that runs on screen, send images in e-mail, order prints, create a photo book, build a web page, and other options. On top of those built-in features, you can also export your photos as computer files in standard formats, and you can print the photos. Let's take a look at all those options in this section.

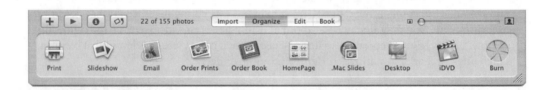

FIGURE 15-3   Here are the different output options that you can activate by selecting images in the main window or by selecting an album and then clicking one of these buttons.

Print Photos

To print a photo or photos, make your selection in the Library or in an album (or select an entire album) and click the Print button that appears at the bottom of the Organize interface; you can also choose File | Print. That brings up the Print dialog sheet.

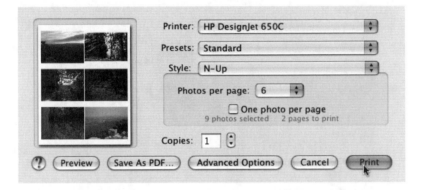

One thing you may notice about this dialog is that you have more options than the typical Print dialog. At the top are some standard menus. In the Printer menu, choose the printer that you want to print to. Then, in the Presets menu, you'll find some preset options for printing to certain types of photo paper; choose one of those if it seems appropriate.

In the Style menu, choose how you'd like to print the selected image or images—options include printing images Full Page, as a Greeting Card (which can be folded), as a Contact Sheet (with multiple thumbnail images), and other options.

After you've chosen a style, you'll see options below that style that relate to the style you've selected. For instance, if you choose Full Page, you'll see a slider for setting the margins around the image; if you choose N-Up, you'll see a menu where you can choose how many images should be printed on each page.

With those choices made, click the Print button to set the print operation into motion.

NOTE *Want to use the more typical Print dialog box options? Click the Advanced Options button. Now you'll see an unlabeled menu with options regarding color and paper type, layout, and so on. In this configuration, choose the iPhoto entry in the menu to see the Style options. To return to the default Print dialog, click the Standard Options button.*

15

Create a Slide Show

Select some images or an album or two, and then click the Slideshow button. That brings up a dialog box where you can make choices about how the slide show will be displayed.

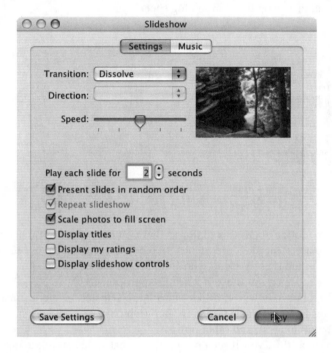

From the Transition menu, choose a special effect to use between each image in the slide show, or choose None if you just want an abrupt cut between images. The Cube, Mosaic Flip, and Wipe transitions have a direction to them, which you can choose from the Direction menu. You can then use the Speed slider to determine how quickly the transition takes place.

In the Play Each Slide For box, enter the number of seconds that each slide should be on screen. Below that entry box you can see a series of check box options. Turn on Present Slides in Random Order if you don't want them to follow the order that you've created in your album organization. If the slides are *not* in random order, then you can determine whether or not the slide show should repeat; if they are randomized, the slide show repeats automatically.

Turn on Scale Photos to Fill Screen if that's what you want; if you turn off this option, the images will appear at their native ratios, with a border around them if they don't fit the dimensions of the screen.

You can also opt to display titles, ratings, and the slide show controls, or you can keep them hidden.

On the Music tab, you can choose a song for your slide show from the list that appears, or use the menu to choose your iTunes Library or a playlist from that library. If you choose a playlist, all of the songs in that playlist will be used for the slide show unless you select a particular song.

NOTE

You can select a song and click the Play button to hear it before making your decision.

With those choices made, click Save Settings if you'd like to have these settings ready the next time you click the Slideshow button; otherwise, click Play to begin the show.

Send Images in E-mail

Want to send a photo in e-mail? It's easy. Select an image (or images), then click the Email button. A dialog box appears. Choose a size for the image(s) from the Size menu. (The smaller the image is, the faster it can be downloaded by your recipients, although they may not mind a large image if they have broadband Internet access.) Then, place a check mark next to the text items that you want to include in the message and click Compose. That exports the image to a JPEG format and automatically brings up a New Message window in Mail. Enter an e-mail address, type a message, and send it along.

Order Prints and Create Books

Highlight images and click the Order Prints button, and if your Mac is connected to the Internet, you'll see a window to the Kodak Print Service that you can use to order a print and have it mailed to you. You may need to set up an account if you don't have a valid Apple ID, but the instructions are on screen and straightforward.

To order a book, you'll first want to arrange that book. Instead of clicking Order Book, you should do the following:

1. Arrange an album that has the images in the order you want them to appear, including a cover image as the first image in the album.

2. Select that album in the Source list.

3. Click the Book tab next to the Edit tab and arrange your book using that interface.

4. Choose a Theme for your book (Catalog, Classic, Portfolio, Picture Book, and so on), and then you can choose which items should appear—Titles, Comments, and/or Page Numbers.

After you've chosen a theme, iPhoto automatically creates and arranges a book for you, which you'll see in the sliding control that appears beneath each page of the book.

15

If you see exclamation points on the images, that means their resolution isn't high enough to be printed in the book. An image that's intended to be a full page in the book should be at least a 3-megapixel image. If you don't have higher-resolution photos, try placing them on pages with multiple images. And note that iPhoto will still allow you to order the book, even if there's a good chance the results won't be what you're hoping for.

Select one of the pages and you can edit the text for that page on the screen. (There's an Edit | Font menu you can use to alter the text.) If you want to change the design of the page, choose a different design from the Page Design menu. You can turn on the Lock Page option if you'd like to lock a page's design and keep iPhoto from reflowing images onto that page if you change other pages.

When you're done making changes, click Preview to see the book in its own window. If you like what you see, click Order Book and you'll be connected to Apple's service for purchasing the book.

.Mac Options

If you'd like to publish your images to the Web and you have a .Mac subscription, then select a series of images or an album and click the HomePage button (to create a page of thumbnail images that can be clicked to show the full-size image) or click the .Mac Slides button (to create a series of pages in the form of a slide show).

Choose the HomePage button and you're connected to the .Mac service, then shown the page that you'll be editing. You can highlight text and edit it directly in the iPhoto window. You'll also see a Theme drawer that enables you to change the look and feel of your page, as well as options to change the number of columns, add a counter, and add an e-mail link to the page. When you've made all your choices, click the Publish button.

You can use .Mac Slides for a screen saver on your Mac. Choose .Mac Slides and a dialog appears asking if you want to overwrite any existing .Mac slide show files. Click Publish if you like the idea. Your images will be uploaded, and at the end of the process, you'll be given a change to announce the new slide show to others via e-mail. Then, head to System Preferences, choose

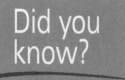

Desktop Images

Want to put an image in iPhoto on your Mac's desktop? Easy enough—select it in the Library or from an album and click the Desktop button. It becomes your desktop image.

Select multiple images and you can have those images change over time. Open System Preferences and click the Desktop & Screen Saver icon. On the Desktop screen, turn on the option Change Picture Every (blank) Minutes and choose the amount of time you want each image to remain on screen.

Desktop and Screen Saver, and select .Mac to use your slide show as your screen saver. To use someone *else's* .Mac slides, click the Options button on the Screen Saver screen and enter another .Mac name in the .Mac Membership Name box, then click OK.

Export Images to iDVD

To export images to iDVD for a slide show, you should first launch iDVD and select the project (or create a new one) to which you want the images added. If you don't choose a project, the photos will be added to the most recently opened project, which may not be what you want.

With the iDVD project open, return to iPhoto and select the images, album, or albums that you'd like to use within iDVD. With those images highlighted, click the iDVD button. The images are collected and sent to iDVD, where they're added as an iDVD slide show. In fact, if you've selected multiple albums, each will be added as a separate slide show.

Now, in iDVD, you can double-click the slide show that's been created to arrange the images, and choose the slide duration, transition, and other features, including adding music or audio (see Figure 15-4). When you're done arranging and selecting for the slide show, click the Return button to return to the main menu; see Chapter 16 for more on finishing your iDVD.

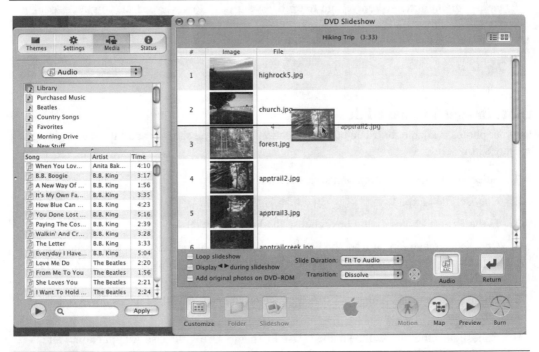

FIGURE 15-4   Building a slide show in iDVD

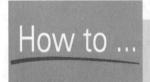 **Export Photos as a Web Page**

The Export dialog box offers another interesting option: click the Web Page tab and you'll see controls that enable you not only to translate your images but also to create a web page that can display those images as thumbnails in a grid of columns and rows.

In the Page section, choose a title for the page, the number of columns and rows, the background color or image (use the Set button to choose a suitable background image), and the text color.

In the Thumbnail section, choose the size that you'd like the thumbnail images to be and whether or not to show the title and comment for that image. In the Image section, choose the width and height that you want the full-sized image to be, and choose whether to show the title or comment.

Click Export and you'll see a Save dialog box where you can choose the folder (or create the folder) where you'd like the web page and images stored. Click OK and the page is created and saved.

One important note—when you go to upload your page to a web server, you need to upload not only the web page that was created, but the subfolders as well, and in the same relative location. That will ensure that your thumbnails and full-sized images will be displayed properly.

Export Images to Image Files

Want your photos available for use in other applications? Then you should export them to an image file. Here's how:

1. Select an image, an album, or a series of either.

2. Choose File | Export.

3. In the Export Photos dialog box, choose the File Export tab.

4. Choose an image format from the Format menu. (Original means that you keep the image in the same format that it was originally imported from, or you can choose JPG, TIFF, or PNG.)

5. Choose a size for the image—either full size or you can scale the images down to a certain size.

6. Choose how the files will be named (Use Filename, Use Title, Use Album Name) and whether you want the file saved with a filename extension.

7. Click Export.

8. In the save dialog sheet that appears, locate the folder where you'd like these files saved, or click New Folder to create one. Then click OK.

That's it—the images will be exported to the file format and sizes that you selected and stored in the folder that you've specified.

NOTE *If you want to get serious about manipulating and translating image files—if, for instance, you're downloading images from a digital camera and need to translate them for display on a web site—I recommend GraphicConverter (**www.lemkesoft.com**), a shareware program that you can download and test before you buy it.*

15

Chapter 16

Edit Your Own Movies

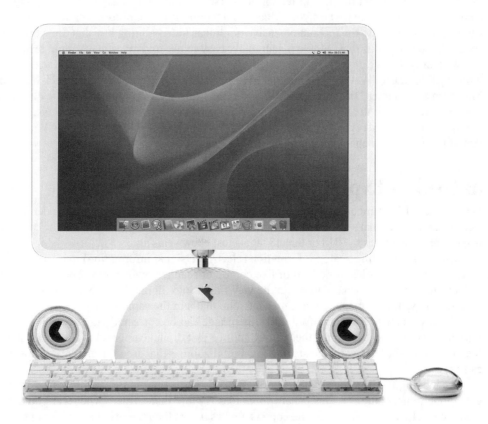

How to...

- Get footage into your Mac
- Edit the clips
- Add transitions, sound effects, and titles
- Lay in your soundtrack and edit your sound
- View, save, and export the movie
- Create your DVD movie disc
- Watch DVD movies

If you have a Mac that includes FireWire ports (and nearly all of today's consumer models do), then you're ready for the next killer app for personal computers: *desktop video*. Using a digital camcorder, the FireWire port on your Mac, and a wonderful little program called iMovie, you can turn your Mac into the most inexpensive nonlinear video-editing bay that the world has yet seen. The funny part is that iMovie is incredibly easy to use and gives really good results.

And, once you've got that movie edited, you can take the next step if your Mac has a built-in "SuperDrive"—you can burn that movie to a DVD that can be played back on your Mac or in a consumer DVD player. iDVD is fun software for doing just that while designing a clever interface for the DVD, to boot. Finally, even if you don't have a SuperDrive, you can still play back commercial DVDs on your Mac if you have a DVD-capable drive. We'll cover that at the end of this chapter.

Digital Video Explained

Digital video (DV) camcorders have hit a magical price point, now coming in well under $500 for a consumer model. That's about the same price that you would have paid for an analog camcorder—one that records images to VHS or Super8 tape—just a few years ago.

Instead of recording analog information (electronic signal information) to a VHS or similar tape, a digital camcorder works sort of like computer scanners with a lens. The DV camcorder immediately translates what you see in the viewfinder into digital data—ones and zeros. That data is then written to magnetic tape on a cassette that's in the camcorder.

The advantage to DV is twofold. First, the image can be corrected digitally as it's brought into the camera. If you shop for them, you'll notice that digital cameras have a lot of interesting features—built-in effects, image stabilizers, digital zoom—that aren't available on most analog cameras.

Second, digital data doesn't lose quality from copy to copy (in the biz, they say "from generation to generation"). This *generational* loss is more than evident whenever you copy from one VHS video to another; the copy is always worse than the original. With digital data, there's nothing to degrade over multiple copies (unless the tape starts falling apart). Because what a DV camcorder stores is basically a computer file like a word processing document or a PICT image file, the quality of a digital video recording doesn't gradually fade as you copy it.

Since the DV camcorder is creating a computer file, that means the video is also easier to work with on your Mac. Since the latest Mac models have FireWire ports—and nearly all DV camcorders have FireWire ports—you can connect your camera directly to your Mac. Now, with iMovie, you can actually control your camera (at least, many models) and copy the video from the camera to your Mac. Then it's a simple matter to cut, paste, add transitions, and lay down a soundtrack. (With analog video, you would first have to "digitize" the video using special equipment. With a DV camcorder, you just plug the camera into your Mac and start copying the video into iMovie.)

Finally, you can save the digital video as a QuickTime movie and put it on the Web, send it in e-mail (if you have a nice, fast connection), or save it on your hard disk. Or you can copy the video back to your camcorder, then use your camcorder as a VCR to play the movie on your TV (or transfer it to typical VHS tape).

> **NOTE** *In this chapter I'll be discussing iMovie 4, which is the version included with Macs starting in early 2004. If you have an earlier version, you may need to upgrade to iLife '04, which is available in retail and online Apple outlets. That said, the basics of iMovie 2 and 3 are pretty close to iMovie 4 in terms of the tasks covered in this chapter, so you shouldn't have much trouble following along.*

Get Video into Your Mac

Before you can edit your movie, you'll need to connect your camcorder to your Mac and launch iMovie. Then you'll copy the video *clips* into the program so you can edit them.

> **TIP** *If you don't have a DV camcorder, some iMovie versions that come on CD or bundled with your Mac include a sample project that you can use to practice your editing. In fact, iMovie has an Apple Help–based tutorial that's pretty good for learning the basics of iMovie.*

Hook Up Your Camera

You can hook up your camera at any point. FireWire is hot-pluggable and iMovie will recognize the camera once the camera is plugged in. So, I'd recommend launching iMovie first (the iMovie icon is on your Dock by default and available in the main Applications folder), just so you can see the status of things. Once launched, you'll see a dialog box with three options: Create Project, Open Existing Project, or Quit. Click Create Project, then give the project a name in the Save dialog box that appears. In the future, you won't see this dialog box, because iMovie automatically opens your most recent project. (To open a different project, you'll need to select File | New Project or File | Open Project.)

Now, use a FireWire cable to connect your DV camcorder to one of the FireWire ports on the side of your Mac. Both of the connectors are designed to fit only in the correct direction.

16

The longer, flatter connector plugs into the FireWire port on your Mac; the smaller, square connector connects to the camera.

Once you've got the camera connected, turn it on. If all goes well, iMovie will recognize the camera, as shown in Figure 16-1.

Depending on the camera, it may need to be in Playback or VCR mode in order for iMovie to control the camera. Then, click the small Camera mode icon (it looks like a little camcorder in silhouette) to put iMovie in Camera mode so it can control the camera. If the camera is in its recording mode, point it around the room and you'll see the image play through the iMovie viewer (called the *monitor* window) in real time.

NOTE   *Apple maintains a list of compatible cameras and manufacturers at http://www.apple.com/macosx/upgrade/devices.html on the Web.*

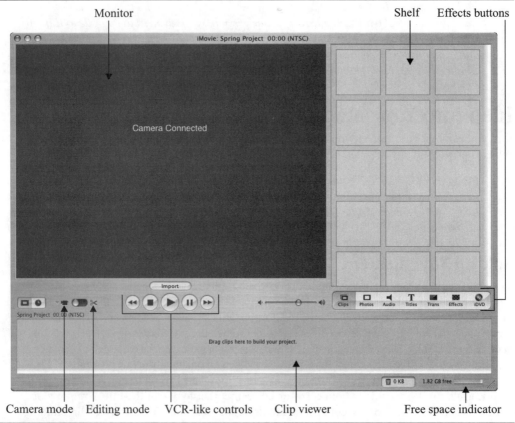

FIGURE 16-1   iMovie has recognized my camera and is ready to import video clips.

Import the Clips

Once you have iMovie connected to your camcorder and iMovie is in Camera mode, you're ready to import clips. With your camcorder in VCR or Playback mode, click the Import button on the iMovie interface and iMovie will fire up your camcorder and start importing clips from the camera.

> **NOTE**   *If you want every clip on your camcorder, make sure you've rewound the tape. You can do so using iMovie, if you like, by clicking the Rewind button in the monitor window while you're in Camera mode.*

iMovie moves through the tape and finds clips to import, then it places them on the "shelf" on the upper-right side of the iMovie screen. Each clip is a distinct segment of video; once you're in iMovie, you'll be able to drag-and-drop movie clips to change the order of the segments in your video.

> **TIP**   *iMovie ends the current clip whenever it encounters a point on the tape where you pressed Pause or Stop. If you'd prefer to have your clips imported as one long clip, choose Edit | Preferences, and on the Import tab, turn off the Automatically Start New Clip at Scene Break option.*

Let iMovie continue to import clips until you've got all the clips you need. When you're done importing, you can click the Import button again to stop the process. Note that you can also use the VCR-like controls (when Import is not selected) to move around on the tape if you need to find additional clips you want.

You should be aware that digital video clips take up *tons* of hard disk space. In the iMovie window, you can see a free space indicator that shows you how much hard disk space is left on your Mac. You'll have to watch this carefully. In raw DV format, video takes around 3MB per *second* of video being created. That means every five minutes of video takes up about 1GB of hard disk space. You should watch the free space gauge to make sure you're not running out.

> **NOTE**   *If you're planning to eventually save the video in QuickTime format (for playback on computers or via the Internet), it will be compressed and take up much less space, but your raw clips still require a lot of hard disk while you're working with them in iMovie.*

Preview Your Clips

Once your clips are imported, you can preview them if you like. Click a clip on the shelf and it appears in the monitor. Now, click Play to see that clip, or use the other VCR-like controls to fast forward, rewind, stop, or pause. There's also a volume control in the monitor window if you need to change the volume.

Toss a Clip

Do you have a clip on the shelf that you don't want? You can toss those clips into iMovie's special Trash receptacle. Just drag the clip from the shelf to the small Trash icon. (This is not the same as

16

the Mac's Trash can.) You can also select a clip and press the DELETE key if that's more your speed. You can empty the Trash by selecting File | Empty Trash or by clicking the small Trash icon and choosing OK in the dialog box.

As you're working in iMovie, the parts of clips that get trimmed while you're editing are put in this Trash as well. And emptying the Trash will reset the Undo function, so you won't be able to undo anything you've done prior to emptying the Trash. So, make sure you're happy with all the edits you've made recently before emptying.

Edit Your Video

Once you have your clips imported into iMovie, you're ready to start editing. You'll do this in two steps: First, you clean up your imported clips, if necessary. Then, you'll lay the clips down in the clip viewer and arrange them to please.

Crop Your Clips

Although you're free to edit your clips once you've placed them in the *clip viewer* (the area at the bottom of the screen where you'll arrange the order of your clips), I think it's best to clean them up while they're still on the shelf. Then you can organize the clips a little more easily.

Select a clip on the shelf by clicking it once. It will appear in the monitor window. Now, you can do some basic cropping to the clip to get it to the rough length you want it to be. To crop a clip, you'll need to get to know the monitor's controls a little more intimately.

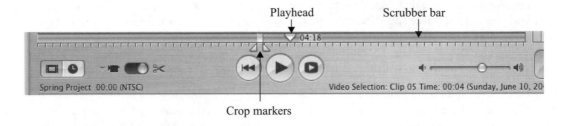

The scrubber bar is a bar that shows you the length of the clip. As the clip plays, you'll see the playhead move along the scrubber bar to show you where you are in the clip. You can drag the playhead to any point in the clip to start at that point. Once you have the playhead in about the right place, you can use the arrow keys on the keyboard to get it to exactly the frame of video you need.

The crop markers appear when you hold down the SHIFT key and click the mouse just below the scrubber bar. These markers can be used to select the area of a movie that you'd like to crop. Just drag the crop markers to the beginning and end of the section of the clip that you'd like to *keep*.

Once you have that portion selected, choose Edit | Crop from the menu. Only the portion of the original clip that was between the two markers will remain.

If you'd like to undo the cropping, you can do that. In fact, iMovie is capable of multiple Undo commands, so you can undo a series of edits or changes if you're not pleased with them. Just select Edit | Undo to undo a change.

Split Your Clips

If you need to split a single clip into two different clips, you can do that, too. Use the playhead to choose the exact point where you'd like to split the clip in two, then choose Edit | Split Clip at Playhead to split the clip. The clip now becomes two clips on the shelf.

TIP *iMovie has a neat trick—select a clip on the shelf and then choose Advanced | Reverse Clip Direction. The clip will now play backwards!*

Rename Clips

If Clip 01 and Clip 02 aren't creative enough for you, you can give your clips new names. Click on the name of a clip on the shelf. Wait a second and the name becomes highlighted, just as if you were renaming an icon in the Finder. Now you can edit the name of the clip; press RETURN when you're finished.

Arrange the Clips

With your clips cropped down to the parts you want, you're ready to drag them from the shelf to the clip viewer. Make sure the clip viewer tab (the one with the eye icon on it) is selected, then drag clips down to the viewer. You can drag them in any order—in fact, you're using the clip viewer to create the order for your video.

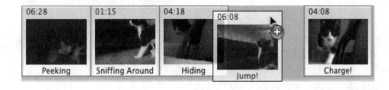

Once you have clips on the clip viewer, you can still move them around all you want. Just drag-and-drop a clip to its new location. And once you've got everything arranged on the clip viewer, you can play the whole movie through if you'd like. Make sure you don't have any of

16

the clips selected (you can use the Edit | Select None command to make doubly sure), then click the Play button in the monitor window. You'll see the video from start to finish.

You can also select one, two, or more clips in the clip viewer and play them back in the monitor window. To select more than one clip, hold down the SHIFT key while you select them. Then, click Play in the monitor window to view the series of clips you've selected.

To remove a clip, drag it back to the shelf. If you're absolutely sure you don't need it any more, you can drag it to iMovie's Trash icon, or you can select the clip and press DELETE.

Transitions, Sounds, and Titles

If you've been reading along so far, you're probably impressed with how easy iMovie is. You've already got an edited video! Well, it's not going to get much harder. Instead, you're just going to easily lay in some transitions and sounds, and add titles to your movie using a little more drag-and-drop.

Transition Between Clips

Transitions are just the fades and wipes between clips in your video. You don't have to use transitions as much as you might think; often, a clean cut between two clips looks fine. But you'll find that transitions are useful in many cases, either to suggest the passage of time, to help the viewer change thoughts along with you, or just to make things a little smoother between two different scenes. Plus, adding a transition is a great way to make your video look like it was edited on expensive professional equipment. And lots of transitions can work well for projects such as music videos or montages.

Before you can add a transition, you'll need two clips between which you can create a transition. Or, with some types of transitions (such as Fade In or Fade Out), you can create a transition at the beginning or the end of your video. In either case, you need to consider where the transition will look good.

Once you've got that location locked in your head, click the Trans button over in the Effects pane. The transition list pops up, along with the preview screen that shows you how your transition will look. Select the transition you'd like to use from the list. Whenever you click a transition, you'll see a small preview in the preview window. Likewise, you can click the Preview button to see the transition previewed in the monitor window.

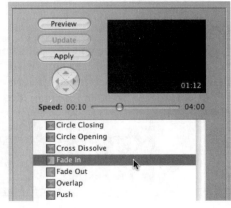

TIP *If I'm planning a transition between two clips, I like to select the two clips in the clip viewer (hold down SHIFT while you're selecting the second clip), and then I select one of the transitions from the list. The preview shows a sample of the transition between the two selected clips.*

Once you've found the transition you like, you should use the slider to select the amount of time you want the transition to take (remember, a number like 2:15 means 2 seconds and 15 frames). Then, drag the transition (you can click and drag the words or the small icon) down between the two clips (or in front of the first clip or behind the last clip) where the transition should take place. A small box appears in the clip viewer, representing the transition. You'll also see a small red line as the transition is rendered. (You'll need to wait for this to complete before you can view the video in the monitor. You can do some other dragging and dropping if you like, though.)

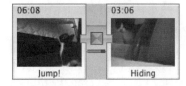

NOTE *Some transitions also use the arrow controls in the Trans pane. The arrows can be used to determine the direction in which the transition will take place. For instance, the Push transition lets you choose a direction.*

Add Titles to the Video

Another pro-level touch is to add titles to your video. You can add titles anywhere in your movie if you'd like to introduce the video, roll some credits, or just have a little fun with written commentary on the screen.

To superimpose titles on a particular clip, select the clip in the clip viewer and click the Titles button. The title controls appear, showing you a list of title styles and some options for those titles.

To get started, select one of the title styles, and then enter text for the title. You can also choose the font, font size, and color for the title text from the pop-up menus, if desired. (Note that if you want to create a new, self-contained title clip, you can turn on the Over Black option, as discussed in the sidebar later in this section.) Whenever you make a change, you'll see what your title looks like in the small preview window, or you can click the Preview button to see the titling in the big monitor window.

There are a number of different types of titles. As you click through them, you'll notice that they offer different ways you can type information, too. For instance, some titling schemes will support scrolling or centered credits, and they offer you multiple lines for those credits. Other options will enable you to create just a single title line. Still others allow for an entire block of text, which can be scrolled, centered, and so on. You can experiment with the different types to see which works best with the type of titling you're trying to do.

16

Also, notice the Pause slider and the Speed slider in the title controller. The Speed slider allows you to determine how quickly the title effect will appear and disappear, while the Pause slider determines how long the title will appear, unchanged, on screen. These may be important if you'd like the title effect to fill the clip that it's overlaying. You'll need to use the sliders to make the length of the titling sequence the same as the length of the clip it's overlaying. If it's longer, the titling will overlap two clips. (You'll notice that the shortest amount of time the title sequence can span is dictated by the effects that are being performed. After all, the title can only scroll or otherwise animate so fast, for instance.)

NOTE *If your titling sequence is shorter than the clip it overlays, then a split is created when you drag in the title style. The titled portion of the clip is followed by the new second clip that represents the rest of the original clip's video.*

Once you've got the length of the title the way you want it (again, you can test by clicking Preview), you can drag the title style from the style list down to the clip viewer. Place the title style in *front* of the clip that the title should overlay. The titled clip appears in the clip viewer. The titling needs to be rendered, so you'll see a small red progress indicator on the clip. You can't play the clip until it's done rendering.

Once the titled clip is rendered, you can view the movie again to see how your new title fits into the scheme of things.

TIP *You can add a transition to a titled clip, but you need to render the titled clip first, then render the transition. For instance, if you want to fade into a titled clip, create the titled clip first, then place the Fade In transition in front of the titled clip.*

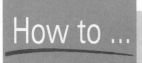

How to ... Add "Over Black" Titles and Credits

If you'd like to create titles or credits on a standard black background, you can do that easily. In the titling window, select a title style that's designed for credits (Centered Title, Centered Multiple, Rolling Credits, Rolling Centered Credits, and Centered Multiple are good choices), then turn on the Over Black option. Choose White (or a slightly more gray-white color, particularly for TV playback) as the text color. In the text area, you'll likely find a number of text boxes for typing your credits; you can click the Add button to add more. (Click the Preview button to see how the credits line up. You may need to type different parts of each credit line in different text areas to make the credits look right.)

When you're done building your credits, just drag the title style to the clip viewer and drop it where you want the credits. (You'll probably place this title clip at the end of all your other clips, since it's being used for credits.) The black-screen credits are rendered, and once they're ready, you can play your video to see them.

Add Special Effects

You can explore some optional special effects by clicking the Effects button. They range from effects to change the colors of your image (including an Old West–style Sepia Tone or Black-and-White effect) to those that change the sharpness, brightness, or focus settings of the image. Using an effect is easy—select the clip in the clip viewer, then select the effect. Now, a few slider bars or other controls will appear in the effects controller area; change them to taste. (Not all effects have sliders.)

When you like what you see, click the Apply button to apply that effect to the clip. Once you've applied the effect, you'll see a small red bar appear on the clip in the clip viewer, and it'll grow as the effect is completed. Note that you have to rerender a clip that already has a transition attached to it if you add an effect, but you can place an effect on a titled clip.

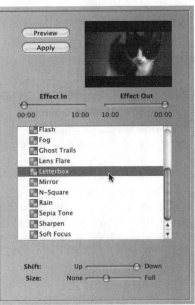

TIP

The effects controls offer another interesting twist. You can choose an Effect In and an Effect Out time for the clip. This causes the effect to take place over time, meaning that, for instance, the frames of the clip will become Sepia Tone or Black and White as they play back, instead of the entire clip taking the effect. You'll find this fun to play with. Set different Effect In and Effect Out times and preview the results to see what might work for your clips.

Drop in Sound Effects

You can create an entire soundtrack for your movie, but, before you do that, you might want to add some simple sound effects. Click the Audio button and choose iMovie Sound Effects from the menu at the top of the Effects pane—you'll see some sample sounds you can add to your video.

To view the sound portions of your movie, click the Timeline tab (the one next to the Clip Viewer tab that looks like a clock face). Now you'll see three different tracks; each looks a little like a bar graph. The top track is the video track—you'll see bars that represent the video clips you've added to the movie. The second track is your first audio track; you can add the sound effects by dragging them to this track. The third track is the second audio track, which you'll generally use for adding underlying music if you'd like it in your movie.

To add sounds, simply drag them from the sound list in the Audio panel to the timeline. Place them on the audio track where you'd like them to occur relative to the video clips. The sound effects show up as small blue boxes with a line between them to indicate the duration of the sound. (Note that sound effects can be placed over other audio clips on either audio track, if necessary.) You can

16

then play the video to see how the sounds are matched up with the video. If the sound isn't in the right place, just drag-and-drop it to a new location in the sound effects track.

To remove a sound from the sound effects track, select it with the mouse and press DELETE.

Edit Your Audio

Not only can you work with external audio, but you can edit the audio that's part of your original camcorder clip as well. You can actually extract the audio, separating it from the video. Then you can change or even delete the audio, if desired. Some of that is beyond the scope of this chapter, but it's worth experimenting with.

First, note that you can simply change the volume level for a particular clip from the timeline. Select the clip on the top track, then use the volume slider at the bottom of the timeline to change the audio level for that clip's audio.

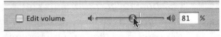

Next, you can extract the audio from your clip. Select the video clip and choose Advanced | Extract Audio. After iMovie has had time to think about things a bit, the extracted audio clip will appear as its own bar—it's now separate from its associated video clip.

Once you have any sort of audio clip on the timeline— whether it's extracted audio, a sound effect, or a music clip (you'll see how to add those in a moment), you can actually dig in and edit the volume of the audio pretty precisely. To do that, select the audio clip in question and click the check box next to Edit Volume. When you do, you'll see a small horizontal line appear in the audio clips. Click somewhere on the line to create a *keyframe,* which you can then drag up and down to change the volume level.

As you can see, adding points gives you a great deal of control and freedom to create a fade-out effect (like you're seeing above) or even to drop the audio abruptly and bring it back up again to deal with a loud sound or some sort of audio problem you want to work around.

Create a Paste-Over Effect

Another neat trick with iMovie is its ability to paste video *over* other video, leaving the audio of the clip intact. This is useful for something called *intercutting,* where you edit in different video scenes while the same audio continues to play. For instance, if you have a long video clip of a park ranger talking about a nature hike, you could intercut with clips of the trailhead, the flowers discussed, and the group as it hikes.

To create this intercut, you need an *original* clip and one (or more) intercut clips. Then, you select an intercut clip that's still on the shelf and highlight a short portion of the clip using the crop markers in the monitor window. Choose Edit | Copy. Now, on the timeline, you place the playhead at the point in the original clip where you'd like the copied video to appear instead of the original video. (When the aforementioned park ranger is talking about flowers, that's when you'd add the flower intercut clip.) With the playhead placed, select Advanced | Paste Over at Pastehead. Now the intercut clip will appear in the place of that portion of the original clip. When you play back that portion of the video, you'll see and hear the park ranger, then you'll hear the park ranger and see the intercut (flowers) footage, then you'll see and hear the park ranger again. Just like a roving reporter on the nightly news!

Lay in Some Music

The last editing step is to lay in your background music. Music is the perfect way to add different interpretations or moods to your clips. And iMovie lets you add them by accessing your iTunes library directly through the interface. Here's how:

1. Place the playhead at the point in your movie where you'd like the music to begin. (This is probably easiest if you've got the timeline showing.)

2. In the Audio pane, choose iTunes Library from the menu at the top. (You can also choose a particular playlist from your iTunes library, or you can choose an audio CD, if one has been inserted in your Mac's CD/DVD drive.)

3. Now you should see a listing of the songs in your iTunes library (or whatever source you've chosen). Select one of those songs and click the Place at Playhead button to add the song to your movie. By default, it's added at the playhead on the third line (the bottom line) of the timeline interface.

That's it. The audio is imported into the program and placed on the second audio track. When you play back the movie, you'll hear the music in the background.

What if that audio doesn't fit? You can actually click and drag the ends of an audio clip to change the length of the clip. (If you're dragging from the end of the song on the right, you can drag to the left to cause the audio to end earlier.) With a fade effect applied to the volume of the clip, you can take an abrupt song ending and make it seem pretty professional.

16

View and Export Your Movie

If you've gotten this far, hopefully you've pulled through the editing phase and you're ready to do something with your masterpiece. You can view it full screen to make sure everything looks good, then you can export the movie either back to your camcorder or as a QuickTime movie.

View the Movie

There's a special button that enables you to preview the movie full screen. It's just to the right of the Play button in the monitor's VCR-like controls.

To stop viewing the movie while it's full screen, simply click the mouse button or press any key.

> **TIP**   *If you choose Edit | Preferences, in the Advanced section you can choose whether the movie playback in iMovie is Standard Quality or High Quality. If the former, you'll see a more pixilated image on screen, but you'll see more frames of video per second. If you choose High Quality, the images will look good, but the video may appear to jump a bit. This only affects playback on screen. Once you get the movie back out to your digital camera, it should be smooth and as high quality as your camera is capable of producing.*

Export to Your Camera

If you plan to view the video on your television or transfer to standard VHS videotape, your best plan is to export it to your camcorder (unless you have a digital video deck, in which case I envy you). Your camcorder is designed to hook up to all that analog equipment quite nicely, so it's the perfect place to put your finished video.

iMovie and AppleWorks

I teach physics and astronomy at a high school of over 1,400 students in Manitowoc, Wisconsin. In physics, I use the tandem applications of AppleWorks and iMovie to help students create high-tech science reports. The students' reports start as simple AppleWorks word processing documents, and the report must adhere to guidelines using traditional fonts and a somewhat standardized format. Along with the text, the students are required to include a diagram of their apparatus, with labeled parts showing visually what is described verbally in their report. They also must include a table of information using organized columns of data and a graph of their results (from multiple trials).

As a final component, the students obtain much of their data by using digital video cameras to record their trials. Once the digital video is imported using iMovie, many students use the time index to obtain measurements far more precise than those traditionally recorded by hand using stopwatches. On-screen measurements of changes in position over time yield high accuracy when tracking objects in motion. Students then export both real-time and slow-motion video clips of their trials as full-quality digital QuickTime videos that are included in the final reports.

Joe Zoller
Physics & Astronomy Teacher
Lincoln High School (Manitowoc, WI)

NOTE *Don't forget that the length of the cassette in your camcorder may limit the length of the movie it can store from your Mac. (Your Mac has the potential to edit a one- to two-hour movie, depending on hard disk space, and some mini-DV cassettes have only a 30-minute capacity.)*

Here's how to export to your camera (in iMovie 4, this command is the File | Share command; in earlier iMovie versions, this command is File | Export):

1. Make sure the camera is connected via FireWire, and, if necessary, put the camera in VCR or Playback mode.

2. In iMovie, choose File | Share.

3. In the Share dialog sheet, choose Videocamera at the top of the dialog sheet.

4. Enter the number of seconds iMovie should wait while the camera gets ready to record. (This is often at least five seconds.) Then enter the number of seconds of black video you want recorded to the tape before and after the movie itself.

5. Click Share.

A progress slider will appear on screen and you'll see the video in the background. You'll also likely see the video on your camera's viewfinder or LCD display.

That's it. iMovie will stop your camera when the video is done recording. Now you can hook up the camcorder to the TV and show the in-laws, or hook the camera up to your VCR and make a videotape for mailing off to friends.

Export to QuickTime

Want to distribute your masterpiece via the Internet or place it on removable media to hand out? You'll need to export it to QuickTime.

CAUTION *Before publicly distributing any videos you create, you should take pains to make sure you aren't violating copyright laws. If you used music from CDs or downloaded images in your video, for instance, it may not be a good idea to distribute your video publicly over the Internet.*

This process can be time consuming, because the QuickTime movie needs to be compressed well beyond the minor compression that happens for the DV format. This compression is sophisticated and processor intensive. Its end result is a much smaller QuickTime movie that can play back with good quality. To create that compressed movie file, though, takes time.

Here's how to export to QuickTime:

1. Choose File | Share from the menu.

2. In the Share dialog box, choose QuickTime from the toolbar menu.

3. Now, select the type of video you want to create in the Compress Movie For menu. You can choose from different recommended compression schemes based on the

16

type of movie you're creating. (Despite its name, the CD-ROM setting is a good choice if you plan to store the movie on your hard disk or place the movie on removable media disks.)

If you know a little something about compression schemes, you might want to select Expert Settings from the Compress Movie For menu. You'll then be presented with a dialog box that enables you to specify the compression settings for your QuickTime movie. Also, if you'll be using this QuickTime movie in another movie editing or compression application, choose Full Quality DV for your export.

4. In the Share dialog sheet, click Share.

5. You'll see a Save dialog box—enter a name, choose a location, and click the Save button.

Now, give yourself a pedicure, go for a bike ride, or hit the phones and see if you can find some friends who'll go bowling with you. You'll be waiting a while, depending on the length of your video and the compression scheme you chose. In the meantime, you can't really use your Mac for much of anything; the whole processor is given over to the complex task of rendering the movie. (You will, however, see the video's progress in the monitor window, so at least you can check in every once in a while and see how things are going.)

When it's done, you'll have a new QuickTime movie that you can view in the QuickTime Player or distribute to your heart's content.

Create Your Movie DVD

If you've got a Mac with a SuperDrive—an optical drive that can write not only to CD media, but to DVD media as well—the system is a little different. To begin, once you've edited your movie, click the iDVD button in the Effects pane. The first thing you want to do is add chapter markers to your movie. These markers are used for the "scene selection" feature that iDVD can use to let people jump to particular scenes in your iMovie. If you've watched many commercial DVD movies, you're probably familiar with how scene selection works.

To add chapters, go back to your movie and place the playhead where a new chapter should begin, then click the Add Chapter button in the iDVD pane. When you do, an entry is added to the iDVD Chapter Markers list and the name is highlighted so that you can begin typing a name for the chapter marker. (iMovie will cleverly name the chapter with the name of the clip, which can make this a very painless process if you've already named some of your clips.)

(Note that you can remove chapters by selecting them and clicking the Remove Chapter button.) Once you've added chapter markers throughout your movie, you're ready to switch over to iDVD—click the Create iDVD Project. That automatically launches iDVD, and, after a moment, you'll see the iDVD interface (see Figure 16-2).

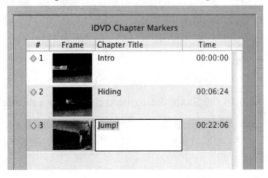

Choose a theme   Choose the media
Change settings   Customize drawer

Preview the disc
Burn the disc

FIGURE 16-2 iDVD enables you to build the DVD interface that viewers will see when they play the movie in their DVD players.

Customize Your Menus

Basically, iDVD does two things. First, it takes a QuickTime movie (including iMovie projects) and burns it to a DVD using standard MPEG compression in such a way that the disc can be viewed on a standard DVD player. That's pretty cool—it used to take a pricey third-party application to do that. Second, iDVD helps you design the interface for your DVD movie, so that viewers can play the movie, play chapter sections, and so on.

Let's start with the second part first. Click the Customize button if the Customize drawer isn't already visible. Then the first place to go is the Themes button, which enables you to dig in and see the general themes that Apple has designed for DVDs. Use the menu to choose from the different collections of themes, then click one to see it previewed in the main window. (See the following illustraton.)

16

Once you've chosen a theme, you can doctor it up a bit by adding a background image (or movie) and audio to the menu. You can do that in one of three ways:

- Drag items to the Background and Audio wells on the Settings pane of the Customize drawer.

- Drag items to the menu window itself (any QuickTime-compatible image, movie, or audio file).

- Click the Media button in the Customize drawer, choose a media type from the menu, and then access the items that have been created by other iApps.

Beyond that, you can double-click the text in the window to edit it. (For button text, click once, wait a second or two, and then click again—that ensures that you don't actually activate the button text by mistake.) And, of course, you can drag those items around on the screen. (At this point, you'll be closer to something a little less generic looking and a little more like Figure 16-2.)

 *Don't forget to save your project every so often. When working with a DVD project, it's sometimes easy to forget that you need to save, just as you do a word processing or spreadsheet document. (By contrast, iMovie saves work for you as you go along, as do iTunes and iPhoto.)*

The next step is to click the Settings button and make some choices about how the menu screen is going to work. The settings options cover three major areas:

- **Menu** In these choices, you can decide how long the menu's media will play before looping (particularly if you add an audio clip to the menu) and how iDVD will transition away from this menu screen when the user opts to view the movie or the chapter selections.

- **Text** Use these controls when you have text selected in the main viewer area. You can change the position, font, color, size, and drop shadow.

- **Button** Select button text and use these controls to change the look and size of the button in your DVD menu.

You'll need to do this customizing for each page in your menu. For instance, if you have a page for scene selections, you'll want to switch to that page and make similar edits to the background, audio, and text. You can usually switch to different pages by choosing the actual interface elements—double-click the Scene Selection button, for instance, to get to the scene selection menu. Another method, however, is to click the Map button, which shows you a flow

How to ... Create a DVD Folder

If you'd like to add to your DVD beyond the controls for simply creating a movie and choosing scenes, you can add a "folder" to the interface, which really gives you a new menu screen to add other movies or movie clips—perhaps even the "outtakes" of your project or something similar. In the main iDVD interface, click the Folder button. Edit the name of the folder just as you edit the other buttons. Now, you can double-click that new folder's name to access the folder menu itself. Make any changes you like.

To add movie clips to that folder, choose the Media button in the Customize drawer and drag movies from the menu listings to the items area on the menu screen. (Depending on the theme that you're using, the menu page probably has a target area where you can drop items to add them as clickable menu items. Other parts of the window may be reserved for the background; if you drop a movie, image, or audio icon on *that* part of the screen, you'll end up changing the background.)

If you don't find everything you want on the Media pane, you can dig into the Finder and drag items to the iDVD window, too—they'll all be gathered up and added to the disc when it's created.

chart of your DVD. That can be handy both for directly accessing the various menu pages and for getting a sense of how your DVD is organized.

Burn Your DVD

When you're done with your menu editing, you should be just about ready to burn the DVD and create your masterpiece. Before you do that, you may want to click the Preview button, which takes you out of Editing mode and puts you into a sort of testing mode. Now you can click around in your menus and act as if you were viewing the final DVD—make sure you don't have any odd issues or orphan menus or anything.

If all that looks good, you're ready to proceed. With a DVD-R disc on hand, click the Burn button in the iDVD interface. You'll click it once to open the iris, and then click it again (the pulsing "Fallout Shelter" icon) and the process begins.

NOTE *Did you get an error? You need a fair amount of free disk space in order to complete the iDVD burning process, because the items need to be encoded. It's best to go into a burning session with a few gigabytes of data free on your hard disk.*

First, you'll be asked to insert a blank DVD—do so and close the drive's tray (if necessary). If the DVD is recognized and everything proceeds as planned, then iDVD begins rendering items and writing the disc. This can take quite a long time—longer, for instance, than it would actually

16

take to play back the movie. That's because your Mac has to do quite a bit of math to take the raw video images and compress them into DVD-compatible MPEG2, then write all that data to the disc. When it's done, the disc will probably pop out of your Mac, and you'll see a dialog sheet in iDVD asking if you want to burn another copy. If you do, put a blank disc in and start the process again; if not, click Done and you're returned to iDVD.

Play a DVD Movie

If you have a Mac model with an internal DVD drive (which includes CD-RW/DVD "Combo" drives as well as DVD-RW SuperDrives), you can play DVD movies using DVD playback software included with your Mac. All you have to do is insert a DVD movie title in your Mac's DVD drive and launch the DVD Player application, which you'll find in the Applications folder on your Mac's hard disk. (In fact, DVD Player is usually launched automatically when a DVD is detected.)

Once you've got the player up and running, you'll see the Viewer window and the DVD controller—a small, sleek, "remote"-shaped window that offers some controls that should be familiar if you've used a VCR or even a tape recorder.

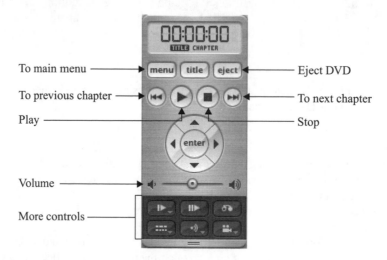

NOTE *You can actually view the controller in two orientations. Choose Controls | Use Horizontal Controller, or Controls | Use Vertical Controller, to switch between the two.*

To begin playing the DVD movie, click the Play button. You should see the movie's opening sequence and then, in most cases, you'll see the movie's main menu. You can then click in the Viewer window itself to select what you'd like to do next—view the movie, see additional features, and so on.

While you're viewing the movie, you can use the different controls to move forward or backward in the film. Most DVD movies are divided into chapters, so you can use the Previous Chapter and Next Chapter buttons to move back and forth between different chunks of the movie. And, at any time, you can click the Menu button on the controller to return to the DVD's main menu.

You can change the size of the movie window fairly easily. Choose the Video menu and choose the size you'd like, or choose Enter Full Screen if you'd like to watch the movie without seeing window controls or the menu bar. To bring the menu bar back, simply move the mouse up to the top of the Mac's screen and the menu reappears.

TIP   *While you're watching the movie you may also want to get that controller out of the way. You can do that by selecting Window | Hide Controller. To get the controller back, choose Window | Show Controller or press* SHIFT-⌘-C.

Many DVD movies include significant additional features, including more than one soundtrack (often in different languages), the ability to display subtitles, and even wackier features like the ability to change the camera angle while you're viewing a movie. To access these controls, drag the two lines at the bottom (or the right, if you're viewing the horizontal controller).

Point the mouse at one of these buttons and leave it there for a moment—you'll see a small label appear, showing you what the purpose of the button is. Click the button to activate that option, and you'll likely see a response in the small indicator in the controller.

When you click the Stop button, your place in the movie is saved; you can click Play again to resume from that point. If you're done with the movie, you can click Eject to eject the DVD from your Mac.

16

Chapter 17

Create Music with GarageBand

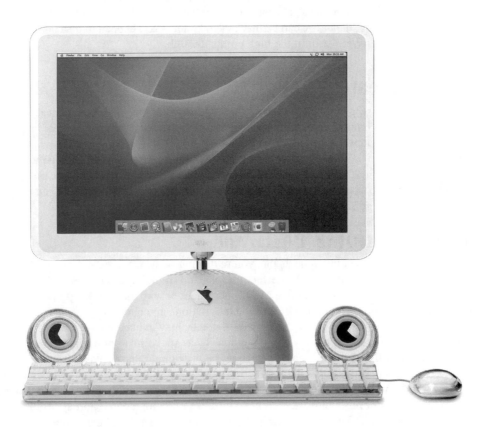

How to…

- Get started with a song
- Add instrument loops
- Change volume and edit sounds
- Connect MIDI and USB controllers
- Record your own instruments
- Export your song

The youngest member of the iLife bundle that's included with consumer Macs is also the youngest at heart—GarageBand, an application that emulates a recording studio, enabling you to piece together instruments and create your own musical compositions. It's a ton of fun if you happen to have an interest in music and some time on your hands. It takes a little learning to get up to speed, and, of course, the music can be made even better if you happen to be a talented musician in a way that I'm not. We'll still hit the high points, though.

Get Started Creating Songs

When you begin working with GarageBand, the "document" that you're creating is a song. In that song you're able to combine three different elements—software instruments, "real" instruments, and software music loops. Each time you add a new instrument or loop, it gets its own track in the song—in that sense, it works a little like iMovie. To build your song, you continue to add *tracks* until you have all of the instruments that interest you and those instruments are playing at the moments in the song when you want to hear them. Figure 17-1 shows a full-fledged song that's been created in GarageBand.

Understand MIDI vs. Digital Audio

So what are these different instruments that you're dealing with? GarageBand can work with both MIDI (Musical Instrument Digital Interface) tracks and digital audio tracks. A MIDI track is a series of software commands that tell a MIDI instrument how to play back a particular melody or bass line. You can sort of think of MIDI as the instructions given to a player piano. In fact, many people have MIDI-capable keyboard synthesizers that they may or may not use with their computers. (Until GarageBand came along, my MIDI keyboard was spending a lot of time in a closet.) With a MIDI track, you'll find that it's easy to change the instrument that is played as well as the way it's played—that's because the MIDI instructions are played back by *music synthesizers*. Apple has some good ones built into QuickTime technology that work with GarageBand. To create a MIDI track, you either use an on-screen keyboard or you connect an external MIDI instrument to your Mac via an interface of some kind. We'll discuss those a little later in the chapter.

FIGURE 17-1   Here's how GarageBand looks when you've put together a song.

The other type of track that GarageBand can deal with is a digital audio track. In this case, it's an actual recorded instrument that is being played back through your speakers via GarageBand. There are two different approaches you can take: you can record real instruments that you connect to your Mac, and you can use instrument *loops*, which are recordings of real instruments, but which can be transposed and otherwise altered to make them fit into your song.

In fact, GarageBand includes two different types of loops that you can use in your songs—software instruments and real instruments. The software instruments are more flexible—you can change a looping software instrument from a piano to percussion, if you want to. The real instrument loops are recorded instruments that are a little less flexible, but tend to sound better.

For other "real" instruments, you'll need to connect the instrument to your Mac, and, most likely, you'll need to do it using an adapter of some sort. We'll cover that a little later in this chapter. One real instrument that doesn't necessarily require special equipment is your voice. You can use your Mac's microphone input to sing, talk, or sample your own voice if you feel that adds to what you're trying to do artistically.

So, that's the background. The first step is to begin a new song and then you can start adding loops, even if you don't have a musical bone in your body.

17

Create a New Song

To get started, you'll need to get started. You do that by launching GarageBand. It should be on your Dock, and if not, there's a GarageBand icon on your Applications folder that you can double-click to launch the application. If you've never created a song before, you'll be greeted with a dialog box asking if you'd like to load an existing song or create a new one. Choose New and the New Project dialog box appears.

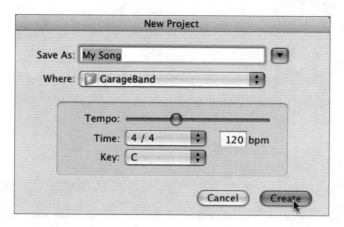

Give your song a name, choose a location for the files that will be created, and choose a tempo, a time signature, and a key for your composition. Click Create and, after a moment, you'll see the GarageBand interface appear. You may notice two things immediately: your song already has a single track, set to Grand Piano, and a keyboard appears on the screen. Using your mouse pointer, you can click on that keyboard and you should immediately hear piano sounds play through your Mac's speaker(s) or headphones.

Save, Quit, Close, or Open a New Song

You may not have done anything yet in your song, but it's worth knowing that you should save your work every so often in GarageBand. Choose File | Save after you've made changes that you want to keep. Note, also, that GarageBand has another interesting command—File | Revert to Saved. You can invoke that command when you've been working in a song and you decide you *don't* like the changes you made. Choose Revert to Saved and you'll return to the most recently saved version of the song.

To quit GarageBand you can do one of two things—choose GarageBand | Quit GarageBand, or choose File | Close or click the close button on the GarageBand window. Oddly, this also closes the application. (I said "oddly" because it doesn't conform to how most Mac applications behave.)

Finally, if you're working in one song and you want to begin work on another (or you want to switch to a different song), you do that not by closing the current song—which, as mentioned, would also quit GarageBand—but by selecting File | Open, or File | Open Recent.

Create Tracks in Your Song

So the burning question is, what's the first step once you've created a song? Actually, I generally start my GarageBand songs by digging into the instrument loops, laying down some rhythm, and getting a sense of the song I want to build from that. But, since GarageBand opens to a piano and some keys, let's start there with a simple recording of a software instrument.

Before we get into that, though, a word about the color coding in GarageBand. As you work with GarageBand, you'll see tracks and instruments in different colors. A green color is a software instrument, while a blue color represents a real instrument. Each reacts a little differently. A real instrument can be transposed in most cases but not edited; a software instrument can be edited (you can go in and change the notes for that instrument), and you can change the instrument sound for a software instrument at any point.

Create a Software Track

If you've ever played piano or keyboard, you probably haven't done it with a mouse pointer. Well, that approach in GarageBand probably isn't the best one, but it can be handy when you're simply trying to record a few notes for a melody line.

The keyboard can be stretched (drag the resize area at the bottom-right corner), and you can click the left and right arrows on the side of the keyboard to change the octaves that you're viewing. To play a note, of course, you click that note.

Once you're ready to record something using the keyboard, simply place the playhead at the beginning of the track in the GarageBand window and then click the Record button, which is the red button next to the player controls (as shown in the following illustration).

GarageBand will begin recording immediately, so it's up to you to play some notes. When you're done, click the Record button again.

17

If you want a little prep time after clicking Record, turn on the command Control | Count In. That will give you a measure's worth of beats before the recording begins.

Like the result? If not, you can click the audio segment that you just created and press the DELETE key on your keyboard. If you do like it but you want to make some alterations, you can double-click the audio segment to change to the editing tools. I'll cover those in the section "Edit Software Tracks" later in the chapter.

You can also resize the clip if you need to. Sometimes there's a delay between the moment that you stop playing and the moment you click the Record button again to stop recording, for instance. If that's the case, you can trim the clip back by simply moving the mouse pointer to the right side of the clip and dragging it backward. Note that you want the mouse pointer to show a vertical line and an arrow:

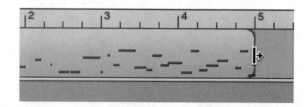

A curly line and arrow is used for looping tracks, which we'll discuss later in the section "Add Instrument Loops."

Add and Delete Tracks

To create a new track so that you can do some additional recording with the on-screen keyboard, click the plus (+) icon at the bottom of the track list. That brings up the New Track dialog box, where you can choose the instrument that you'll be adding. By default it's set to the Software Instrument tab so that you can move through the options and select the instrument that you'd like to use.

If you decide you don't need a particular track in your composition, click to select that track in the GarageBand window and then press ⌘-DELETE. That deletes the track and any segments that have been recorded on (or otherwise added to) that track.

Change Software Instruments

When you're working with software instruments, you can immediately change that instrument for a particular track and have the notes that you've recorded play in that new instrument. So, if you've created a melody line in the Grand Piano instrument and you'd like to have it play as an organ, instead, you can change the instrument. To do so, simply double-click the instrument's name in the Tracks column on the left side of the GarageBand window. (You can also choose Track | Show Track Info or press ⌘-I.) When you do, the Track Info window appears.

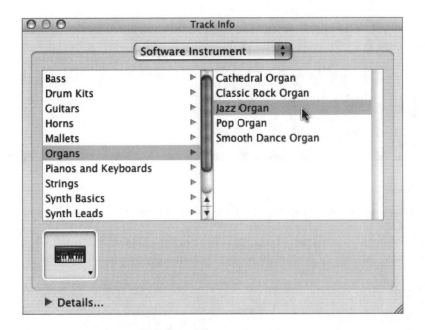

The Track Info window uses a Finder columns-like interface. Click an instrument group on the left side and you'll see a list of specific instruments from which you can choose.

You can click the Details button to see more about the instrument and its settings. The Details settings are ultimately used to define the sound associated with this instrument. They're complex and beyond the scope of this chapter, but you can dig in and play with the various effects and settings to see if you can get the exact sound that you want.

Add Instrument Loops

To me, this is the fun part. I'm not much of a mouse pointer keyboardist, myself. So when I work in GarageBand, I like the drag-and-drop approach to building a song.

The loops are essentially predefined *measures* of music that are designed to "loop" well, meaning they can play over and over again and sound like they're being played continuously. Obviously, this can work well for drums and percussions, which tend to be played that way in many types of music. But you'll find that loops can also sound pretty good for other instruments—a base line, a rhythm guitar—to help you build toward a complete song. And while the song that you create probably won't win a Grammy, it's not a half-bad way to create an original composition for use behind an iPhoto slide show or in an iMovie video.

To find the loops, you'll dig into the Loops Browser. To do that, either click the eyelike icon in the GarageBand interface (I'm not sure why it's an eye, unless maybe that means "browse")

17

or choose Control | Show Loops Browser. When you do that, you'll see the GarageBand window retool and the Loops Browser appear at the bottom of the screen.

How to Browse

The browser works in an interesting way. When you first open it, you should see that all of the buttons are active except, perhaps, the Favorites button. This means you can choose any of the options shown to begin limiting the loops that you look at. You can click Guitars or Urban or Relaxed, for instance, and when you do, you'll see options that are limited by whatever keyword you selected.

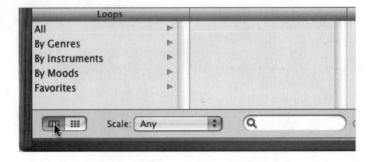

Now, you'll see a list of items appear on the right side of the browser pane. If you'd like to limit your browsing further, you can do that—click another of the remaining active buttons. For instance, if your first choice was Urban, you could now click Drums to see just those options; or, conversely, if you had picked Drums, you could click Urban to limit the drum choices momentarily.

To turn off a keyword, click it again. That should take you back to a point that reveals more instruments.

Play with this interface a bit and you'll get used to it. Note also that there's a small search box at the bottom that you can use to search for loops by name, and you can choose to limit the results to a particular scale in the Scale menu—major, minor, or loops that are good for both. Finally, the browser offers you the option of a Finder columns-like interface if you prefer it. At the bottom-left corner, click the Columns icon to change to a columns-based interface for choosing loops:

Add Loops to Your Song

Once you find the loops that you like, the next step is to add them to your song. There are a few rules to consider here. Each unique instrument that you add should be on its own track. This is particularly important for software instruments. The main reason is that if you put a software instrument on an existing track, it will play back using that track's instrument, not its original sound. (For instance, if you add a software instrument labeled Drums to an existing track that's defined as a piano, that drum sequence will play as if piano keys were being played.)

NOTE   *Remember the color coding as you browse instruments and add them to your song. Instruments labeled with a green musical note icon in the Loops Browser are software instruments, and those labeled with a blue sound-wave icon are hardware instruments. Also, recognize that loops have a base tempo, but they are automatically adjusted to the tempo of the song that they're added to.*

Here's how to add an instrument on its own track:

1. Place the playhead in GarageBand where you're going to want this loop to begin. (If you're just starting out, make sure the playhead is at the beginning of the song.)

2. Drag the loop from the browser up to the main song interface and drop it below any existing tracks. Note, as shown in the next illustration, that you can drop the loop at a place other than the playhead. You'll see a thin line appear to show you where the loop will be dropped.

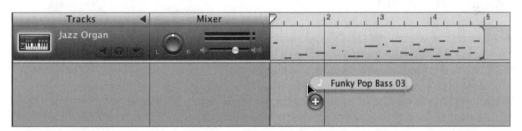

That should create a new track with your loop on it.

Now, it's possible that the loop you've added suits your needs; if that's the case, you can browse for another loop and repeat the previous steps to add another loop to another track of your song. In many cases, though, you're going to want this particular loop to repeat a few more times—that's how you can create a driving bass or drum track. To repeat a loop, you need to move the mouse pointer to the right side of the loop. Move the pointer around a little until you see the curly line pointer.

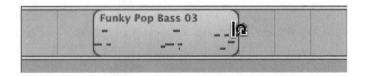

17

That's the loop tool. Click and hold the mouse, and drag to the right. You'll see an identical clip begin to form next to the previous one, and they'll be attached.

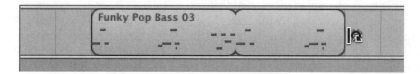

Keep dragging and you'll see that an indentation appears to show you when another full loop has been completed.

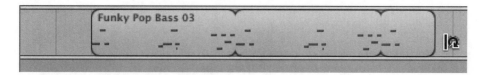

Keep dragging until you have as much of that loop as you want. You can also click and drag the loop itself to reposition it within the song if necessary. To delete a particular loop, select it so that it's highlighted, then press the DELETE key on your keyboard.

Arrange Your Song

We're digging a little deeper into the parts of GarageBand that will allow you to explore your talent for putting musical instruments together. As you're adding tracks—whether they're recorded using the on-screen keyboard or loops that you drag in—you'll be building your song. You build the song by adding tracks that represent the instruments you're adding to your "garage band." (The fact that some of those instruments can replicate an entire symphonic strings section is just icing on the cake.)

When you look at the GarageBand interface, you can see that it's very focused on time. The stretched instruments' representations show you when an instrument will be playing and for how long. It's up to you to move those gaps around so that the song sounds good and isn't too repetitious. So, for a typical rock-and-roll song, you may have a consistent drum track and bass line, but you'll have other instruments—guitars, pianos, keyboards, maybe a sax—that don't play in every measure of the song. Figure 17-2 shows how a song is composed of different instruments coming in at different times.

 *Figure 17-2 also shows the slider that you can use to view more or less of a song at one time in the interface.*

As you play back a song—which you do by placing the playhead and pressing the Play button in the interface (you can also press the SPACEBAR to start and stop playback), you'll see the playhead sweep along the song. Any loop that appears on a track at the moment the playhead hits it will be

Other instruments play at
different times in the song

Beat line is
continuous

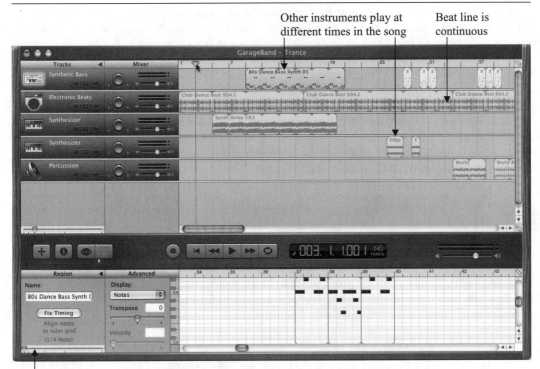

Slide control to display more or less
of the song in the window

FIGURE 17-2   In this techno song, you can see that the "beat" line is consistent, but other
instruments are played only at certain points during the song.

played at that moment. That's how you time different instruments to start and end playback, to add
interest to the song. So, for instance, if you need to add an electric guitar lick in part of a song—
or an orchestra hit at just one or two spots—you place them on the timeline so that they begin to
play at the moment in the song when you want them to play. It's all about timing.

NOTE   *One more point of interest in Figure 17-2. Because the Club Dance Beat tracks use the
same instrument (the Electronic Beats instrument), it's okay to put different loops on
the same track. That's true in any case where you want to use different loops that are
played with the same instrument.*

17

Track Volume and Master Volume

GarageBand offers some fairly advanced options for editing loops and recorded instrument sounds
that we'll get into a little later in the chapter. For now, though, let's quickly cover setting the volume.

You set the volume for your song in two different places—a master volume level for the whole song and a separate volume level for each track, as desired. The volume levels can be set to change throughout the song, so they're handy for creating effects like a Fade In and Fade Out.

To set the master volume, choose Track | Show Master Track from the menu. Now, place a check mark next to the Master Volume check box. That makes the volume editable. Now you have two choices. First you can click and drag the master volume line up and down on the master track to change the overall volume for the song.

The other trick is to add *keyframes* to the volume line, so that you can change the volume between two keyframes. To create a keyframe, click somewhere on the line; a small purple dot appears. Now, you can drag these dots to cause the volume level to change over time. In this example, the audio level will fade out:

You can make the same choices about individual instruments. You can make a particular instrument louder, for instance, or you can put fade-in and fade-out effects on certain instruments. To do that, you need to reveal the volume line for a particular instrument, which you do by clicking the small triangle icon below the instrument's name.

Now, click the check box to turn on the volume controls for that instrument, and you're free to make changes the same way you made them to the master volume.

Record Your Own Tracks

GarageBand offers you two ways to record instruments as you play them. You can use a MIDI controller (usually a keyboard) to create software tracks, or you can connect an external electronic instrument—or an instrument with a microphone pickup—directly to your Mac for recording. (It may not be *directly*, as you may need some go-between electronics. I'll cover those in this section of the chapter.)

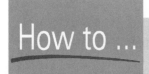

Use Sound Playback Tricks

As you're playing back a composition, you might find it handy to listen to only one track at a time. To do that, click the small Headphones icon under the track's name. That causes only that track to be audible as the song plays. To mute a track, click the small Speaker icon that's to the right of that Headphones icon.

Also, you'll find some keyboard shortcuts handy for playback. The left and right arrows move the playhead back a full measure with each press; the ⌘ key can move you to the beginning of the song, while OPTION-⌘ takes you to the end of the song. You can also use the PAGE UP and PAGE DOWN keys to move one entire screen back or forward (respectively).

Using a MIDI controller is interesting, because what you're essentially doing is feeding notes to GarageBand, not sounds. Once those notes are stored as a software instrument, you can change the software instrument to something completely different. (In fact, you can even change the notes once they're recorded.) So, a MIDI instrument offers flexibility. The downside is that you're ultimately playing a computerized instrument, so you're at the mercy of the quality of Apple's MIDI library. (Which, for the record, is pretty good.)

When you record an instrument directly into iTunes, you get what you play. If you have a good instrument, a good connection to your Mac, and you've got some talent, then this may be the way to go.

Connect MIDI and USB Controllers

How you connect your keyboard and your Mac depends on your keyboard and your Mac. If your keyboard is a USB-based MIDI keyboard that's designed for Mac OS X, you can connect it directly to a USB port on your Mac and it should work directly with GarageBand without any special modifications.

If you've got a keyboard that doesn't have its own USB connector (like mine), then you can get a MIDI-to-USB adapter like those made by M-Audio (**http://www.m-audio.com/**), Mark of the Unicorn (**www.motu.com**), or DigiDesigns (**www.digidesigns.com**). With such an adapter, you should be able to plug your keyboard into the adapter and the adapter into an available USB port. (On the device I use from M-Audio, the USB adapter needs to be connected to the side of the Mac, not a keyboard or hub, because it requires power from the USB bus.)

But, before you do plug in a device or adapter, if it requires driver software, you'll probably want to install that software first. (Check the instructions that came with the device.) Either

17

download the driver from the manufacturer's web site (which is the best way to make sure you have the latest version) or launch it off the included CD and install it on your Mac. Then, if it's recommended, restart your Mac; otherwise, plug in the MIDI device.

To find out if GarageBand recognizes the device, choose GarageBand | Preferences. In the Preferences dialog box, click the Audio/MIDI button. Now, you should see something like 1 MIDI Input(s) Detected on the MIDI Status menu. That means your keyboard is recognized.

Just because your keyboard is recognized doesn't necessarily mean it will play through. Check carefully to make sure the In and Out cables and ports are configured correctly. On my keyboard, I plug the cable labeled Out into the port labeled In on my keyboard. That's fairly standard, but might be confusing. (And, on some adapters, it might be reversed.)

Record and Play Back MIDI

Once your keyboard is connected and recognized, all you have to do is create a new track (Track | New Track or OPTION-⌘-N) and you'll see the New Track dialog box. In the dialog box, choose a Software Instrument. When you do, that instrument appears as a new track in the song.

Now, tickle the ivories. You should hear notes playing as if they were played on the selected software instrument. You can practice for a while if you like.

To record, place the playhead where you want to start recording and click the Record button. (You might first choose Control | Count In so that you get a four-beat count before you have to start playing the keys.) Now, play. When you're done, click the Record button again.

That's it—you'll have a recorded segment. To play it back, place the playhead at the beginning of the recording and press the SPACEBAR or click the Play button. To stop it, press the SPACEBAR or click the Play button again.

Want to change the instrument? Just double-click the name of the instrument in the Tracks list and you'll see the Track Info window. Select an instrument type on the left side and then select the instrument that you want to use on the right side. Close the window and the instrument has been changed. Play it back to hear the difference.

Edit Software Tracks

Once you've played and recorded a software track, you can dig into it and do quite a bit of editing. You can fix the timing automatically in some cases, or you can actually dig in and change the notes themselves.

To do that, select the recorded segment on its track and choose Control | Show Editor, or click the Editor button on the GarageBand interface. It's the icon that looks like a pair of scissors and a sound wave. When you do, you'll see the Editor interface.

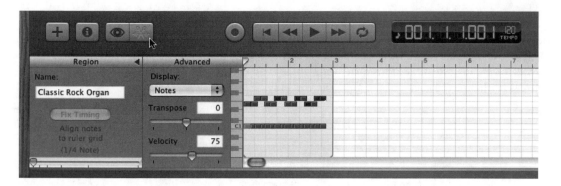

The editor gives you a few different tools. Select the Fix Timing button and GarageBand will attempt to even out the notes that you've played so that they align to a quarter-note grid. (It tends to work only with fairly simple melody lines.) You can also edit individual notes. Select a note (one of the small boxes) and you can change the velocity of the note, or you can drag the note around to place it elsewhere in the music segment. This can be handy for evening things out nicely.

You can also transpose an entire segment using the Transpose slider. Simply select it and slide around to change the key in which the musical segment plays.

When you're done with the editor, click the Editor button again to close the interface.

TIP   *As with any other instrument or loop, you can click the down-pointing triangle to set the volume for the clip that you've recorded.*

Record Actual Instruments

Probably the biggest problem you'll encounter when it comes to recording an actual instrument is figuring out how to connect it to your Mac. Some current consumer models include an analog line-in port, although many recent consumer models don't include such a port. (For instance, the iBook G4 doesn't include a line-in port, and iMac G4 models with processors slower than 1GHz also don't include them.) If your Mac has such a port, then you'll find some solutions for connecting instruments directly to your Mac, such as the Monster Instrument Adaptor (**www.monstercable.com**).

For Macs that don't feature such a port, a more comprehensive audio-to-USB translator box is a good idea. Such adapters are made by companies such as M-Audio and DigiDesigns. These options can get pretty sophisticated, enabling you to input more than one instrument at once, for instance, and giving you various preamplification options.

TIP   *For one-stop shopping, check out the Apple Store, which offers a number of accessories designed to work with GarageBand.*

17

With your instrument connected to your Mac, you can create a track for the instrument you'll be playing. Choose Track | New Track. In the New Track dialog box, choose the Real Instrument tab. Now, choose the instrument you plan to record—note that you can also choose some preset effects for the instrument. For instance, for a guitar, you can use the built-in amplifier and effects settings to change the sound of the guitar as you play.

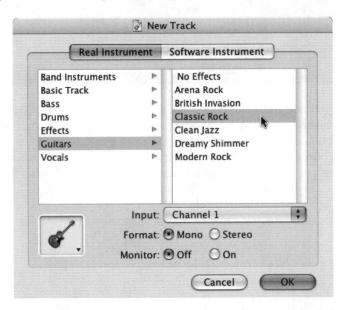

If none of the preset instruments works for you, then you can choose Basic Track and No Effects. Otherwise, from the Input box, choose where the instrument is located (what you choose depends on the adapter or port that you're using), choose whether to record mono or stereo, and whether you want to monitor the playback (do you want to hear it through the Mac's speakers as you record?). Then, click OK.

Now you should see the instrument on a track in GarageBand. When you're ready, you can record. Click the Record button. The button will illuminate, but recording may not actually start—the recording begins when you start playing. Play a note and you're off to the races.

When you're done, click the Record button again. Now you can change the volume or dig in and edit the sound the same way you do with other tracks.

Export Your Song

There's not quite enough room in this chapter to dig deep into some of the theory and science of arranging music, which is good because I don't know a lot about it. But once you've experimented and played and tested and figured things out, perhaps you've got a decent little arrangement. The last step is to get it out of GarageBand and off to somewhere else.

The easiest solution is to select File | Export to iTunes. When you do, you'll see a dialog sheet that shows GarageBand is creating a *mixdown*, which simply means putting all instruments in a digital audio format so they can be saved as a single AAC (Advanced Audio Codec) song that's compatible with iTunes. When the mixdown is complete, iTunes will be launched automatically and you'll see that the song has been added to your library.

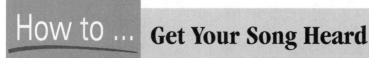

| ☑ Groovy Tune.band | | 1:20 | Todd Stauffer | Todd Stauffer's Alb... | | |

Once you have the song in iTunes, you can translate it to another format or otherwise access the file that's created and stored in your iTunes music folder. Plus, you can access your iTunes library from programs like iMovie, iDVD, and iPhoto and use your song in movies or slide shows.

Of course, you can also save your song in GarageBand format. That allows you to store the song and retrieve it as necessary. To play it back on another machine, you may need to ensure that the machine has the same loops and software instruments available, particularly if you've added any of your own.

How to ... Get Your Song Heard

Got a composition that you're proud of? Since the release of GarageBand, a number of web sites have sprung up to support promoting and swapping songs that are created within the program. Check out iCompositions (**www.icompositions.com**), where you can find hundreds of songs posted by participants, as well as news about GarageBand, tips for finding and using loops, and other exciting bits.

MacJukeBox.net is a similar site that offers news and commentary regarding GarageBand and other iApps, as well as a "Jukebox" where you can hear other people's songs. MacJams.com is more of the same, including forums, top songs, and prizes. Finally, there's Mac Idol (**www .macidol.com**), which purports to be a contest for original GarageBand compositions. Check the site for details on the file formats they accept and how you are expected to submit them.

17

Part III

Get Online

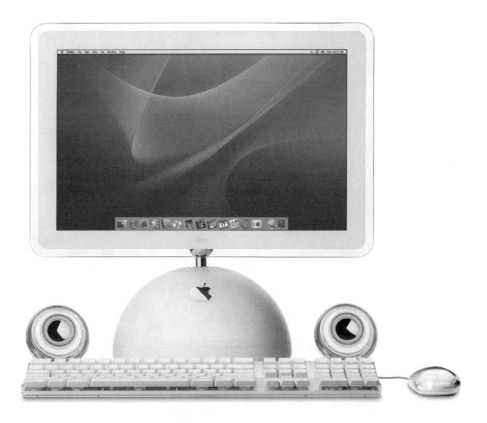

Chapter 18

Get Serious About E-mail and Mac.com

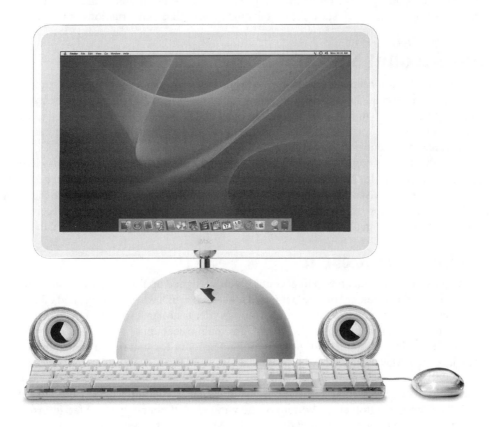

How to...

- Set up your e-mail account(s)
- Use Mac.com mail
- Organize your e-mail
- Get attachments, add signatures, build rules

You may have bought your Mac for the express purpose of getting e-mail—a lot of people do. Even if it wasn't your primary goal, you probably think e-mail is a big part of the computing experience. Electronic mail (e-mail) gives you the opportunity to communicate inexpensively and rather quickly in a written format. What were once letters between family, friends, and business associates have become electronic messages. What used to take days now arrives in seconds.

In this chapter I'll focus on Apple Mail, Mac OS X's full-featured e-mail program, and we'll build on the discussion that started with the quick-start Internet instructions in Chapter 5.

Is Your Account Set Up?

The first thing you'll need before you can send and receive e-mail is an e-mail account. Most likely you already have one—an e-mail account is created for you when you sign up for Internet access. And the best part is, with most ISPs, you'll have an e-mail account that corresponds to your Internet account name. If you were given the user name *myusername* when you created the Internet account, for instance, then your e-mail address is probably *myusername@myisp.net*.

If you've walked through the Setup Assistant discussed in Chapter 1, then you may already have your account set up. In that case, you can just fire up your e-mail application and begin sending and receiving. Likewise, if you've added your .Mac information to the .Mac pane in the System Preferences application of Mac OS X, then you're automatically set up to send and receive Mac.com mail. If not, then you may need to dig deeper into your e-mail settings, as discussed in this section.

Set Up a .Mac Account

Apple provides you with an e-mail account if you've signed up for its subscription .Mac service. The service offers a number of Internet-based tools such as iDisk, HomePage, and others, including a Mac.com e-mail account. The e-mail account is your user name followed by @mac.com as in steve@mac.com. (That's Apple CEO Steve Jobs' public account.)

Apple Mail will automatically configure that account for you if you've set up your Mac to recognize your .Mac user name. You can do that via the .Mac pane of System Preferences, as shown in Figure 18-1. Simply enter your .Mac user name and password, and all of your .Mac-related features in Mac OS X will be activated; if you don't have .Mac service but would like it, you can click the Sign Up button at the bottom of the window. (Of course, your .Mac information may already be entered if you submitted or created a .Mac account when you set up your Mac.)

Here's the System Preferences pane where you set up your .Mac account.

Set Up an E-mail Account

If you work with a third-party Internet service provider, you likely have an e-mail account through them—it may be the service that you use for dial-up or broadband Internet access, or it might be an ISP that provides you (or your company) with web hosting space. Or, you might be trying to access an Internet e-mail box that's managed by your company or organization.

Setting up any of these is straightforward, as long as you know certain things about the e-mail account:

- ■ **E-mail address**   Any Internet e-mail account has an e-mail address, generally in the form of *myname@myisp.net* or *myname@mydomain.com*. For instance, my main e-mail account is todd@macblog.com. Note that your e-mail address isn't always the same as your account name for the service, although they're often similar.

- ■ **Incoming mail server**   This is the address of the mail server computer where your incoming e-mail should be retrieved. Usually it's in the form of *mail.myisp.net* or *pop.myisp.net* for POP e-mail accounts.

18

Did you know?

Access Your Mac.com Mail Online

Apple offers a special web-based interface for accessing your Mac.com mail when you aren't near your Mac but do have access to a web browser. If you're a .Mac subscriber, you can visit **http://webmail.mac.com/** in most any web browser. Log in and you should have access to your .Mac account. Apple does a fairly good job of making the Webmail interface similar to Mail, but there are some definite differences. You'll notice, for instance, that clicking a message entry causes the page to open that message in the browser window—you can use your Back button to return to the message list.

In the Webmail message list, note that each message has a check box next to it. You can use those check boxes to select more than one message if you want to move them or delete them. Also, instead of a Mailboxes drawer, you can access the folders you've created by clicking the Show Folders icon at the top of the screen.

Apple offers a few other options for your Mac.com e-mail account, which are accessible by clicking the Preferences icon at the top of the Webmail screen. The Preferences offer you options for customizing the look and feel of Webmail, but also hide these extras in the Account section:

■ **E-Mail Forwarding**   You can select this option if you'd prefer that any messages sent to your Mac.com address are forwarded to another e-mail account. Forwarding has the advantage of allowing you to check your Mac.com e-mail from anywhere that you can check your other e-mail account. (For instance, you could forward to a Yahoo!, Excite, or Hotmail account, if you're already used to checking those accounts.)

■ **Auto Reply**   Select this option if you'd like .Mac to reply to all received messages with an automatic message you select. Enter an Auto Reply message that says "I'm out of the office for two weeks…" or "I'm on a meditation retreat in Nova Scotia…" and turn on the Auto Reply option. You'll still receive the e-mail messages whenever you check them in your e-mail program, and you'll still be able to reply to messages you've received, but, in the meantime, your senders won't be left wondering what happened to you and why you don't love them anymore. (Don't forget to turn *off* Auto Reply once you're back and functioning again in your day-to-day life.)

■ **Check Other POP Mail**   Enter the appropriate addresses, user name, and password and you can check mail from other POP accounts using the Webmail interface. You can choose to leave the e-mail on its server so that you can still retrieve it from a different application (like Mail), but this can be handy if you need to check more than one account while you're away from your Mac.

- **Account type**   You likely have one of two e-mail account types, either a POP account (Post Office Protocol) or an IMAP account (Internet Message Access Protocol). Which you choose depends on the type of account provided by your ISP. The main difference between the two is that a POP account is generally designed to download all incoming mail from the server to your Mac, while an IMAP account enables you to browse your e-mail while it's still on the server, downloading it to your Mac only when you want to read it.

- **User name**   This is the user name used to log you into your ISP's mail server. In many cases it's the same as the first part of your e-mail address, but not always.

- **Password**   This is the password that, along with the user account ID, enables you to log into your ISP's mail server and retrieve your e-mail.

- **Outgoing mail server**   This is the mail server used for outgoing messages, usually in the form of *smtp.myisp.net*. (SMTP stands for Simple Mail Transport Protocol.) This address is often different from your incoming mail server.

TIP   *In most cases, you should use the outgoing mail server provided by the ISP that you actually sign into for Internet access, not necessarily the ISP that hosts your e-mail account. For instance, if you sign onto the Internet using a cable modem, but you access an e-mail account provided by a different hosting provider, then you should use the cable modem ISP's outgoing mail server to send your e-mail. Otherwise, you may get "forwarding" error messages from the outgoing mail server at your hosting provider because you aren't recognized as a valid user.*

So what do you do with this information? If you're setting up your first account, you'll enter it in the Welcome to Mail screen that appears after you launch Mail. If you already have an e-mail account set up (for instance, if you have a Mac.com account or you signed up for Internet service when you first started up your Mac), then you will enter this information in Mail's Preferences, as described in the next section.

Use More Than One Account

Do you have more than one e-mail account? You'll be happy to know that Mail can handle messages from more than one e-mail account, allowing you to download from all your accounts at once, manage your messages from one inbox, and, as you've already seen in Chapter 5, send your e-mail from the account of your choice. (For the record, I use 10 accounts; our technical editor notes that he's managing 12 accounts from his copy of Mail!)

NOTE   *You can use Mail to access different people's e-mail accounts in your household or organization, but a better approach is to create multiple users, as discussed in Chapter 21. In that way, each individual can have his or her own e-mail preferences and archives— in fact, you can use different e-mail programs altogether, if desired!*

Here's how to add an account to Mac OS X's Mail:

1. Choose Mail | Preferences.

2. In the Mail Preferences window, click the Accounts icon. You'll see a window like Figure 18-2.

3. To create a new account, click the small plus symbol (+) at the bottom of the Accounts list.

4. You'll see New Account appear in the list, and the Description entry box will be highlighted. Begin typing to give a description for this account.

5. Now, choose an account type from the Account Type menu—your choices are Mac.com, POP, IMAP, and Exchange. Most standard-issue ISP-based accounts are POP accounts (which means e-mail is downloaded from a central mail server), although some can be accessed as IMAP accounts (which means the e-mail and sometimes your personal folders

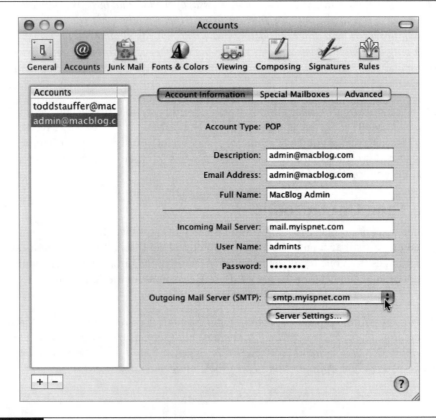

FIGURE 18-2   Here's the Mail Preferences window set to Accounts where a new account is being created.

are left on the server). IMAP is more likely for corporate or organizational accounts. Exchange is used if you have a Microsoft Exchange e-mail server that you need to access.

6. After you've chosen the account type, fill in the rest of the entries using the information described in the previous section, "Set Up an E-mail Account." (You can press the TAB key to move between the entry boxes.)

7. Note that the SMTP server entry is a menu, since you can sometimes use the same SMTP server for multiple e-mail accounts. (Generally you'll use the SMTP server provided by the company that offers you Internet access.) To add to that menu, select the Add Server command. You can then enter a new server address (and a user name and password, if necessary) in the SMTP Server Options dialog box.

8. Choose the Special Mailboxes tab if you'd like to customize how this account deals with messages that are moved to the Trash and Sent folders. By default, your deleted messages are moved to the Trash folder; here, you can set how long Mail waits before deleting them. You can also make choices regarding junk mail, which we'll cover later in the section "Manage Your Junk E-mail."

9. If you'd like to set advanced options for this account, click the Advanced tab at the top of the window. You'll see a number of interesting options, including the option to "Remove copy from server after retrieving a message:" that enables you to set a time frame for how soon messages should be deleted from your mail server after they've been retrieved from the server computer. (This is handy because it leaves your recent e-mail on the server computer so it can be retrieved in other ways, such as via a Webmail interface. But, it can also take up space on your mail server, which may be limited.) You can also enable and disable the account and determine whether it should be included when Mail automatically checks for new mail.

Close Mail Preferences and the account is created. Now, whenever you create a new message, you have the choice of using the new account to send the message (via the Account menu in the composition window) instead of your original one. When you click the Get Mail icon in the Mail viewer window, both (or all) of your e-mail accounts will be accessed and the new e-mail will show up in the inbox, unless you opt to change these options on the Advanced tab discussed in step 9 above.

You can also check this account individually. Choose Mailbox | Get New Mail | *Account Name* to check messages for a particular account.

18

Organize Your E-mail

You saw the basics of reading, responding to, and creating e-mail messages in Chapter 5. Once you've received more than a few messages in Mail, you'll probably want to start organizing them. Mail makes that easy enough to do, via the Mailboxes drawer and the multiple personal folders (which Mail calls *mailboxes*) that you can create for storing messages.

Create and Delete Mailboxes in Mail

To create a new mailbox in Mail, first select the *top level* where you'd like the new mailbox to appear. Most likely you'll select On My Mac, although you may wish to select a particular e-mail account if you have more than one that appears in the Mailboxes drawer (such as a Mac.com account).

Creating a new mailbox is simple—just choose Mailbox | New. (You can also CONTROL-click the account on On My Mac and then choose New.) In the dialog box that appears, confirm that the location for the new mailbox is correct in the Location menu, then enter a name for the new mailbox and press RETURN or click OK. The mailbox appears in the Mailboxes drawer, complete with a small folder icon (suggesting that this is a personal mailbox that you've created to organize messages).

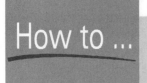

How to ... Customize the Toolbar in Mail

Delete, Reply, Reply All, and New are handy commands to have on the Mail toolbar, but they're not the only commands possible. What's more, you can decide exactly what commands appear on the toolbar and in what order. And, if you've read Chapter 3, you'll recognize the system that's used to customize Mail's toolbar—it's the same approach you can use to customize a Finder window's toolbar.

Select View | Customize Toolbar and you'll see a large dialog sheet appear, featuring many different icons and controls that you can add to the toolbar. Now, just drag items up from the dialog sheet to Mail's toolbar—you can even drag existing icons around on the toolbar itself to change the icons' positions. Also, at the bottom of the dialog sheet, you can select from the Show menu what you'd like to see in the toolbar: Icon & Text, Icon Only, or Text Only, as well as the option to Use Small Size (icons). To return to the default toolbar, simply click the default set of icons near the bottom of the dialog sheet. When you're finished customizing, click the Done button.

Want even more customization? You can choose View | Customize Toolbar when you're viewing an open composition window—either during a reply or while creating a new e-mail message. There, you can use the same process to customize the toolbar for editing and sending your messages.

 **Rebuild Mailboxes**

After working with mailbox folders for a while in Mail, you'll find that it's a good idea to *rebuild* those folders—a process that cleans up the database entries and recovers the storage space that had been used for deleted files. This is especially true if it seems to take a long time to view a particular mailbox or if you believe odd things are happening—messages don't seem to appear correctly or deleted messages remain in the mailbox folder.

To rebuild a mailbox, select the individual mailbox folder (it can be a mailbox you use for storing older e-mail or an inbox for one of your accounts), then choose Mailbox | Rebuild. You'll see the progress of the rebuild indicated on the status line. Each individual subfolder that you decide to rebuild needs to be rebuilt separately.

NOTE   *Wondering why you can assign mailboxes to a particular e-mail account? If it's a Mac.com or IMAP account, it's because those folders are stored online, on the mail server computer, instead of on your Mac. That makes them accessible from multiple computers—but, of course, it means you may fill your storage allotment more quickly, if you have one. For long-term storage, you can move items from the Mac.com inbox to mailboxes that are stored under On My Mac. But for short-term organization, you can use mailboxes that are created under your Mac.com account if you want them stored on Apple's servers.*

To move messages to the new mailbox folder, select them in the message list, then drag-and-drop items from the message list to that mailbox. You can also CONTROL-click on a particular message, choose Move To from the contextual menu, and then select the target mailbox folder.

TIP   *If you'd like to create nested mailbox folders (that is, subfolders inside the main mailbox folders), you do that by selecting the folder in the Mailboxes drawer and then choosing Mailbox | New. (You can also CONTROL-click the folder to create a subfolder.) The mailbox that you create will be stored as a subfolder of the mailbox you highlighted.*

To delete a mailbox, select it in the Mailboxes drawer, then choose Mailbox | Delete. You'll be asked if you're sure—click Delete if that's what you really want to do. Note that when you delete a mailbox, any messages in that mailbox are deleted immediately—they are *not* moved to the Deleted Messages mailbox folder.

Manage Your Junk E-mail

Is your inbox filling with "spam," or junk e-mail? Junk e-mail runs the gamut from annoying to offensive, and there's only so much you can do about it. Apple Mail offers a special feature for dealing with junk e-mail that can make things a bit more palatable. You can train Mail to move

18

your junk from the inbox to a special folder, thus de-cluttering your inbox quite a bit. That's how the junk mail filter works.

By default, junk mail filtering is enabled, and when you first get started with Mail, you'll see that junk mail in your inbox, but the text will be colored brown. When you select a message that Mail has decided is junk, you'll see a banner at the top of that message telling you so.

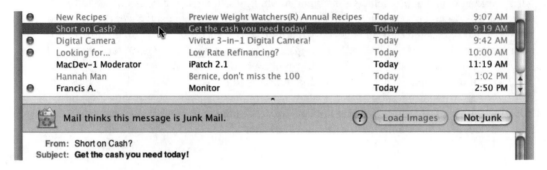

You have some choices at this point. You can click the Load Images button if you'd like to see the images in the e-mail message. (The button is only active when there are images in the message; the load images feature is designed to block images you don't want to see in distasteful junk e-mails.) Or you can click the Not Junk button if the message that Mail has labeled junk actually isn't. That helps Mail train itself. Otherwise, for junk that's correctly marked, you can delete the message by clicking the Delete button in the toolbar or pressing the DELETE key on your keyboard.

While you're training Mail, you have another responsibility—select any junk messages that aren't labeled as junk and click the Junk button in the toolbar or choose Message | Mark | As Junk Mail. That, again, helps train Mail to determine what is junk and what isn't. (You can also CONTROL-click a message and choose Mark | As Junk Mail.)

After a few days or weeks of use this way, you can decide that Mail has a good idea what's junk and what isn't, and at that point you can help Mail change its behavior. To do that, open Mail Preferences and click the Junk Mail icon. On the Junk Mail screen, under When Junk Mail Arrives, choose the option Move It to the Junk Mailbox. That creates a special mailbox in Mail and moves all of your junk mail to it automatically whenever Mail retrieves more. That places it in a central spot where it isn't intruding on your inbox, but you can still access it to check for stray messages.

Also, when you access the Junk Mail preferences, note that you can make a few other tweaks to how Mail determines whether a message is junk, including whether the message comes from someone in your address book or someone from whom you've previously received a message. In fact, you can click the Advanced button to see a special Mail Rule that's created to manage incoming junk mail, and, if you feel up to it, you can change that rule with your own criteria.

Did you know?

Encoding and Compressing

By definition, Internet e-mail programs are designed to send text, not computer files like documents, programs, or system code. There is a way to get around this limitation, though, and it's exactly what Mail does to send an attached file—it's called *encoding*. Through the process of encoding, a file made up of binary data (ones and zeros) is literally translated into a transmittable format following a particular encoding method and then is decoded on the other side.

Mail uses a specific type of encoding, called *Base64/MIME*, which is the most popular encoding/decoding format for most types of computers, including Macs and Microsoft Windows PCs. If your recipient asks you what format you're using, however, you may need to tell her, because not all e-mail programs handle these attachments automatically.

It's also recommended that you compress files—particularly large documents or groups of documents—before sending them. That's discussed more in Chapter 20.

> **TIP** *The fact that Mail keeps learning means it's important to continue to mark messages as junk even once you're out of "training" mode. When a new junk message shows up in your inbox, select it and click the Junk button in the toolbar or choose Message | Mark | As Junk Mail. That way you stay on top of the filter, and it should continue to improve.*

Learn Mail Tricks: Attachments, Signatures, and Rules

Beyond the basics of managing your e-mail, you may want to customize the experience further. In this section, we'll talk about sending and receiving documents as attachments to your e-mail messages. You'll also see how to add custom signatures to your messages, and you'll see how to automate certain e-mail tasks with Mail's built-in rules feature.

Send and Receive Attachments

Most any Mac e-mail application, including Mail, lets you send a file—a document, application, or compressed archive of different sorts of files—to recipients through Internet e-mail. In fact, you can even send attachments to recipients using Intel-compatible PCs. The only major limitation is that it can take a while to upload and download attachments. While most e-mail messages are about 5–10 kilobytes in size, the typical graphical image document—a photo, for instance—begins at 50,000 kilobytes and spirals upward from there. Sending and receiving such documents over a modem connection can seem to take forever.

There are two rules about sending attachments to someone. First, netiquette dictates that the person should be expecting the attachment. It's important to remember that a lot of people pay for their time online and for their e-mail service, and a very large download could cost them time or money. Also, some clever computer viruses are sent as e-mail attachments and can even appear to have come from a trusted friend. So, if your recipient knows ahead of time that you intend to send an attachment, she is less likely to simply toss your message as a safeguard against infection from a virus.

Second, you should make sure that the attachment arrives in the correct format for your recipient to use. Ideally, you should try to store documents in formats that will be easily translated on the other computer. If you're sending a Microsoft Word document to the other user and he also has Microsoft Word, the conversion should work. If you don't have the same word processing program, it might be best to send the document in RTF (Rich Text Format) instead, which can be handled by most word processing programs, including AppleWorks.

Add the Attachment

In Mail, you add an attachment to an outgoing message by dragging it from the Finder into the composition window, clicking the Attach button in the toolbar, or by selecting Message | Attach File. (In either of the latter two cases, you'll see an Open dialog box where you should locate the file to attach.) Once the file is attached, you'll see the file's icon appear in the message window.

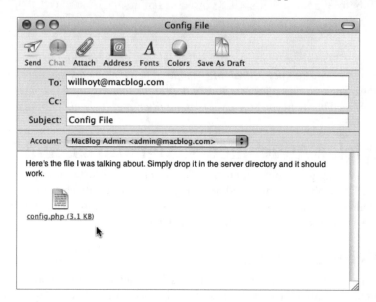

Now, send your e-mail as usual and the attachment goes right along for the ride. If you decide you don't want to send a document that you've already attached, select Message | Remove Attachments.

 *In Mail, a number of document types will actually display in the composition window—instead of an icon, you'll see the whole thing. That's true of PDF documents and many types of image files, for instance.*

Get an Attachment

If you receive an e-mail message that includes an attachment, you'll see the attached file's icon appear in the message area (in Mail) when you read the message. (If it's an image or certain document types, you may actually see the image or document displayed in the viewing window.) To work with the attachment, you can drag it from the message window to your desktop or to an open Finder window. In Mail, you can also single-click the name of the attachment (you'll notice that it looks like a hyperlink), which will load the file in its associated application, if possible. If an application can't be found, you'll see a dialog box asking if you'd like to save the attachment. Click Save and you'll be presented with a Save dialog box.

Opening attachments to e-mail messages is one known way to contract a computer virus. You should only open or use attachments from known senders and only when the attachment is expected from that user. It's possible for some viruses to automatically send virus-infected attachments automatically from a user's e-mail program, making it look like the user sent the message to you. If you're not expecting an attachment, don't open it until you've talked to the sender and confirmed that he or she meant to send you the attachment.

Create and Add Your Signature

A signature, in e-mail parlance, is a block of text that you add to the end of your e-mail messages to help identify you. For professional purposes, people will often put their corporate title, address, and phone numbers; for personal signatures, you might put your name, web site, and a favorite quote. In either case, signatures are generally composed ahead of time so they can be easily reused. In general, you should use about three to five lines of information, but make sure it's not too personal (home phone numbers and so on) for the Internet.

To create a signature in Mail, open Mail Preferences (Mail | Preferences) and click the Signatures icon. Now, click the Add Signature button to open a new signature dialog sheet. In the Description box, enter a description for the signature, and then in the main entry area, enter your signature.

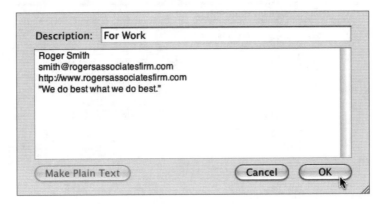

Click OK when you're done editing. Back in the Mail Preferences window, you can opt to create additional signatures if you'd like to be able to rotate between them—just click Create Signature again. If you do create multiple signatures, you can use the Automatically Insert Signature menu to determine which signature is used by default (or randomly) in your messages; or, if you'd prefer to choose the signature in the composition window, turn on the Show Signature When Composing Email option. (Click the Mail Preferences' close button to close the window.) With this option selected, you'll find a Signature menu in the composition window, where you can choose which signature to use for that particular message.

Automate Your E-mail Using Rules

Need to automate your e-mail? Mail enables you to create *rules*, or filters, that look at incoming mail and compare the messages against criteria that you specify. If an e-mail message matches the criterion, a certain action is taken—the message is deleted, moved to a particular mailbox folder, or automatically forwarded, for instance.

To create a rule in Mail, choose Mail | Preferences. In the Mail Preferences window, select the Rules icon. Now you'll see a list of the current rules. By default, Apple has a rule here to change the color of messages sent to you by Apple. (Nice of them, eh?) You can open that rule (select it and click Edit) to see the basic structure of a rule.

You'll also notice in the rules list that you can turn a rule on or off by clicking its check box in the Active column. You can also drag rules around to change their order. Each incoming message is applied against the rules in order, starting with the first rule on the list.

To create a new rule in Mail, click the Create Rule button. You'll see a dialog sheet appear, where you can begin building your rule (see Figure 18-3).

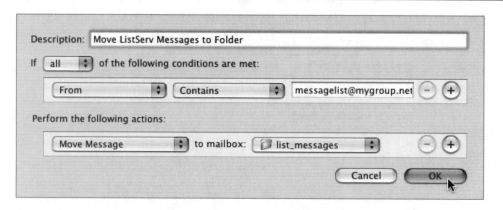

FIGURE 18-3 Building a rule in Mail

Building rules can be a thinking game. In a sense, it approaches the logic you need for creating an AppleScript or a similar computer program. It's a basic IF…THEN statement—in order to use mail rules, you'll have to think that way.

Once you get your mind set to the problem, you'll find solutions. For instance, consider the idea of automatically moving messages to a particular folder. In this case, let's focus on mail that you get as part of a *message list* (sometimes called a "listserv"). When you're on a message list, where e-mail messages are broadcast to all members so that they can read and discuss matters that interest them, each message generally has a common From entry. So, you could set up a criterion like:

```
From Contains messagelist@mygroup.net
```

Now, if the criterion is met, actions can be put into place. (Note that you don't have to be as specific as the example. You could use a partial approach, such as `messagelist@my` or `list@mygroup`, if you thought that would do a better job of catching various permutations.) To enable an action in Mail, click its check box, then complete the options. (You can activate any or all of the actions, if desired.) For instance, to move the message to a new folder, you'd choose Move Message and select the destination mailbox folder from the menu, as shown in Figure 18-3.

When you're done creating the rule, click the OK button. Now, whenever new messages are received, they'll be compared against the active rules, and if criteria are met, the actions will be put into place.

TIP   *In Mail, if you'd like to run a rule against e-mail messages that you have already received, select those messages in the viewer window (hold down the SHIFT key while clicking to select multiple messages), then choose Message | Apply Rules to Selection. In Outlook Express, choose Message | Apply Rules.*

18

Chapter 19

Learn Cool Web Tricks and Build Web Pages

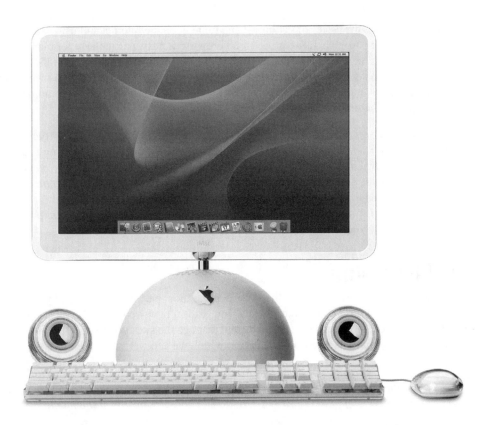

How to...

- Surf multimedia and frames
- Choose a home page
- Fill in a form and buy things online
- Use Java and plug-ins
- Manage passwords and the keychain
- Stay secure on the Internet
- Create a web page with HomePage
- Upload your own web pages
- Check out Sherlock

In Chapter 5, you saw the basics of getting up and running on the Internet and using a web browser. Indeed, using Safari, Apple's full-featured web browser, is easy, particularly for plain old surfin'. But Safari—and the greater Web itself—offers some prospects for going deeper with the technology. In this chapter, you'll see some of the interesting things you can do with most any web browser, including trying out some advanced browsing techniques, customizing your web home page, and using some special features of Safari.

NOTE   *Aside from Safari, most Macs include a copy of Internet Explorer (IE), Microsoft's web browser. Microsoft no longer plans to update IE, but it can be handy as a back-up browser, particularly for sites that don't display correctly in Safari. (My bank's online check register is one example.) A number of other browsers for the Mac, including Netscape (**www.netscape.com**), Mozilla (**www.mozilla.org**, the open-source version of Netscape), Camino (**www.mozilla.org/projects/camino/index.html**), and OmniWeb (**www.omnigroup.com**), offer interesting alternatives to Safari and IE.*

Advanced Browsing

Chapter 5 showed you how to browse the Web. For the most part, you just click hyperlinks or images, and, in turn, your web browser locates and loads a new web page. You can then use the bookmarks feature of the web browser to store and manage the sites you visit often. But as you're browsing, you'll encounter some other behavior, which we'll cover in this section.

TIP   *Need to set Safari as your default browser so that links that you click in Mail or another application open in Safari? Choose Safari | Preferences and click General. At the top, you'll see the Default Web Browser option—choose Safari from the menu.*

Click a Multimedia Link

Most of the time when you click a hyperlink in your web browser, you'll load a new web page. But a hyperlink can be used to load other things, such as images or multimedia, or you might even click a link that enables you to download a file. Other than loading a new web page, four different things can happen when you click a link:

- ■ *A helper program is invoked.* Your web browser recognizes many types of files and passes them on to the appropriate application. For instance, if you click a link to a Microsoft Word document, the document might be downloaded and handed over to Microsoft Word to display, assuming you have Word installed. Similarly, clicking a hyperlink that leads to an e-mail address (using what's called a "mailto:" URL) activates your e-mail application.

- ■ *A plug-in is activated.* The most common plug-in is QuickTime, which enables you to watch movies from within your web browser's window. Or, you can choose plug-ins for Macromedia Flash documents, virtual reality documents, audio and video formats, Java applets, and more. The plug-in takes over a portion of the browser window and displays its data as part of the web page.

NOTE   *Plug-ins are discussed in more depth later in this chapter.*

- ■ *A file is downloaded.* If a link points to a file using an FTP protocol URL, the file is then downloaded to your iMac's hard disk, often directly to your desktop. You can view it with another application, decompress it with StuffIt Expander (which is often done automatically), or perform a similar task. (In some cases, an FTP link shows you a list of files you can then click to download.) In Safari, downloaded files appear in the Downloads window (Window | Downloads).

In the Downloads window, you can see the progress of an item as it downloads. You can also click the small magnifying glass icon to view the downloaded file in a Finder window, and you can click the X icon to stop a download that's in progress.

- ■ *The item isn't recognized.* Sometimes, you click a hyperlink to a particular file and the web browser won't recognize it. In this case, you'll usually see a dialog box, where you

19

can choose to download the file, ignore it, or search for the correct application to view it, as instructed by a dialog box that appears when errors are encountered.

Work with Frames

With some web sites, you encounter an *HTML frames* interface, which is a special sort of page that actually breaks a single web browser window into different window panes (hence *frames*) used to display different pages. In most cases, the idea is to click a link in one of the frames and then have the page change in another frame. Frames enable you to view many pages' worth of information without refreshing the entire window every time (see Figure 19-1).

If necessary, you can choose commands to let you go Back, Forward, and so on within that particular frame. Click-and-hold the mouse button within a frame to see a pop-up contextual menu. (You can also hold down the CONTROL key and click within the frame.) You can then choose Back, Forward (if applicable), and other commands that affect only that frame.

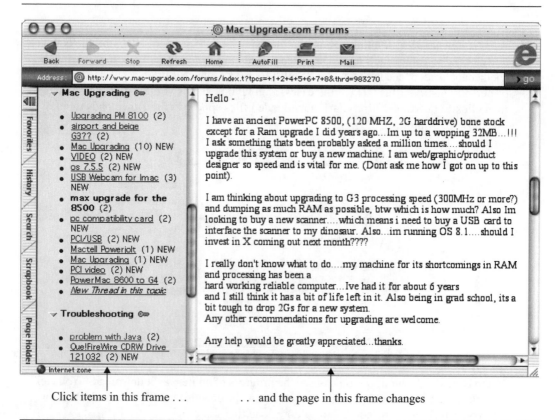

Click items in this frame . . .   . . . and the page in this frame changes

FIGURE 19-1   The Forums section of my web site uses an HTML frames interface.

Use Tabbed Browsing

Safari offers a special feature that you may find appealing—Tabbed Browsing, which enables you to access more than one web page from within the same browser window, switching back and forth between them by clicking tabs at the top of the browser window.

This is a convenience, and it's something of a matter of taste. (I don't use tabs much, but it's handy on smaller screens or if you simply don't like clutter.) You could have multiple Safari windows open at once, but the tabs enable you to manage those multiple pages—for research, comparison shopping, or simply for quickly thumbing through some favorite pages. (Or if you tend to keep the same pages open and refer to them regularly, tabs can be handy. In fact, maybe I'll start using them more.)

To turn on Tabbed Browsing, open Safari Preferences (Safari | Preferences) and click the Tabs icon. Now, place a check mark next to the option Enable Tabbed Browsing. With that option turned on, you get two more options: Select New Tabs as They Are Created is used to cause new tabs to appear in "front" of the current tab, so that the new document is viewed; Always Show Tab Bar means you'll see the tab controls even if you only have one page open in the browser window.

With Tabbed Browsing turned on, you'll get some new commands to think about. Simply clicking a link in the browser window causes a new document to appear on that same tab. If you want to create a new tab by clicking a link, hold down the ⌘ key as you click it or hold down ⌘-SHIFT and click to create a new tab for the linked document *and* make that tab active so you view it immediately. You can also CONTROL-click on the Tab Bar to get a small contextual menu with options that include creating a blank tab, reloading tabs, or closing tabs.

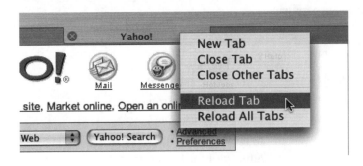

 *You can also use keyboard shortcuts to open links in new windows instead of new tabs. Use ⌘-OPTION-SHIFT-click to open a link in a new window that stays behind the current one.*

Create a SnapBack Page

One of my favorite Safari features is the SnapBack Page feature. What this does is create a page that you can return to quickly at any time, even if you've surfed away from it quite a bit. Often, this is a search results page such as a list of Google results, but other times it might simply be a page with lots of links and resources that you find handy.

To turn a page into a SnapBack page, display it in the browser and choose History | Mark Page for Snapback (or press ⌘-OPTION-K). Now you can click links and surf away. When you get far enough away from the original page and you want to "snap back" to it, choose History | Page SnapBack (or press ⌘-OPTION-P). You'll be sent right back to the original page, ready to start more surfing adventures.

Use a Home Page

If you plan to spend a lot of time online, you want to get organized. The best starting place I know for getting organized is a good home page. In Safari, deciding on a particular home page where you want to start your Internet adventure every time you sign on is easy. (In fact, the home page is usually loaded every time you open a new browser window.) You can link to your company page, a page you particularly enjoy reading, a professional *portal* page (a home page with news, sports, and other topical headlines) from one of the big Internet companies, or even to a page you create yourself.

Change Your Home Page

If you use Safari for your web surfing, your home page is already set for you—it's the Apple Netscape home page. If you don't need or want to change from these defaults, skip down to the section "Edit the Home Page." You can change the home page, though, if you find one you like more or if you want to experiment.

Popular sites that enable you to customize your own home page include the following:

My Excite	**http://my.excite.com/**
Apple Excite (offers Apple news)	**http://apple.excite.com/**
My Netscape	**http://my.netscape.com/**
Microsoft Network	**http://www.msn.com/**
My Yahoo	**http://my.yahoo.com/**
Earthlink Personal Start Page	**http://start.earthlink.net/**

You needn't go with one of the big names. Equally useful may be a smaller site you enjoy visiting—one associated with a hobby or interest of yours. Of course, the site should also be the sort of page that changes often. Making a home page out of a page that's never updated is a little dull, unless it's filled with interesting hyperlinks.

Making any page into your home page is simple:

1. Open your potential home page in your browser.

2. Open Safari Preferences (Safari | Preferences) and click the General icon.

3. Click the Set to Current Page button underneath the Home Page entry box.

> TIP   *If you're working with a browser other than Safari, check its preferences for a home page setting.*

Now, the Home button in Safari should lead you to the new home page whenever you click it. Similarly, you see the home page every time you open a new browser window while you're connected to the Internet.

Edit the Home Page

If you're using one of the major services for your home page, you can probably edit it, if desired. Look for a link that says "Personalize This Page" or something similar. Click that link and you'll

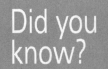

The Cookie Issue

For most custom home pages to work—along with many other customization features and, sometimes, even e-commerce features, such as online shopping carts—you need to have the cookies feature enabled in your browser. *Cookies* are small bits of data that a web server can store on your hard disk, making it possible for the site to identify and remember you. Some users don't like to enable cookies because they allow web servers to track their browsing, store personal information, and so forth. Although cookies are generally harmless, you can enable and disable them in Safari Preferences. Choose Safari | Preferences, and then click the Security icon. Now click the Show Cookies button to see the cookies that Safari has stored. If you want to change how Safari accepts cookies, use the radio buttons next to Accept Cookies. The option Only from Sites You Navigate is an interesting one, as it keeps you from getting cookies from pop-ups and advertisers. If you want more control, you may need to opt for a different browser— Netscape, Mozilla, and OmniWeb are better at managing cookies.

19

likely find tools that enable you to change what you view on the home page and the order in which you view it.

In most cases, you place a check mark next to items you want on the page. Then, you enter a number next to each item to choose how you want it prioritized—whether you want the item to appear at the top or the bottom of the page, for instance. You should be able to choose from a variety of topics, financials, types of news, entertainment, and so on.

You'll also probably be asked for some demographic information, as well as for your ZIP code and perhaps your birthday (especially for horoscopes). If you're worried about the information getting out, look for a link to the company's privacy statement. Also, look for an option you can check telling them they can't sell or use your information for advertising and junk mail purposes.

Fill in Forms and Buy Things Online

Web browsers are capable of displaying web pages that include *HTML form* elements. Interface items you might find in a dialog box within the Mac OS can be added to a web page, so you can send information back to the web server computer. These elements include familiar items like entry boxes, menus, check boxes, radio buttons, and regular buttons. All these form elements are used much as they are within the Mac OS.

The difference is, you're usually filling in personal information, which you plan to send to the web server computer so it can be processed in some way. Perhaps you're buying computer software or subscribing to an online newsletter—or maybe you're setting up a home page, as discussed earlier in this chapter.

Fill in the Form

Filling in a form is usually pretty easy. You just enter the information necessary by typing in entry boxes and choosing items in lists or menus (see Figure 19-2). Other elements should also be familiar. Press TAB to move among most parts of the form. (You'll probably have to use the mouse to choose items from pull-down menus.)

Once you fill in the form, you need to look for a way to submit that form. Your data needs to be sent to the web server computer, but it can't go until you say it can. In most cases, you can see a Send or Submit button that you click with the mouse. You might also see a Clear button, which clears the form of everything you just entered. Don't click that button unless you're sure you want to clear the form.

Click Submit (or Send, or Search, and so on) and your data is sent over the Internet to the web server computer where it's processed. In most cases, clicking the Submit button also loads a new page into your web browser that includes either results from your data or a page telling you that your submission has been received.

Did I say your data is sent over the Internet? But what if it's private data like credit card numbers, salary figures, or e-mail addresses? Are you sure you want them floating around?

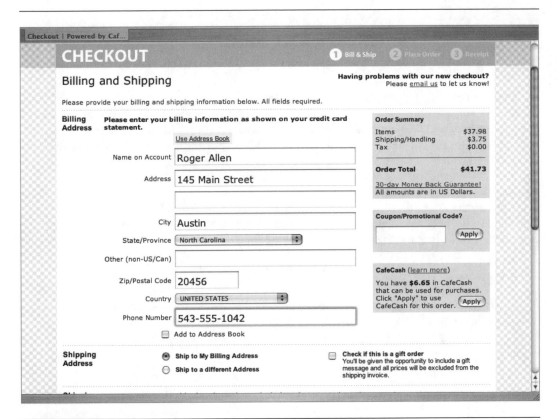

FIGURE 19-2 Web pages can enable you to fill in information and send it across the Internet.

Check for a Secure Connection

In most cases, when a web site wants you to send financial or private information, it does so over what's called a *secure* server. What this means is simple: the web site and your browser establish a connection over which data is encrypted. Your data is coded like a military transmission. The code can only be broken once your data gets to the server computer.

In Safari, you see the locked padlock icon at the top right on the screen, and you'll see that the URL you're using for the connection will have https:// before the web address.

19

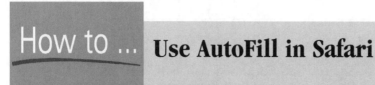

How to ... Use AutoFill in Safari

In Safari, you may sometimes see that it attempts to help you fill in the entry blanks on your forms. It's using a feature called AutoFill that enables it to automatically fill in common form data (your name, address, phone number, and so on) based on your entry in the Address Book or from other forms that you've filled in previously. If you like this feature, you don't have to do anything special—it's turned on by default. If it ever fills something in incorrectly, simply delete what it added and type something yourself. If you encounter a form that won't fill on its own, try the Edit | AutoFill Form command.

You can turn AutoFill off or change the way it works in the Safari Preferences dialog box. Choose Safari | Preferences and then click the AutoFill icon. Now, you can access three choices for how AutoFill will work in your copy of Safari:

- Turn on Using Info from My Address Book Card if you have such a card created in Address Book (see Chapter 13).

- Turn on Use Names and Passwords if you want to use AutoFill to remember your web passwords. (Be careful with this; anyone with access to your Mac will gain access to your password-protected sites.)

- Turn on Other Forms if you want AutoFill to learn your personal info from the other HTML forms you fill out while surfing.

- Turn off all the options if you don't want to use AutoFill at all.

Only enter your password and other personal information—particularly account names, ID numbers, and credit card or bank accounts—if you initiated the connection. In other words, don't click a link in an e-mail or an instant message and then offer personal information. It's too easy for a nefarious soul to spoof a known web site (like eBay or AOL or Amazon) and use their images and text to make it look real. When in doubt about an e-mail message you receive regarding "your account" or asking for personal information, be suspicious and communicate directly with the company that purported to send the message.

Internet Plug-Ins and Java

You've already seen that your web browser is capable of displaying and arranging images and text in the browser window. But web browsers can also give over part of the browser window to other mini-applications that enable you to interact with an online program of some sort. These fall under the heading of *embedded* content, which just means they're small programs that enable you to perform a simple task. Some of them rely on *plug-ins*, or special add-ons that different companies make for browsers. Other embedded programs rely on Java, which works with your browser to enable small applications, such as calculators, interactive content, and even full-fledged programs.

Embedded Plug-In Files

Using plug-in technology, the web browser can actually give control of part of the browser window to another little program, which can be responsible for dealing with user input and displaying things on the screen. In most cases, these plug-ins add more multimedia, perhaps offering animated graphics, a unique interface to the web site, and so on. One popular plug-in technology is Macromedia's Flash plug-in (**http://www.macromedia.com/software/flash/**), which enables you to view animated graphics within the browser window (see Figure 19-3). Flash plug-ins are already included and installed on your Mac. You will occasionally want to visit the web site and update the plug-in, however.

Other plug-ins let you view a variety of embedded multimedia documents, like Real Network's RealOne Player (**http://www.real.com/**). With RealOne Player, you can view streaming audio and video (audio and video played as they arrive across the Internet in a data stream, so you don't have to wait a long time for the data to download). Other popular plug-ins offer 3-D vistas, Virtual Reality Modeling Language (VRML) controllers, and so on. A great place to find many of the plug-ins available today for web browsers is at Netscape's browser plug-in web pages (**http://home.netscape.com/plugins/index.html**).

Add Plug-Ins

You install plug-ins differently depending on which Mac OS you're using. (Indeed, the plug-ins need to be specifically compatible with the Mac OS version you're using.) In Mac OS X, plug-ins need to be placed in one of two folders—either the Internet Plug-Ins folder located in your personal Library folder inside your home folder, or in the Internet Plug-Ins folder in the main Library folder on your startup disk. To install the plug-in in the main Library folder, you need to be logged into an administrator's account, but doing so makes the plug-in available to all users on your multiuser Mac (assuming you have multiple users).

FIGURE 19-3   Plug-in technology adds interactivity (and visual effects) to web pages.

If the plug-in has an installation program, just let it do its thing. But if you simply downloaded the plug-in to your desktop, you need to drag it to the appropriate Internet Plug-Ins folder. Once the plug-in is installed there, you can restart your web browser, which then automatically searches for and detects new plug-ins. The plug-in's functionality is noted, and the next time you encounter an embedded multimedia document, the correct plug-in is loaded and the multimedia content is displayed in the browser window.

Use the QuickTime Web Browser Plug-In

Along with the Mac OS's built-in QuickTime technology layer (which allows it to display digital movies) comes the QuickTime plug-in, an addition to web browsers that allows them to display QuickTime movies directly within the web browser's document window.

QuickTime movies must be embedded in the web page for them to appear in the browser; otherwise they're downloaded to your Mac first, and you view them in the QuickTime Player. If they're embedded in the page with special HTML codes, the movie, QuickTime VR, or QuickTime audio movie plays from within the browser screen itself. This works great for streaming QuickTime, which allows you to watch a movie *while* it is being transmitted over the Internet.

If you've upgraded to QuickTime Pro (currently $29.95, **http://www.quicktime.com/**), you'll be given a few other options with the plug-in, including the ability to save movies directly from web pages. Click and hold the mouse button on an embedded QuickTime movie (or CONTROL-click the movie), and a pop-up menu appears. Choose Save as QuickTime Movie to save the movie to your Mac's hard drive. Then you're free to view it in the QuickTime Player.

Work with Java

As you may know, one type of application—say, one written for Microsoft Windows—won't easily run on another type of computer, such as a Mac. *Java* changes that by allowing a Java program to run using a *virtual machine*—an emulator of sorts—that runs on top of the operating system. That means Java applications don't have to be written for a specific operating system—instead, they're written to run in the virtual machine. The Java virtual machine, in turn, is written specifically for the particular OS—Mac OS X has its own virtual machine, which makes it possible to run Java applications on your Mac.

In most cases, Java works seamlessly on your iMac—there's nothing in particular you need to do. In fact, if you download and install a Java application on your iMac, it should work just like any other iMac program.

Often, though, Java applets are loaded over the Internet and displayed in your web browser. To use a Java applet, if it requires any user interaction, simply point and click the mouse like you would with any Mac application.

Turning Java and Plug-Ins On and Off

In Safari, you have the option of turning support for Java and plug-ins on and off. It isn't often needed except in special circumstances—some online calculators and product viewers, for instance, require Java. For day-to-day surfing you can live without it, particularly if it seems to slow down or crash your browser. To turn Java off, open Safari Preferences, choose Security, and turn off the Enable Java option. To turn off plug-ins, remove the Enable Plug-Ins check mark.

NOTE *Java and JavaScript are not the same thing—in fact, they're not really related except that JavaScript has a somewhat similar syntax (form and keywords). JavaScript is a type of script that can be embedded in a web page and do automatic things like react to your mouse pointer or check an HTML form for bad input. It's generally okay to leave JavaScript turned on, but if you have trouble with your browser on JavaScript pages or you don't often access web applications (like searches for homes, online banking, web stores, and so on), you can turn it off in Safari Preferences as well.*

TIP *If you have trouble with Java in one browser (such as Safari), try it in another (such as Internet Explorer), as differences in their Java support may work to your benefit.*

Manage Passwords and the Keychain

Have trouble remembering your passwords for the Web? After a while, you'll accumulate quite a few if you ever do any online shopping or access your credit card statements or even if you sign up for web-based discussion forums. Where do you keep all of those passwords?

Apple offers a built-in solution in the *keychain*. Actually, the keychain is used by default for a number of passwords, such as the passwords for your e-mail accounts and for some networking connections. In essence, it's a central password-protected database that stores your personal passwords on your Mac. You have a single password—usually your login password—that can also

19

be used to secure your keychain. And, aside from the passwords that the Mac automatically stores in your keychain, you can add your own for safekeeping. It takes a minute or two to get used to the keychain, but once you do, you'll find it handy.

To access your keychain, you'll need to launch Keychain Access, which is an application inside the main Utilities folder (a subfolder of Applications) on your Mac's hard drive. Double-click the Keychain Access icon and you'll see the application launch. When Keychain Access opens, you're shown your current keychain and the items in it, as seen in Figure 19-4.

Select an item in the keychain, and you have two tabs in the window—Attributes and Access Control. The Attributes tab shows you the specifics of the keychain item. You can click the check box next to Show Password if you'd like to see the password that's stored for that item. The Access Control tab is used to control what applications can access this item and whether or not they need

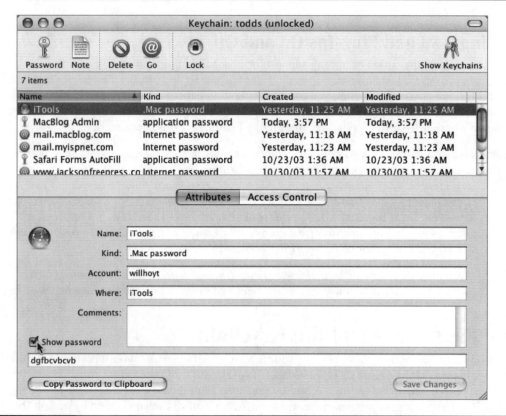

FIGURE 19-4   The Keychain Access application and the items on my keychain

to ask permission. If you turn on the option Confirm Before Allowing Access, you'll see a dialog box whenever an application attempts to access this keychain item.

So how do you add passwords to the keychain? One of two ways. The first way is via another application—Safari, for instance. When accessing certain types of web servers, you may be asked for a user name and password via a dialog sheet. In that sheet, if you see an option like Remember This Password, or Add to Keychain, you can add the information in that way; hopefully the login will be more automatic the next time around.

Second, you can add a password directly via Keychain Access. To do that, click the Password icon in the toolbar or choose File | New Password Item. In the New Password Item dialog box, enter a name for the password item in the Name entry box, then enter the account name for the item in the Account entry box. Finally, in the Password entry box, enter the password. Now, click Add.

This doesn't make the item work automatically in your browser. Instead, it allows you to access the password in the future via Keychain Access. You select the item in the main keychain window and click the Attributes tab. Just turn on Show Password and you'll be able to see that password (after you enter your keychain password). Now you can use the password wherever you need to.

Keychain Access can also be used to store a secure note (click the Note icon), which can include other things such as credit card numbers, account numbers, and so on—anything that you want to keep secure.

Of course, this info can be accessed as long as your keychain is accessible, so it's a good idea to "lock" your keychain every so often. Choose Edit | Change Settings for Keychain and you'll

19

see a dialog box with a number of options, including the option to lock the keychain after a few minutes of inactivity or when the Mac goes to sleep.

You can also lock the keychain in its window. Click the Lock icon on the toolbar in Keychain Access. Now you'll need to enter your keychain password again before you can see and access the keychain items.

 *You can use the AutoFill feature in Safari to store account names and passwords, even those that use an HTML form for input. Realize, however, that doing so means anyone who gains access to your Mac might be able to access those items, too.*

Build Your Own Web Page

Interested in building your own web page? Apple has an easy way for you to do it if you're signed into the .Mac subscription service—a tool called HomePage. You'll need to sign into iTools and launch the HomePage tool. You'll then select a template for your page and begin editing the text that will appear on that page. Next, you'll edit links, add images, and make some other basic choices. Finally, you'll preview the page and publish it on the Web.

 *If you don't have the HomePage service, you can use any of a number of free services to build a simple home page, such as Yahoo! GeoCities (**http://geocities.yahoo.com**), Angelfire (**http://www.angelfire.lycos.com/**), or Blogger (**http://www.blogger.com/**) for a weblog (personal web journal) site. Those and many others have online tools to make your site easy to build.*

Here's how to begin a HomePage site:

- Connect to the Internet (if necessary), launch your web browser, and enter the URL `http://www.mac.com`.

- Click the HomePage button (or image) to launch the HomePage tool. If you haven't recently signed into iTools, you'll see a screen asking for your member name and password. Type them and click the Enter button.

Now you'll see the main HomePage screen. If you haven't created any pages thus far, you won't see anything in the Pages section of the HomePage screen. Scroll down to the Create a Page section, though, and you can begin to see how HomePage works.

HomePage enables you to create web pages based on templates that Apple has created for you. The templates are arranged by topic, with the topics appearing as buttons down the left-hand side. HomePage offers a number of different types of templates that can change anytime Apple gets the urge (so they may be different from what's pictured here). Categories include Writing (newsletters mostly), Invite, Baby (different types of pages for featuring a newborn), Resume, and Education for teachers and students. Other categories—Photo Album, iMovie, and File Sharing—are different types of pages we'll discuss more later in the chapter.

Select one of the topic buttons, and the page will reload, showing you the different template choices you have, as in Modern Resume, Classic Resume I, and so on for the Resume topic. When you see a template that you like, click it.

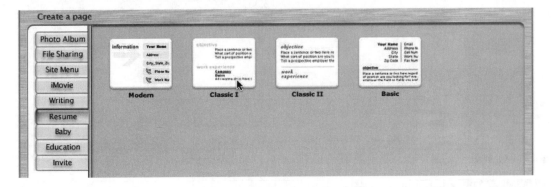

Edit the Text

After you've selected a template, you'll see a screen that enables you to edit the page. In the top-right corner on this screen you'll see the Themes button, which enables you to change to a different template at any time. If you click this button, you'll see the same template options you saw previously (such as Modern Resume, Classic Resume, and so forth). The only difference is, when you use the Themes command, any changes on your page will be saved and will appear in the new template, which is handy if you change your mind about the design of your page, but you still want to publish this text and information.

You'll also see the Edit button, which you should click so that you can edit the text that appears on the page. After you've clicked Edit Text, you'll see entry boxes that enable you to edit the contents of the page. Make the changes that you'd like to make by clicking in each entry box and editing the text (see Figure 19-5). When you're done with your alterations, you can scroll back to the top of the page and click the Preview button to see how things are shaping up.

Note that you can add hypertext links while editing some portions of your page, by enclosing them in the standard HTML anchor tags, such as `<a href="http://www.apple.com/">Click to visit Apple's site</a>`. Likewise, you can use a mailto: URL if you'd like

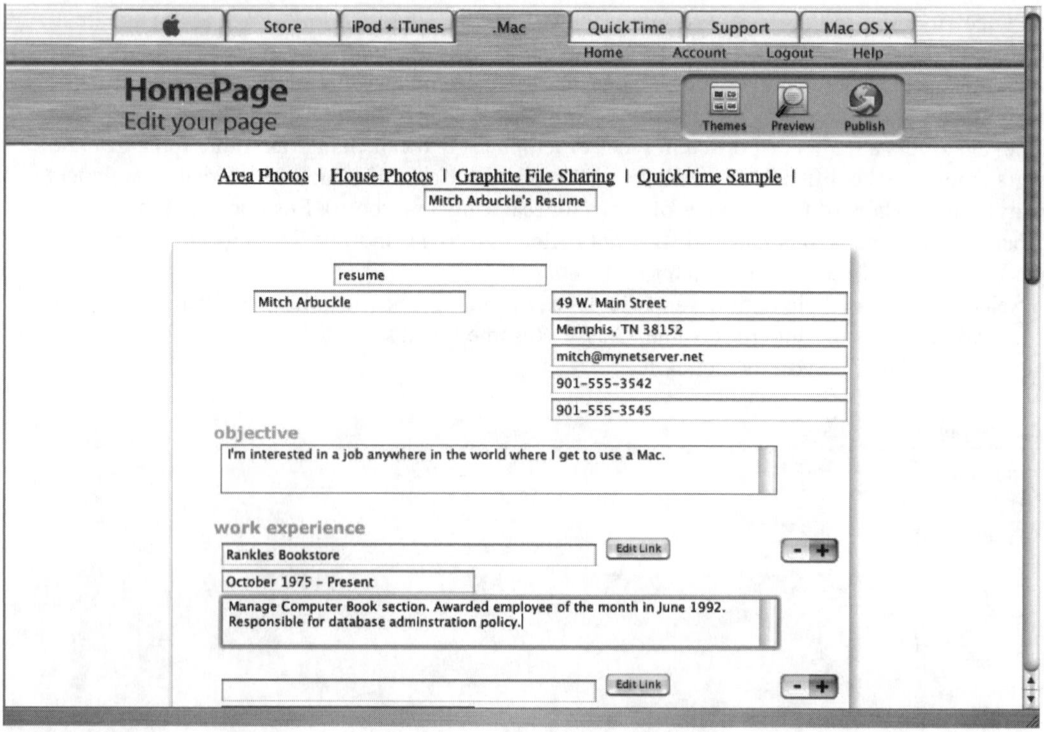

FIGURE 19-5   Click Edit and you can begin to change the text for your web page.

the clicked link to lead to an e-mail address, such as `<a href="mailto:todd@macblog .com">Click to send me your reply.</a>`. In some cases, you can use other HTML tags, such as `<b>boldface</b>` or `<i>italics</i>`, to alter your text. (HTML tags usually work in larger text areas that support a lot of text, but short lines for addresses and names may not properly recognize the HTML tags—instead, display those codes as part of the text. Just reedit that line to remove the unrecognized tags.)

Alter the Layout, Links, and Images

You may have other options within the template besides just altering text. For instance, on some templates you can click an Add/Remove button (with a plus sign and a minus sign) to add or remove a particular line from the site. Click the plus-sign button to add a new line or element with those same features, or click the minus-sign button to remove an item if you don't need it for your page.

work experience

| Rankles Bookstore | Edit Link | − + |
| October 1975 – Present | | |

Manage Computer Book section. Awarded employee of the month in June 1992. Responsible for database adminstration policy.

You may also see Edit Link buttons at various points on your page, where you can click to edit the URL to a particular item on the page that HomePage believes should have a hyperlink associated with it. (On a resume, for instance, it will assume you want a link to the company names listed in your work history.) Click the Edit Link button and a small entry box appears: enter the URL for the associated item, then click Apply. Now, once published, the underlined text will be a hyperlink to the URL you entered.

NOTE   *Some special links are specifically designed for e-mail addresses, such as those used for the RSVP section of party invitation pages. In those cases, simply enter the e-mail address you want to use. Don't use* `http://` *or* `mailto:` *as part of the entry.*

Some templates offer yet another option for adding individual images to the page you're creating. The Choose button enables you to choose a single graphic image that you've previously uploaded to the Pictures folder on your iDisk (see Chapter 20). Click Choose, and then use the Select a File screen to locate the image (or QuickTime movie) you want to use. (To open folders, click the folder name and click the Open Folder button.)

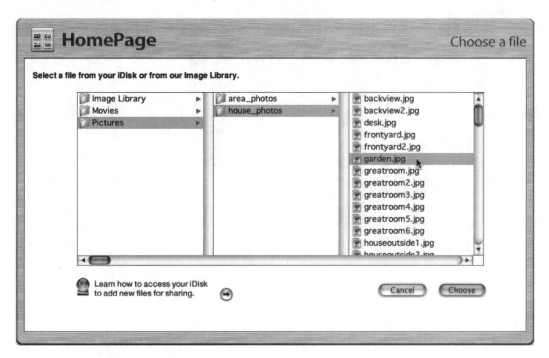

The Image Library button leads to a number of clipart and free images that Apple makes available for you to add to your pages, if desired.

When you select an image, you'll see a preview in the rightmost column; you can click Choose to add the image to the web page. Once you click Choose or Cancel, you'll be returned to your page's main editing screen.

Preview and Publish

When you're done with all of your changes, you can click the Preview button in the top-right corner of the HomePage interface, which will cause the page to appear much as it will to your site's visitors. If you don't like the way things look, you can click the Edit button to return to the main editing screen.

Otherwise, you're ready to publish your page—just click the Publish button. You'll see a confirmation page that congratulates you for finishing the page and shows you the URL by which that page can be accessed. To test, open another web browser window and enter the URL given. You'll see the page just as your visitors will in the future!

Are you in a spot where you've created a page you don't want to keep? Just click the word "HomePage" or the HomePage button at the top of the screen, or close the browser window. When you return to the main HomePage screen, you'll be able to start over again or start on a different page.

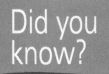

Publish Your Own Pages

The web pages you create in HomePage are the same type of HTML documents you could create on your own using an HTML or web-page editing application such as Adobe's GoLive or Macromedia's Dreamweaver.

So, it would follow that you can post pages you create without HomePage and still display them using your .Mac server space, right? That's true. All you have to do is copy the HTML documents (and any associated files, such as image files) to the Sites folder on your iDisk, and they become immediately available on the Internet at the URL **http://homepage.mac .com/membername/pagename.html** (mine is **http://homepage.mac.com/toddstauffer/ mypage.html**). Remember to name one of your pages `index.html` if you'd like it to load automatically as the index page for the site. And see Chapter 20 for more on iDisk.

From the confirmation screen, click the Back to Home button to return to the main HomePage screen, where you'll see the page you've just created (along with any others you've created in the past) in the Edit a Page section. If you'd like to change the page, you can select it and click Edit Page. To delete a page, select it and click Delete Page. To set the page as your Start Page (meaning users will see it when they access your base URL at **http://homepage.mac.com/***membername*/), select the page in the list and drag it to the top of the list. Once it's bold, it's the main page.

Publish Movies and Images

Aside from the pages discussed thus far, HomePage offers a few other special types of templates that require a little preparation. One of those is an iMovie page, which can be used to display an iMovie (or, actually, any QuickTime movie) that you've uploaded to your iDisk and placed in the Movies folder.

> **NOTE** *Although the HomePage screens often say you can display "iMovies" on a web page, you're actually displaying a QuickTime movie, not an iMovie project file. Using iMovie, you should export using the Web Movie, Small option, as discussed in Chapter 16 in the section "Export to QuickTime." QuickTime movies should be 240 × 180 pixels, although HomePage can stretch the templates to fit larger movies. (Movies can be saved as "hinted" if desired, using QuickTime's Expert options, as discussed in Chapter 16.) Remember, too, you have a 100MB limit in a standard .Mac subscription, as QuickTime movies can take up a lot of space.*

If you've selected a template designed for a QuickTime movie, you'll see a Choose button when editing the page. Click it and the contents of the Movies folder on your iDisk will be displayed. Select a movie file, then click either Preview (to see the movie play back on screen) or Apply to add the movie to your page. Now, use Edit Text to change the text on the page, and once you've clicked Apply Text, you can then click the Publish button to add the page to your site.

If you're working with a page designed to display a photo album, you'll need to do a little prep work. Photo album pages work by either displaying the entire contents of your iDisk's Pictures folder, or displaying the contents of a subfolder that you create within the Photos folder. So, your first order of business should be to open your iDisk and copy a series of images to your Pictures folder; or, better yet, create a subfolder within the Pictures folder and copy images into that folder. The images should be in GIF or JPEG format.

> **TIP** *Images for the Web should be relatively small in both dimensions and file size. If you have an image-editing program (GraphicConverter, $35 shareware from **http://www.lemkesoft .com**, is a great option), edit your images down in size. If you used a digital camera, somewhere between 320 × 240 and 640 × 480 is a good size for the Web. Then set the resolution to 72 dots per inch. That way, the images will be relatively small in file size so they take up less space on your iDisk and less time to download to your visitor's browser.*

Now, once you have the subfolder set up, select a Photo Album template from the main HomePage screen. On the "Choose a folder of images" screen, you can either click Choose Folder immediately to select your main Pictures folder on your iDisk, or you can highlight the name of a folder and click Choose Folder. By default, every image in that folder will be included on the photo album page(s) that you create.

Once you've selected the folder, you'll see all the images in that folder appear as *thumbnails* (smaller versions of the images) on a photo album page. If there's a particular image you don't want to show in the album, remove the check in the Show check box for that image.

Don't like the order of the images? You can drag one image to the location of another to place it there. Click and hold the mouse button on the first image you want to move, then drag it to another image. When the second image becomes highlighted, release the mouse button, and all of the images will scoot over one spot so that the dropped image will appear in the new location.

Once you've gotten all the images in the right order, click Preview to see the page, and/or Publish to add the photo album page to your growing web site. Now, when visitors access this page, they can click the thumbnail images to see them full size in their web browsers.

Check Out Sherlock

I need to touch on one other web-related tool in this chapter, but I won't say much about it because it's more fun to explore than it is to read about. That tool is Sherlock, Apple's built-in web services application.

Sherlock can be found on your Dock (by default) or in the Applications folder—it's the Sherlock Holmes–style hat and magnifying glass icon. Once launched, you'll see an interface that's a little like a web browser and a little like some of Apple's other iApps, such as iTunes or iPhoto. (See Figure 19-6.) What Sherlock does, in a nutshell, is act as an interface for tons of little web applications that let you do all sorts of things, including search for movies and dictionary entries, check stocks, and access creative third-party tools. You can even search Apple's AppleCare support site.

The major channels can be found in the Toolbar, but you'll also be able to access and manage other channels in the Collections list. Add items to the Channels Menu collection, for instance, and you'll find them for quick access in the Channels menu in Sherlock. Choose the Other Channels collection and you'll see third-party channels that you can access. You can then drag those elsewhere—Toolbar or My Channels, for instance—to organize them.

Play around and get to know Sherlock. If you can find the right channels, it can be a handy way to access some interesting Internet-based information.

TIP   *Web sites can offer Sherlock channels that can be automatically installed in Sherlock by simply clicking on them. In my experience they aren't terribly popular, but you can find some by searching for Sherlock channels at Google.com or a similar search service.*

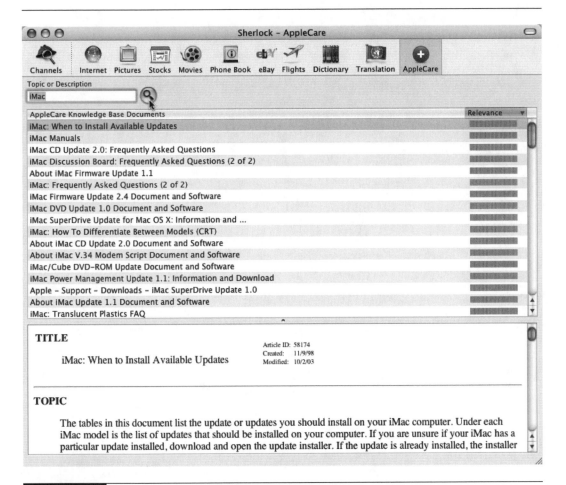

FIGURE 19-6   Here's Sherlock being used to search AppleCare.

Chapter 20

Access iDisk, Transfer Files, and Chat

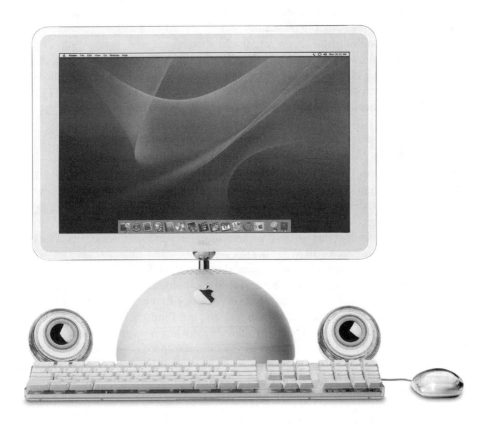

How to...

- Access your iDisk
- Share files on the Web
- Transfer files over the Internet
- Compress and decompress files
- Work with disk images
- Talk it up with iChat

Your Mac is designed to live on the Internet. It's built to transfer files online, back up files online, and get most of its updates, new installations, and new tools online. While many of these tasks are accomplished via built-in features—particularly iDisk and Software Update—you'll also find it useful to download third-party applications, such as an FTP program, so you can access the wealth of files available on the Internet for downloading.

In this chapter, you'll see how to use your iDisk—if you've signed up for Apple's .Mac service—to store and retrieve files over the Internet. You'll also learn how to upload to and download from the Internet using an FTP application. And, you will see how to work with some of the unique archiving file formats often used for transferring files, besides learning some ways to get new applications and application updates into your Mac over the Internet.

Work with Your iDisk

It's just my opinion, but I think iDisk is the coolest .Mac tool that Apple offers. For one, iDisk is an interesting solution to the conundrum of how to transfer and back up your files in as convenient a way as possible. You can actually store files online, using Apple's servers, enabling you to access those files from another Mac when necessary. iDisk also enables others to download those files (if you choose to make them public) for easy file exchange, as you'll see. And, iDisk can be accessed by using Mac OS 9 and Microsoft Windows, as well.

iDisk is essentially a bit of server disk space (by default, 100MB) that you can access over the Internet. It's sort of a combination of FTP and Apple file sharing. (In fact, it's a slightly different technology, called WebDAV, but it's similar to networking in the way it works.) When you sign into your iDisk, you access it using the small icon in your Finder's Sidebar (in Mac OS X 10.3 and above). You can drag files and folders to the iDisk; when it's synchronized with the remote server, it sends those files over the Internet to your storage space on Apple's computers. In fact, iDisk is great for backing up your most important files so that they're saved in two places—on your Mac and remotely on Apple's servers. That way, if some catastrophe strikes your Mac, you can still get to those important documents.

TIP *Want more than 100MB of storage space? Apple has an option (at the time of writing) that lets you pay monthly for additional storage. Check the iDisk page online at **http://www.mac.com** for details.*

Access Your iDisk

If you have a .Mac account, you already have an iDisk available. All you have to do is access it, and Mac OS X gives you two easy ways to do that. In Mac OS X, the most basic way to access your iDisk is from within the Finder. You'll need to have your .Mac account set up in System Preferences. (If you don't, launch Apple | System Preferences and access the .Mac pane, then enter your .Mac member name and password.) If everything is configured, choose Go | iDisk in the Finder, or simply click the iDisk icon in a Finder window Sidebar in Mac OS X.

When you do this, your Mac will connect to Apple's servers and display your iDisk, as shown in Figure 20-1. What you're seeing is your storage space on Apple's servers and the folders that are preset for you. You'll notice that they're a little like the subfolders of your home folder on your Mac.

There are actually two different ways that you can work with your iDisk, and which one you choose may depend on the speed of your Internet connection. The first you've seen. The second method allows you to work with a *local* version of your iDisk and then synchronize the contents with Apple's servers only every so often. This may work better if you have a modem-based Internet connection (instead of a fast broadband connection) or if you want to be able to work with the contents of your iDisk when you're both on- and offline. The downside to the local-version system is that the files that you place on your iDisk for safekeeping aren't always *instantly* on Apple's server.

FIGURE 20-1   iDisk's folders

20

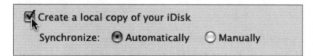

To turn on the local option, open System Preferences and choose the .Mac pane. Now click the iDisk tab. On that tab you'll find not only information about your iDisk, but the Create a Local Copy of Your iDisk option. (Note that this requires 100MB of disk space on your Mac's hard disk if you have a default-sized iDisk.)

Turn on that option and you've got another choice to make—whether the iDisk should synchronize automatically or manually. If you choose Automatically, you'll find that the iDisk

synchronizes at set intervals while you're connected to the Internet. If you choose Manually, it won't synchronize on its own, but you can synchronize it by clicking the small icon that appears in the Finder window's Sidebar next to the iDisk icon.

With your choices made, close System Preferences (or switch to another preference pane). When you do, a dialog box appears to inform you that your iDisk contents are being copied to a new local version of your iDisk. Depending on how much is stored on your iDisk, that process can take a while. Once it's done, however, you'll access your iDisk as you normally would—you'll just notice that it's usually a bit faster. When you're logged onto the Internet, you should find that it updates itself, unless you've chosen to handle that manually. (When you select the iDisk in the Sidebar of a Finder window, the bottom of that window will show the iDisk status, including when it was last synchronized.)

In Mac OS X 10.3 you can launch someone else's iDisk (that is, one that isn't set in the .Mac preference pane) by choosing Go | iDisk | Other User's iDisk in the Finder. You'll need a user name and password to access that iDisk, which will then appear as a mounted volume in the Sidebar. If you don't have the password for it, you can access their Public folder by choosing Go | iDisk | Other User's Public Folder.

Explore Your iDisk

Once you have the iDisk on your desktop, you can start taking a look around. You'll notice right away that the iDisk is pre-organized for you. You'll find a Documents folder (where you'll store a lot of your files) as well as folders for specific uses: Music, Pictures, Movies, Public, Sites, and Software.

The .Mac service includes an application, called Backup, that can be very handy for automating the backup process so that your important documents are duplicated automatically to your iDisk. (And, Backup can be used for backing up to CD-R or DVD-R discs as well.) If you've subscribed to .Mac, I encourage you to look into Backup.

So what are each of these folders for? Here's a rundown:

■ **Documents** This folder is for storing anything you'd like to save or back up online. Others can't access this folder—it's your private spot for storing and backing up documents. You can create subfolders and organize your files in whatever way that you'd like.

- **Library**   You won't have to dig into this folder if it appears. It's used for iSync to synchronize data between applications on your Mac and your iDisk.

- **Music**   Place files here for use with iTunes or if you'd like to add music to a web site you create with the HomePage tool.

- **Pictures**   Copy image files to this folder (in JPEG or GIF format) to use with the HomePage tool, discussed in Chapter 19. (You can also use photos stored here with iCard, which enables you to send electronic greeting cards.) Note that you can store your pictures in titled subfolders within this folder (Vacation, New Car, Baby's Steps), and tools such as iCard and HomePage can still access them within the subfolders.

- **Movies**   If you create a movie with iMovie (in fact, any QuickTime-format movie will work) and you'd like to use it on your HomePage web site, you can copy that movie to this folder.

- **Public**   Copy files to this folder if you'd like to share them with others on the Internet. (You'll also need to create a file-sharing web page, which is discussed later in this chapter.)

- **Sites**   This is the folder where your web pages are stored if you use the HomePage tool. You can also upload your own HTML files to this folder, if you know something about HTML. Place a file called `index.html` in the root of the Sites folder, and it will be accessible at **http://homepage.mac.com/*membername*/index.html**, where *membername* is your iTools member name. All other files and folders will be similarly accessible using that base URL.

- **Software**   The Software folder is a special case. Here, Apple has made available a number of shareware, freeware, and demo applications that you can copy *from* the Software folder *to* your Mac. You can then run the installers and work with the software. Note that you can't copy files *to* the Software folder, only from it. It's simply a convenient way for you to gain access to shareware and similar applications.

For the most part, you can work with your iDisk just as you would any removable disk (such as a Zip disk or external hard disk) or any network volume. A few caveats exist, however. First, you can't add folders or files to the first level of the iDisk; if you want to create subfolders for arranging your personal files, you should do so inside the Documents folder. And remember that you're accessing your iDisk over the Internet, so some operations can feel slow—painfully at times. That's just the nature of the beast. If you can't stand the slow speeds, the best plan is to upgrade your Internet service. (See Chapter 22 for details.)

NOTE   *When you delete items from your iDisk, they're deleted immediately; they aren't stored in your Trash (unless you're using the local iDisk approach, in which case, files deleted from the local iDisk remain in your Trash). Also, you can't delete items from the Software folder or its subfolders, and you can't delete any of the first-level folders discussed above.*

Close Your iDisk

When you're done working with your iDisk, you don't have to close it or eject it if you're working with the local iDisk option, since you only connect to Apple's servers when you synchronize.

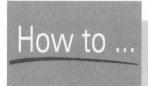 **Share Files with Others via iDisk**

If you have files on your iDisk that you'd like to share with others, you can place them in your Public folder, which is the only folder that is accessible to outsiders who don't have a password. Any files you place in your Public folder can be read by outsiders—even without your knowledge, so be careful with that folder. Likewise, within the Public folder is a folder called DropBox, where others can place files on your iDisk. Again, be careful—it's conceivable that someone could put a file in your DropBox that included a computer virus, worm, or other problematic code. If you don't know why you've received such a file, it may be best to delete it.

If you don't like the idea of allowing that public access, you can password-protect your Public folder so that others can access it only if they know the correct password. To do that, launch the .Mac preference pane in System Preferences and choose the iDisk tab. You'll see an option to password-protect your Public folder as well as to decide if visitors can only read (copy) files or if they can read and write (copy and save) files to your Public folder.

If you'd like to use your iDisk to make files available on the Web, you can do that using the HomePage tool, as discussed in Chapter 19. Begin by placing the files you want to share in your Public folder, then launch HomePage, and in the Create a Page section, select one of the file-sharing templates. Doing so automatically shares your Public folder, although you're free to choose subfolders within your Public folder. Then, click Edit to edit the text on the page, and choose Publish. Note also that password-protecting your Public folder doesn't protect it if you've posted a file-sharing page, although HomePage does allow you to password-protect your entire site, if desired.

If you don't use the local iDisk feature, then you're technically connected to your remote iDisk space when you have your iDisk mounted. However, iDisk and the .Mac servers use WebDAV technology for this connection, which isn't quite as active as other types of networking. (It uses web protocols for the connections, so accessing your iDisk is like accessing a two-way web site.) So, you can work with it as if it were connected to your Mac.

If you've connected to someone else's iDisk (or if you're connected to your own iDisk in an earlier version of Mac OS X), then, in that case, you may want to eject it. You can do that by clicking the small eject icon that appears next to the remote iDisk in the Sidebar of a Finder window. You can also drag the iDisk icon to the Trash if it's mounted on the desktop, or you can select the iDisk icon and choose File | Eject.

Use File Transfer Protocol

File Transfer Protocol, or FTP, is a client-server system for transferring files via the Internet. Like a web browser, an FTP application is designed to access special FTP server computers on the Internet. But instead of viewing pages and images, the FTP application's sole purpose is to upload and download files.

If you're using FTP to access online FTP resources (such as an FTP server at your organization or a public FTP server for shareware downloads), then all you really need to worry about is getting an FTP application. If you want to use FTP for storing your personal files, you'll need both an application and a virtual "place" where you can send your files. In this second case, you need to get some FTP storage space, most likely through your Internet service provider (ISP).

The FTP Application and Server Space

So which FTP application should you use? It's up to you, although any of them must be downloaded from the Internet before you can use them. My personal favorite is an FTP application called Transmit, shown in Figure 20-2. First, I like the way Transmit looks, and, second, I like the way Transmit makes it easy to see what's on your computer versus what's on the computer you're reaching over the Internet.

Transmit is written by Panic Software and can be downloaded from **http://www.panic.com**. It costs $24.95 to license the software if you like it. (Transmit is shareware, meaning you can download it and try it before you buy it.)

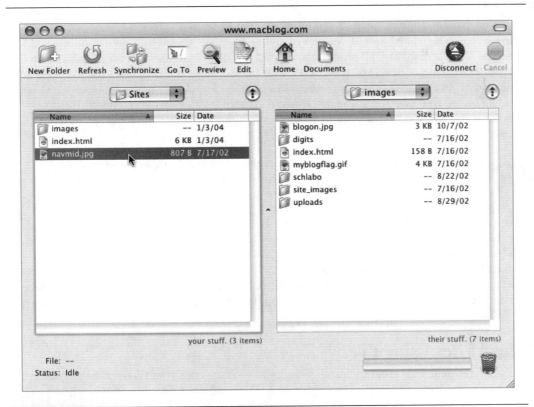

FIGURE 20-2   Transmit makes transferring files via FTP easy and visual.

20

Other popular FTP programs available for Mac OS X include Fetch (**http://fetchsoftworks.com**) and Interarchy (**http://www.interarchy.com/**), both of which are shareware programs with a long history on the Mac platform. They work a little differently from Transmit, but the concepts are the same.

Once you have the FTP application, you may also want some FTP storage space, most likely through your ISP. You may also want to have two different folders in that space—public and private—with different privilege settings (ask your ISP how to set these). The public folder on the server will be accessible to other Internet users—perfect if you need Bob in San Francisco to be able to log in and download a long report. The private folder is accessible only to you. The private folder can be used for backing up your important documents and applications in a secure, online location, so your files are accessible if you ever have trouble with your Mac.

If your ISP offers storage space for a web site that you can access via FTP, you may also be able to use that space for personal file storage. In that case, you should ask your ISP to help you create a private folder on the FTP site, so others can't access your files via the Web (unless that's what you want them to do, of course). Otherwise, you might ask the ISP if you can rent private FTP storage space—it's often available for a small fee.

The FTP Address

FTP servers have an address, just as web servers do. The difference is, some FTP servers require you to log in as a registered user of that server, and then you get access to certain or all files on that server. You can use the FTP program to upload and download files stored in your Internet space. So, the burning question you need to ask your ISP is, "What is the address I use to access my Internet space?" In most cases, this is an address like *ftp.mac-upgrade.com* or *www.companyname.net*, depending on the type of server computer. (Most dedicated FTP servers start with "ftp" in their name, but if you're uploading directly to a web server computer, it may have "www" as part of its name.)

 Some FTP servers, called anonymous *servers, allow you to log in and download files without having a specific account on the system. For servers where you'll upload files, you generally need to be a registered user.*

To access a non-anonymous FTP server, you'll need an account on the remote computer, and you'll need to know your user name and password. (If you're trying to access space made available by your ISP, then your user name and password are most likely the same as your user name and password for the dial-up connection, but they may be different. Ask your ISP.) Usually when you access an anonymous FTP server, you don't need an account or password, although some systems request that you enter anonymous as your user name and enter your e-mail address as a password.

Upload Files Using FTP

Once you have your FTP program installed and you've made sure your Internet connection is active, you're ready to transfer files to the distant site. Uploading is done in two steps: first you prepare the file(s) for uploading, and then you send them.

In most cases, files must have a proper filename extension to work correctly when uploaded and downloaded from FTP servers. For instance, if you upload a TIFF image from your Mac, called `Image01`, to your FTP server, and then subsequently download it, your Mac won't immediately know this is a TIFF image. If you include the filename extension .tif or .tiff, as in `Image01.tif`, however, then your Mac (or any other computer) should be able to work with the file properly. The same goes for AppleWorks (.cwk) or Microsoft Word (.doc) documents. And, you should always add filename extensions if you're making the files available to Microsoft Windows or Unix users.

> **TIP**
>
> *For best results, you might also want to compress the file(s) into an archive, as discussed in the upcoming section "Compress and Decompress Files."*

Now you're ready to upload. In FTP parlance, uploading a file uses the Put command, and downloading a file requires the Get command. If you're using Transmit, you won't see these commands by default, but Interarchy and Fetch both use them.

1. Start up the FTP application and enter an FTP server computer address. (In some programs, you may need to choose File | Connect or a similar command first.) You should also enter user name and password information, if relevant. Click the button that enables you to log on.

2. Once you successfully log on, you see a file list. On the remote server, you should create a folder you can use for uploading and downloading files. (In Transmit, use File | New Folder; you then select Their Stuff in the New Folder dialog box.) I like to call my folder Transfer because that's what I tend to use it for.

> **NOTE**
>
> *If the FTP space offered by your ISP is for a web site, then you may be shown, by default, a folder available to everyone on the Web. If you're not uploading web documents that you want publicly available, you'll need to create a private folder for your files. Consult your ISP.*

3. Double-click the new folder.

4. Now, if you're using Transmit, you can select the files you want to upload in the My Stuff file list, and then click-and-drag the files to the Their Stuff file list. If you're using Fetch or Interarchy, you can drag files from the Finder to the open window in that application. (You can also use the Put command in Fetch or Interarchy.)

> **CAUTION**
>
> *Some FTP applications may reveal hidden folders or files (such as .FBCIndex in Mac OS X) on your Mac's hard disk. Don't delete or move these files, because they're used by the Mac OS at the system level for important tasks. (They should not be copied to remote servers, either.)*

That's it—you should see the files available now in the remote folder.

Download Files Using FTP

To retrieve or download a file, the process is reversed—you can drag-and-drop a file from the server folder to your desktop or a folder in the Finder. Or, you can select the remote file and drag it to the

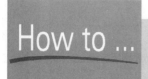

How to ... Access FTP Servers from the Finder

Actually, you can download files from an FTP server *without* special software, if you'd like to, using the Finder. In the Finder, choose Go | Connect to Server. In the Connect to Server dialog box, enter an FTP address (in the form `ftp://computer.domain.ext`—don't forget the `ftp://` part) and click Connect or press return. You'll see a dialog box appear asking for a user name and password. Enter those and click OK. If they're correct, you should see the FTP server's folders appear in a Finder window; you'll also see that the FTP server is mounted like a remote network volume.

So why did I recommend that you download third-party software? Because, at this writing, the FTP service within Mac OS X simply doesn't always work. Sometimes you can't log into servers that you should be able to access, and sometimes you can't upload files using the Finder—you can only copy them from the FTP server to your Mac. That's handy, but it's only half of FTP, which is why you need an FTP program.

OK…actually, you don't *need* an FTP program to upload—*if* you're willing to use the Mac's Terminal to access the command line. If you're intrepid like that, then launch Terminal (it's in the Applications folder), and when the prompt appears, type `man ftp` and press return. That's the online "manual" that will tell you about command-line FTP. (Press any key to scroll each screen after reading it.)

My Stuff window (in Transmit), click the Get button (in Fetch), or choose the File | FTP Download command (in Interarchy). The file is downloaded and saved on your hard disk.

Compress and Decompress Files

Because large files take a long time to transmit over the Internet, sometimes it's preferable to compress them. Using sophisticated algorithms, the compression software can reduce redundant information in a document or program and make the file more compact. The catch is that the file is completely useless until it's expanded, using the reverse of the compression scheme.

The other thing you can often do with most compression schemes is create a compressed archive of more than one file, so a number of files, or an entire folder, can be stored and sent within a single archive file, almost as if it were a shipping envelope. Once the file arrives at its destination, the decompression program is used to separate the files and bring them back to full size.

To do all this, you need to pick a compression scheme. Three major schemes are used for compressing files on the Internet:

■ **StuffIt**   This format (with the filename extension .sit) is used almost exclusively by Macs, although a Windows version of StuffIt Expander is available. Windows users who have Expander for Windows can expand stuffed archives created on a Mac.

- **Zip**   This format is used almost exclusively in the Windows world. Utilities are available on the Mac to create PKZip (or just .zip or ZIP) files, and StuffIt Expander can expand .zip files. In Mac OS X 10.3, you can even use the Finder to create Zip archives.

- **Gzip and UNIX Compress**   These formats are generally used by Unix machines (the files have .gz and .Z extensions). Because Mac OS X is based on Unix, you occasionally encounter these types of compressed files, although most day-to-day compression in Mac OS X uses the StuffIt format. StuffIt Expander can decompress these formats.

StuffIt and DropStuff

For decompressing files you download, StuffIt Expander works with any files created on a Mac, even older formats like Compact Pro. It can also decompress most common Windows ZIP and Unix archives. DropStuff is a shareware program, available from Aladdin Systems, that's used for compressing StuffIt archives. Because DropStuff is shareware, you should pay for it (about $25) if you find it's useful.

NOTE   *Your Mac includes StuffIt Expander by default, but newer versions might be available. Check **http://www.aladdinsys.com** to find a new version of StuffIt Expander or to download DropStuff. Remember to get the native Mac OS X versions if you're using Mac OS X.*

The procedure for *decompressing* most archives is simply to drag-and-drop the archive onto the StuffIt Expander icon. When you drop an archive on StuffIt Expander, it expands the archive, if possible. And StuffIt knows quite a bit about expanding archives.

SHORTCUT   *You can usually decompress .sit files easily by double-clicking them. Also, many web browser and e-mail applications, including those bundled with your Mac, automatically decompress .sit files by sending them to StuffIt Expander when you download them.*

How about *compressing* files? If you're sending a file to a Macintosh, compress it as a StuffIt file. To do this, simply drag-and-drop the file, folder, or group of files (and folders) to the DropStuff icon. When you release the mouse button, DropStuff goes into action, stuffing the files into an archive.

If you're only stuffing one document, then the archive file is named for that document with a .sit filename extension. If you're stuffing more than one document, you get a file named archive.sit. You can rename the file, just as you can rename any other file. One suggestion, however: keep the .sit part in the name so that your receiving party (assuming you're sending this to someone else) knows to drag it to StuffIt Expander.

TIP   *If you encounter a file with the extension .sea, it's a self-extracting archive. This doesn't require StuffIt Expander to decompress; however, it will have to launch the Classic environment to open. Your best bet is to drag such a file to the StuffIt Expander icon.*

CAUTION   *Because of a known bug in the software, you should avoid using StuffIt Expander 8.0, StuffIt Deluxe 8.0, and DropStuff 8.0 to decompress archives that include applications. Use versions either prior to 8.0 or 8.02 (which fixed the bug) or higher if you have trouble.*

20

Compress Using PC/Unix Formats

If you're sending a file to a user of a Microsoft Windows machine, you'll probably want to use the PKZip format instead of the StuffIt format. And, if you're sending to a Unix machine, third-party utilities are available. The main ones are listed in Table 20-1.

Work with Disk Images

When the iMac was first released so many years ago, the lack of a floppy drive was much maligned. While most of that has died down now (particularly with the latest models sporting writable CD drives), the legacy of the floppy disk lives on in something called disk images. A *disk image* is a special sort of document: when you double-click it, it gets "mounted" on the desktop, almost as if the file itself was a removable disk, like a CD or a floppy. If you've installed software downloaded from Apple (along with many other companies that write Mac software), you've probably used a disk image.

Once the disk image is mounted, it acts like any other disk. You can drag files to its icon, for instance, to copy files onto the disk image. Similarly, you can double-click the disk image to open its window and copy files from (and sometimes to) that window. But the disk image isn't a disk at all; it's a special kind of file, which you can copy to other disks, copy over a network connection, or even send over the Internet.

In this sense, a disk image can be used much like a Zip or StuffIt file. And, using Disk Utility on your Mac, you can create your own disk images in a process that's similar to burning data to a CD. The result is a single file that takes up less space when in its compressed form, making it easy to transfer across the Internet or store on removable media.

Utility	Description	URL
StuffIt Deluxe	Deluxe version of DropStuff—creates and decompresses StuffIt, ZIP, and Unix-style archives	http://www.aladdinsys.com/
Finder	Creates and decompresses Windows ZIP archives	http://www.apple.com/
ZipIt	Creates and decompresses Windows ZIP archives	http://www.maczipit.com/
DropZip	Creates Windows ZIP archives	http://www.aladdinsys.com/
Pack Up and Go	Creates Unix-style archives and compressed files	http://www.stone.com/PackUpAndGo/PackUpAndGo.html
OpenUp	Compresses (via the Services menu) and decompresses a variety of formats, including Unix-style archives	http://www.stepwise.com/Software/OpenUp/

TABLE 20-1   Compression/Decompression Utilities

Mount a Disk Image

There are two different kinds of disk images—self-mounting images (.smi) and regular disk images (.img or .dmg). A *self-mounting image* can be used on any Macintosh because it mounts itself. This is how most electronic software updates are distributed by Apple these days, which makes it easy to download the images and double-click to mount them. Then you can install from them as if they were actual disks.

To use regular image files, you need the Disk Copy software, which comes preinstalled with Mac OS X. Then, you need to find a disk image file—one with those extensions discussed above. Once you have one, double-click it to mount the disk image on the desktop. In the example at the right, for instance, the disk image file is on top and the mounted disk image below it.

Once the disk icon appears on the desktop, you can work with it, just as if it were another removable disk. Double-click it to open a Finder window and reveal its contents. Then, double-click installer applications to launch them, or drag-and-drop files from the disk image's window to another Finder window or to the desktop. When you finish with the disk image, drag its disk icon to the Trash and it will be *unmounted*, or removed, from the desktop. (Dragging the disk image file itself to the Trash places it in the Trash for deletion.)

Create a Disk Image

The easiest way to create a compressed disk image that's good for transmitting to others is to use an existing folder filled with files. Here's how:

1. Gather together all of the files that you want to add to that disk image in a folder.

2. Launch Disk Utility, which is found in the Utilities folder inside your main Applications folder.

3. Choose Images | New | Image from Folder.

4. In the dialog box that appears, locate the folder, select it, and choose Open.

5. In the Convert Image dialog box (see Figure 20-3), enter a name for the disk, choose a location where it should be stored, and choose a type of disk image from the Image Format menu. You'll likely want to choose Compressed, unless you have a different purpose in mind.

6. In the Encryption menu, choose a style of encryption if you'd like the image only to be accessible via a password.

7. Click Save. You'll see a Progress dialog box appear and your disk image will be created and saved. If you chose encryption, you'll be asked to assign a password to the disk image.

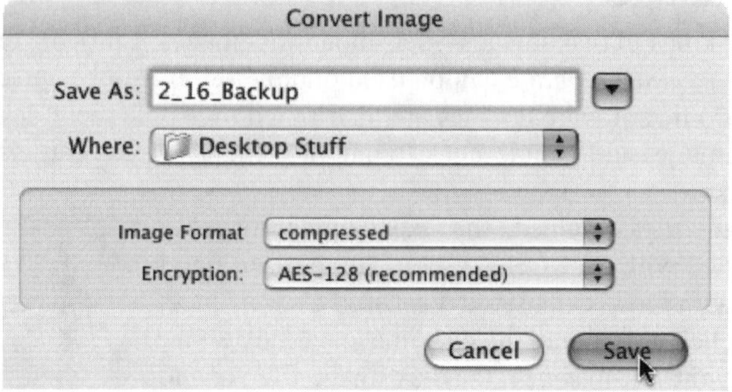

FIGURE 20-3   Here's a disk image I'm creating.

That's it. The image is created and can now be accessed and manipulated as a file, or you can double-click it to mount it.

While the existing-folder approach is a convenient way to create a disk image, it's not the only way. In Disk Utility, choose the Images | New menu to explore the other ways you can create disk images, including creating a blank image of a certain size that you can gradually fill with files. Some users will create a disk image the size of a CD-R, for instance, and slowly drag files that they want to back up to that image. When the disk image is filled, the Images | Burn command can be used in Disk Utility to burn that disk image to a CD.

Talk It Up with iChat AV

The last major feature I'd like to discuss in this chapter is iChat AV, an all-around chatting application that comes with Mac OS X 10.3 and is available for Mac OS X 10.2 for $29.95 from **http://www.apple.com/ichat/** on the Web. iChat AV is a deceptively simple application that started out as a text-chatting client application—one that worked with the popular AIM (AOL Instant Messaging) service to allow you to type messages back and forth between members of AIM and those with .Mac accounts.

When Apple appended the "AV" to iChat AV's name, however, it did so for good reason, as iChat was upgraded from instant messaging to audio and video conferencing capabilities. When Apple announced iChat AV, it also announced the iSight camera (**http://www.apple.com/isight/**), which works with the software to enable you to transmit video over the Internet. Coupled with an incredible ability to transmit good-sounding, two-way audio for discussions, iChat AV makes for a rather impressive all-around communications center.

Launch iChat AV

When you launch iChat AV for the first time, you're asked for some info. iChat needs to know what service you intend to use as the foundation for your chatting, and it needs to know your user name and password for that service. In the assistant that appears after launching iChat, walk through the steps required to set up iChat AV by viewing the screens, and then click the Continue button.

On the first screen after the intro is the Set Up a New iChat Account. You do that by entering the information for either a .Mac account name and password or an AIM account name and password. (You can switch between the types using the Account Type menu.) If you don't have either, you can click the Get an iChat Account button, which takes you to the .Mac site. Apple lets you create a new iChat account without subscribing to the .Mac service.

Once you set up that account and click Continue, the next question is whether you want to set up Rendezvous messaging. *Rendezvous* is a technology that automatically discovers things on your local network—other people who have iChat running, for example. If you're set up for Rendezvous chat, then anyone on your local network—in your home or dorm or office or organization—will pop up as available for chatting if they have iChat open and Rendezvous chat enabled. So, if you've got a network and you think you might want to chat with the people on that network, enable Rendezvous messaging and click Continue.

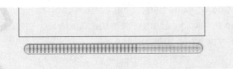

The last screen is the Set Up iChat AV screen. If you have a camera connected, you'll see an image on screen; you'll also see an indicator showing you the levels that your Mac's microphone is hearing. Speak while looking at this screen and you'll see the indicator respond.

Now you should see the Conclusion page. Click Done and you're ready to work with iChat.

Navigate Your Buddy and Rendezvous Lists

If you've set up Rendezvous messaging, you'll see two windows when iChat appears; if you've only set up AIM/.Mac messaging, you'll see one window. In either case, what those windows are showing you are other chat-users who are available for you to chat with. In the case of Rendezvous, those individuals are people on your local network who also have iChat and Rendezvous messaging active; for AIM/.Mac messaging, you're seeing your Buddy List, which is people you've set up iChat to track. (If you don't have anyone, it's simply because you're working with an account where you haven't set up buddies. If you *do* have buddies and didn't expect them, it's likely that you set them up using a different chat interface, such as AOL.)

As mentioned, people in the Rendezvous list come up automatically when they're detected, but Buddies have to be added manually. To do that, click the plus (+) sign on the Buddy List window. In the dialog sheet that appears, you can select someone from your Mac's Address Book, or you can click New Person, which enables you to enter the account type (.Mac or AIM), account name for that person, and some other specifics so this person can also be stored in your Address Book. When you're done, you can click Add to add them to your Buddy List.

TIP   *You can change your iChat picture by choosing the Buddy List window and then choosing Buddies | Change My Picture. You then drag in a picture that you want to use, or if you have an iSight or similar camera attached, you can take a video snapshot of yourself (or anything else you want as a stand-in).*

Clearly the point of these lists is to make it a simple matter for you to begin a chat with one of the people listed. If their entry is not grayed out, then they're online; if they have a green icon next to their name, then they're available for chatting. A red icon means they're connected to the server but have chosen a message to tell you that they're busy or away. You can do the same thing in either list by clicking the small menu beneath your name in the window.

 *Your "away" and "available" messages can be customized by choosing one of the Custom commands from that pop-up menu.*

Chat Online

To initiate a chat, simply double-click the name of a person in one of your lists. That causes the Instant Message window to pop up. This is where you'll see the text of your chat session, and at the bottom of that window is a small entry box, where you can type your message.

You begin by typing a message and pressing RETURN, which sends your initial message to the recipient and allows her or him to either accept the message or ignore it. Your recipient will see a window something like this:

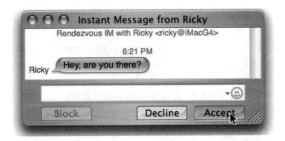

This window allows the recipient to respond or decline the instant message session. If accepted, then the text in the entry box gets added to the discussion. To continue, simply enter text and press RETURN. You can also use the small smiley-face menu to choose from the different built-in *smilies* that iChat allows, which can be used to express emotion in your chat. (For instance, you can use a smiley face to soften the blow when you're being sarcastic in your typing. You'll find them useful.)

> **TIP**   *You can also type certain emoticons and they'll be turned into little smiley images when you submit the message. For instance, :-) is turned into a smiley face, and :-P is a face with its tongue sticking out.*

You can also send links and even images through the iChat interface. When you type a full URL, such as http://www.macblog.com/, it's made clickable for the recipient. To send an image, you can simply drag it to the area where you type your message. (Don't drag it to the message window itself, as you'll simply add it as a background image for the chat window.)

> **TIP**   *You can change or clear the background images—and accomplish a lot more customization we don't have space to cover—in the View menu within iChat.*

What's more, you can send files and file folders to others via iChat. (You can't send a group of files, at least not in the current version, although you can send a folder that has multiple files in it.) Simply drag a file's icon either to the text entry box in the chat window or to the person's name in your Buddy or Rendezvous list. Drop the file and you'll see a small dialog box appear telling you iChat is waiting to send the file; when your recipient accepts the file, it will begin to download to him or her.

> **TIP**   *It's best to compress large files (using built-in Finder compression in Zip format or DropStuff, as discussed earlier in the chapter) before sending them through iChat, as compressed archives will transmit a bit more quickly.*

When you're done with a chat, you can simply click the close button on the chat window. That closes the window and disconnects the chat.

Clicking a Buddy or Rendezvous name isn't the only way to begin a chat. If you'd like to chat with someone who isn't in one of your lists, choose File | New Chat with Person. That opens a new

20

window, as well as a dialog sheet that lets you enter the person's AIM or .Mac address so that you can attempt to contact them.

Another possibility is a group chat or a conference. You initiate such a chat by choosing File | Open and then, in the Participants drawer, clicking the plus (+) symbol. That lets you add multiple people to your chat, including those in your lists (Buddy and Rendezvous) or those for whom you enter an AIM or .Mac address. When you type a message and press RETURN, that message will be sent to everyone in the Participants list.

Initiate Audio and Video Chat

Of course, text chatting is not the only type you can do. In order to audio chat, you and the other party need to be configured to do so, and you both need to be running iChat AV, since early iChat versions only support text chats. When an audio chat is possible, you'll see a small audio chat icon next to that person's name in your Buddy or Rendezvous list.

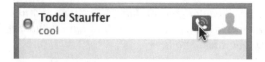

Click that icon and iChat attempts to connect for an audio chat. A query window is sent to the other party, who can then accept, decline, or opt for a text discussion instead.

As you chat you'll notice the audio bar that reacts to audible input. That acts as an indicator that your Mac is hearing you and, therefore, the other party should be getting good volume as well. (The window has a mute button that you can click if you need to talk to someone who is physically in the room with you, or answer the phone, for instance.)

For a video chat, you'll do the same thing, but with the small video icon, which looks a little like a movie camera or camcorder. When you click that icon, a video chat is requested of the other party, and if they click Accept, you should see their video window appear. (You can view your own at any time by clicking the video icon that's next to your own name.)

If you have trouble with your connection at any time, you can choose Video | Connection Doctor to see a diagnostic screen that tells you what the various connection rates are working out to, which may help you determine the exact problem.

Part IV

Improve and Maintain Your Mac

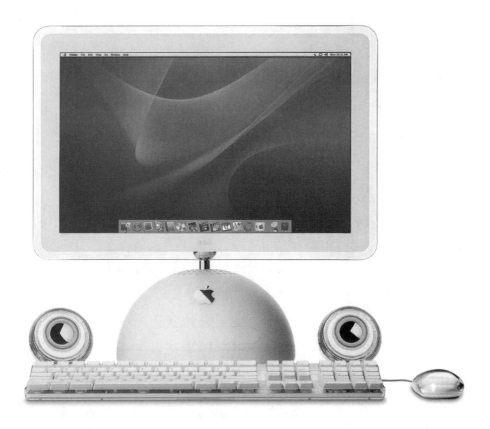

Chapter 21

Network, Share Files, and Manage Users

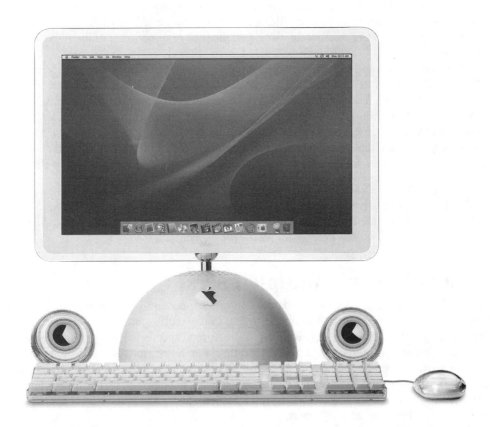

How to...

- Create and manage multiple users
- Connect your Mac to a network
- Enter the settings for your network protocols
- Connect to any network server
- Share files on the network
- Network two Macs together
- Create your own local network

A Mac running Mac OS X can be shared by multiple users in a variety of ways, including local accounts for multiple users or connections over network cabling (or wireless connections) that enable you to share files with other computers. You've got a few different ways to let multiple users collaborate using a single Mac or a room full of them—or something in between.

To understand how all this works, we first need to take a look at user accounts in Mac OS X. Those accounts are the key to both sharing a single Mac among multiple users *and* making files in your Mac available to others on a network. Then, if you're interested, we can dig into the cabling and settings that make file sharing between Macs (and other computers) possible. A *local area network (LAN)* is two or more computers connected by special cabling (or, these days, wirelessly) for the purpose of sharing files and resources like printers. With a file-sharing network, you can place files on other computers that are attached to yours either via cabling or using a wireless technology.

 Most modern Macs support wireless networks. The file-sharing and user issues are the same, but the configuration of the wireless devices is a little different. Chapter 23 covers actually setting up wireless hardware; this chapter covers setting up user accounts, connecting computers, and activating file sharing.

Create and Manage Multiple Users

In Mac OS X, you can create two fundamental types of accounts—an administrator account and a standard account. A standard account is for day-to-day stuff—getting work done. You can't use it to install applications in the Applications folder, for instance, and it only has access to a limited number of the options and settings available in the System Preferences application. By contrast, an administrator account (one that's in the Admin group) has enough *privileges* to install applications in the Applications folder, make changes in the main Library folder (where fonts, driver software, and other important files are installed), and make system-level decisions in the System Preferences application.

Within the "standard" category are two other types of accounts in Mac OS X 10.3—Managed and Simplified. We'll touch on those briefly, but they essentially allow you to limit a user to certain types of operations and applications—great for minimizing the damage a child could do to files on your Mac, for instance, or for setting limits for Macs in a computer lab.

The first user account created in Mac OS X is automatically placed in the Admin group. That means that this account has the capabilities to do all of the above tasks, as well as create other user accounts. When you create a new user, you're also creating a new home folder for that user, giving that user a "virtual workspace" of sorts on the Mac. And, you're separating that user's files and preferences from those of any other users, so that each individual who accesses your Mac can have a personal space that's free from meddling by others.

Being an Admin user means you have to be careful. Deleting items in the Applications or Library folders can lead to problems for your iMac, as can choosing the wrong settings in the System Preferences application. And, if you're digging into other administrative utilities—particularly the Terminal application and the NetInfo Manager application—you could cause your Mac's underlying system files some damage. Be sure to educate yourself about these more technical utilities and what their capabilities are before you take any drastic actions.

Create Users

If you've decided you'd like to have multiple user accounts on your Mac, you're ready to begin creating them. To do so, launch the System Preferences application by either clicking its tile in the Dock or selecting System Preferences from the Apple menu. Then, in the System Preferences application, click the Accounts icon to launch the Accounts pane.

You'll notice immediately that all of the currently created accounts are listed on the left side of the Accounts pane. You can also see which of those accounts are Admin accounts and which are Standard (and Managed or Simplified, for that matter). If your account is not an Admin account, then you'll need to log out and log back in using an Admin account. Alternatively, you can *authenticate* by clicking the small padlock icon at the bottom of the pane and entering the user name and password of a valid Admin account. (Remember that the first account created, during the Setup Assistant discussed in Chapter 1, is an Admin account.)

If the padlock icon is already unlocked, you're signed into an Admin account. (If the padlock *is* locked, you can click it to authenticate.) You're ready to begin creating and managing users. Click the plus (+) button at the bottom of the user list and you'll see an entry for a new user appear, along with blank entry boxes for that user's vitals. From there, creating a new user is easy:

1. Enter the user's first and last name in the Name entry box. Press TAB.

2. In the Short Name entry box, you'll see a suggested short name. You can press TAB again to accept it, or edit it before pressing TAB.

3. Enter a password for the user. It should be at least eight characters long (it can be shorter, but not much) and not easily guessed. The best passwords are combinations of nonsensical words or names and numbers that aren't part of your daily life. (For instance, don't user your birth date or anniversary.) Press TAB.

4. Since you can't see what you typed in the Password entry box, you'll type the password again in the Verify box to make sure they match. When you type, use the same capitalization— passwords are case sensitive in Mac OS X. Press TAB.

5. If desired, you can type a hint in the Password Hint entry box. (Don't let the hint be a giveaway!) Later, when this user attempts to log in, the password hint may appear in the Login window (see the section "Set Login Options").

6. Click the Picture tab and you'll see options for selecting a picture that will be associated with this new user. Click one of the pictures you see, drag one from the desktop to the small picture well next to the Edit button, or click that Edit button and you'll see a window that lets you customize the picture.

7. Click the Security tab and ignore FileVault for now (more on that in Chapter 22). Instead, note the option at the bottom of the screen. You can turn on Allow User to Administer This Computer if you want this new account to be an Admin account.

NOTE *FileVault is encryption for your home folder, which makes your personal data impossible to access without the correct password. It can be turned on after you've set up an account, so I recommend reading up on it in Chapter 22 before making the final decision to use it— it requires some trade-offs.*

8. Finally, if you plan to make this account a limited one, click the Limitations tab and consult the upcoming sidebar.

When you're done entering user information, you can either click another user in the pane, choose another preference pane, or close System Preferences. (It may seem odd, but Apple opted against a Save or Apply Now button in this particular pane.) The user is saved, a home folder is created for the user, and a new entry will appear for this user in the Accounts pane.

One other thing may happen: if your Mac is currently set for *automatic login*, which means you don't see the Login window when you first start or restart your Mac, then creating a user will cause the Users pane to prompt you to change this. Now that you have two (or more) users on your Mac, you may want to display the Login window every time the Mac is started or restarted so that different users can log in. In the dialog sheet that appears, click the Yes button if you'd like to enable the Login window. If you'd prefer that automatic login for your main account continues, click the No button.

Did you know?

Limit User Accounts

When you're creating a new user account in the Accounts pane, you'll find options on the Limitations tab that allow you to govern the behavior of an account a little more closely. Click the Limitations tab and you'll see three buttons—No Limits, Some Limits, and Simple Finder. No Limits is the standard user account; Some Limits is a Managed account, which means you can limit the applications that the user can access and some of the basic tasks that the user can perform, such as opening System Preferences or burning a CD. To allow a user to do something on the Some Limits tab, you place a check mark next to that item; to disallow something, make sure the check mark is unchecked.

Click the Simple Finder tab and you're going to more severely limit what that user can do—he or she will only be able to access the items accessible via a simplified Dock. This is best for young children or for people who use your Mac in a public space where accessing the underlying files isn't a good idea. Once you've chosen Simple Finder, you can dig through the folders in the bottom half of the window and place a check next to any application that the user should be allowed to launch.

TIP *Need to change a user's info? As long as you're an Admin user, you can dig in and change things in the Accounts pane, including the Admin status or password of other users.*

Delete a User

To delete a user, you'll need to be logged into an Admin account or authenticated as an Admin user. Then, select that user and click the minus-sign (–) button. An alert sheet immediately appears warning you that the user will be permanently deleted. If that's what you want to do, select an Admin account to which you want the privileges for that user's home folder assigned, and click the Delete Immediately button. If you'd prefer to simply deactivate the user and save his or her files, choose the OK button.

CAUTION *You should only choose Delete Immediately if you're absolutely sure that no important documents or data will be lost when you delete the user's account and home folder. If you choose OK instead, that user's home folder is stored in a compressed image file that can be accessed later if you need to get something from that folder. (It can also be made available to the user if he or she ever returns to the system.) Of course, you don't want the disk image cluttering your system forever, but it's a nice stopgap for a few months.*

After clicking either Delete Immediately or OK, you're returned to the Accounts pane (it may take a minute or two), and the deleted user will no longer appear in the list of users. Behind the scenes, if you've chosen OK, that user's home folder is moved to the Deleted Users folder, inside the main Users folder, where you'll be able to access the contents of that folder.

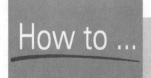 **Re-Create a Deleted User**

To re-create a user you've deleted, follow the procedure for creating a new user. You can enter the user's original name, short name, and password, if desired. When you're finished creating the user, click the Save button and that user is created. Now, in the Finder, locate the user's old folder—the one with "Deleted" as part of the name. Open the folder and drag the disk image to the Drop Box folder that's inside the Public folder in the user's new home folder. Items copied to the Drop Box folder automatically become "owned" by that user so that the user, once logged in, will have full permission for launching the disk image and accessing all the files that were in the original home folder.

Log in

Now, with multiple users, you're likely to see the Login window when you start up your Mac. When confronted with the Login window, you'll need to select a user name in the list of users and type the associated password in the Password entry box. Then, press RETURN or click the Log In button. If you don't enter a valid user name or password, the Login window shakes from side to side, almost like a toddler saying "No." Try again. If you're entering a valid user name, but your password is entered incorrectly three times, the password hint for that user name will appear. This will continue (every three failed attempts will result in the password hint being displayed) until you give up.

If you successfully enter a valid user name and password, the Login window disappears and the desktop appears. After a few seconds, the Finder appears and you're ready to begin working with your iMac and your personal home folder.

Use Fast User Switching

Mac OS X version 10.3 offers a new feature for multiple users—fast user switching. What this enables you to do is to switch between user accounts without requiring that you first log out of accounts that are already open. That lets more than one user switch between their accounts quickly—hence the name.

To turn on fast user switching, click the Login Options button at the bottom of the list of users in the Accounts pane. Now, turn on the Enable Fast User Switching option. That creates a new menu at the top right of the menu bar.

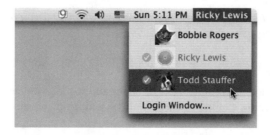

Now, to switch to a user account other than the current one, you simply choose a name from the menu. When you do, a Login window will appear, requiring you to log in with the correct password for that user. If you do, you'll be switched to that user account, complete with the home folder, desktop, and configuration settings for that new user. (You'll also see a fancy animation as Mac OS X moves from one account to the next.)

To return to other accounts, you can do one of two things. First, you can choose Apple | Logout from any account that's open if you'd like to log out and allow someone else to return to their work. Or, you can remain logged in, but select another user account from the menu in order to switch to it. Regardless of whether or not that account is already logged in, you'll be asked for the password to verify that you deserve access.

There's one other important circumstance—restarting the computer when multiple accounts are active. Ideally, you should log out of all open accounts before restarting the computer to ensure that no data is lost. (The corollary to that rule is that you should always save data in open applications before allowing the Mac to switch away from your user account.) If you have an Admin account and you need to restart or shut down the Mac, you can do that, including any open accounts, by choosing Apple | Restart or Apple | Shut Down. If any other accounts are open, you'll need to authenticate in a special dialog box to prove that you're an administrator. If you succeed, the Mac will restart or shut down.

Log Out of Your Mac

In a multiple user scenario, it's important that you log out of your account whenever you're done working on the Mac. (Unless, of course, you're using fast user switching. Your data is safer when you log out completely, however.) In fact, logging out gives you better security even when you're not switching users, as it password-protects access to your account.

To log out, choose the Log Out command from the Apple menu. An alert box will appear, asking you to confirm your decision. Click Log Out if that's what you really want to do, or click Cancel to stop the logout process.

If you've clicked Log Out, your applications will automatically quit, and you'll be asked to save any unsaved changes in your open documents. Then, eventually, the Finder and desktop will disappear and you'll see the Login window. Now you can log in again, allow another user to log in, or click the Restart or Shut Down buttons to restart or shut down your Mac, respectively.

 *The Restart and Shut Down buttons may not be displayed if you are not an Admin user and they have been turned off for your account.*

Set Login Options

If you'd like to customize how the Login window looks and works, you can do that by choosing the Login Options button below the list of users in the Accounts pane. You'll see some options appear:

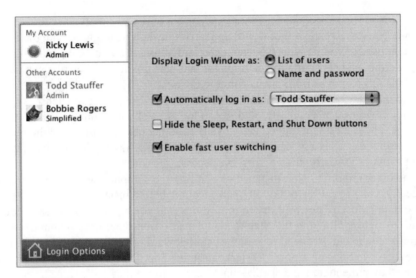

One we've already discussed is Enable Fast User Switching. At the top of that pane, however, you'll see Display Login Window As, which enables you to choose whether the Login window will have a list of users or blanks for a name and password. The blanks are a little more secure, because they require that a user know what the available user names are. With the list, it's a little more convenient to log in, but someone trying to break in can simply select a user and start guessing at the password.

Next, you can turn on or off the option Automatically Log in As if you'd like Mac OS X to bypass the Login window and automatically log in a particular user whenever the Mac is started up or restarted. By default the option is turned on if you haven't created additional users. If you've added users, you may have turned off the Automatic login option at that time.

 *Turning on the Automatically Log in As option means any user who restarts the Mac will have access to the main user's files, folders, and settings. It's on by default, so if your Mac runs in an environment where you'd prefer a bit more security, turn the option off so that others can't reach your desktop automatically.*

The other options on the Login window tab enable you to change the way the Login window looks and works. Turning on the Hide the Sleep, Restart, and Shut Down Buttons option is generally done as a security measure to keep users who don't have a valid user name from restarting the Mac and starting up from a different hard disk or startup CD that's been inserted in the iMac. (Restarting from a CD is covered in Chapter 24.)

Set Up Networking Hardware

Now you've seen how to create user accounts—those same user accounts are used for either accessing your Mac locally or connecting to it over a network. So, if a network is your desire (or if you want to be able to access other Macs over networking cables from yours), then you'll need to set up some network hardware.

Each Mac or other computer or printer on your network needs to have a way to connect to that network—either via Ethernet cable or an AirPort wireless card. Once you have those cables and cards installed, you'll need to configure them using the Network pane in System Preferences.

Connect Using Ethernet

Regardless of the size or complexity of your network, your Mac gets connected the same way. If you're using cabling (as opposed to AirPort wireless cards, which are discussed in the next section, "Connect Using AirPort"), you'll connect to other Macs via an Ethernet cable. If you're connecting the iMac to *one* other machine, you can use something called a *crossover cable*.

If you're connecting to more than one machine, you'll use a regular Ethernet *patch* cable (called "Category 5") to connect your Mac to an Ethernet hub, an external hardware device that allows you to connect your Mac to many other machines. A hub is required to connect more than two Macs or other devices, like network printers and Windows PCs.

You'll notice that the connector on the end of an Ethernet cable looks a lot like a phone cable connector, only it's larger. When you're connecting it to your Mac, make sure you're plugging that cable into the Ethernet port, not the modem port. (The connector won't fit in the modem port, but you could create trouble by trying to squeeze it in.) Once it's connected, you can connect directly to the Ethernet port of the other Mac (if you're only connecting two computers using a crossover cable), or you can connect it to an open port on the Ethernet hub.

To remove the Ethernet connector, press the small tab on the connector in toward the connector, then pull the cable out. This works just like removing a phone cable connector from a wall jack.

TIP   *If you want all computers on your local network to have Internet access, you'll need to have an Internet router as part of your network. The router can take data from the Internet and "route" it to different computers on your network. Some routers also have small hubs built in, meaning they can be used as your sole networking solution. See Chapter 22 for details on Internet router setup and use.*

Connect Using AirPort

For an AirPort connection, you'll need an AirPort card properly installed in your Mac, as discussed in Chapter 22. You'll also need an AirPort device to connect *to*—that can be either an AirPort Base Station or another Mac that's AirPort capable. The AirPort Base Station is a small, UFO-shaped device that Apple makes available for AirPort networks. It acts as a hub, like an Ethernet hub, allowing AirPort-enabled Macs within a 150-foot radius to communicate with it.

The AirPort Base Station needs to be configured, which you do by running the AirPort Setup Assistant, found in the Utility folder inside the Applications folder. The Setup Assistant must be run from a Mac that has an AirPort card installed; it will guide you through the process of communicating with the Base Station and configuring the AirPort network. (I'll discuss this in a little more detail in Chapter 22.)

Once the Base Station is configured, you should be able to locate it from your AirPort-enabled Mac. You can do that in one of two ways. If you have the AirPort menu bar icon active, you can select it and see if a named wireless network is available in that menu; if so, select it. (In this example, the name that's been given to the wireless network is "FastestNet.")

The other way to locate and connect to a wireless network is using the Internet Connect application found in the Applications folder on your Mac. At the top of the Internet Connect window, click the AirPort icon; that switches the display to the AirPort-related controls. Now, you can turn the AirPort card in your Mac on or off, select a network, and see that network's connection strength and status. You can also use the Show AirPort Status in Menu Bar option to turn on and off the menu bar item for AirPort.

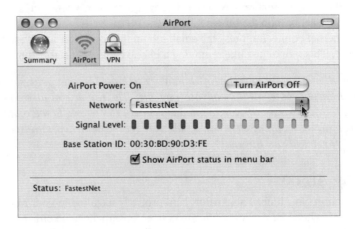

Choose Your Protocol

Once you have the network connection set up between your Mac and other computers—whether that connection is wired or wireless—you need to choose the protocol you're going to use to pass data between them. There are two major protocols in use today by Macs: AppleTalk and TCP/IP. AppleTalk is the traditional favorite of Mac users. It tends to be easier to configure on smaller networks and can allow newer Macs to network with much older (10 years or more) Macs. It's also useful for connecting to older laser printers, but it's a slower protocol, particularly with today's high-speed Ethernet networks.

TCP/IP, the protocol used over the Internet, has become the standard option, however. Mac OS X, for instance, is designed to use TCP/IP, even though it offers backward compatibility with AppleTalk.

Fortunately, in Mac OS X, you can use both protocols at once over your network connection. In fact, if you have things set up correctly, you can use the same connection for both Internet access and local network access. (Or, you can use two different connections, such as a modem for Internet and Ethernet for a network.) In most cases, you'll probably stick with TCP/IP for your networking unless you specifically need to access an AppleTalk-based resource, such as an older Apple or Mac-centric laser printer.

Set Up TCP/IP

You set up TCP/IP in the Network pane of System Preferences, by selecting the Network icon. When you do that, you're shown the Network Status screen. The Network Status screen displays any connections into your Mac that are currently active, including those that aren't fully configured. (If you don't see Ethernet, for instance, it may be because an Ethernet cable isn't plugged into your Mac.) Figure 21-1 shows a sample Network Status screen.

If the port you plan to use (AirPort, Ethernet, etc.) has a green dot and says it's properly configured, then it's possible you can simply move on to the "Connect to a Server" section of this chapter. These days, that's often the case—simply plugging in an Ethernet cable or choosing an AirPort network can allow your Mac to automatically configure itself using your Ethernet hub or router.

If things don't seem to configure automatically, you'll need to configure the port yourself by choosing it from the Network Status list or from the Show menu. That will reconfigure the screen so that you see the individual settings for that port.

For example, if you choose Built-in Ethernet, you'll next see the TCP/IP tab for that Ethernet connection. In the Configure IPv4 menu, you'll likely choose either Manually, Using DHCP with Manual Address, or Using DHCP. Which you choose, again, depends on circumstances and your network administrator:

■ **Manually** If you have a fixed IP address on your network (which can be used for both Internet and LAN access, for instance), you'll enter that IP address, a subnet mask, router address, and name server, if appropriate. In most cases, you'll need to consult your network administrator to learn the correct numbers for this entry.

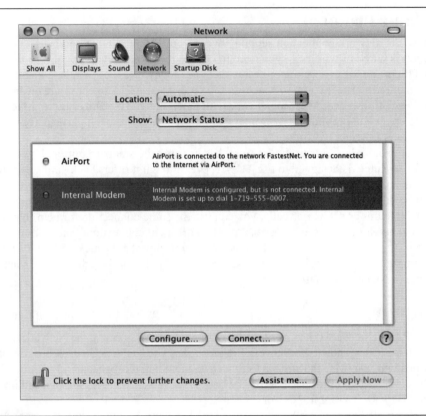

FIGURE 21-1 Here's my iMac's current network status according to the Network pane in System Preferences.

■ **Using DHCP with Manual Address** This setting means your Mac will consult a DHCP server on your network in order to get most of its settings, but you will be specifying an IP address. This is useful for situations where you don't want your IP address to change internally, which can make certain applications difficult.

> NOTE *DHCP stands for Dynamic Host Configuration Protocol, and it's a way of assigning IP addresses on a network. Many small office routers and/or server computers include DHCP capability. And, a local network of Macs without a DHCP server can still use their DHCP setting to generate addresses and talk to one another automatically.*

■ **Using DHCP** If you're setting up a LAN for your home or organization, and Internet access isn't a factor, you can set the Configure IPv4 setting to Using DHCP. Do this on all Macs connected to the network, and assuming you don't have a DHCP server, your

Macs will choose IP addresses for themselves. File-sharing and web-sharing servers can then be turned on, and those Macs can be accessed using the Network icon on the Finder or via the Connect to Server command.

NOTE *Mac OS 9 was the first Mac OS version to support file sharing over TCP/IP. You can use the TCP/IP control panel on a Mac OS 9–based Mac to connect using DHCP on the same network where Mac OS X–based machines exist, and they can connect to one another.*

If you have a router or gateway for Internet access, you may need to set up TCP/IP using the Manually setting and enter that router address in the Router entry box. Alternatively, you can usually set up your router to act as a DHCP server, in which case you can set up TCP/IP for Using DHCP. Once the router is accessible from your iMac, you should be able to access both local file sharing and remote Internet data over the same network connection.

NOTE *More on Internet access and LAN routers in Chapter 22.*

Turn on AppleTalk

So why activate AppleTalk? Turning on AppleTalk is necessary for printing to AppleTalk printers, and it can be useful for accessing older Macs that aren't capable of file sharing over TCP/IP. You probably won't need to turn on AppleTalk in most situations, although in my office, for instance, I have it on to access an AppleWriter laser printer.

In Mac OS X, you'll activate AppleTalk in the Network pane of System Preferences. Select the port you want to use from the Show menu (either Built-in Ethernet or AirPort), then click the AppleTalk tab.

NOTE *AppleTalk can only be turned on for one port at a time.*

Turn on the Make AppleTalk Active option, and if appropriate, select the AppleTalk Zone where you'd like your iMac to reside. (Again, you'll only see this in larger organizations.) If you need to configure AppleTalk's node and network ID manually, you can do that by choosing Manually from the Configure menu; otherwise, Automatically is standard for most users.

NOTE *Zones are designations that network administrators use to artificially separate Macs from one another, which is both more efficient for the network data and easier for users to handle. For instance, you can separate Accounting computers and Human Resources computers in different zones so that users are less likely to access a hard disk or printer that isn't in their AppleTalk zone. If you're at home setting up your own network, you won't see zones, because they require hardware—either a router or a server computer that acts as a router.*

Click Apply Now or close the System Preferences utility; AppleTalk is now ready to be used on that port.

Connect to a Server

Once you've got your network set up and TCP/IP (or AppleTalk) configured for Ethernet or AirPort, you're ready to log into any server computer that offers compatibility with the Apple Filing Protocol (AFP), as long as you have a valid user name and password for that server. Such a server can be something as complex as an Apple XServe device running Mac OS X Server, or something simple, such as another Mac that has its file-sharing options turned on.

To access a server on your local network in Mac OS X 10.3, you simply switch to the Finder and click the Network icon in the Sidebar of a Finder window. After a moment, you'll see all of the server computers that your Mac is able to locate on your network.

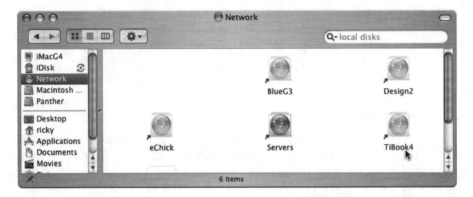

To access one of those servers, double-click its icon and the Connect to File Server dialog box appears. Enter your name and your password, and then click Connect to connect to the server. Note that the password is case sensitive, so don't use uppercase if your original password used lowercase.

If you've entered your user name and password correctly, you'll see an icon that represents your home folder on that computer. If you've logged into an Admin account, you'll also see the icon for any hard disks that are attached to that remote computer. Now, just double-click one of those icons (or single-click in Columns view), and you can access what's on that drive. In this example, I'm viewing the contents of the hard disk of one of the machines in my office:

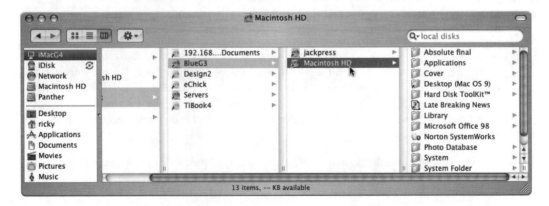

When you're done with your access to a particular server computer, you can select it in the Network window and choose File | Eject or drag that computer's icon to the Trash icon in the Dock. That will unmount the server, and you'll have to enter a user name and password to access that server's resources again.

Connect Using "Connect to Server..."

In versions of Mac OS X prior to 10.3, connecting to servers worked a little differently. You used the command Go | Connect to Server in the Finder. That command still exists in Mac OS X 10.3 and higher, but it's specifically used for accessing servers that require an Internet address (as opposed to those that are directly connected to your local network).

First, let's talk about the older Connect to Server window. When you choose Go | Connect to Server in Mac OS X 10.2 and earlier, you'll see a window that shows local servers and network "neighborhoods" in the left column of a Finder columns-like interface. You select one of the servers listed and click Connect to access it.

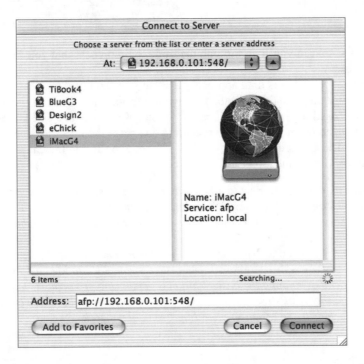

When you do, you'll see a Connect to File Server dialog box where you enter a user name and password. When you get past that box, you'll be asked to select the volume you want to access; that's a little different from Mac OS X 10.3, which automatically gives you access to any volumes for which you have the proper OS-level permissions. Finally, that volume is mounted on the desktop and in Finder windows for you to access.

Now, in both the 10.3 and earlier version of the Connect to Server window, you have another option: you can directly enter the URL for a particular server. That allows you to access servers over the Internet, for instance, or servers that use protocols other than the AFP protocol that Macs tend to use. So, for instance, you could enter the URL to a remote computer on the Internet in order to access it as a file-sharing server:

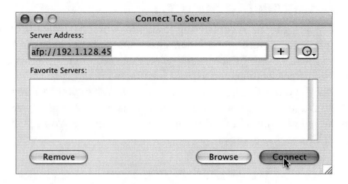

When you click Connect, you'll go through the same login process that you would with other sorts of network access.

If there's a difference with this final approach, it's that you can use it to access not only AFP servers, but servers that use other protocols as well. For instance, you can access certain Microsoft Windows–based servers using the smb:// protocol; you can access FTP servers using the ftp:// protocol, and some WebDAV servers let you access them for file sharing using an http:// protocol. The Connect to Server window is where you'll find the entry box for this sort of specific networking connection.

> NOTE
>
> *As mentioned, you can connect to Microsoft Windows–based computers that have file sharing turned on using the* smb:// *protocol, as in* smb://192.168.0.1, *in the Connect to Server dialog box. In most cases, you need to add a* share *to the smb URL, so that something like* smb://192.168.0.1/todds/ *would work well. Want something a bit simpler? If you access Windows machines day in and day out, try Dave from Thursby Software (**http://www.thursby.com/**). Dave allows your Mac to log into a network of Windows machines running the basic Windows file-sharing protocols. If Macs dominate your network, then Thursby has a similar solution, called TSStalk, which enables the Windows machine to access an Apple Filing Protocol network.*

Share Your Files

Once you have your network connections in place and TCP/IP (or AppleTalk) up and running, you're ready to set up file sharing and share folders from your Mac on the network. When you set up file sharing, you're actually turning your Mac into a server computer. Other users attached to your network will be able to sign onto your Mac, access any folders that you make available to them, and copy files to and from your Mac.

CAUTION

Once again, remember that turning on file sharing poses a security risk, particularly if you turn it on over TCP/IP (which is the default in Mac OS X) and you have an active Internet connection. If you turn on file sharing, make sure all of your users have hard-to-guess passwords and that you don't create any users that don't have passwords.

Turn on File Sharing

File sharing in Mac OS X is simple. All you need to do, once your network is configured, is launch the Sharing pane of the System Preferences application. You'll see the Personal File Sharing entry at the top of the list of services. Click the On button next to Personal File Sharing (or, if the listing is already selected, you can click the Start button), and sharing will be started. When the message changes to Personal File Sharing On, your Mac is set up as a server.

NOTE

The Sharing pane also has other options, including Remote Login, FTP Access, and even Windows Sharing. In general, it's recommended that you leave these options off unless you intend to use your Mac as an Internet server or in a cross-platform environment. If you don't need them, enabling these services while your Mac is connected to the Internet is an unnecessary security risk.

Unlike Mac OS 9 (if you've worked with it previously), you don't need to set up users, groups, passwords, and so forth. Instead, file sharing in Mac OS X uses the same users discussed at the beginning of this chapter. By default, however, regular users can only see the Public folders of other users and the Shared folder that's located in the Users folder. Also, Mac OS X doesn't have an option to turn off Guest access, so realize that anyone who gains access to your Mac's IP address could access Public folders, Shared folders, and even upload items to user's Drop Boxes. It's important to remind users not to launch items that appear in their Drop Boxes if they're not sure of the item's origin.

Users with Admin accounts can see nearly all folders on the hard disk and have access privileges similar to when you're working directly on the Mac. (Actually, an Admin account has slightly more power, so make sure you don't accidentally delete important files when you're logged into a Mac OS X computer via file sharing.)

NOTE

Any Admin user who accesses your Mac via file sharing can access other volumes attached or mounted on that Mac, including removable disks and external disks. If you think it's important, you should eject them, disconnect them, or set privileges as discussed next.

Set Sharing Privileges

The final step in setting up file sharing is to determine which items you're willing to share with others. Select a folder (or a disk) that you'd like to share with a particular user or group and choose File | Get Info. In the Info window, click the Ownership & Permissions disclosure triangle.

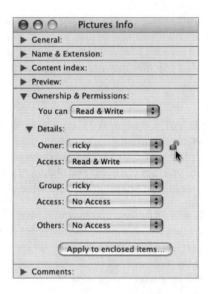

To set permissions for a folder, you must be the owner of that folder. If you are, click the padlock next to the owner's name. Now you can set a Group and the access level for that group, and you can set the access level for Others (which means everyone not in that group) as well. The access options are as follows:

- Read & Write means full access, meaning the user can copy files from the folder and save them to that folder, including changes that overwrite existing files.

- Read Only means the user can launch or copy documents in this folder but can't save them.

- Write Only, also called Drop Box, means that the user can save files to this folder, but can't access, launch, or copy existing items.

- No Access means the user can't open this folder at all.

After making your choices, you'll see one other button—Apply to Enclosed Items. Click this button if you'd like these settings to be applied to items inside this folder, including subfolders and their contents.

When you're done changing settings, close the Info window. That's it—you're ready for others to log into your Mac.

Chapter 22

Go Faster, Go Wireless, Go Portable

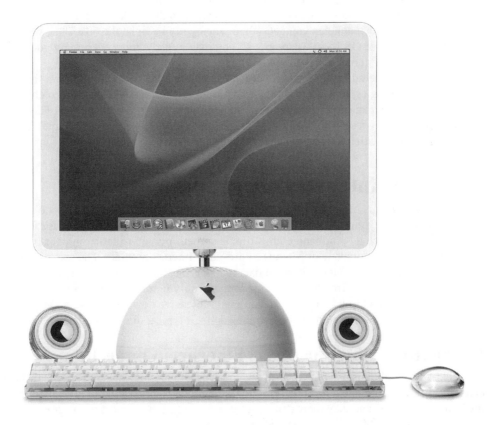

How to...

- Go broadband
- Change network locations easily
- Add Internet access to your LAN
- Use wireless Internet points
- Create a wireless network
- Outfit your iBook survival kit
- Encrypt your home folder

The Mac is usually simple to get up and running with an Internet service provider (ISP)—that's part of the reason I've left all the gritty details to this chapter, instead of explaining all the Internet-related settings and control panels earlier in the book. After all, there's the Setup Assistant (Mac OS X) that helps you get online when you first open the box. Plus, we discussed Internet Connect (Mac OS X) in Chapter 5, so you may already know everything you need to know to make your Internet connection work.

But if you need to add a new connection or you're interested in exploring new, faster Internet connection technologies, read on, as I'll cover them in this chapter. I'd also like to cover some other fun things you can explore with your Mac, including wireless connections. The hardware necessary to make a wireless version of file sharing possible is discussed in Chapter 21. And, we'll wrap it all up with a look at some hints for using an iBook on the road.

Get a "Faster" Internet Connection

The term *broadband* is meant to suggest any Internet connection that offers a "wide pipe" for data that, under many circumstances, makes your Internet connection work faster. For most household users, such a broadband connection is something you order from your local phone company or cable TV company or perhaps a third-party Internet provider. The result is a connection that can handle a much greater volume of data than a typical modem connection can, making the connection seem faster. (Broadband connections are only nominally faster in a technical sense, but they let more data through at once, making data-intensive downloads such as audio and video connections move much more quickly than they do over typical dial-up modem connections.)

Configure a Cable (or Direct Ethernet) Connection

One high-speed option is a cable modem, which gives you high-speed service over the same coaxial cable as your cable television service. Cable modems are available in many large and medium-sized cities, and they represent a pretty popular option. In most of the deals I've seen, cable access is $40-$50 a month (sometimes less, particularly for more limited access), and most cable company technicians are reasonably comfortable around Macs these days, thanks to the iMac's and iBook's popularity.

Because a cable modem (or any Ethernet-based Internet solution) needs to plug into your Mac's Ethernet port, you won't be able to use Ethernet for a local network. If that's a problem, though, there's a solution—an Internet router, which is discussed later in this chapter.

The majority of cable modem connections are "always-on" connections that work directly with the TCP/IP protocols built into Mac OS X—you don't need additional software. (These steps also work for other types of Ethernet connections that don't require additional software, such as corporate T-1 and other hard-wired Internet connections.) Once you've gotten the cable modem hooked up and an Ethernet cable between the cable modem and your Mac, you'll either configure your Mac with manual settings (from the ISP), or you'll select DHCP (Dynamic Host Configuration Protocol) to have your Mac configured automatically. Here's how to set up access in Mac OS X:

1. Launch System Preferences and choose the Network pane.

2. Select Built-in Ethernet from the Show menu in the Network pane, then make sure the TCP/IP tab is selected.

3. In the Configure IPv4 menu, choose either Using DHCP or Manually, depending on your ISP's (in most cases, the cable company's) instructions.

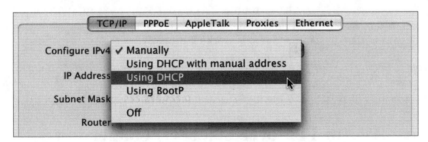

If you choose Using DHCP, you may need to enter a code in the DHCP Client ID entry box that appears. Some ISPs require an ID number to help uniquely identify your Mac on the network.

4. If you chose Manually (which you won't do often unless you've specifically set up a static IP address), enter an IP address, subnet mask, and router address, as specified by your ISP. With either Manually or Using DHCP, you should enter DNS addresses in the Domain Name Server entry box, if your ISP requires them.

5. Click Save at the bottom of the Network pane and close System Preferences. You should now be able to access the Internet.

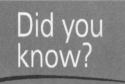

Cable Speed and Security

The way cable-based Internet connections work is a little weird: because cable television is installed for individual neighborhoods at once, cable modems operate on that same neighborhood *loop*. That means that the Internet *bandwidth* (which loosely translates as downloading speed) is shared between households in a given neighborhood. The more people in your area that access a cable modem at once, the slower your connection will seem. That fact leads to the cardinal rule of cable modems—never brag about them at neighborhood barbecues.

The other issue is security. Because of this local networking loop, everyone in your neighborhood is actually on something similar to a local area network. That means, with some cable services, others may be able to see and access your Mac if you have file sharing or web sharing enabled. While that generally isn't a problem (particularly if you have good passwords for all your remote users), it's still something to think about if you use a cable modem. If you don't have any reason to share files, turn off file sharing and web sharing (as well as FTP, remote access, and others) just to be safe. (See Chapter 21 for more details on file sharing.)

To test your Internet connection, launch a web browser and check to see if you're able to access web sites. You can also launch your e-mail application and try to check for e-mail. If all goes well, you're connected. If you have trouble, check your settings again (particularly your DNS addresses), and make sure the Ethernet cable is properly connected to the cable modem (or similar device) and that the cable modem is working properly.

 *If you're talking to your provider's technical support, you might find it handy to use the Network Utility, found in the Utilities folder inside the Applications folder, to perform some common tests such as Ping and Traceroute operations.*

Configure a DSL (or PPP-over-Ethernet) Connection

Digital Service Line (DSL) connections use your home or business phone line to provide high-speed access to a special DSL modem, which you then connect to your Mac via Ethernet. You can even continue to use the phone line for voice conversations. DSL is generally offered by the phone company in small-to-large cities, although you'll find some other ISPs that offer DSL, including national companies such as Earthlink. (The ISP still has to work with your phone company, which ultimately provides portions of the service.) The location where you plan to have DSL service needs to be reasonably close to the phone company's local buildings (usually within 15,000 feet), which means that it's a less likely option for rural areas.

If DSL is available in your area, you should find that the phone company is familiar with Macs and capable of installing the service. While some DSL connections are as easily configured as cable modems, in general DSL service can be a bit more complex. That's because DSL tends to use a protocol called PPP-over-Ethernet in order to complete the connection. PPP-over-Ethernet (PPPoE) is similar to a modem connection, in that the DSL modem "dials out" to the ISP's server, but PPPoE connections are generally negotiated within a few seconds, instead of the minute or so it can take your Mac's built-in modem to connect.

NOTE *Some ISPs require your Mac's Ethernet ID number (the MAC number) to configure the service. You can find this one of three ways. The easiest way is to look on the bottom of your Mac, where the Ethernet ID is printed. In Mac OS X, the ID number is shown on the TCP/IP tab when you've selected Built-in Ethernet from the main Show menu of the Network pane in System Preferences.*

You configure a PPPoE connection by opening the Network pane of System Preferences, choosing Built-in Ethernet from the Show menu, and selecting the PPPoE tab. In the PPPoE tab, click the check box next to Connect Using PPPoE.

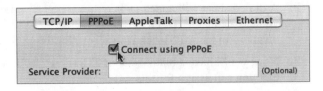

This automatically changes your TCP/IP settings (on the TCP/IP tab) to Using PPP, and it enables you to enter more information about your PPPoE account. Now, enter an account name and password. (The Service Provider and PPPoE Service Name entries are optional.) You can have your password saved (using the Save Password check box) if you don't want to be forced to enter your password each time you connect.

Click the PPPoE Options button if you'd like to change some of the advanced options. You may, in particular, wish to check Connect Automatically When Starting TCP/IP Applications if you'd like the connection to come up automatically whenever you work with an Internet application. When you're done making changes, click Save in the Network pane.

NOTE *If your ISP requires that you manually enter DNS addresses, click the TCP/IP tab and do so before moving on.*

The next step is the cool part—you can use Internet Connect to initiate the PPPoE connection. Launch the Internet Connect application (inside your Applications folder) and choose Built-in Ethernet from the toolbar. Now, click Connect. If everything is properly configured in the Network pane and you've successfully connected your DSL modem to your Mac via Ethernet, you should see the connection completed in Internet Connect. To disconnect, click the Disconnect button.

TIP *You can turn on the option Show PPPoE Status in the Menu Bar in either Internet Connect or the Network pane of System Preferences.*

Change Locations (or Configurations) Quickly

Mac OS X features another trick that you might find handy for customizing network connections— the Location Manager. The Location Manager allows you to create different saved *location sets*, which you can then switch back and forth between easily. For instance, if you often move your

Mac between your beach house, your pied-à-terre, and regular residence, you could create a location set for each of those, with different ISP phone numbers, TCP/IP settings, and so on.

Then, you can quickly switch between the settings by choosing a location. Note that this is also useful if you don't move your Mac, but, for instance, you have two different dial-up ISP accounts you'd like to be able to switch between easily.

Here's how to create a new location set in Mac OS X:

1. Choose New Location from the Locations menu in the Network pane of System Preferences.

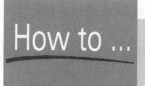

2. A dialog sheet will appear, where you can name the set. Give it a meaningful name ("Beach House" or "Earthlink Settings") and click OK.

3. Now, you'll have a blank slate of TCP/IP, PPP, PPPoE, and Modem settings that you can assign for this set.

4. Repeat as necessary.

Once you have more than one location set created, you can switch between different sets by selecting them in the Locations menu of the Network pane, or you can choose the location from the Locations menu in the Apple menu. Once you've switched, you can immediately begin using the new settings.

How to ... Get Internet Access for Your LAN

If you'd like to use a broadband modem or similar solution with your network of Macs (and other PCs), you can do that by adding an *Internet router* to your network. The router sits between your cable or DSL modem and routes Internet data from that modem to your network, depending on the requests being made by your Macs.

Routers are generally hardware devices. Popular models in the $100–$150 range for Mac networks include those made by Macsense (**www.macsense.com**) and D-Link (**www.d-link.com**), although it's worth noting that routers are generally cross-platform and can work with any type of computer. Note that many Internet routers include additional Ethernet points that enable you to connect from four to seven computers and printers.

Note also that some cable and DSL providers prohibit Internet routers on their networks or require you to pay for additional computers that you're connecting—consult them for details. And, if you do opt to provide Internet access to your entire network, you should learn the workings of your router to configure any *firewall* features that are built into the router to block unwanted access. (Also, sometimes you need to turn on your router before turning on your cable modem so that your router is correctly recognized by the modem.)

Once you've configured your router to connect to the Internet via DSL, cable, or similar broadband solution, you'll generally set up your Mac using one of the two ways described earlier—either Manually (if you want to specify the IP address of the Macs on your network), or Using DHCP (if your router is configured to work as a DHCP server).

Go Wireless

Apple's wireless AirPort technology is based on the IEEE 802.11 standard and, thus, widely compatible with other wireless technologies. It's also a boon for all sorts of networking situations. As discussed in Chapter 21, it can be used for networking on a local network—in fact, in my office, I use AirPort or other wireless products for about half of the computers. It keeps me from needing Ethernet cabling snaking around to the computers that are tough to reach without drilling through walls.

But having an AirPort card in your Mac isn't only handy for your local network; it also works great with most public wireless Internet access points, such as those in airports, public buildings, libraries, hotels, and, of course, coffee houses. With an AirPort card in your iBook (since I know you're unlikely to drag your iMac or eMac to a coffee shop), you can take advantage of these mobile access points. And if you *do* move your desktop around a bit, then AirPort is a handy way to get networked quickly.

Install an AirPort Card

If you want to access wireless networks or wireless Internet points, you'll need an AirPort card in your iMac, eMac, or iBook. The cards are designed by Apple to fit most of their models— the one caveat is that you need to know if your particular model supports AirPort or AirPort Extreme. Since your Mac only supports one or the other type of card, you'll need to get the right one. Table 22-1 offers a quick guide.

Model	AirPort Technology	Requires Circuit Board?
iBook G3	AirPort	No
iBook G4	AirPort Extreme	No
iMac G3 (Tray Loading)	None	N/A
iMac G3 (Slot Loading)	AirPort	Yes
iMac G4 (15 inch and 17 inch)	AirPort	No
iMac G4 (17 inch, 1GHz and later)	AirPort Extreme	No
iMac G4 (20 inch)	AirPort Extreme	No
eMac (original)	AirPort	No
eMac (ATI Graphics and later—intro May 2003)	AirPort Extreme	No

TABLE 22-1   AirPort Support in Apple's Consumer Macs

NOTE

AirPort Extreme is capable of communicating at a faster standard, called 802.11g, than regular AirPort, which uses 802.11b. Regular AirPort communicates at a top speed of 11 Mbps (megabits per second), which means it can transfer about 1.5 megabytes of data in one second. AirPort Extreme (802.11g) can transmit data at 54 Mbps. The 802.11 standard is often called Wi-Fi in computing circles.

Once you have the correct card, how you install it varies from model to model. If you don't have the original manual that came with your Mac, you can access Apple's Support site for specifics on adding the card to your model. (The method has changed from model to model.) The document **http://docs.info.apple.com/article.html?artnum=50053** on Apple's Support site offers some clues. If you don't find your model listed there, try **http://www.info.apple.com/ usen/airport/**, the main page for AirPort support.

With your card installed and your Mac powered back on, you should be able to test to make sure the card is recognized. In System Preferences, launch the Network pane. You should see AirPort on the Network Status screen; if you don't, try choosing it from the Show menu. It should appear there if the card has been recognized. If not, choose Network Port Configurations from the Show menu and see if AirPort has been turned off. Otherwise, you may need to shut your Mac back down and double-check your AirPort's physical installation.

When you know AirPort is working, you can use the Internet Connect application or the AirPort menu bar icon to connect to any wireless networks in your vicinity, as discussed in Chapter 21. If you don't yet have a wireless router configured, you might want to do so, as described in this chapter.

Use Wireless Internet Points

Even if you don't have a wireless router (like the AirPort Base Station) at home or in your office, you may still find that having an AirPort card in your iBook is handy for accessing wireless Internet points. To access one, generally all you need to do is turn on the AirPort card in Internet Connect or via the AirPort menu bar icon, then see if a named wireless network appears as an option. When it does, select it. If your AirPort card is set to using a DHCP server in the Network pane, it should gain Internet access from the wireless point.

NOTE

If there's anything that you may be limited in doing while you're accessing the Internet wirelessly, it's sending e-mail from Mail or a similar program. That's because for most e-mail accounts you need to know the SMTP (outgoing) mail server address of the ISP through which you're currently accessing the Internet. If you can learn that about your connection, then you can add that SMTP server in Mail's Preferences. If you can't find out that address, the best solution is to use a web mail interface (such as .Mac Webmail, or a web mail interface provided by the ISP that manages your e-mail account) to send e-mail.

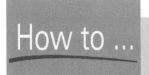

Connect Two Macs Wirelessly

If you have an AirPort card installed in your Mac, you can use that card to connect directly to another AirPort-enabled Mac without a base station. In Mac OS X, launch Internet Connect, choose AirPort from the toolbar, and then choose Create Network from the Network menu. In the dialog box that appears, enter a name for the network. Now, you can set each Mac's AirPort settings to TCP/IP or AppleTalk, as appropriate, and share files as discussed in Chapter 21.

So how do you find wireless access points? Some web sites try to track locations, such as **http://www.wi-fihotspotlist.com** and **http://www.wifinder.com**. Apple's AirPort pages offer a special page about hotspots at **http://www.apple.com/airport/hotspots.html**, where you'll find some other tips.

Set Up a Wireless Base Station

If you'd like to create a wireless network for your home or office, you'll want to set up a wireless base station or wireless router. Apple makes the AirPort Base Station that, obviously, is designed for optimum compatibility with Macs and AirPort technology. But other 802.11-compatible routers will often work well with AirPort.

With the AirPort Base Station, you get a UFO-style device (in current incarnations) that enables you to connect your AirPort-based Macs to other computers on a wired Ethernet network (the AirPort Base Station has an Ethernet port for connecting to an Ethernet hub) and/or to a wired broadband connection, such as a cable or DSL modem. Just like your Mac, the AirPort Base Station can be configured to make PPPoE connections. In fact, most AirPort Base Stations include a dial-up modem, so that even a dial-up connection can be shared among the networked Macs.

To configure an AirPort Base Station, you simply turn it on and make the appropriate cable connections, then you launch the AirPort Setup Assistant, which is found in the Utilities folder inside your Applications folder. Choose to set up an AirPort Base Station, and then walk through the assistant, which helps you to configure the base station for your Internet connection. When it's done, you should be able to use it for both Internet access and for accessing other computers via file sharing, as discussed in Chapter 21.

Once you have the base station configured for the basics, you can use the AirPort Admin Utility—also located in the Utilities folder inside your Applications folder—to fine-tune your settings. The Admin Utility offers some more specific security and custom settings, including whether and how the base station works as a DHCP server (see Figure 22-1), what computers are allowed to access the base station, and so on.

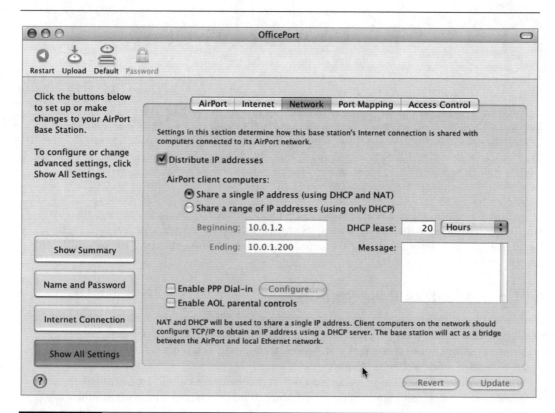

The AirPort Admin Utility lets you specify some of the nitty-gritty details of how your AirPort Base Station manages its connected Macs (like mine, here, which I've nicknamed "OfficePort").

Your iBook Survival Kit

While we're covering some topics—like the Locations menu and AirPort connections—that tend to affect iBook owners, I'd like to take a quick look at some suggestions for managing life with your iBook, including some general advice on getting the most out of it. For starters, I've compiled a list of items you might want to think about having for your iBook if you plan to travel with it much:

- **A padded carry case** Some of the better models actually suspend your iBook in the middle of the bag or pack so that if it's dropped, additional items, or air, will cushion the iBook.

- **Power adapter** Don't leave home without it.

- **Extra battery** Although not a 100 percent requirement, the second-generation iBook (including the iBook G4) makes battery swapping a little easier than the first edition. Swapping batteries can be handy for long trips away from power outlets.

■ **Phone cable**   Many computer stores offer handy retractable cable that can be used to connect for modem-based Internet access or for faxing.

■ **Phone numbers**   If you plan to use phone lines for Internet access (or even if you don't plan to, but want a backup solution), you'll need phone numbers for your ISP. At the very least bring the 800 customer service number with you so you can call and find local numbers.

TIP   *AOL's ability to help you locate local numbers by calling an 800 number first can be very handy while traveling. While I'm not a huge AOL fan, I do like that fall-back option; so, I keep my account active.*

■ **Recovery disks**   I recommend you travel with whatever disk utility program you use, particularly one that's designed for emergency data recovery. (See Chapter 24 for details.) If you have recent backups, you might want to travel with those as well (unless they're your *only* backups, in which case they should probably be in a safe deposit box or similar).

Aside from those items, two other important steps should be taken regularly when you're working with an iBook. First, you should back up regularly. If you have a .Mac account, backing up to your iDisk may be the perfect solution because it lets you quickly access those important documents from any machine in a pinch. Even if you don't have a .Mac account, I suggest you put your important business presentation or spreadsheets (or Quicken data, or iCal, and so on) somewhere on a secure FTP server so that you can access them if something goes wrong with your iBook.

Second, you should learn to manage your battery power to get the most out of your iBook. Some of that comes from choosing conservative settings within the Energy Saver pane of System Preferences. Setting your computer to sleep and your display to dim relatively quickly will help save battery power.

Here are some other tips:

■ Be aware that the AirPort card uses a lot of power. When you're not accessing a wireless network, turn the card *off* either from the Internet Connect application or from the AirPort menu bar icon.

■ Also know that having file-sharing servers turned on can drain some extra power and open your Mac up to vulnerabilities while you're traveling, particularly if you also have your AirPort card activated.

■ Run fewer applications than you normally would if you're trying to stretch battery life. That way, you limit the thrashing your hard disk takes when you switch among many different applications. Accessing the hard disk requires additional battery power compared to simply accessing data that already fits in the computer's memory. (The more RAM you have installed, the less hard disk access as well.)

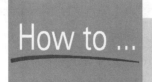 **Encrypt Your Home Folder**

In Mac OS X 10.3 you can encrypt the home folder on any Mac model—iBook or otherwise—using the FileVault technology. It so happens that it's a particularly good idea for iBooks, however, if your data is sensitive, because an iBook is a little more likely to be lost or stolen than is a desktop Mac. (Note: Using Software Update, discussed in Chapter 24, you should update to Mac OS X 10.3.1 or later before activating FileVault, as the initial 10.3 version had a nasty bug that could cause data loss.)

Encryption uses a special key to turn your data into something that's unreadable without that deciphering key—depending on the technology used, the keys can be sufficiently complicated to make it unlikely someone will crack the code and access your data. Apple makes FileVault available as a technology that will encrypt the data in your home folder on the fly and behind the scenes. When you log into your account on your Mac, you automatically make the data accessible. Others who don't know your login password can't access the unencrypted data.

FileVault has its drawbacks. Encrypting the data introduces a level of risk: if you forget the password to your account (as well as a master password that Mac OS X requires), you could lose your data. Likewise, because of the background operation of encrypting and decrypting, there's a slightly higher chance of data loss or corruption during that process. Finally, FileVault will, by necessity, slow your Mac down a bit.

If it all still sounds worth it, then launch System Preferences and choose the Security pane. Read the on-screen warnings. If a master password has not been set, click the Set Master Password button and choose that password, including a hint. (This actually isn't mandatory, but it's recommended.)

When that's done, you're ready to activate FileVault. Click the Turn on FileVault button. That begins the process—the Mac will begin encrypting the contents of your home folder. When it's done, you now have a new level of security for your data. Just don't forget your password!

Chapter 23

Upgrade Your iMac, eMac, or iBook

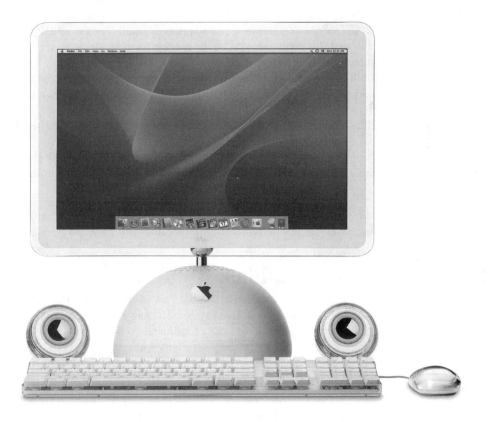

How to…

- ■ Install applications
- ■ Run DOS and Windows programs
- ■ Add USB and FireWire peripherals to your iMac
- ■ Add a removable drive
- ■ Add a CD-R or CD-RW drive
- ■ Add speakers or a USB microphone
- ■ Upgrade your RAM

When the iMac was introduced back in 1998, one of the revolutionary gambles Apple took was abandoning older *port* technologies in favor of two simple Universal Serial Bus (USB) ports. USB ports were faster than those they replaced, and less troublesome, but the market for USB devices (printers, keyboards, CD burners, and so on) was small. Fortunately, it worked out tremendously, as the original iMac's success drove the market for USB devices, and hundreds of peripherals are available for all new Macs, all of which support USB these days.

In addition to USB, the slot-loading iMac models began offering another option for upgrading—FireWire. FireWire ports offer very high speed data transfer with similar convenience to USB, making FireWire perfect for certain demanding devices, such as digital camcorders, high-speed external disks, and removable storage drives. Again, today, all new Macs feature FireWire as well as USB.

If you absolutely must connect older peripherals that don't support USB or FireWire, that's possible, too. You simply need the right adapter for the job. We'll take a look at all those options in this chapter.

> **NOTE** *This chapter doesn't cover printers, although many of them use a USB port on your Mac. See Chapter 12 for information on installing and configuring a printer.*

Install Your Own Applications

While your iMac, eMac, or iBook comes preinstalled with a host of applications—as evidenced by the middle section of this book—you'll eventually come across a reason to install some of your own. Generally, installation is simple: you launch an installer application, choose a disk and/or a folder for the application, then let the installer do its work.

> **NOTE** *For many installations you'll also need to authenticate the installer so that it can gain access to the Applications folder and change permissions settings as necessary.*

Installing in Mac OS X can be a little demanding due to its multiuser nature. If you're the original user of your Mac and/or you have administrator permissions, you can use an installer application to install native Mac OS X programs in the main Applications folder (or in a subfolder such as the Utilities folder). Once installed here, the applications are made available to all users on your Mac, regardless of their permission level. If you're installing an application that you don't want or need to share with other users on the Mac, you install that application in your personal home folder, or in a subfolder within your home folder. (You can create a subfolder called My Applications, for instance.)

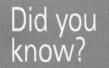

Mac OS X's reliance on permissions means that only administrator-level users can install software in the main folders, such as Applications and Library. The first user created on your Mac is an administrative user, so if you remember the password you used in the Setup Assistant, you can install applications that require a password. See Chapter 21 for more details on creating and using administrator accounts.

In some cases, you won't have much choice—the standard installer built into Mac OS X generally requires an administrator's password and will automatically install in the main Applications folder. With others, you simply drag-and-drop the application to a folder for which you have write permissions. The third case is the typical third-party installer, which will enable you to pick your target folder, often by choosing a Select Folder option in the installer.

Now you'll see a standard Open dialog box, where you can choose the folder where you'd like the application installed.

Did you know?

Run DOS and Windows Applications

Have a need to run an application that hasn't been written for Mac OS X? If it's compatible with Microsoft DOS or Windows versions, you may be able to run it using a product called VirtualPC, from Microsoft (**http://www.microsoft.com/mac/products/virtualpc/**). Virtual PC runs as an application on your Mac, but it emulates a Windows-compatible PC. Then, depending on the version you buy, you can use Virtual PC to run Windows 98, ME, 2000, XP, and later. For more information, visit Microsoft's site, as well as MacWindows.com, an excellent site for information about integrating Mac and Windows applications and computers.

Add Devices with USB and FireWire

All modern Macs include USB ports for connecting to peripherals. USB is a technology designed to allow other technologies that have traditionally been connected to Macs via "serial" ports to connect to a faster, more modern equivalent. The connector, the speeds, and the methods of connection have all been updated.

iMac DV and later slot-loading iMac G3 models also include FireWire ports—as do all iMac G4 models, eMacs, and second-generation iBooks—another technology that enables you to hook up peripherals easily and quickly. FireWire is much faster than USB, meaning it's better suited for devices that transfer a lot of data to and from your Mac. Those devices include hard disks, removable drives, scanners, and similar devices.

Why USB?

There are three major improvements that USB offers over the serial ports that have been used in both Windows-based PCs and older Macintosh computers for nearly two decades:

- **Speed**   Each USB bus on a consumer Mac can transfer data up to 12 megabits per second, or over 12,000 kilobits per second. USB is fast enough for external removable disks and other devices that require reasonably high speed connections.

Beginning in late 2003, the iMac G4 and iBook G4 offer USB 2.0 ports, which provide a much faster transfer speed of 480 Mbps, or speeds slightly faster than FireWire. That makes USB 2.0 good for the same sorts of connections that FireWire is good for—external drives and removable media.

- **Ease of use**   Aside from being *hot-swappable* (meaning you can plug and unplug devices without damaging them or your Mac while the Mac is turned on), USB ports can also provide power to some peripherals, meaning fewer of them require their own power cords and adapters.

- **Device support**   Old serial ports offered one peripheral per port; USB can support up to 127 devices per bus, as long as those devices don't mind sharing the connection. That means you'll easily be able to hook up a scanner, joystick, printer, Zip drive, digital camera, mouse, keyboard, and most anything else without much trouble.

With these improvements you can see why USB is a boon for the Mac—not only is it quick and extensible, but it's also simple to use.

Why FireWire?

If you have a slot-loading iMac G3 or later—or any iMac G4, eMac, or second-generation iBook—you have FireWire ports available for connecting devices. FireWire is very fast compared to USB 1.1 and older external port technologies. FireWire can transfer data at up to 400 megabits per second, which is quite a bit more than USB, older serial ports, or even external SCSI ports.

(At the time of this writing, Apple doesn't offer FireWire 800, a newer and faster version, on its consumer Macs. It likely soon will if it doesn't already by the time you read this.)

That makes FireWire ideal not only for connecting external DV camcorders, but also for high-speed devices like external hard disks and removable disk drives.

> NOTE   *As noted, USB 2.0 is slightly faster than FireWire, although it's a little less popular on the Mac platform. USB 2.0 is not, however, commonly used for DV camcorders, even for PCs, where FireWire is called by its standard name, IEEE-1394, or Sony's name for the technology, i.Link.*

FireWire is just as easy to hook up as USB, with up to 63 devices supported between the two ports. Even better, FireWire devices don't require a hub—you can actually *daisy-chain* them together by plugging one device into the Mac, the next device into the first device, and so on. (That works with most FireWire devices; some, such as the iPod, don't offer a second FireWire port. USB, by contrast, requires a hub.)

> NOTE   *Although FireWire hubs are available, hubs aren't necessary for FireWire devices; they're simply convenient. A FireWire hub allows you to connect and disconnect FireWire devices without affecting other devices. If you have devices arranged in a daisy chain, disconnecting one of them may interrupt others on the chain until you get the whole thing plugged back in again.*

The real advantage, though, is choice. With a FireWire-supporting Mac model, you can choose to buy higher-speed peripheral devices that use FireWire for best performance. Then, you'll also have USB ports available for Zip drives, input devices, and other lower-performance external devices. You've got the best of both worlds!

USB Ports and Hubs

Your Mac has two or three USB ports on the chassis of the computer, and depending on your model, you may have one or two on your keyboard, as well. One of those ports on the Mac probably has your Mac's keyboard plugged into it, with a mouse plugged into one of the additional ports on the keyboard.

That leaves one port open on the keyboard (for desktop models) and two ports open on the side of the iMac, eMac, or iBook. (You may only have one port for earlier iMac G3 and colorful iBook models.) After a rough count, that's either one or two ports available for devices—hardly comes close to the 127-device USB limit, does it?

In order to use more than two devices, you'll need to get a device called a USB hub. This device will probably have its own AC adapter so it can provide power to the USB ports. It'll also have four, eight, or more USB ports that you can use for additional devices.

Hubs are reasonably inexpensive, but you won't even need one until you have more than two additional devices for your Mac—one can plug into the keyboard, which is a passive hub in its own right (it doesn't supply power), and the other can plug directly into the Mac. If all you have is a printer and a stick, for instance, you might plug the joystick into your keyboard and the printer into your Mac's side or back. Once you get more than two devices, though, it's hub time.

A number of vendors sell hubs. Here's a partial list of the vendors and their web sites:

Asante	**http://www.asante.com/**
Belkin Components	**http://www.belkin.com/**
CompuCable	**http://www.compucable.com/**
Keyspan	**http://www.keyspan.com/**
MacAlly	**http://www.macally.com/**

Install a USB or FireWire Device

Some, although not all, USB and FireWire devices require a special driver, called a *kernel extension*, that needs to be installed using the manufacturer's installation application. Keyboards and mice don't necessarily require you to install software (plug them in and they should work with built-in drivers), although they will require special drivers in some cases—for example, to program more than one mouse button or to remap the Windows key to the ⌘ key. All of these require special driver software.

 *Even if the peripheral comes with a CD that includes driver software, it's a good idea to check the web site of the manufacturer to see if any updates are available for download, either to fix bugs in the software or to update the driver for your version of Mac OS X.*

The normal game plan is to install the driver software, then connect your device to the Mac. If all goes well, your device will be recognized and the driver will be properly loaded and used with the device. (This can sometimes appear to freeze the Mac while the driver gets situated. You should always wait a few seconds after you've plugged in a device before you panic.) If your Mac doesn't recognize the attached device, then you can take some troubleshooting steps, including:

- Unplug and replug the device.
- Use (or double-check) the device's external power supply to make sure it's getting the power it needs.
- Try a different USB or FireWire port. (In particular with USB, you should try a port on the side of the device instead of the keyboard if you're having trouble.)
- Restart (or start up) the Mac with the device attached.
- Check the manufacturer's web site for driver or software updates.

Add a Mouse, Keyboard, or Controller

All controllers and input devices use USB for their connection, since FireWire is overkill for a mouse, keyboard, or controller. Mice and keyboards are generally the easiest devices to add—in many cases, they don't even require special drivers. Apple's USB software has built into it some generic drivers that can recognize nearly any USB mouse or keyboard that's been plugged into an available USB port and use it easily.

In other cases, though, you will need a driver. (Or, sometimes a driver can activate special features for the input device.) Such drivers are simple to use—simply launch the installation application that came with the device, usually on CD-ROM. (You may want to check the manufacturer's web site for a newer driver that may be available.) In most cases, installing a driver doesn't require a restart; the software should let you know if it does require or recommend that your Mac be restarted before the device is connected.

Keyboards usually require even less customization, unless the keyboard has special features like a built-in pointing device. Some keyboards originally designed for Windows require a special driver that allows the Windows keys and other keys to be used as Mac OS equivalents. Although the keyboards are basically the same, the Mac OS recognizes the ⌘ and, in some cases the POWER or EJECT keys, which are unique compared to many Windows-oriented keyboards.

NOTE   *Wireless keyboards and mice are becoming more and more popular. Most wireless keyboards are still USB based. A small wireless receiver is connected to USB, and the keyboard and/ or mouse are positioned so that they can communicate with that receiver.*

A number of companies offer unique pointing devices and keyboards for the Mac. Here are a few of those companies and what they offer:

Apple	http://www.apple.com/	Mouse, keyboard, wireless options
Belkin	http://www.belkin.com/	Mouse, keyboard
CompuCable	http://www.compucable.com/	Mouse
Contour Design	http://www.contourdesign.com/	Mouse, keyboard
Kensington	http://www.kensington.com/	Mouse, keyboard, trackball, wireless options
Keyspan	http://www.keyspan.com/	Presentation/media remote
MacAlly	http://www.macally.com/	Mouse, keyboard, trackball, joystick
Microsoft	http://www.microsoft.com/	Mouse, keyboard
Wacom	http://www.wacom.com/	Pen tablet

NOTE   *What's a pen tablet? It's a flat surface that allows you to use a pen for moving the mouse cursor—great for drawing, touch-ups, or just a familiar interface for moving the mouse pointer.*

Add an External Drive

A removable drive can be an important addition, since modern Macs lack a floppy drive and many users aren't connected to local area networks. Online file transfer is certainly one option, especially if you have a higher-speed connection. (Online storage is discussed in Chapter 20.) But if you'd like to be able to back up on physical disks, a removable drive is a good idea.

NOTE *External drives come in both USB and FireWire varieties. In most cases, FireWire is preferable to USB 1.1 if you have a Mac that supports FireWire, since it is much faster for copying data to and from the drive. That said, if you have a Mac model that supports USB 2.0, then you can opt for a USB 2.0 drive, which may even be a bit faster than a FireWire 400 drive. (These days, many external drives are USB/FireWire switchable, which can be very handy.)*

There are two basic approaches to removable media—removable disks and writable CD technology. These days there are very few removable drives that you can buy new for use with consumer Macs. The Iomega Zip drive (**http://www.iomega.com/**), which was once a dominant form of removable media, is still available for Macs. Zip disks come in capacities of 100MB, 250MB, and 750MB, although you must have a drive that's specifically capable of reading those larger capacities. (The original 100MB disks can be read by any compatible drive.) Aside from Iomega Zip, you'll find very few removable solutions left—the Jaz, Orb, Imation SuperDisk, and other technologies of the recent past just aren't as popular, largely because most modern Macs are capable of storing data on writable CD and DVD media.

You'll will find some external drives on the market that don't quite fit the "removable" mold but are popular ways to extend your Mac nonetheless. A few companies make USB floppy drives for Macs, allowing you to use a typical 1.4MB floppy disk. And a number of companies make external hard disks that can be used for backing up and/or transporting files from one computer to another. In fact, the low cost of today's hard disks makes external options—using both FireWire and USB 2.0—very popular upgrades for Mac users.

If your older iMac or iBook doesn't support FireWire, you may opt for a USB-based hard disk. Be warned that USB 1.1 is a little slow for use with a hard disk; the external disk will never be as fast as your Mac's internal disk. That doesn't mean it won't be useful, though, since having such a large capacity for backup—along with the option of unplugging the drive and using it with another computer—is a convenient touch. Here are some manufacturers of floppy and hard disks for Macs:

EZQuest	**http://www.ezquest.com**	External hard disks
Fantom Drives	**http://www.fantomdrives.com**	External hard disks
LaCie	**http://www.lacie.com/**	External hard disks, floppy drive
MacAlly	**http://www.macally.com/**	Floppy drive
Maxtor	**http://www.maxtor.com/**	External hard disks
Teac	**http://www.teac.com/**	Floppy drive

If you have a Mac model that does support FireWire 400 or USB 2.0, you'll find external hard disks that are fully as fast and useful as your Mac's internal disk. In fact, FireWire hard disks are a great addition to your Mac, since you can easily back up to the disk, transport the disk, and move the disk between Macs that support FireWire.

NOTE *One incredibly popular FireWire hard disk is one that you might not immediately think of—Apple's iPod. The iPod doesn't just interface with iTunes software, it can also be used as a hard disk, as discussed in Chapter 14.*

There are also some unique USB storage options—even at USB 1.1 speeds—that are interesting to look into. Often called "keychain drives," a number of manufacturers offer small USB flash RAM drives that can be easily transported. They're often about the size of something that would fit comfortably on a keychain, but can hold many megabytes worth of data—enough for your important documents, for instance. They're also generally cross-platform, so they can be used much as floppy disks were used in the past, to create a "sneaker net" method of moving files from one computer to another. Popular USB flash RAM drives are made by MacAlly Peripherals, Kingston (**http://www.kingston.com**), Sonnet Technology (**http://www.sonnettech.com**), and Lexar Media (**http://www.lexarmedia.com**), among many others.

Install an External Drive

Hard disk drives often don't require additional drivers, as the Mac OS has built-in drivers to support hard disks; but removable and floppy drives (including the Zip) are a little more finicky and tend to require their own drivers.

CAUTION *Before connecting any external FireWire hard disk to a Mac running Mac OS X Panther or later, you should update the drive's firmware. (Visit the manufacturer's web site and download the firmware update, then follow instructions.) Doing so will help avoid a possible data loss bug that occurred with FireWire drives (mostly FireWire 800 models) and early versions of Mac OS X 10.3.*

Once the driver is installed, hooking up the drive should be simple. Just plug the USB or FireWire cable into the drive, then into the appropriate port on your Mac's side or back. USB devices can also be plugged into a USB hub; FireWire devices can usually be plugged into the back of another FireWire device, if you're creating a chain of FireWire devices (a daisy chain).

Right after you plug in the drive, you'll either have success, or you'll see a message that suggests you haven't correctly installed the drive's software. Success is generally indicated by the appearance of the disk on the desktop or in a Finder window Sidebar. In the example at right, my FireWire hard disk has mounted.

CAUTION *If you're connecting multiple FireWire devices in a daisy chain, make sure that none of the connections loop back on any of the already connected devices. Device one should be connected to the iMac's FireWire port, device two to device one, device three to device two, and so on.*

You'll want to be careful with your removable drives, because some of them don't react well in certain configurations. In some situations, you also need to consider *where* you put your removable drive on the USB bus. Some removable drives work better with older iMacs if they have access to their own port, for instance. With slot-loading iMacs and later models, you may get better performance from USB devices if you try different ports on the side of your Mac. Those models have *two* internal USB buses, so if you're having performance trouble on one of them, choosing a different port may result in better performance. Plugging USB devices into their own ports (instead of USB hubs) is definitely a good idea when possible, particularly for storage devices.

 *Earlier versions of Mac OS X have trouble with many external USB devices, and using them may cause* kernel panics, *or system crashes that result in text on the screen. If this happens, remove the device and restart your Mac, then check the device manufacturer's web site or customer service for details or improved drivers.*

If you can't dedicate a whole USB port to the removable or hard drive, it's best to connect and use your drive while other peripherals on the same connection are inactive. That is, you'll see worse performance if a scanner, removable drive, keyboard, mouse, or gaming device are all being used on the same bus at the same time. It's not a huge problem, although there's a chance it could result in data loss.

With slot-loading iMacs and all later models, it is possible to boot from external USB hard disks, thanks to the dual-channel nature of the USB implementation; likewise, you can often boot from FireWire devices. If you'd like to boot from a removable disk, insert, connect, or otherwise mount a disk that includes a valid Mac OS installation, then open the Startup Disk pane in System Preferences. Select the removable disk and close the pane. Now, when you restart, your Mac will start up from the removable disk.

With any Mac model, you can still boot from a CD in the internal CD-ROM or DVD-ROM drive. Place a valid Mac OS startup disc in the drive and restart your Mac. Immediately after you hear the startup tone, hold down the C key until the Apple logo screen appears.

NOTE *Another option is to use the Boot Picker screen—hold down the* OPTION *key as your Mac starts up. You'll see a screen that shows the various drives connected to your Mac. Select the drive you want to use for starting up your Mac and click the right-arrow button.*

Use an Optical Drive

Optical drives are those that use flat discs—usually writable CD and DVD technology—to store data. A CD-RW drive can write once to a CD-R disc, which can then be read by nearly any CD-ROM drive. This is a convenient way to transfer files or send files great distances because CD-R discs are cheap, they can hold as much as 650MB of data, and they're pretty resilient. CD-R discs are also a great medium for archiving important documents from your hard disk since the CD-R disks store well, don't take up a lot of space, and can be popped into any Mac if there's trouble with your consumer Mac.

CD-RW disks are slightly more expensive, but allow you to erase information on the disc and write to it again. In this way a CD-RW is very much like a Zip or similar removable drive. CD-RW drives tend to be capable of writing to CD-R media, too, so you can have the best of both worlds.

These days, most consumer Macs come with at least a CD-RW drive built in—some have CD-RW/DVD "combo" drives (which can write to CD media and play back DVD media), while others have Apple SuperDrives, which can write to both CD and DVD media.

Not all of us have CD-RW capability built in, however, so you may find that you want to add an external model. Companies making CD-R and CD-RW drives for the consumer Mac (via USB and/or FireWire) include

EZQuest	**http://www.ezq.com/**
Fantom Drives	**http://www.fantomdrives.com/**
Formac Electronic	**http://www.formac.com/**
LaCie	**http://www.lacie.com/**
QPS, Inc.	**http://www.qps-inc.com/**
SmartDisk	**http://www.smartdisk.com/**
Sony	**http://www.sony.com/**

Some CD-RW drives are compatible with Apple's Disc Burner software, which enables you to burn data CDs from the Finder, as well as audio CDs using Apple's iTunes software. In order to fully gauge compatibility, it's good to know the manufacturer of the CD-RW mechanism inside your drive—often that's a large, recognizable company such as Sony, Panasonic, Pioneer, or Yamaha. Check your drive's documentation and consult **http://www.apple.com/itunes/** to see which devices are supported directly by Apple. If your external CD-RW drive works with Disc Burner, you can use the commands discussed in Chapters 3 and 14 to create data and audio CDs.

In other cases, or when you want more features than Disc Burner offers, you'll need to turn to a third-party solution. The most popular option is Roxio Toast (**www.roxio.com**), a program that allows you to burn an entire CD at once. You can also write to CDs in *sessions*, meaning you can write to the disc at different times, storing data sequentially on the disc. Toast also lets you create audio CDs, video CDs (that can be played back in some commercial DVD players), and CDs designed to use the file format that Windows computers generally read. Discribe by CharisMac (**http://www.charismac.com/**) is also an interesting option.

Back Up to an External Drive

The Iomega Zip drive comes with special software (**http://www.iomega.com/software/autobackupmac.html**) to help you manage backing up to the drive—other removable drives may include the same. For backing up to writable CD or DVD discs, you can use Apple's own Backup application, shown in Figure 23-1, which comes with a .Mac membership. (You can also use that same Backup software to back up to your iDisk, a FireWire hard disk, or your iPod.)

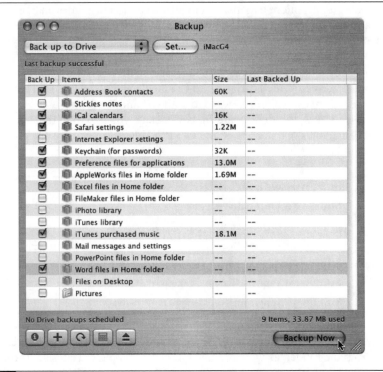

Apple's Backup software is handy for backing up either to your iDisk or to writable CD or DVD media.

Backup is also nicely intuitive in that it knows many of the important items on your Mac that need to be backed up in order to fully recover from a catastrophic disk failure. If you have access to it, I recommend you use it.

TIP *If you don't have a .Mac account, or you want software that will help you back up to other removable disks or external hard disks, you have some options. FolderSynchronizer (**http://www.softobe.com/**) and Synk (**http://www.decimus.net/synk/**) are interesting shareware options, while Prosoft Data Backup (**http://www.prosoftengineering.com/**) and Dantz Retrospect (**http://www.retrospect.com/**) are good commercial solutions.*

You've already seen (in Chapter 20) that online backup can be automated in this way, and with great success. When you're dealing with disks, though, there are some things to consider:

■ **Rotate media** If you can, rotate backups between three or more different disks. If you need to back up often, you can back up Mondays, Wednesdays, and Fridays. Then, the next week, you can use your software to do an incremental backup, which simply adds files that have changed since the last backup. If you don't want to back up that often, back up once a week and rotate new media in each week for three or four weeks, then start over.

- **Archive** This is important: every so often (say, once a week in a business situation, once a month at home) archive one of your removable disks—that is, drop it out of the rotation and store it somewhere safe. This does two things. It gives you a reasonably up-to-date emergency copy of your data. It also gives you a copy of your data that's fixed in time. If your iMac subsequently gets infected with a virus, or if you accidentally delete or change a file, you still have the older copy to return to.

NOTE   *If you're serious about archiving disks, you should consider a CD-RW (or DVD-RW) drive. CDs are much better for long-term storage than many removable disks. CDs are also cheaper than most removable disks, making it less expensive to back up to CDs over the long haul. Plus, the latest Mac models have CD-RW (and sometimes DVD-RW) drives built in, as discussed in this chapter and in Chapter 3. You should also have a fireproof, weatherproof repository for your discs, ideally in a different location from your Mac.*

- **Test** Especially in a business situation (or even with your thesis, business plan, novel, or personal investment portfolio), test the backup media occasionally to make sure they're working okay.

Once you get into the swing of things, you should find it's easy to automate the backup process. In many cases, it's just a question of telling the backup software when to schedule the backup, then leaving the right disk in the drive when it's time for the backup.

Scanners and Digital Cameras

If you want to work much with digital images—either professionally or as a hobbyist—you're going to need some way to get those images into your Mac. Scanners allow you to place an image or document flat on the glass bed of the scanner's top—like a copy machine—and digitize the image or document so that it can be used on your Mac's screen. In fact, some scanners include special Optical Character Recognition (OCR) software that allows a scanned document to be turned into a regular word processing document, enabling you to edit and store the document in an application like AppleWorks.

Add a Scanner

Scanners for today's consumer Macs tend to be inexpensive and they include decent bells and whistles. If you're comparison shopping, look for high-end color support (32-bit color or better), high *true* resolution (600 × 600 or better), and extras like Photoshop plug-ins and OCR software. Here are some scanner manufacturers with Mac-compatible products:

Canon	**http://www.canonusa.com/**
Epson	**http://www.epsonusa.com/**
Hewlett-Packard	**http://www.hp.com/**
Microtek	**http://www.microtek.com/**
Nikon	**http://www.nikon.com/**

For some scanners you'll need to install a software driver before it will work properly. Accessing the scanner can be done in a number of ways. The most common is to use a plug-in for Adobe Photoshop, Photoshop Elements, GraphicConverter, or a similar application, particularly if that software is bundled with the scanner. That's handy because it brings the images directly into the editing application, eliminating a step if you intend to edit or alter the image.

Second, you can use other software that came with the scanner. It may have a standalone application that's used for a variety of scanning purposes, such as using the scanner with your printer to make copies and so on. Finally, you can use the Image Capture application bundled with Mac OS X with some scanners. Launch Image Capture, and if a scanner is detected, you'll see a window appear that enables you to control that scanner. From there, you can import images from the scanner and save them for use in other applications.

Add a Digital Camera

There are two different types of Mac-compatible digital cameras. One is a *still-image camera*, designed to be carried around and used just like a typical 35mm point-and-shoot camera. The difference with a digital camera is that instead of taking pictures on film, it takes pictures that are stored in a computer-compatible format, often TIFF or JPEG. These images can be downloaded from the camera and used immediately in a photo-editing program, in a desktop layout, or for web pages.

The other type of digital camera is a *digital motion camera*. These all come in two varieties— DV camcorders and low-end video capture cameras. Nearly all DV camcorders support FireWire, making it simple to transfer digital movies from the camcorder to your iMac DV model. If you plan to make home movies, corporate videos, or other high-quality video, a DV camcorder that supports FireWire is the best choice.

 Attaching a FireWire-based DV camcorder to your FireWire-equipped Mac is covered in Chapter 16.

Digital Still Camera

In the case of a digital still camera, you get the images into your Mac in one of two ways. The first way is via a USB connection and software (such as iPhoto, discussed in Chapter 15) that enables you to acquire the images the same way you acquire a scanned image. (In Mac OS X, you can also use the Image Capture application, included in the Applications folder, to capture images from USB-based still cameras. Connect the camera and launch Image Capture, and you'll see a window that lets you select and download those images to your Mac.)

The other method is to remove the memory card from the camera and plug it into a card reader. This causes the card to pop up on the desktop as if it were a removable disk, enabling you to copy the images directly from the card. Popular formats for these cards include SmartDisk, CompactFlash, Secure Digital (SD), MemoryStick, and others. Card readers are made by a number of companies, including Kingston, Lexar Media, SanDisk (**www.sandisk.com**), and many others.

Today's top digital still cameras are made by some familiar companies—Nikon, Canon, Fuji, Kodak, Sony, Hewlett-Packard, for example. You'll find such cameras in nearly any electronics store, and most of them use USB for communicating with computers. Just make sure the camera that you're considering is known to be Mac compatible. One place to look for that confirmation is **http://www.apple.com/macosx/upgrade/devices.html**, where you can learn about camera compatibility with iPhoto and Mac OS X.

Video Conference Cameras

With the popularity of iChat AV software and the Apple iSight camera that works with it, there's been a slight surge in third-party conference cameras as well. These are cameras that connect to the Mac over a USB or FireWire connection and input a relatively low resolution image that can be used for transmitting over the Internet or phone lines during a video chat.

Along those same lines, you can also purchase *video capture* devices that enable you to hook up a VHS camcorder and digitize video via the USB port. You'll generally do this if you want to create QuickTime movies from videos you've filmed using a traditional camcorder.

Here's some of what's available at the time of this writing:

Apple	**http://www.apple.com/**	iSight video conference camera
Daystar Technology	**http://www.daystartechnology.com/**	Video capture device
Formac Electronic	**http://www.formac.com/**	Video capture device
Logitech	**http://www.logitech.com/**	Video conference cameras
Orange Micro	**http://www.orangemicro.com/**	Video conference cameras
XLR8	**http://www.xlr8.com/**	Video capture device

USB-based digital video cameras, like removable drives and still cameras, can be demanding on the USB bus, so it's recommended that you use digital video cameras and similar devices on a different USB port from removable disks and/or while the removable disk isn't operating. You'll get better performance that way.

Special USB and FireWire Adapters

If you've got an older device that you want to hook up to your Mac, my first advice is *don't*. It's best to use USB- and FireWire-based devices that have been designed and certified for use with Macs and Mac OS X. That will (hopefully) give you the least trouble, and newer devices mean you can (usually) upgrade to new versions of the Mac OS and other software without running into as many problems.

But if you must use an older device—such as one that uses a Mac serial connector or a SCSI port—there are a number of companies that make adapters for the USB or FireWire ports on your Mac to allow you to connect other sorts of devices that don't natively support USB or FireWire.

We already saw some adapters for hooking up printers in Chapter 12. Here's a list of some adapter manufacturers and the types of adapter products they offer:

Belkin	**http://www.belkin.com/**	USB-to-serial, USB-to-parallel, USB-to-SCSI, FireWire-to-SCSI
CompuCable	**http://www.compucable.com/**	USB-to-serial, USB-to-parallel, USB-to-ADB
Griffin Technology	**http://www.griffintechnology.com/**	USB-to-ADB, USB-to-serial
Keyspan	**http://www.keyspan.com/**	USB-to-serial
Mark of the Unicorn	**http://www.motu.com/**	USB-to-MIDI
2ndWave Technologies	**http://www.2ndwave.com**	FireWire-to-SCSI, USB-to-SCSI

What are all these technologies? Here's a quick look:

- **Serial** Pre-iMac Macs use serial ports for many connections, including external modems, some digital cameras, PDA synchronize cables, and non-PostScript printers.

- **ADB** Apple Desktop Bus is used to connect keyboard, mice, and other pointing devices for pre-iMac Mac computers.

- **SCSI** Used by Macs and PCs to connect external drives and scanners to the computer, SCSI is a faster technology than USB, so a USB-to-SCSI connector isn't recommended for daily use (although a FireWire-to-SCSI adapter should work okay). USB-to-SCSI is one way to hook up an older scanner or hard disk occasionally, if only to get a few files or images transferred to your Mac.

- **Parallel** Parallel adapters are used on Intel-compatible PCs to connect to many printers (and some other devices). These adapters can be used to connect PC printers to your Mac, as long as you have a driver that allows your Mac to print to that printer.

- **MIDI** The Musical Instrument Digital Interface allows you to connect MIDI keyboard synthesizers and other devices to your Mac to edit music and play back songs.

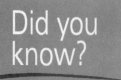

Video Out

Most of the Mac models we're talking about—the iMac G4, iBook, and eMac—include video out capabilities that will allow the image on the Mac's screen to be *mirrored* to another display (so that you could use a larger external monitor, for instance) or, with the correct adapter, to a television screen or similar device for presentations or teaching. This is possible because of a

23

small "mini-VGA" port on the side or back of the Mac. That port requires an adapter—either the Apple Video Adapter or the Apple VGA Display Adapter—which enables it to send the image to the external device. The Apple VGA Display Adapter is for connecting the Mac to a standard VGA computer display; the Apple Video Adapter is for connecting the Mac to a TV or similar device via either S-Video or composite RCA-style connectors.

When you make such a connection, the Displays pane in System Preferences can be used to select an appropriate screen resolution and to turn on mirroring if necessary.

One thing that's a little less known is that there's actually a workaround that allows many of the latest consumer Macs not only to mirror their display to an external one, but actually to use a second display to *expand* the screen, so that your mouse can travel across two screens that are side-by-side. (This is common for pro-level Macs, but not something Apple makes the default in consumer machines.) All it takes is a small utility program available from **http://macparts.de/ibook/**. Read the web site carefully and note that the author doesn't take responsibility for the hack—it could mess up your Mac or cause damage, so try it at your own risk. If it works for you (and it doesn't work for all models, so, again, check closely), you end up with a feature—screen spanning—that some folks pay good money to have with the PowerBooks or desktop Power Macintosh models.

Add Microphones and Speakers

Some first-generation iMacs can support microphones via a special port, and all Macs support USB-based microphones; likewise, all desktop Macs and some iBooks can support external speakers. (And, of course, the iMac G4 includes them.) The only caveat is this: for speakers, choose powered, computer-shielded speakers, preferably those designed to be used with your Mac model. This is important because speakers not designed specifically for a computer can affect the monitor picture and other aspects of the computing experience.

The output for speakers on desktop Macs is actually a *line-level output*, which means you can plug your Mac directly into a stereo amplifier, if you have the right audio cable adapter, and listen to Mac sounds through your stereo system. To connect, you'll need an adapter from the Mac's 1/8-inch RCA stereo mini-plug connector to the inputs on your stereo system.

The microphone port on earlier iMacs and the eMac is also a line-level device, meaning you'll need either a special Apple PlainTalk microphone (available in Mac-friendly computer stores) or a signal from a powered microphone or from a line-level device, such as an external receiver or even an external device like a CD player. Typical karaoke-style microphones won't work. If you want to use an inexpensive microphone, Griffin Technology (**http://www.griffintechnology.com/**) offers a special adapter for connecting such microphones to your Mac.

NOTE   *For Macs that don't include a microphone port, the solution is a USB microphone, such as the models made by MacAlly, Griffin Technology, and others.*

Upgrade RAM

With Mac OS X, having a lot of RAM is vital to your Mac performance. In this section I'd like to briefly touch on the types of RAM and the procedure for upgrading RAM in your iMac G4, iBook G4, or eMac. (For earlier models, consult Apple's Support pages at **http:// www.info.apple.com**.)

 *Whenever you access the insides of a computer, you need to guard against static electricity discharge, which can damage computer components. The best way to do this is to buy and wear a grounding strap, which attaches to your wrist and discharges static. You can get a grounding strap from most computer and electronics stores.*

There are two different types of RAM technology that have been used in the machines we're covering—SDRAM and DDR RAM. SDRAM (which stands for Synchronous DRAM) is the older and slower technology found in early iMac G4 models and most eMac models thus far; DDR (Double Data Rate) RAM is found in later iMac G4 models and the iBook G4. Here's a chart with a brief rundown:

Model	RAM Type	Open Slots
iMac G4 (700-800 MHz)	PC133 SDRAM	1 SO-DIMM slot
iMac G4 (1 MHz+)	DDR PC2100 or PC2700	1 SO-DIMM slot
eMac G4	PC133 SDRAM	1 DIMM slot
iBook G4	DDR PC2100	1 SO-DIMM slot

The term PC133 SDRAM refers to a DIMM (Dual Inline Memory Module) that uses SDRAM suitable for a computer that has a 133 MHz memory bus; because that RAM is backward compatible with Macs that have 100 MHz buses, it works in those as well. The term SO-DIMM is important, however, as it means a *small outline* DIMM—the RAM slot requires a smaller DIMM than the standard size.

DDR PC2100 RAM is designed to run on computers with bus speeds of 133 MHz; DDR PC2700 runs on computers with 167 MHz buses. In the case of DDR RAM, you can add PC2700 modules to a Mac that supports PC2100, if you like, but not vice versa.

Perhaps most important is simply to buy your RAM from a vendor that can specify the correct size and style of RAM module for your particular Mac model. A few places that are great for configuring Mac RAM include Other World Computer (**http://www.macsales.com/**), ClubMac (**http://www.clubmac.com**—look for the Memory Configurator), and TransInternational (**www.transintl.com**) among many, many others.

NOTE *The handbook that comes with your Mac includes step-by-step instructions and drawings to help you install RAM. Likewise, Apple's Support pages include detailed PDFs that you can access. I recommend you check those out to figure out exactly how to get into your particular Mac model and perform the upgrades.*

Chapter 24

Troubleshoot and Maintain Your Mac

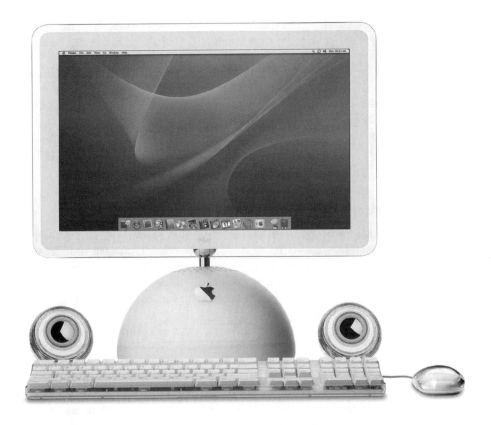

How to...

- Find technical support resources
- Troubleshoot your hardware
- Troubleshoot software
- Deal with errors
- Fix freezes and hangs
- Solve problems with permissions and files
- Use the Software Restore discs
- Use Software Update
- Maintain your Mac

It's never good when your Mac starts giving you serious trouble. Hopefully, you won't encounter this much, although the likelihood is that, eventually, you'll have to troubleshoot something. The nature of today's computing is that it isn't all flawless.

Not that it has to be an intolerable experience, either. One of the tricks is adhering to a good maintenance schedule. If you do that, you'll probably have fewer instances of trouble. The other is knowing how to attack problems when they occur—and, more to the point, where to diagnose problems and then find answers.

So, let's take a look at both troubleshooting and maintenance as ways of keeping your Mac healthy and happy. Using these steps, you can keep your Mac running well, or get it up and running again after you've had some trouble.

Find Tech Support Online

Since this is the Internet-savvy iMac, iBook, and eMac we're talking about, I recommend that you get to know online resources for troubleshooting your Mac right at the outset. Apple's Mac-specific support pages are very useful and offer some great features, including online message areas for Mac users. These sites offer a great way to learn more about your Mac, identify potential problems, and do what is probably the most important step in keeping your Mac tuned—stay up on the latest news and information.

Enter `http://www.apple.com/support/` in a browser, then look around for the Select Your Product control. Choose your Mac model and click Go. Once you reach the support page for your Mac model, you'll find all sorts of information about your Mac, including the latest news, articles on different technologies, and pointers to any software updates that have been released for your model (as well as for Mac OS X and the standard bundle of applications).

I won't harp specifically on certain parts of the Mac Support site because the site is likely to change. You'll probably always find a link to the Discussions message area that allows you to exchange messages with other Mac users and Apple Tech Support specialists. (I highly recommend the Discussions section if you're having a specific problem—there are tons of helpful folks in there.) You'll probably also find links to the latest updates, including updates to your Mac model's firmware, to the Mac OS, to the applications that came with your Mac, and to the modem's firmware, among others.

 Firmware *is a type of software/hardware driver combination that can be installed to update your Mac. The firmware updates usually fix bugs or add new features and capabilities to hardware like your Mac's modem or the Mac itself.*

While you're online, you might also want to check out some of the popular Mac-oriented sites, where you'll find news and help on various issues affecting your Mac as well as the entire Macintosh industry. Here's a sampling of them:

Macworld	**http://www.macworld.com/**
MacCentral	**http://www.maccentral.com/**
MacAddict	**http://www.macaddict.com/**
MacFixIt	**http://www.macfixit.com/**
MacBlog	**http://www.macblog.com/**

All of these sites can help you find new peripherals, follow the news regarding Apple, discuss Mac and Mac troubleshooting issues, and so on.

Troubleshoot Hardware Problems

There are a couple of telltale signs that something has gone wrong with your Mac. Here's what they are, what might cause them, and a few things to try before sending your Mac off to the repair shop.

Get Past a Blank Screen or Tones

If you've just tried to turn on your Mac and you've gotten no response, you're seeing a blank screen, and/or you're hearing tones, it's possible there's something wrong with the internals of your Mac, like a RAM module that's not properly installed or something that has come loose. Before you send it to the shop though, test a few things:

- Make sure the Mac is plugged in properly and the surge protector (if you're using one) is turned on.
- Check for signs that your surge protector is working correctly and that it hasn't absorbed a power surge, which might cause a fuse to blow on the power strip.
- Restart the Mac by pressing CONTROL-⌘-POWER (on the keyboard).
- Unplug all USB (and FireWire, on later Mac models) peripherals and network connections other than the mouse and keyboard. Try restarting.
- If that doesn't work, restart the Mac with the Power button on the front of the Mac or via the reset button or reset hole, as discussed in the sidebar "How to…Restart Your Mac" later in the chapter.

If none of that works, you may need to take your Mac in for service.

Fix a Blinking Question Mark

If a question mark is blinking in the middle of your screen, it's a sign that the Mac can't find a disk with a working version of the Mac OS on it. Here's what you can do:

- Wait a minute or so. It may resolve itself. (If this happens, check your Startup Disk control panel and make sure it's set to start up from the Mac's internal disk.)
- Restart with CONTROL-⌘-POWER.
- Unplug the Mac, wait a minute, then plug it back in and press the POWER key.
- If none of the previous steps does away with the blinking question mark, consider performing a step called "zapping the PRAM" to see if that gets your Mac to notice the drive and boot from it. Do that by restarting the Mac. After the startup tone, hold down ⌘-OPTION-P-R until you hear the startup chime five more times. Then, release the keys. That may cause the Mac to find the internal hard disk and start up normally.

If these things don't work, start from a recovery CD, launch Disk Utility (see the "Fix Your Disks and Permissions" section later in this chapter), and use Disk First Aid. You might also want to start up from a disk doctor application.

Start Up from a Mac OS (or Recovery) CD

Your Mac has the ability to start up from a CD-ROM, which is useful if you need to troubleshoot your main disk, install a new Mac OS version, or if you need to start up from a recovery CD such as those included with Norton Utilities or a similar utility program. If you need to start your Mac from a CD-ROM, here's how:

1. Place the CD (the Mac Restore CD, a Mac OS X CD, or a recovery CD) in the drive tray or in the CD's slot.

2. Restart. You can use the Apple | Restart command, or if your Mac is frozen or hung and you're willing to lose data, press CONTROL-⌘-POWER or CONTROL-⌘-EJECT. (For more details, consult the sidebar "How to…Restart Your Mac.")

3. As the Mac starts, hold down the C key right after the Mac plays its startup tones until you see the Mac OS startup screen and/or hear the CD drive being accessed.

The Mac will start up and the CD will be the main disk that appears in the top-right corner in the Finder. Now, locate and launch the disk doctoring utility. (If it's a Mac OS X CD, you can select Disk Utility from the Installer menu.)

Did you know?

PRAM

Parameter RAM (PRAM) is a small portion of RAM that the Mac uses for special settings in control panels, as well as some other internal settings. This RAM always has a little power trickling to it, thanks to a battery inside your Mac. PRAM can also become corrupted, which requires a reset. A reset is usually a last line of defense—but you can try zapping PRAM using the method described in "Start Up from a Mac OS (or Recovery) CD," or using MicroMat TechTool (discussed later in the chapter).

The battery that powers PRAM eventually runs out, usually after three to five years. When that happens, your AppleTalk, Date & Time, screen resolution, and other settings will sometimes seem to change randomly. That's a sure sign it's time to replace the battery, which any Apple Authorized service center can do for you.

Fix a Problematic Peripheral

If a USB device isn't working, check to make sure it's installed correctly. If the nonworking device is connected to a USB hub, turn the hub on and off to reset it.

If everything is plugged in correctly, reset the device by turning it on and off. Also, unplug and replug the device's USB connector (which will often reset its USB driver) and follow the manual's instructions for resetting the device.

If you're having trouble with your printer, check to make sure it's selected (highlighted) in the Print Center. Turn it on and off again, or check the printer's manual for a command that allows you to restart the printer.

If none of these work, unplug the device and restart your Mac. Now, with the Mac OS loaded, plug the device back into the USB port. Hopefully it will be detected and begin working again.

With FireWire devices, you can plug and unplug them if they're not recognized, but be sure you don't plug and unplug devices while they're in use. Also, if a FireWire device requires power from the FireWire bus, plug it directly into the Mac's FireWire port or into a powered hub.

TIP   *Keep up with Mac OS X updates from Apple and software driver updates from your peripheral manufacturers, and you'll likely have better luck with peripherals.*

Disk Cannot Be Ejected or Renamed

If you're having trouble ejecting a removable disk, it may not be a problem with the media. This often happens when the disk is still in use—you may be using it, or if file sharing is active, someone else on your network could be using the disk. Try closing all active applications and check for network users.

Heat Buildup

One thing that's important to keep an eye out for with any computer is a rising internal temperature, which can lead to erratic performance, crashes, and even component damage. This is particularly true of iMac and eMac models that have strategically placed vent holes for heat dissipation. It's important to make sure your Mac is in a well-ventilated area, that it's operated at room temperature, and that you don't cover those air holes with paper, books, cloth, cats, or other obstructions.

NOTE *If you have trouble renaming disks, that may also be because file sharing is turned on. Turn it off momentarily and attempt to rename the disk again.*

If no one is using the disk, try restarting your Mac, and as the Mac starts up, hold down the EJECT key. (You can also try holding down the mouse button if the EJECT key doesn't work.) That may cause the disk to come free.

The other side of this problem is a CD that doesn't appear to be recognized and/or won't eject when you select the eject commands in the Finder or on your keyboard. (I've noticed this particularly with CD-RW discs that haven't been completely or properly erased by the Disc Burner software.) If you've encountered such a disc on a slot-loading iMac or iBook, your best plan may be to physically eject the disc by inserting a straightened paperclip into the small hole at the far right of the slot. That should activate the mechanism, popping the disc out.

Troubleshoot Software Problems

There are three basic causes of software problems. Let's define those quickly, then we'll take a look at the symptoms your Mac may be experiencing. Here are the problems that software can encounter on your Mac:

- **Bugs** These are the result of mistakes or oversights by programmers who created applications for the Mac OS. Usually the only fix is to stop using the program and/or update it.

- **Conflicts** When two pieces of software—usually an application and a system component—don't get along, you have a conflict. Conflicts cause crashes and freezes and are usually solved by finding the culprits and updating or disabling them.

TIP *Read the Read Me file that accompanies any application causing you trouble. The Read Me file might tell you that the software is known to conflict with other software on your Mac.*

■ **Corruption** This problem occurs when data is overwritten with either bad or nonsensical information. Corruption can cause all sorts of trouble, but typically causes crashes and freezes. This is solved by deleting or finding the corrupt data file and fixing it with a disk doctor program.

Understand Software Symptoms

These are the common symptoms and the first aid you should perform for the problem:

■ **Error** This is an error message in the form of an alert dialog box (outlined in red) that includes an OK button. It tells you the last command you attempted could not be executed because something went wrong.
First Aid: Click OK and save your work. If the error sounds like data is threatened—you're out of memory or disk space, a disk couldn't be found, or you receive an error number—you should keep an eye on that application in the future and see if the problem repeats itself. If so, consult the web site or technical support staff for that application.

■ **Crash** In this case, you get an error message and the application shuts down. Sometimes the application itself tells you about the problem; sometimes the Finder tells you there was an "Unexpected Quit."
First Aid: There's nothing you need to do except be careful with this application in the future and make a point of saving your working documents fairly regularly.

■ **Hang** An application no longer responds to input.
First Aid: Wait. Note if any activity in the frontmost application occurs. If your data is important (and not recently saved), you should wait at least ten minutes before forcing the application to quit, as described in "Fix Freezes and Hangs."

Once you've gotten past the immediate first aid, you can move on to diagnose the cause of the problem and attempt a long-term solution.

Respond to Error Messages

These are the best sorts of errors to encounter, since they give you some indication of what's going on. If the error didn't crash the application, you'll likely already have some idea what's wrong. A printing error means you should check out your printer or the Chooser; an error loading a web site or getting your e-mail might have something to do with your Internet connection.

Most of the time, the error message is your guide. Read it, then consult the rest of this section or check out the part of this book where that application or issue is discussed. Something may be wrong with your Mac's settings or hardware configuration.

Some errors aren't as specific—let's take a quick look at those.

24

Disk Is Full Error

If your hard disk gets full or close to full, you'll start to see all sorts of errors, including "Disk is full." Most applications, Internet programs, and games write temporary files, preference files, and other sorts of data to your hard disk, even when you're not actively saving a document. If your hard disk gets full, your applications and the Mac OS will encounter unexpected trouble.

If it happens to you, the best plan is to delete any old documents (or any that you have backed up already) and uninstall any applications or games that you don't immediately need. (You'll find that most application installers also have a Remove or Uninstall choice in their Custom Install menu.)

You should also consider getting rid of image files and QuickTime movies. These are culprits that can take up a lot of disk space, as can games and educational software.

> NOTE *All of Apple's iLife applications—iMovie, iTunes, iPhoto, iDVD, and GarageBand— deal with large multimedia files. If you're editing a lot of video or working with a lot of digital photos or songs, then you may be filling up your hard disk quicker than you realize. If you encounter a full disk problem, the best solution may be to purchase an external hard disk and start to offload some of those large files.*

Insufficient Permissions Errors

Permissions problems generally crop up when you're trying to copy items back and forth in the Finder. The basic issue is this—in Mac OS X, thanks to its Unix-like infrastructure, each file has certain permissions assigned to it when it's created or copied. Each file has an owner, a group associated with it, and permissions assigned to "everyone."

> NOTE *Permissions problems can happen in the background as well, and they can have an odd effect on your files and applications. If you suspect that you have a folder or file with incorrect permissions settings, see the section "Fix Your Disks and Permissions" later in this chapter.*

If you don't have the proper permissions for a file, you often can't move or delete it. In some cases, you may not even be able to access a file so that you could load the file in an application and view it. Likewise, permissions can be assigned to folders, where you may not be able to read (view) the file, write (move, delete, or save) to the file, or both.

You have a couple of solutions to permissions problems. If you are using a regular Mac OS X account and you have access to an administrator's account, you can log in as an administrator and work with many files, particularly those in the main Applications and Library folders on your Mac. If you don't have access to an administrator's account, or if that still doesn't work, you may need to ask the owner of the file to move or delete the files. (For instance, if you create a folder in the Shared folder, that folder is owned by you. Another user, not even an administrator, can move or delete it.)

There's a third solution for changing ownership of files. Copy a file to a user's Drop Box, located inside the user's Public folder, and that file becomes owned by that user. This is a great way to make sure that a person you're working with on your Mac has full control over the file, including the ability to delete it if necessary.

NOTE
Sometimes a removable disk or an external drive may be inaccessible because of privilege problems on that disk. If that's the case, you can do the following. Select the disk, then choose File | Show Info in the Finder. Select Permissions from the pop-up menu in the Info window. At the bottom of the window, turn on the Ignore Ownership on This Volume check box. Now you should be able to access the disk. (If security is a concern, copy the files to another location, then turn the Ignore option back off when you're done.)

Deal with Crashes

There are a couple different kinds of crashes you'll encounter. Often they'll include an error message or an alert, but sometimes they just happen. Here's a look at what could occur:

- **Error message or code**   When an error message appears within the application itself, it means the application *noticed* the error. This can lead you to the source of the problem. It may be a bug in the document or corruption of the document.

- **Unexpected quitting**   The program disappears, followed by a message in the Finder. This sort of crash often happens because there's a bug in the program or the program encountered a corrupt data file.

- **No message**   In this case, the program just quits or disappears. This could be corruption, but it's likely a bug or a conflict.

Test for Crashing

So what can you do about a crash? In Mac OS X, it's generally OK to continue computing after a native application crashes. (The exception is the Classic environment—if a Classic application crashes, you should restart the Classic environment. See the Appendix for details on Classic.) After that, your priority is isolating the crash—figuring out when the crash occurs and any factors that contribute to it. Here are some questions to consider when it comes to crashes:

- *Have you added anything recently?* If you've recently installed a new application or utility program, it's possible that it installed a new kernel extension or startup item that's causing trouble. (See the section "Kernel Extensions and Drivers" later in this chapter, for details.)

- *Is the crashing consistent?* If your Mac crashes every time you do something in particular— load a QuickTime movie, check your e-mail, load a particular game—then you may be closer to a solution.

If you can reproduce the error fairly consistently, there are a few things you can try to test for the error and isolate it further. Here's what to try:

- *Test different documents.* It's possible that a particular document is corrupt, especially if the crash occurs as you're opening a document, as you're saving a document, as you're printing, or when you move to a particular page in a document. Find a similar document or two and test the application with those to see if the same crash occurs. If it doesn't, you can try running a disk doctor utility (or a special file fixer utility), or just avoid using that document.

■ *Remove the preferences file.* Most applications have a preferences file stored in the Preferences folder inside the Library folder that's in your home folder in Mac OS X. Quit the application, move the preferences file to the desktop or another folder, and restart the application. Some of its default behavior may change, and the crashing may also stop. If it does, throw away the preferences file and reset your preferences within the application.

■ *Restart without third-party kernel extensions.* As your Mac starts up, hold down the SHIFT key until you see the message "Safe Boot" in the startup window. This only disables third-party kernel extensions, not Apple's own extensions. Still, it can be useful if you believe a third-party driver is crashing your Mac.

■ *Check the fonts.* Sometimes a font can become corrupt and cause problems with your documents or applications. If you find that applications crash as they're starting up—particularly word processing or desktop layout applications—the problem may be a font. Fonts are also a possibility if you encounter problems with a particular document or when attempting to change the fonts in a document. The best troubleshooting is to get an application designed to deal with font corruption, such as Extensis FontReserve (**http://www.extensis.com/fontreserve/**), and test your fonts. Or, if you suspect a particular font, try removing it from your Fonts folder (inside the main Library folder), or use the Font Book application to deactivate that font, then test for crashing,

Fix Internet Crashing

Did the crash happen while you were browsing the Web? The preferences file or a file in your browser's cache may be corrupt. In Safari, you can easily delete your browser's cache by choosing Safari | Empty Cache. For Safari's other files, check the Safari folder inside your personal Library folder.

The Apple Support knowledge base also points to another possibility: some browser crashing occurs when your browser attempts to launch multimedia content, plug-ins, or Java content. If you suspect QuickTime (you repeatedly get crashing when you try to play QuickTime movies online), you might try this:

1. Quit Safari if it's open. (You can force quit if necessary.)

2. Dig into the Preferences folder inside the Library folder in your home folder and locate the file `com.apple.quicktime.plugin.preferences.plist`.

3. Drag that file to your desktop.

4. Restart Safari and try to access the QuickTime movie that crashed it previously.

If that solves the problem, you should delete the plug-in preferences file—QuickTime will automatically generate a new one.

If you notice that Safari crashes when accessing JavaScript of Java pages—particularly if it's a site you must access, but you can get by without those features—you can open Safari Preferences, click Security, and turn on or off those features.

TIP   *Safari isn't perfect—there are some sites it simply doesn't work with correctly. I find that such sites often work well with Internet Explorer, so I'll run it to access a few select sites. (Safari is faster, though, so I use it most of the time.) I even have one site I visit regularly that doesn't work with Safari or Internet Explorer. For that one, I have to launch Mozilla (**http://www.mozilla.org**) or Netscape (**http://www.netscape.com**), both of which work fine with the bank's web application.*

For other Internet applications, open the Preferences folder inside the Library folder inside your personal home folder in Mac OS X. Generally, you can delete "cache" and "history" files without causing too much trouble; but think twice before trashing bookmarks or favorites.

Fix Freezes and Hangs

A freeze will bring the mouse cursor to a halt, and nothing else will happen on the screen. A hang is a little different—the mouse pointer moves, even though things otherwise seem frozen. Why the difference? A hang results when an application has gone into an endless loop of some sort and can't break out to give control back to the Mac OS X. A freeze occurs when an application goes bad and causes the Mac OS itself to seize up.

Freezes are extremely rare in Mac OS X, although they do happen occasionally. Hangs happen more often, and it's important to be able to differentiate between the two. Here's how to test that:

1. Make sure the mouse and keyboard haven't been unplugged accidentally. Try unplugging and replugging them to see if there is a USB problem.

2. Check the screen carefully for any activity.

3. Attempt to switch to another application using the Dock or by pressing ⌘-TAB.

4. Wait. Get up and grab a cup of coffee or check to see if the mail has come. Five minutes or more might be a good idea.

5. Press ⌘-. (period) to see if you can interrupt the program. Press ESC. If that doesn't work, try ⌘-Q to quit. If none of those keyboard combinations are working, you can try a force quit—press ⌘-SHIFT-ESC. If you see the Force Quit Applications window, select the application that appears to be frozen and click Force Quit. If you're having trouble with the Finder, you can even select it and click Restart.

If none of the above work, the Mac may be frozen. (Or, at the very least, an application has managed to hang badly enough that you can't get past it.) Try to restart using CONTROL-⌘-POWER or CONTROL-⌘-EJECT to force the Mac to restart, or hold down the Power button on the front or side of the Mac until it restarts.

If the freeze or hang recurs after you've restarted and launched the application again, check the application's Read Me file for known conflicts with other applications or Mac OS extensions. Start with kernel extensions off (hold down the SHIFT key through the startup process) and see if the freeze recurs. Check with the software publisher's web site to see if there are any bug fixes or other suggestions. Contact the publisher's technical support folks to see if they have any suggestions.

Kernel Extensions and Drivers

For the most part, Mac OS X does away with the entire *extensions* concept that was a big part of the Classic Mac OS (and its troubleshooting), and Mac OS X, in theory, doesn't allow third parties to "patch" the operating system. This is probably a good thing, as Mac OS extensions, while historically useful, can also be exceptionally problematic.

That said, there are extensions to Mac OS X—called *kernel extensions*—that can be installed by third parties. Instead of adding capabilities to the system, however, these extensions are generally just low-level device drivers for working with third-party peripherals. (I've also seen these extensions installed by very low level utility applications such as disk repair or recovery software.)

If you're having trouble with such an extension, the first solution is to boot with extensions off. Hold down the SHIFT key as Mac OS X starts, and only Apple's kernel extensions will load. If you notice that the trouble has ended, you'll need to get in touch with the company that wrote the extension and let your displeasure be known (or, simply see if they have a newer version of the driver).

How to ... Restart Your Mac

With most of today's Macs, you can force a "soft reset" by pressing either CONTROL-⌘-POWER or CONTROL-⌘-EJECT, depending on which your keyboard offers. That's the first thing to try after you've exhausted your force quit and shut-down options.

For a hard reset, most modern Macs will reset if you hold in their Power button (on the front or side of the Mac) for about seven to ten seconds. The Power button, however, doesn't restart some of the earliest iMac models. If you have an original Revision A Mac, you'll need to straighten a paperclip and insert it in the reset button hole (labeled with a triangle) to restart your Mac. You may also need to do this—or press the raised reset button on some models, which is labeled with a triangle—for other Macs that don't respond when you press the Power button on the front or side.

<table>
<tr><td>

Did you know?

</td><td>

Kernel Panic

</td></tr>
</table>

Mac OS X is built on top of a tiny, low-level operating system called a *kernel*, and it's this OS that's used to talk directly to hardware devices; that's why many device drivers are kernel extensions. This also opens up a vulnerability. When there's a problem with the kernel, it's one of the few problems that can truly crash the entire Mac OS X system, meaning a freeze or full-blown crash. That's called a *kernel panic*.

In most cases, there isn't much you can do to resolve a kernel panic other than follow the instructions for restarting, if you see any on screen. Otherwise, restart the Mac using the instructions discussed earlier in this chapter in the sidebar "How to…Restart Your Mac." Now, you should carefully watch your Mac to see if it shows signs of trouble, and try to either locate a solution (a new device driver, for instance) or to avoid reproducing the error in the future.

Reinstall, Restore, and Update

Eventually, you may get to the point that you need to reinstall your applications, reinstall Mac OS X, or even update the Mac or Mac OS X. As far as reinstalling and restoring go, you can do those things easily using the software CDs that came with your Mac. You can also update your Mac using the Software Update feature or by accessing updates posted by Apple on the Mac Support web site.

Uninstall and Reinstall Applications

If you want to get rid of an application, the best way to do it usually is to launch the application's installer program and choose Uninstall or Remove from the Custom Install menu. That's the best way because it removes any special extensions or control panels the application added to your Mac.

If you need to manually uninstall an application, that shouldn't be too much harder. Just drag the application's folder to the Trash. Now, open the Library folder in your home folder in Mac OS X, then the Preferences folder, and drag the application's preferences file to the Trash, too.

Before doing this, it's a good idea to check the application's folder (if it has one) and make sure you didn't store any important documents in that folder. You can reinstall the application, if necessary, but you can't recover the documents you delete accidentally. You should also stop to consider whether you have another application that can read documents created in the uninstalled application. If you don't have one and you think you may need to read those documents at some point, then you might want to translate them to another document format before tossing the application for good.

If you've uninstalled an application in this way, it's usually pretty simple to reinstall the application—just run the installation program. Before reinstalling, you should probably make sure that the old preferences file has been deleted, and that there isn't another version of the application already on your hard disk. (Two versions of the same application could cause trouble, and will definitely cause confusion.) Other than that, reinstalling is pretty easy to do.

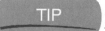 *You can also get utility programs that help you uninstall applications, such as the popular Spring Cleaning (**www.aladdinsys.com**).*

Software Restore

If you ever get in real trouble with your Mac, you have an out that can save you, get things up and running again, and hopefully go a long way to solving your problems. It's called Software Restore, and it allows you to reinstall Mac OS X (and, in many cases, the Classic environment) and your applications to the state they were when you first pulled your Mac out of the box and set it up.

Even if that sounds enticing, realize that this is a recourse of last resort. Doing this will wipe out any changes you've made to Mac OS X, settings you made in various preference panes, updates you've made to your applications, and so on. It's important that you not perform a Software Restore lightly, since you're in for some extra work—reconfiguring and reinstalling extras—once you've performed the Restore. Still, it's there if you need it.

How, exactly, this works depends on the model of Mac that you have. For a flat-panel iMac and other models that came with Mac OS X but that can boot into Mac OS 9, the process will be something like this:

1. If your Mac is on, insert the Software Restore CD in your Mac's CD or DVD drive.
2. When the disc's window appears, launch the file SoftwareRestore.pkg.
3. Now, walk through the installer application. (You'll need to authenticate with an administrator's account name and password.)
4. The Software Restore application will be installed and launched.
5. Follow the on-screen instructions.

One major component of those instructions is deciding what you're going to restore. You'll need to select whether you want all files restored or a subset. Use the on-screen controls to make those choices.

 In some versions of the Software Restore program, I've noticed it will occasionally ask for the CD that's already in the drive. Press the EJECT button on your keyboard once to open the tray and then press it again to have the Mac recognize the disc. (If this happens on a slot-loading iMac or iBook, press the EJECT button and then gently press the CD back into the drive.)

If you have an earlier version of Software Restore, things go a bit differently. To perform the Software Restore, you'll be restarting your Mac and booting off the Software Restore CD. Here's how the Software Restore works:

1. If your Mac is on, insert the Software Restore CD in your iMac's CD-ROM drive and restart the Mac. If your Mac is off, start it up, then quickly open the CD-ROM drive. Place the Software Restore CD in the drive and close it back up.

2. If your Mac doesn't automatically start up from the CD, restart the Mac and hold down the C key after you hear the startup tone.

3. Once the Mac has started up from the CD, double-click the Apple Software Restore icon on the CD.

4. Now choose between the two basic ways to perform a Software Restore. Click the Restore in Place check box if you'd like the Mac to restore the Mac OS and applications to their original state. Choose Erase Mac HD Before Restoring if you'd like the hard disk to be erased before the restoration takes place.

NOTE *Choosing Restore in Place won't erase your Documents folder or most of the other folders on your hard disk. It will, however, change settings in the Mac OS and erase anything other than the original Mac bundle. Choosing Erase Mac HD Before Restoring will wipe out everything on the disk, including documents, games, and so on. If you've installed a newer version of the Mac OS or any of its components, you'll need to reinstall it after the Software Restore.*

5. If you've chosen Erase Mac HD Before Restoring, you can also choose how you want your hard disk formatted—with Standard or Extended Mac OS format. The Extended Mac OS format gives you more efficient use of the hard disk so that you can pack more files onto the drive. (Extended is the best choice, but you might want to choose Standard for some reason that you're not willing to share with the rest of the class.) Make your choice from the menu.

6. Once you've made all your decisions, click Restore to begin the process.

Your Mac starts the process of formatting your hard disk (if you chose that option) and restoring the original Mac OS and applications to your hard disk. After this process is over, your Mac is restarted and, hopefully, starts up from its internal hard disk again in all its splendid, restored glory.

Now it's up to you to go through the process of restoring everything, setting up the Mac again, and copying over documents from your backups. You may also need to reinstall applications, reapply updates, and basically spend an afternoon getting everything back into shape.

 **Reinstall Mac OS X**

Earlier versions of Software Restore don't reinstall Mac OS X, so you'll need to do that from the Mac OS X CD-ROM—either one that came with your Mac or one that you've gotten subsequently for upgrading purposes (as long as it's a full version of the Mac OS). Note that you may have other reasons to do this as well—unlike previous versions of the Mac OS, the Mac OS X installer is fairly adept at fixing problems and replacing corrupt files when it's run. If you're noticing trouble with Mac OS X that seems to be at the system level, you might try reinstalling from the CD-ROM.

Of course, you should use the most recent CD-ROM version that you have, and if you've downloaded updates to the Mac OS using Software Update (discussed later in this section), you may need to perform those updates again. Also, the reinstallation can actually take quite a bit longer than the initial installation, because it requires the installer to check each file for changes.

Update Your Mac

Early in this chapter we discussed the fact that you can update the firmware in your Mac. You can also update applications and, occasionally, the Mac OS. In most cases, those software updates use an interface that's exactly like the typical software installer—you choose the installation and tell the installer which drive you want to install on. They aren't tough to use. Check Apple's Mac Support web site for details on the various updates available for Mac software and the Mac OS.

Firmware Update

A firmware update is a slightly different story. You'll also find these on the Apple Support site, but they're installed slightly differently. First, you'll want to download the update from the Web. Then, once the update has been processed by StuffIt Expander, it appears as a disk image. Double-click it to mount the disk. Once the disk appears on the desktop, double-click the Firmware Updater icon.

 As of this writing, the iMac G3 and iBook G3 models require firmware upgrades to run Mac OS X and some other technologies. Later models tend not to follow this procedure, as the necessary updates tend to be accessible via Software Update.

Here's how the process goes:

1. If your firmware is up-to-date already, you'll immediately see a dialog box letting you know that. If it's not, all applications are quit in the background and the Updater continues.

2. You'll see a dialog box explaining the process. When you click Update, your Mac restarts.

3. Now, after the Mac has restarted, you'll see a small indicator bar that tells you that the update is progressing.

4. When the update is finished, PRAM is automatically zapped (you'll hear a series of startup tones), then the Mac starts up.

5. When you get to the desktop, the Mac should tell you that the firmware was updated successfully.

If all doesn't go well, you may need to go through the process again. Apple also warns of a situation in which you may be asked by the Updater to shut down your Mac and press the programmer's button using a paperclip. (The programmer's button is the one under the recessed reset button on certain iMac G3 models.) To do this, click Shut Down in the dialog box.

Once the Mac is shut down, insert a paperclip in the programmer's button's recessed slot and press the button. Hold the paperclip in and press the POWER key on the front of the Mac. Now the Mac will start up and the Updater will be able to update the firmware. (You'll see the progress bar.)

> **NOTE** *Apple maintains a technical document that should help you determine whether your Mac requires a firmware update. Visit the Tech Info Library (**http://til.info.apple.com/**) and search for article n58174, titled "Mac: When to Install Available Updaters."*

Update with Software Update

Mac OS X includes a system software component that enables you to update your Mac over the Internet. Called Software Update, it comes in the form of a System Preferences pane in Mac OS X.

> **TIP** *If you use the Classic environment within Mac OS X, you should check the Software Update control panel separately whenever you're booted into Mac OS 9. The Mac OS X Software Update pane doesn't automatically update Classic or Mac OS 9.*

If your Internet connection is active, launch the Software Update by choosing Apple | Software Update. (You can also choose the Software Update pane in System Preferences to access the tools.) Software Update will check with special Internet servers at Apple to see if there are updates available that you don't yet have installed on your Mac. If there are items, you'll see a window for installing the software:

Place a check mark next to the items you'd like to download and install, then click the Install button. Those items will be downloaded (which can take a while over a modem connection) and installed. (You should stick around your Mac, just in case you need to read and agree to licensing agreements and do some other clicking.)

You may see some items that are unchecked by default. Those are items that Software Update believes aren't necessary for your Mac. If you think it may be incorrect in that assumption, you can download and attempt to install those updates.

You can also automate Software Update, so that it checks for system updates regularly. In Mac OS X, turn on the Check for Updates check box and choose a frequency (Daily, Weekly, or Monthly) from the Check for Updates menu.

Maintain Your Mac

One of the best ways I know to help you get the most out of your Mac is a maintenance schedule. It's important to any Mac that some basic steps take place every week, every few weeks, or once every couple of months.

Here, then, are some of the things you do in the course of Mac maintenance. Let's begin with a schedule for the maintenance, then we'll take a close look at what each schedule item entails.

24

The Mac Maintenance Schedule

A lot of the problems that occur with your Mac's hard disk, Mac OS system files, and other arcana occur slowly—a little file corruption starts to sneak in, causing more problems. Pretty soon things cascade.

What are the things you should do? There are two lists: the daily stuff and the time-based issues. Daily, you should do the following when you're working with your Mac:

- *Turn your Mac on and off no more than once a day.* If you want to shut down your Mac every evening and turn it on in the morning, that's fine. Otherwise, the settings in Energy pane of System Preferences (Mac OS X) will conserve energy. After all, it's the Mac's monitor that consumes most of the power. You can also choose Apple | Sleep in Mac OS X when you walk away from your Mac.

NOTE *Ideally, Mac OS X should be left on all the time, including overnight, because it occasionally runs maintenance tasks at night. The Sleep mode is a good low-power mode that should save enough power while letting the Mac remain functional. Also, for security reasons, if you do leave your Mac on all night, it's a good idea to disable your DSL or cable modem connection by disconnecting from Internet Connect or pushing the Standby button on your Internet modem, if it has one.*

- *When shutting down or restarting the Mac, use the commands in the Apple menu.* You shouldn't just turn off your surge protector or throw a light switch to turn off your Mac. Instead, use the Shut Down and/or Restart commands in the Finder. If your Mac doesn't shut down in an orderly way, system files and configuration files can be left open, data can be discarded, and problems can ensue.

- *Restart the Classic environment occasionally.* After starting and quitting many Classic programs, your Mac's memory can become fragmented, which leads to errors. If you restart (using the Special menu) after lunch or before a major Internet surfing session, you'll get better performance with fewer errors. (Note that Mac OS X doesn't need to be restarted regularly as a maintenance task, unless you're running very low on available disk space.)

- *Check your hard disk space frequently.* If your hard disk ever fills up or comes close to it, you'll start to see errors in your applications. Make a point of throwing away documents that you're done with. That way you won't fill up your drive, plus you won't have to commit to major purging sessions every few months to regain disk space. Check disk space by looking at the Finder window's information area, just under the toolbar, to see how much space is available on the disk. You can also highlight the disk's icon (in a Finder window Sidebar or on the desktop) and choose File | Get Info to learn more about the drive's capacities.

```
Format: Mac OS Extended (Journaled)
Capacity: 27.94 GB
Available: 15.86 GB
    Used: 12.08 GB on disk (12,976,394,240
          bytes)
```

■ *Back up.* You may not do it daily, but I recommend that you use an automated solution and back up your important documents every few days. See Chapters 20 and 23 for details.

In the rest of this chapter, I'll discuss tasks you should perform weekly and monthly.

Check for Viruses

Since your Mac is designed to live on the Internet, chances are that you're downloading and working with many different files from different sources. This is a great way to catch a computer virus. So, you should buy a virus-checking application and set it to automatically scan your disk and files on a regular basis.

A computer *virus* is a program that attaches itself to other programs and attempts to replicate itself as much as it can, preferably by being transferred via disks, network connections, and the Internet. Not all viruses are designed to cause harm, although they can, anyway, by accident. Others really are designed to infect your files, rendering them useless or sometimes deleting or destroying them.

In one sense, viruses on computers work the same way that physical viruses work. The more you're exposed to high-risk situations—the Internet, swapping Zip disks, and using a large computer network—the more likely you are to be infected. And with your Mac, you're probably spending enough time online to be high risk.

NOTE   *In case you're curious, viruses are computer programs written by people. Virus authors are usually interested in causing consternation and fear around the world. Sometimes that's enough—other times, it's important to the virus author that they also cause trouble and loss.*

If you're online a lot with your Mac, consider getting yourself a virus-protection program. These programs generally run in the background, checking files as they appear on your hard disk or from a removable disk. You can also schedule them to check while you're not using your Mac—late at night or on the weekends, for instance.

There are at least three major virus packages for the Mac OS—Norton AntiVirus (**http://www.norton.com/**), VirusBarrier (**http://www.intego.com/**) and Virex, which is included with a .Mac subscription. The first two are available from online Mac stores as well as in computer stores and superstores that carry Mac OS products.

Most of the time the scans take place in the background. When the virus program detects a file that it thinks may be infected, it lets you know. Sometimes the detector will automatically move infected files to a particular folder. Other times, it may be able to "clean" the virus from the file after it's been isolated.

I wouldn't even try to clean a file unless you absolutely need access to its data and you don't have a good backup. (Remember, the backup might be corrupted as well—you should check.) If the infected file is a document that you need, you can try to clean the virus from it.

Both of the major virus protection utilities give you the choice of scheduling scans, scanning files as they're added to your Mac (from the Internet or from removable media), or only scanning when you actively ask the program to scan. For maximum protection, you should leave the scanner on all the time to check programs as they're downloaded. If you find this is annoying, I'd recommend scheduling regular scans for when you're away from the computer.

One thing you should definitely do is update your virus definitions. The virus-protection publishers come out with updates, usually every month, that allow the software to detect more viruses, fight them better, and protect against new types of infections. In both utilities, you can have the antivirus check automatically for updates.

Fix Your Disks and Permissions

Part of your maintenance routine will require the use of special utility programs designed to help you find corruption, fix disks, and so on. A few of those utilities are free, but others will cost some money. Let's take a look at both.

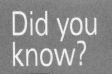
Did you know?

Virus Hoaxes

Viruses are a popular topic for e-mail hoaxes—e-mail messages distributed in chain-letter form, telling you to "pass it on" and "spread the word." These messages offer spurious information about some dire problem. The e-mail warnings generally show up in the form of a virus alert that's been released by "the U.S. government," "Microsoft," "a university lab," or some other organization that seems credible. A dead giveaway is misspellings or grammatical errors in the message.

Most of them also claim that reading a particular e-mail message or loading a particular web page causes a virus to spread to your Mac. This really isn't the case; a virus can't be spread through the text of a message, so simply reading an e-mail message will not give your Mac a virus. If you *execute an attached document or program*, then it's possible to get a virus, so don't use attachments from people you don't know.

The "open an e-mail" virus alerts are hoaxes, though. Read carefully and you'll see that, in spite of their supposed source being a reputable organization, they probably have misspellings or bizarre grammatical constructs. For the official word on viruses (and many virus hoaxes), the best place to turn is the Symantec Anti-Virus Research center at **http://www.symantec.com/avcenter/index.html** on the Web.

 *Other tools not mentioned here include Alsoft Diskwarrior (**www.alsoft.com**), which can sometimes magically recover disks that suddenly can't be booted, as in those showing a blinking question mark. DataRescue (**www.prosoft.com**) is touted as another solution for drives that have encountered serious corruption or a failure to start up.*

Disk First Aid

At least once a month you should run Disk First Aid (see Figure 24-1), which is included with your Mac and designed to find problems with the directory structure of your Mac. Run it every month or so since it allows you to find directory problems before they crop up. To run Disk First Aid, launch the Disk Utility application that's found in the Utilities folder inside the Applications folder on your hard disk.

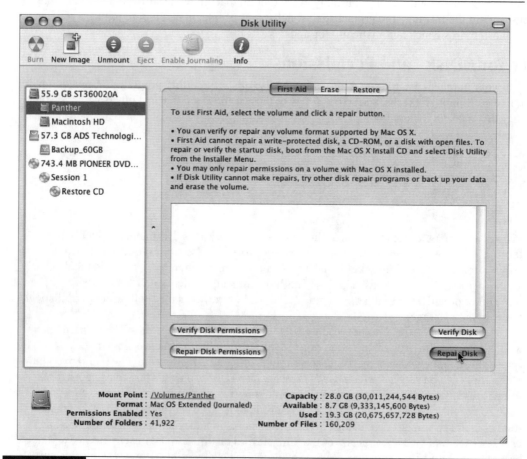

FIGURE 24-1   The Disk First Aid tools in Disk Utility in Mac OS X

On the left side of the window, select the disk you want to verify—most likely it's the Macintosh HD volume. You can now click the First Aid tab at the top of the right side of the window. Click Verify Disk to simply have Disk First Aid take a look at the drive and see how everything is doing. If you want to repair the disk while it's being verified, click Repair Disk. This accomplishes two steps in one click.

Now Disk First Aid runs through the disk looking for corruption in the directory structure. If it finds a problem, it alerts you, asking if you want to fix the problem. (This is true in some cases; in others, it just goes ahead and fixes things.) Otherwise, you'll get through your session and, hopefully, receive a clean bill of health.

24

NOTE *Disk First Aid can't always fix your startup disk if it's launched from that disk. The solution is to start up from either another volume or from a Mac OS X installation CD. Insert the CD, restart your Mac, and hold down the C key, then wait for the Installer to appear. When it does, choose Open Disk Utility from the Installer menu.*

Permissions First Aid

On the same screen as the disk tools, Disk Utility offers Permissions First Aid as well. These options comb through your disk and check for files that appear to have the wrong permissions and then set them correctly. It happens occasionally that a program, installer, or system component simply sets the permissions for a file incorrectly—depending on what the file is, the result could be some odd crashing or error messages—or you may have trouble with a particular file or group of files. Permissions First Aid can stop some of those problems and is an important maintenance step to keep your Mac relatively trouble free.

To use Permissions First Aid, simply select a disk volume from the list and click the Verify Disk Permissions button to see if any are found; you can click Repair Disk Permissions if you just want to fix any problems that are found without first seeing what they are.

Periodic Tasks

Mac OS X has a few special maintenance tasks that occur at the Unix-level core of the operating system that need to happen daily, weekly, and monthly. They are designed to run automatically, but that only works if you leave your Mac on 24 hours a day. If you're the type that shuts your Mac down, then you should get the freeware MacJanitor, available at **http://personalpages .tds.net/~brian_hill/downloads.html** on the Web and run that software on a regular basis.

Explore Commercial Solutions

It's a good idea for you to have at least one commercial disk-fixing solution available to you at all times. I'm not a huge believer in running a utilities suite constantly in the background, although they tend to have some interesting tools, and virus checking is definitely something you should do vigilantly, as is backup of your important data. (If you have a .Mac account, you have access to both Virex and Backup, which can help you with those two tasks.) For emergency recovery, though, it's a good idea to have a third-party solution. Here's a look at some of the contenders.

- MicroMat TechTool Pro (**http://www.micromat.com**) is a good all-around solution for maintaining a Mac, as it looks not only at fixing and optimizing files and directories on your hard disk, but also at testing the mechanism, testing CPU, memory, power, and many other items that contribute to the overall "health" of your Mac.

- Alsoft Diskwarrior (**http://www.alsoft.com**) is a focused tool that's designed to rebuild the disk directories for a hard disk that has a lot of corruption or failure. In my experience it works great to recover a disk that otherwise won't start, and it's a great tool to have in such an emergency.

- Prosoft Data Rescue (**www.prosoft.com**) is touted as another solution for drives that have encountered serious corruption or a failure to start up. Data Rescue is designed to recover files from a drive that won't start up, giving you a chance to retrieve important data. It's an interesting secondary solution when other utilities can't recover the disk.

- Norton Utilities (**http://www.symantec.com/product/home-mac.html**) offers a number of different programs that help you keep your Mac running smoothly, including Norton Disk Doctor to analyze and fix hard disk trouble; Volume Recover and FileSaver to track and save data from files or entire disks, including removable disks; Speed Disk to defragment and optimize your hard disk for better performance; UnErase to track and retrieve files you've deleted accidentally; and Wipe Info to delete sensitive files permanently.

NOTE *Norton Utilities also comes bundled in Norton SystemWorks, which includes antivirus and backup tools along with Norton Utilities.*

Appendix

Dig into Classic

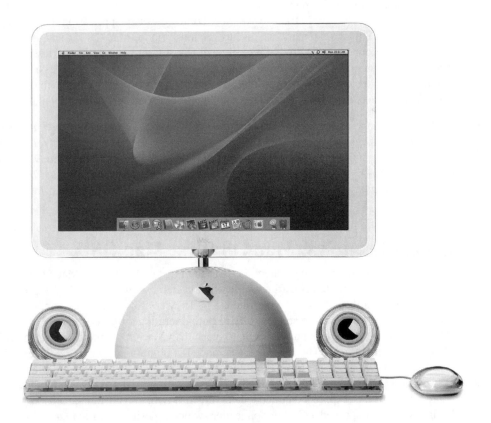

How to...

- Understand Classic vs. Mac OS 9 vs. Mac OS X
- Identify Classic applications
- Start and manage Classic
- Use the Classic Apple and Application menus
- Boot into Mac OS 9

When Apple introduced Mac OS X, it introduced an operating system that was radically different from the Mac operating systems that had come before it. The differences weren't just cosmetic—in fact, to the casual viewer, they're somewhat similar looking. Mac OS X, based ultimately on Unix, introduced an extremely powerful and capable operating system to Mac users, all while maintaining a friendly interface.

So why discuss the old stuff? Because you may come across an application that's designed for the classic Mac OS (that's the name we give to versions prior to Mac OS X), and you may need or want to run it on your Mac. To do that, you'll need to configure and activate Classic mode so that the application can run. You'll then find there are some differences between Classic applications and regular ones, so we'll go over that in this Appendix. And, finally, we'll touch on the ability that some Macs (particularly older models) have to "dual-boot" between Mac OS 9 and Mac OS X.

NOTE   *You'll find Mac folks tossing around the term "Classic" a lot in the Mac universe. It can mean a few different things. A* Classic application *is one that is designed for Mac OS 9; the* Classic environment *is an instance of Mac OS 9 run from within Mac OS X; and the* classic Mac OS *(or components of it, like the classic Apple menu, classic Finder, and so on) refers to any and/or all pre-Mac OS X versions of the Mac OS, including Mac OS 9 and later.*

Understand Classic vs. Mac OS 9 vs. Mac OS X

Mac OS X, Apple's latest operating system, is more than just an upgrade to Mac OS 9 and earlier versions. It's actually a completely different operating system, with underlying components that are very different from those that make up Mac OS 9. They're so different that applications need to be rewritten before they can run successfully in both operating systems.

Mac OS X is more powerful and less likely to crash than Mac OS 9, and designed for efficient networking and Internet tasks. Those advantages made the upgrade to Mac OS X an exciting move for Apple. But at the same time, Apple (particularly soon after it debuted Mac OS X) needed a solution that enables older Mac applications, which users have invested in heavily, to run in Mac OS X. In fact, Apple's engineers came up with two.

The first is something called a *Carbon* application, which is designed to run in both Mac OS 9 and Mac OS X. This is accomplished by rewriting an application so that it only uses a subset of programming commands, called the Carbon APIs (Application Programming Interfaces) that both Mac OS 9 and Mac OS X support. While this results in an application that doesn't have every Mac OS X advantage of a fully native application (called a *Cocoa* application), it does allow the application to run in both operating systems while still taking advantage of advanced features in Mac OS X. For instance, AppleWorks 6.1 is a Carbon application, and it's certainly a very useful application, as discussed in Chapters 7 through 11.

The other solution to the OS conundrum is called the *Classic environment*, which is simply a way in which Mac OS 9.2 or higher is run as an application within Mac OS X. Once launched, the Classic environment can run Mac OS 9.2–compatible applications that haven't been altered to run in Mac OS X. Or, when the Classic environment isn't good enough for you, you may be able to boot into Mac OS 9.2, depending on your Mac model. (Most models manufactured in 2003 or later cannot be used to start up in Mac OS 9.x.)

A

NOTE
Why can't newer Macs boot into Mac OS 9? For at least two reasons—one is to encourage users to use Mac OS X, while the other is for security. A Mac that runs Mac OS X but can boot into Mac OS 9 is less secure because the underlying files in Mac OS X are accessible from Mac OS 9 without the same permission and ownership limits.

Identify Classic Applications

So how can you tell which application is a native Mac OS X application and which is a Classic application? Classic applications will give you two telltale signs. First, they look like older Macintosh applications, if you've seen them (see Figure A-1). They have a different menu bar and slightly less colorful windows and controls. Second, when you start up a Classic application from within Mac OS X, you'll usually need to launch the Classic environment, which means a delay of a minute or more before the application pops on the screen.

Work with the Classic Environment

Whenever you launch a Classic application from within Mac OS X, the Classic environment will first be launched, if necessary. What is the Classic environment? It's really just an *instance* of Mac OS 9 being loaded from the hard disk and placed into memory, just as if the Mac were starting up from a power-off state. The major difference is that this version of Mac OS 9 loads as a *process* within Mac OS X, thus enabling Classic applications to run side-by-side with native applications.

Once the Classic environment is launched, it can handle one or more Classic applications. You can continue to launch Classic applications until system memory isn't able to accommodate more. (Although, by then, you'll likely see a severe slowdown in application response.)

TIP
If you work with the Classic environment a good deal, you can also set it to automatically load when Mac OS X starts up on your Mac. In Mac OS X, select System Preferences from the Apple menu, then click the Classic icon. In the Classic pane, turn on the option Start Up Classic on Login to This Computer.

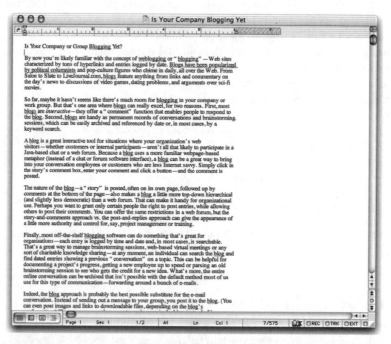

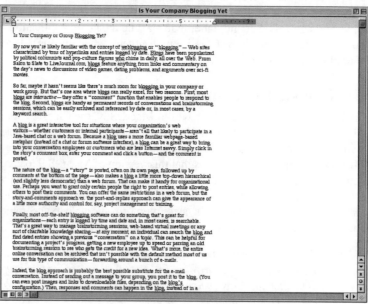

FIGURE A-1   At the top, a native Mac OS X application; at the bottom, a Classic application has older-style menu bar and window treatments.

One caveat of the Classic environment is that trouble in one Classic application can cause trouble for all Classic applications, because they don't have the protected memory and other features of both Carbon and Cocoa Mac OS X applications. If you encounter trouble, you should save data in all your other Classic applications, if you can, and then restart the Classic environment from the Classic pane. If you can't restart, you may need to force quit the environment.

Use the Classic Apple and Application Menus

Whenever you switch to a Classic application in Mac OS X, you'll see a slightly different menu bar from the standard one in Mac OS X. In Classic, the menu bar has two familiar menus—the Apple menu and the Application menu—but they're arranged a bit differently, and they have different purposes and tasks, as well.

A

Explore the Classic Apple Menu

Overall, the Apple menu works like any other menu. You move the mouse pointer up to the Apple icon, click the mouse button, and the menu appears (see Figure A-2). Then, move the mouse pointer down the menu until you're pointing at the item you want to select. If it's a submenu, it will have a little arrowhead pointing to the right—another menu will appear directly to the right once the mouse reaches the arrowhead. You can then move to the right and choose something from the new menu.

FIGURE A-2   The Classic Apple menu is sort of a junk drawer for your Mac.

If there's anything that's remarkably different about the Apple menu, it's the simple fact that you're usually launching something—a desk accessory, a control panel, an alias—instead of choosing a command. Most commands in the Finder and in other applications are for performing a task; the Apple menu, on the other hand, is pretty much a quick-launcher.

So what's on this menu? Lots of things, in four basic categories, including Desk Accessories, Control Panels, Aliases, and Menus.

Desk Accessories

Originally, desk accessories were the only types of program that could multitask on the Macintosh. Very early Macs could only run one application—like a word processor—at a time. So, Apple had to create desk accessories to help out with important tasks that you need to perform while still using the application. That's why they're small, single-function programs like Calculator or Note Pad. Here are some of the desk accessories you'll find on the Apple menu in Mac OS 9:

- **Chooser** The Chooser is a special desk accessory that helps you select printers and connect to networked computers. Select it in the Apple menu and then choose the printer to which you'd like to print; if you don't see that printer as an option, you'll need to install its Mac OS 9 drivers. (See Chapter 12 for a brief discussion on printing from Classic applications.)

- **Key Caps** This little program helps you figure out what key combinations you need to press in order to type certain characters. Launch it, then choose the font you want to use from the Font menu. Now, try different modifier keys—⌘, OPTION, CONTROL, SHIFT— in various configurations. The letter keys will change to show you the character that will appear when you press that same combination of modifier keys and that letter key.

- **Scrapbook** The Scrapbook is designed for cutting and pasting multimedia elements that you'd like to save for the future—stuff like pictures, drawings, audio clips, even QuickTime videos. All you have to do is highlight the desired item in an application, then choose Edit | Copy or Edit | Cut. Switch to the Scrapbook and choose Edit | Paste and your clipping is added at the end of the Scrapbook's pages. Now, when necessary, you can copy the multimedia clipping out of the Scrapbook and into some other applications. (Note: The Scrapbook is fully drag-and-drop aware, so you can drag-and-drop from applications to the Scrapbook, and vice versa, if you prefer.) To close the Scrapbook, click its close box. Anything you've pasted into the Scrapbook will be there the next time you launch it—it's saved automatically. To remove something from the Scrapbook, view it, then choose Edit | Clear from the menu.

- **Stickies** These ought to look familiar. Launch Stickies from the Apple menu and you've got little sticky notes you can add to your screen, sort of. Just type your message on a note, then position it on the screen; you can choose File | New Note if you need more little colorful opportunities to express yourself. (Choose the colors by selecting a note and then choosing the color from the Color menu.) Stickies don't need to be saved unless you want the note off the screen. In that case, click the note's close box and you'll be asked if you want to save the note as a text file. You can quit Stickies by choosing File | Quit in the Stickies menu.

Control Panels

Control panels are used to customize and make choices about your Mac. They can range from the droll, like setting the clock or deciding what sort of text the OS should use, to the fun, like the Appearance Manager, which allows you to change the colors and appearance of your Mac's interface. Not all controls panels are active when you're working in the Classic environment, as some of their functions are overseen by preferences panes in Mac OS X's System Preferences application. But you'll find that some work in the Classic environment, and if your Mac supports dual-booting, you may need to delve into these settings when you're working directly in Mac OS 9.

 You might also be interested to know that control panels are stored in the System Folder on your Mac's hard drive in the folder called Control Panels. Any control panels in that folder will appear in the Control Panels menu on the Apple menu.

Aliases

In the Apple menu, you'll also find aliases to applications or utilities that are actually stored elsewhere on the hard drive. Most of these are added by non-Apple installation programs, but you can add items to the Apple menu yourself, including aliases to files or even folders (which appear as submenus). Simply drag them to the Apple Menu Items folder inside the System Folder. You'll see the items the next time you access the Apple menu.

Recent Menus

The Recent menus enable you to quickly relaunch or re-access an item you've been working with recently. To use the Recent menus, just click the Apple menu, then point the mouse at Recent Applications, Recent Documents, or Recent Servers (see Figure A-3) that you've used within the Classic environment. (Applications and documents that are native to Mac OS X don't show up in these menus.) Then, select the item you'd like to relaunch. Your Mac will switch back to the Finder (if necessary) and launch the application and/or open the document you've chosen.

If you'd like to change the behavior of the Recent menus, you can do so through the Apple Menu Options control panel (Apple | Control Panels | Apple Menu Options). In the control panel, you can decide if you want to use the Recent menus; if not, click to make sure there's no check mark in the check box next to the Remember Recently Used Items option. If you are using Recent menus, you can select how many items your Mac remembers—the default is ten.

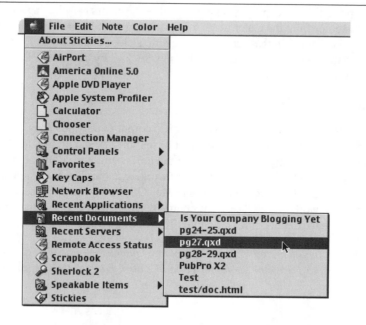

The Recent menus let you pick documents, applications, or servers that you've worked with recently in the Classic environment.

If you want to change that number, just click in the entry box and edit the number. When you're done, click the close box in the Apple Menu Options control panel. Your changes are noted and put into action.

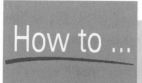 **Delete Entries from the Recent Menus**

Open the Apple Menu Items folder that's stored in your System Folder. Now, open the folder that corresponds to the Recent menu you want to clean out. In that folder, each alias corresponds to an entry on that Recent menu; drag any of the aliases to the Trash. Check the Recent menu in the Apple menu; those trashed items should be gone from the menu.

The Classic Application Menu

Up in the top-right corner of the Classic (and Mac OS 9, if your Mac is dual-boot capable) screen, you'll always find the Application menu, a menu dedicated to switching between your open applications. Which menu is it? It's the one with the name and icon of whatever applications you're currently running. Point to that icon and name, then click the mouse button to open the menu.

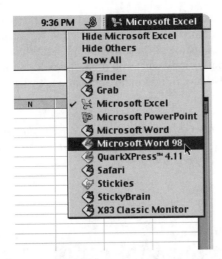

A

As you can see, the Application menu allows you to see both Classic and native Mac OS X applications, although the native applications lack a detailed icon. You can use the Application menu to switch from a Classic application to a native one if you like (although be aware that the Application menu will then disappear from view).

Choose one of the applications in that menu and it will move to the *foreground*—you'll suddenly see that new application's menus and windows in front of you, ready to be worked on. While this is most useful when you're working directly within Mac OS 9 (on Macs that support dual-booting), it also works in the Classic environment of Mac OS X, giving you an alternative to the Dock for switching applications.

 *You can switch between applications with a keystroke, too. Press ⌘-TAB to switch from application to application. You can press ⌘-SHIFT-TAB to switch back in the opposite order. Again, this works in both Mac OS 9 and Mac OS X.*

Hide and Show Applications

The Application menu has some other useful commands that help you when you switch between applications. If you've switched applications, and windows from another application are getting in your way or cluttering up the screen, you can pull down the Application menu and choose Hide Others, which hides all applications except the one you're currently working in. The applications are still running and you can still switch to them using the Application menu—only their windows are currently hidden.

You can also hide the application that you're working in—perhaps so you can see an open window in a background application. To do that, pull down the Application menu and choose Hide ... (the ellipsis represents the name of the current application).

The Show All command does exactly what you think it would—it reveals the windows of all hidden applications. You can also reveal individual applications by switching to them using the Application menu.

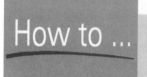

Want to hide an application as you switch away from it? Just hold down the OPTION *key as you switch between applications. The application you're switching from gets hidden as you switch to the new application.*

How to ... Float the Application Menu

If you select the Application menu and hold down the mouse button, then drag straight down the menu right off the bottom edge, you'll "tear away" the menu. Suddenly it becomes a floating window that includes the icons and names of the currently running applications. (Note that this only works when you've booted into Mac OS 9, not from within the Classic environment.)

The window will always float *on top* of all your other applications, so you'll always be able to see it. To switch to a different application, all you have to do is click once on that application's icon.

You can also customize the window somewhat. Do you want just icons and no words? Click the zoom box and the menu shrinks down to small icons. If you'd like the icons bigger, hold down OPTION and click the zoom box. If you'd like to change from vertical to horizontal, hold down SHIFT-OPTION and click the zoom box.

Need to get rid of the floating menu window? Click its close box and it's gone. You can still, as always, use the Application menu the next time you need to switch applications.

Boot into Mac OS 9

If your Mac has the ability to boot directly into Mac OS 9 (which means, loosely speaking, that it was made before 2003), then you can do that when you'd like to run Classic applications. Your Mac will run faster and it's more compatible with older applications when booted into Mac OS 9—the downside is that you lose the advanced features and interface elements of Mac OS X. More than likely you'll want your trips to Mac OS 9 to be temporary—to play a game or work in an older copy of an expensive application such as QuarkXPress.

To boot into Mac OS 9, launch the System Preferences application (Apple | System Preferences). In System Preferences, choose the Startup Disk pane. The window should reconfigure and you'll see a few different options:

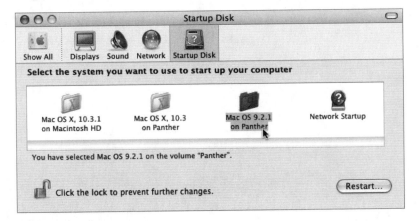

Select the System Folder that you want to use to start up Mac OS 9. In most cases you'll only see one, unless you've installed multiple System Folders for some reason. (Some people like to boot into a different System Folder from the one they use for the Classic environment, for instance.) With your selection made, click the Restart button if you want to restart immediately in Mac OS 9. In the dialog sheet that appears, click Restart again.

> **NOTE**   *If you don't want to restart immediately, simply make your startup disk selection and then close System Preferences. You'll boot up using your selected System Folder the next time you restart your Mac. Also, note that the first time you start up in either Mac OS 9 or Mac OS X, you'll be greeted by a Startup Assistant.*

Once you've successfully reached Mac OS 9, you'll eventually find yourself in a situation where you want to switch back to Mac OS X. To do that, you'll access a similar control panel in Mac OS 9. Choose Apple | Control Panels | Startup Disk. In the Startup Disk control panel that appears, select the Mac OS X System Folder that you'd like to use for booting. Select it and click the Restart button in the control panel.

Index

INTERNATIONAL CONTACT INFORMATION

AUSTRALIA
McGraw-Hill Book Company
Australia Pty. Ltd.
TEL +61-2-9900-1800
FAX +61-2-9878-8881
http://www.mcgraw-hill.com.au
books-it_sydney@mcgraw-hill.com

CANADA
McGraw-Hill Ryerson Ltd.
TEL +905-430-5000
FAX +905-430-5020
http://www.mcgraw-hill.ca

GREECE, MIDDLE EAST, & AFRICA
(Excluding South Africa)
McGraw-Hill Hellas
TEL +30-210-6560-990
TEL +30-210-6560-993
TEL +30-210-6560-994
FAX +30-210-6545-525

MEXICO (Also serving Latin America)
McGraw-Hill Interamericana Editores
S.A. de C.V.
TEL +525-1500-5108
FAX +525-117-1589
http://www.mcgraw-hill.com.mx
carlos_ruiz@mcgraw-hill.com

SINGAPORE (Serving Asia)
McGraw-Hill Book Company
TEL +65-6863-1580
FAX +65-6862-3354
http://www.mcgraw-hill.com.sg
mghasia@mcgraw-hill.com

SOUTH AFRICA
McGraw-Hill South Africa
TEL +27-11-622-7512
FAX +27-11-622-9045
robyn_swanepoel@mcgraw-hill.com

SPAIN
McGraw-Hill/
Interamericana de España, S.A.U.
TEL +34-91-180-3000
FAX +34-91-372-8513
http://www.mcgraw-hill.es
professional@mcgraw-hill.es

UNITED KINGDOM, NORTHERN, EASTERN, & CENTRAL EUROPE
McGraw-Hill Education Europe
TEL +44-1-628-502500
FAX +44-1-628-770224
http://www.mcgraw-hill.co.uk
emea_queries@mcgraw-hill.com

ALL OTHER INQUIRIES Contact:
McGraw-Hill/Osborne
TEL +1-510-420-7700
FAX +1-510-420-7703
http://www.osborne.com
omg_international@mcgraw-hill.com

Sound Off!

Sneak Peek

Mc

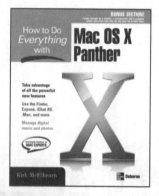